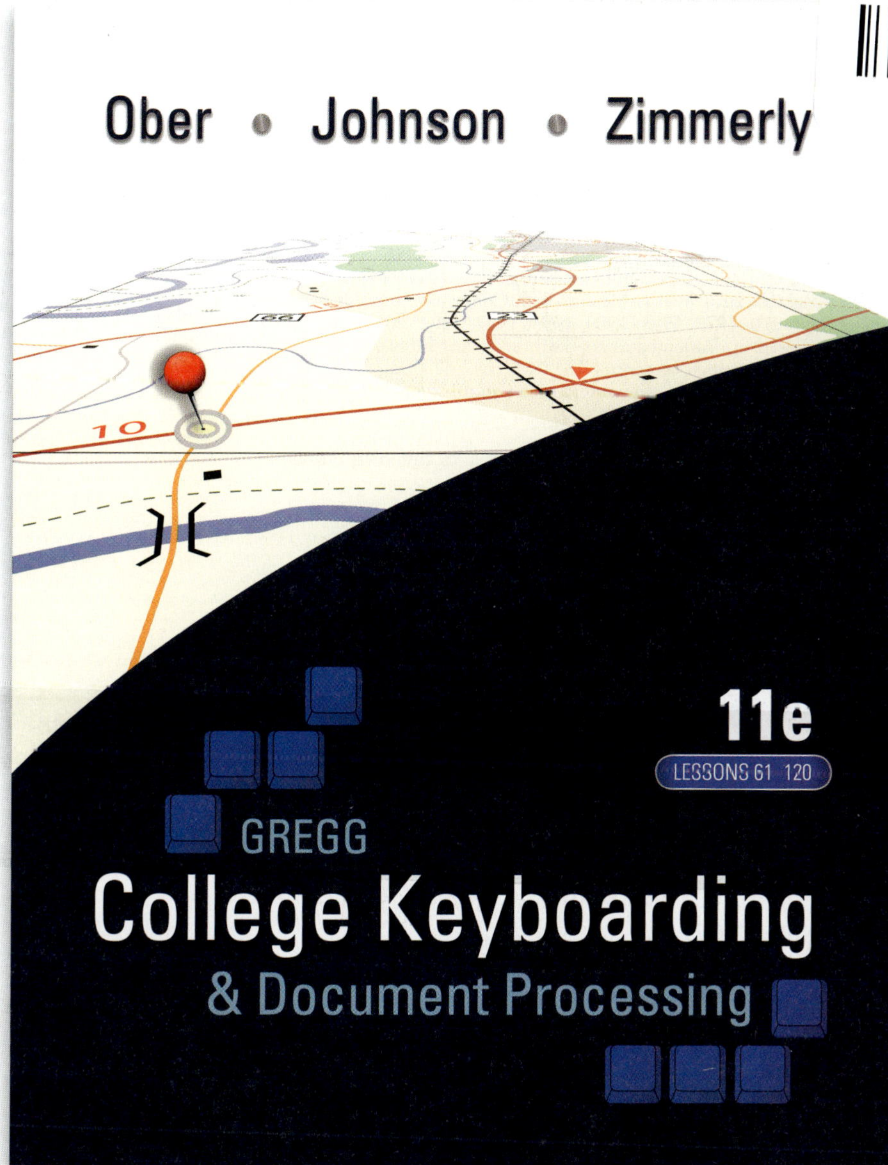

Scot Ober
Ball State University
Jack E. Johnson
University of West Georgia
Arlene Zimmerly
Los Angeles City College

Visit the *College Keyboarding* Web site at **www.mhhe.com/gdp11**

Mc Graw Hill
Connect Learn Succeed™

The McGraw-Hill Companies

Connect Learn Succeed™

GREGG COLLEGE KEYBOARDING & DOCUMENT PROCESSING, LESSONS 61–120

Published by McGraw-Hill, a business unit of The McGraw-Hill Companies, Inc., 1221 Avenue of the Americas, New York, NY, 10020.

This book is printed on acid-free paper.

7 8 9 0 RMN/RMN 1 0 9 8 7 6 5 4 3 2

ISBN 978-0-07-731940-3
MHID 0-07-731940-0

Vice President/Editor in Chief: *Elizabeth Haefele*
Vice President/Director of Marketing: *John E. Biernat*
Executive editor: *Scott Davidson*
Director of Development, Business Careers: *Sarah Wood*
Editorial coordinator: *Alan Palmer*
Marketing manager: *Tiffany Wendt*
Lead digital product manager: *Damian Moshak*
Senior digital product manager: *Lynn M. Bluhm*
Digital product specialist: *Randall Bates*
Director, Editing/Design/Production: *Jess Ann Kosic*
Project manager: *Marlena Pechan*
Senior production supervisor: *Janean A. Utley*
Senior designer: *Marianna Kinigakis*
Senior photo research coordinator: *Lori Kramer*
Digital production coordinator: *Brent Dela Cruz*
Digital developmental editor: *Kevin White*
Outside development house: *Debra Matteson*
Cover credit: © *Robert Adrian Hillman/Shutterstock*
Cover design: *Jessica M. Lazar*
Interior design: *Jessica M. Lazar and Laurie J. Entringer, BrainWorx Studio, Inc.*
Typeface: *11/13.5 Adobe Garamond Pro*
Compositor: *Lachina Publishing Services*
Printer: RR Donnelley, Menesha
Credits: The credits section for this book begins on page I-12 and is considered an extension of the copyright page.

The Library of Congress has cataloged the single volume edition of this work as follows

Ober, Scot, 1946–
Gregg college keyboarding & document processing. Lessons 1–120 / Scot Ober, Jack E. Johnson, Arlene Zimmerly. — 11th ed.
p. cm
Includeds index.
ISBN-13: 978-0-07-337219-8 (Lessons 1–120)
ISBN-10: 0-07-337219-6 (Lessons 1–120)
ISBN-13: 978-0-07-734422-1 (Lessons 1–20)
ISBN-10: 0-07-734422-7 (Lessons 1–20)
ISBN-13: 978-0-07-731936-6 (Lessons 1–60)
ISBN-10: 0-07-731936-2 (Lessons 1–60)
ISBN-13: 978-0-07-731940-3 (Lessons 61–120)
ISBN-10: 0-07-731940-0 (Lessons 61–120)
1. Word processing—Problems, exercises, etc. 2. Keyboarding—Problems, exercises, etc. 3. Commercial correspondence—Problems, exercises, etc. 4. Report writing—Problems, exercises, etc. I. Johnson, Jack E. II. Zimmerly, Arlene. III. Title. IV. Title: Gregg college keyboarding and document processing.

Z52.3.G74 2011
652.3'0076—dc22 2009037843

www.mhhe.com

Welcome to
Gregg College Keyboarding & Document Processing 11th Edition

Your complete learning/teaching *system*
Your guide to success

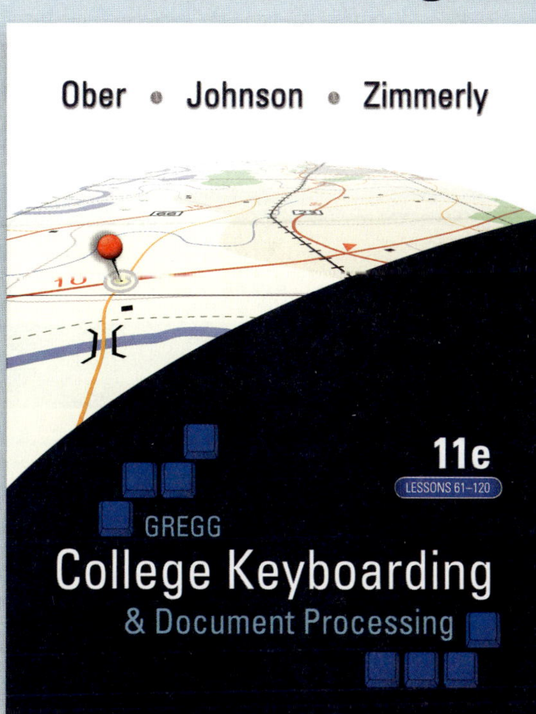

Textbook

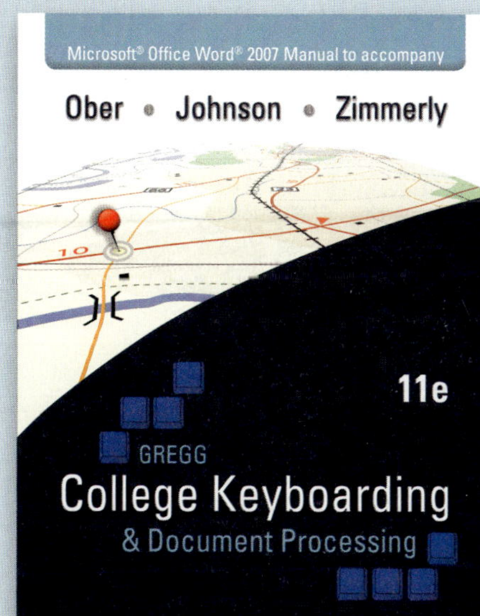

Word Manual

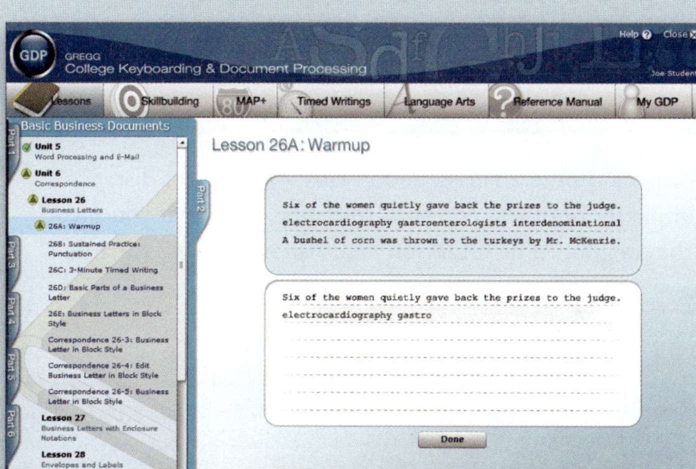

GDP (Gregg Document Processing) Web-Based Software

Instructor Wraparound Edition

Online GDP Software

New! Online functionality
Same program; *now* Web-based

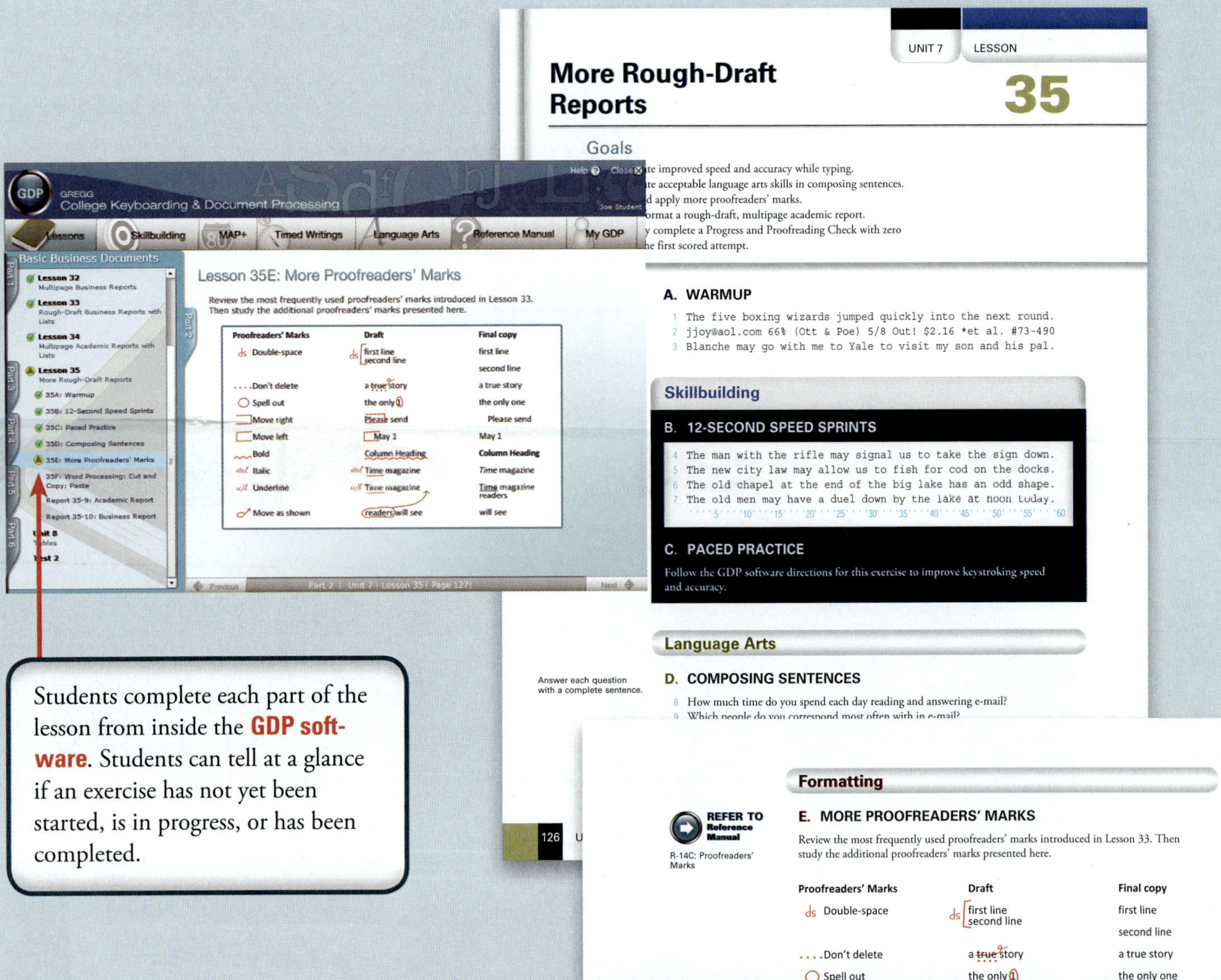

Students complete each part of the lesson from inside the **GDP software**. Students can tell at a glance if an exercise has not yet been started, is in progress, or has been completed.

This online software now offers greater accessibility for use at home, in class, and in labs—perfect for distance learning! Its easy-to-use interface makes this system simple for both you and your students . . . so that you spend more time teaching the skills you want, not learning the program. The GDP software also now allows for automatic keystroking and format scoring.

With GDP's new online functionality, updates are now seamless.

MAP+
The best just got better!

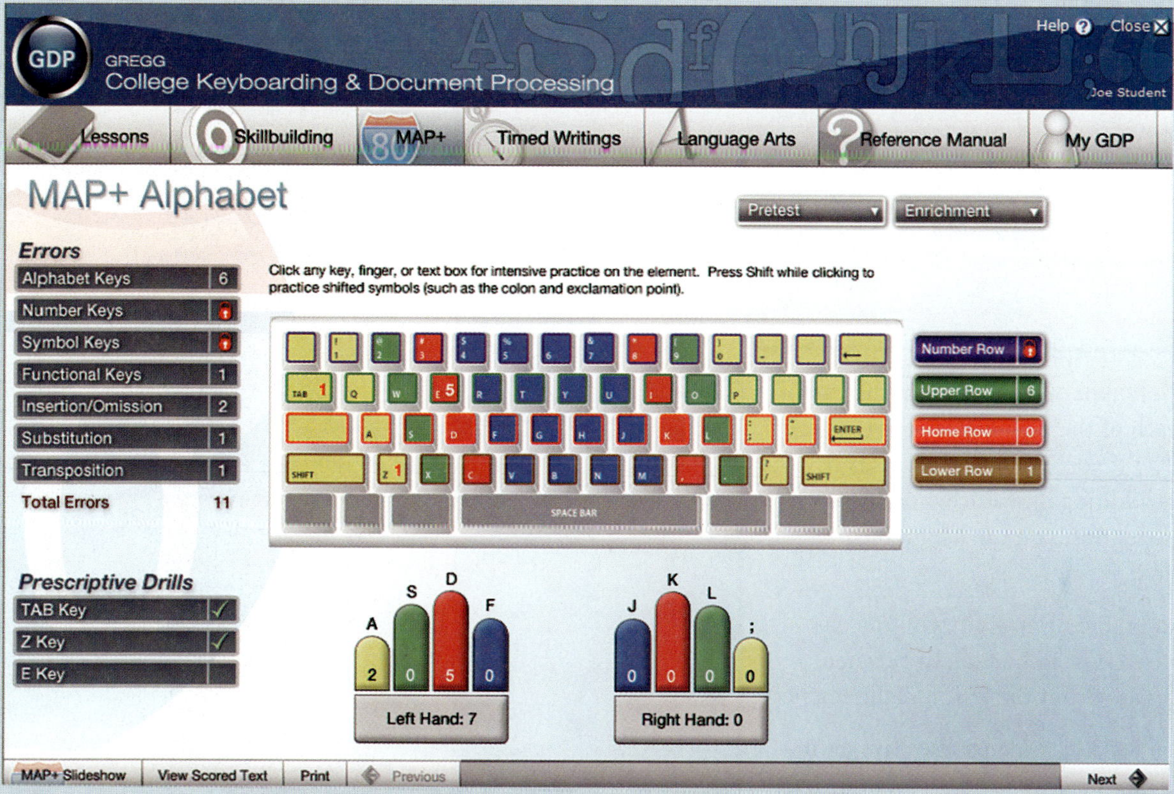

MAP+ (Misstroke Analysis and Prescription) is a *diagnostic tool* within GDP/11 that analyzes each student's pretest misstrokes and prescribes individualized remediation drills based on a powerful new scoring algorithm. MAP+ includes these features:

- **New! Unlimited drill lines**—*Now begin with Lesson 1.*
- **Interactive**—Features a streamlined interactive screen, which allows students to click anywhere for intensive practice on that key or kind of reach.
- **Continuous new drills**—Generate three *new* drill lines every time the student clicks a key or specific reach.
- **New! Deeper content**—Allows students to take a pretest and practice either alphabetic copy, numbers, or numbers and symbols.
- **Integrated**—Is a required part of each unit, although students can access MAP+ at any time from the lesson menu.

New! Enrichment Pages

More drill lines for faster touch-typing skills

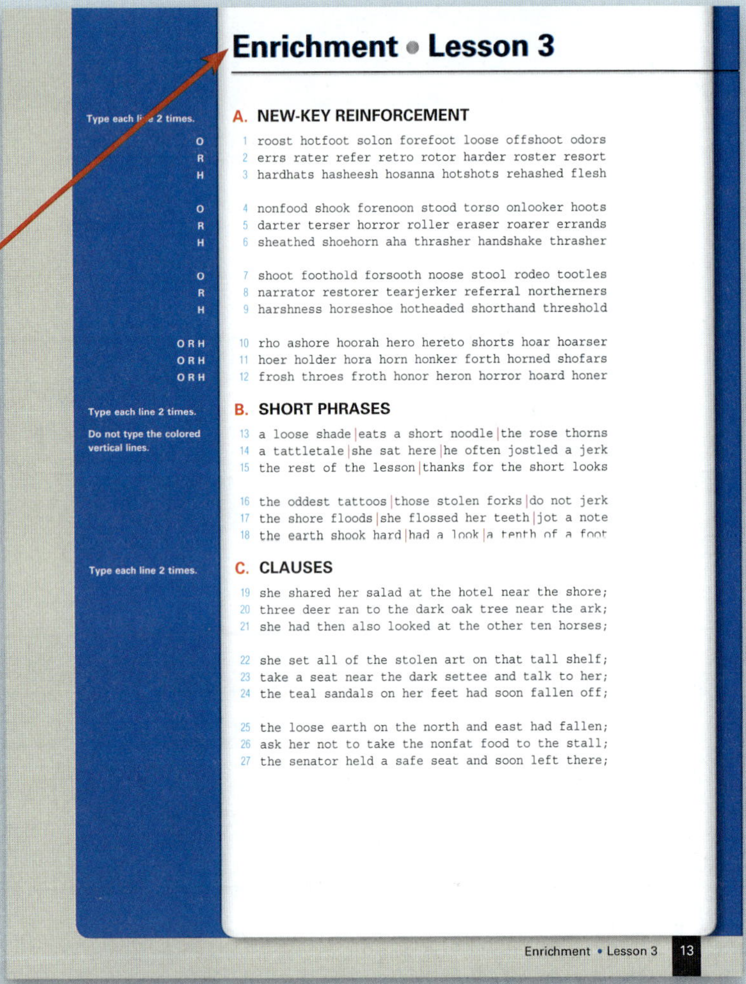

Enrichment • Lesson 3

Type each line 2 times.

A. NEW-KEY REINFORCEMENT

O 1 roost hotfoot solon forefoot loose offshoot odors
R 2 errs rater refer retro rotor harder roster resort
H 3 hardhats hasheesh hosanna hotshots rehashed flesh

O 4 nonfood shook forenoon stood torso onlooker hoots
R 5 darter terser horror roller eraser roarer errands
H 6 sheathed shoehorn aha thrasher handshake thrasher

O 7 shoot foothold forsooth noose stool rodeo tootles
R 8 narrator restorer tearjerker referral northerners
H 9 harshness horseshoe hotheaded shorthand threshold

ORH 10 rho ashore hoorah hero hereto shorts hoar hoarser
ORH 11 hoer holder hora horn honker forth horned shofars
ORH 12 frosh throes froth honor heron horror hoard honer

Type each line 2 times. Do not type the colored vertical lines.

B. SHORT PHRASES

13 a loose shade|eats a short noodle|the rose thorns
14 a tattletale|she sat here|he often jostled a jerk
15 the rest of the lesson|thanks for the short looks

16 the oddest tattoos|those stolen forks|do not jerk
17 the shore floods|she flossed her teeth|jot a note
18 the earth shook hard|had a look|a tenth of a foot

Type each line 2 times.

C. CLAUSES

19 she shared her salad at the hotel near the shore;
20 three deer ran to the dark oak tree near the ark;
21 she had then also looked at the other ten horses;

22 she set all of the stolen art on that tall shelf;
23 take a seat near the dark settee and talk to her;
24 the teal sandals on her feet had soon fallen off;

25 the loose earth on the north and east had fallen;
26 ask her not to take the nonfat food to the stall;
27 the senator held a safe seat and soon left there;

Enrichment • Lesson 3 13

Enrichment pages appear at the end of each of the new-key lessons (Lessons 1–20). If you want your students to have additional practice on each of these lessons, you can assign them as desired.

Using the GDP system, you can customize GDP to include Enrichment pages as part of the lesson requirements.

With **MAP+**, students also have unlimited new practice drills—*beginning with Lesson 1.* Every time they access MAP+ for a specific lesson, new drill lines appear that contain only those words students can type up to that point.

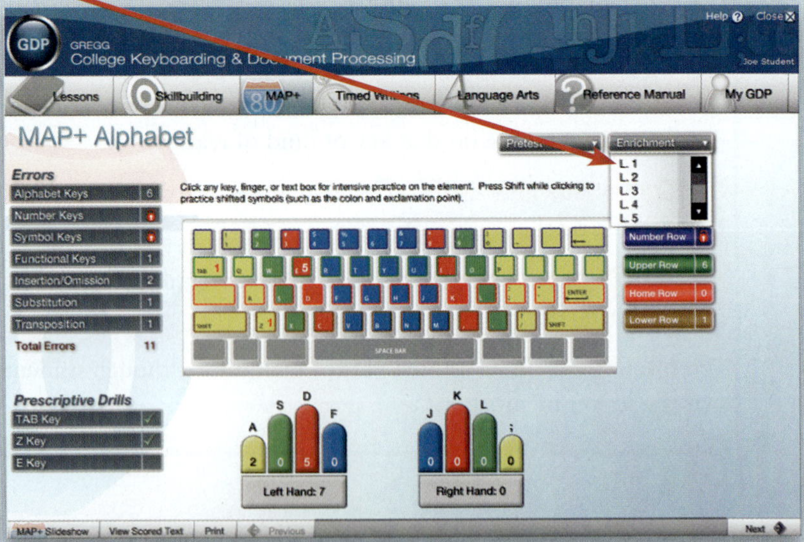

Individualized Skillbuilding
In every lesson

Warmups at the start of each lesson comprise 3 lines. Line 1 is an alphabetic sentence to review all reaches; Line 2 practices a particular type of reach; Line 3 contains easy words to help build speed.

Skillbuilding (building straight-copy speed and accuracy) is built into *every lesson*—15′–20′ of *individualized* skill-building routines.

Each student always practices on the type of drill that is appropriate for him or her and for which the **individualized** goals are challenging—but attainable.

The **timed writings** in every even-numbered lesson are controlled for difficulty, contain all letters of the alphabet, and are the exact length needed to achieve that lesson's speed goal.

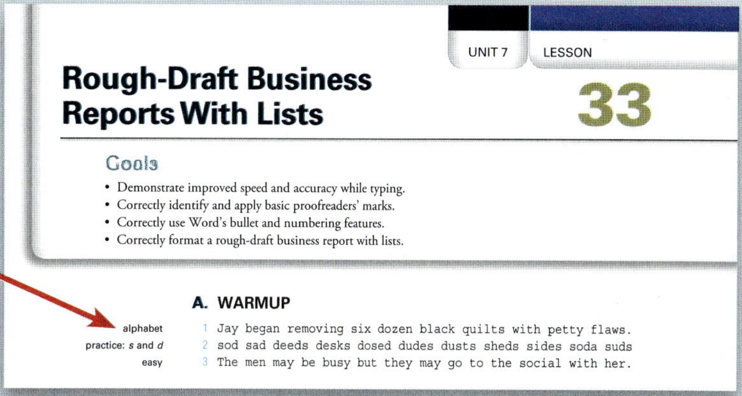

UNIT 7 LESSON 33

Rough-Draft Business Reports With Lists

Goals
- Demonstrate improved speed and accuracy while typing.
- Correctly identify and apply basic proofreaders' marks.
- Correctly use Word's bullet and numbering features.
- Correctly format a rough-draft business report with lists.

A. WARMUP

alphabet Jay began removing six dozen black quilts with petty flaws.
practice: *s* and *d* sod sad deeds desks dosed dudes dusts sheds sides soda suds
easy The men may be busy but they may go to the social with her.

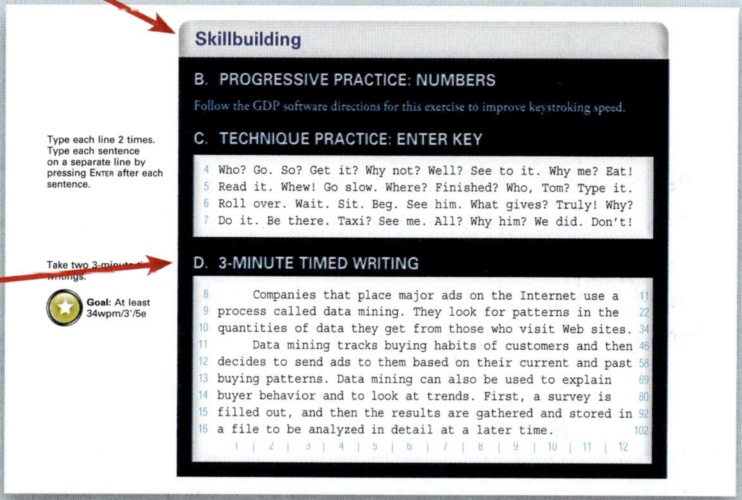

Skillbuilding

B. PROGRESSIVE PRACTICE: NUMBERS

Follow the GDP software directions for this exercise to improve keystroking speed.

C. TECHNIQUE PRACTICE: ENTER KEY

Type each line 2 times. Type each sentence on a separate line by pressing ENTER after each sentence.

Who? Go. So? Get it? Why not? Well? See to it. Why me? Eat!
Read it. Whew! Go slow. Where? Finished? Who, Tom? Type it.
Roll over. Wait. Sit. Beg. See him. What gives? Truly! Why?
Do it. Be there. Taxi? See me. All? Why him? We did. Don't!

D. 3-MINUTE TIMED WRITING

Take two 3-minute writings.

Goal: At least 34wpm/3′/5e

Companies that place major ads on the Internet use a 11
process called data mining. They look for patterns in the 22
quantities of data they get from those who visit Web sites. 34
Data mining tracks buying habits of customers and then 46
decides to send ads to them based on their current and past 58
buying patterns. Data mining can also be used to explain 69
buyer behavior and to look at trends. First, a survey is 80
filled out, and then the results are gathered and stored in 92
a file to be analyzed in detail at a later time. 102
1 | 2 | 3 | 4 | 5 | 6 | 7 | 8 | 9 | 10 | 11 | 12

Language Arts

A critical document processing skill

Language arts (punctuation rules, usage, proofreading, composing, and spelling) are systematically covered. Short, easy-to-grasp exercises are incorporated throughout Lessons 21–120 with increasing difficulty.

The rules are presented, practiced, and then illustrated in the documents that students type in that lesson—for immediate reinforcement.

Language Arts

Study the rules at the right.

RULE
, independent clause

The underline calls attention to a point in the sentence where a comma might mistakenly be inserted.

D. COMMAS AND SENTENCES

Use a comma between independent clauses joined by a coordinate conjunction (unless both clauses are short).

Ellen left her job with IBM, and she and her sister went to Paris.
But: Ellen left her job with IBM and went to Paris with her sister.
But: John drove and I navigated.

Note: An independent clause is one that can stand alone as a complete sentence. The most common coordinate conjunctions are *and, but, or,* and *nor.*

RULE
, introductory expression

Use a comma after an introductory expression (unless it is a short prepositional phrase).

Before we can make a decision, we must have all the facts.
But: In 2008 our nation elected a new president.

Note: An introductory expression is a group of words that come before the subject and verb of the independent clause. Common prepositions are *to, in, on, of, at, by, for,* and *with.*

Edit each sentence to correct any errors.

```
If you agree I will let Mr. Hancock know.

On Friday we will meet to discuss the upcoming campaign.

Mr. Ray will lead the delegation and Ms. Guy will be the
interpreter.

Ella dictated and I typed.

Melvin accepted a job in Miami that starts in July and then
left for a two-week vacation.

Now that it is light outside we can begin moving the
furniture.

It was a well-deserved victory and it didn't come any too
soon.
```

Correspondence
27-8
Business Letter in Block Style

, introductory expression

, independent clause

October 10, 20-- / Mr. Nick Limpett / Marketing Manager / Secure Investments Inc. / 398 East Wacker Drive / Chicago, IL 60601 / Dear Mr. Limpett:

¶ Are you searching for a suitable conference site for your next corporate meeting? If so, the Paradise Valley Resort in Scottsdale, Arizona, offers you every amenity imaginable.

¶ Our luxury resort accommodations and stunning Sonoran Desert views are minutes away from the largest mall in the Southwest and hundreds of shops, galleries, and Scottsdale eateries. We are conveniently located only 12 miles from Phoenix Sky Harbor International Airport. Paradise Valley Resort has 40,000 square feet of flexible meeting space, including stunning outdoor venues. Our in-house audiovisual staff will make sure that your event is flawless.

¶ I've enclosed several brochures for your convenience. Let me know if I can be of service in any way. Your success is our success, and I hope to hear from you soon.

Sincerely yours, / Ms. Julie Mays / Corporate Event Specialist / urs / Enclosures

New! Expanded Ten-Key Practice

Students learn to touch-type the entire ten-key pad—a frequent job requirement. After Lesson 20, a new **Ten-Key Numeric Keypad** supplementary lesson teaches the touch typing of both the number keys *and the arithmetic operators* (+ - * and /)—for a total of 55 new lines of drills.

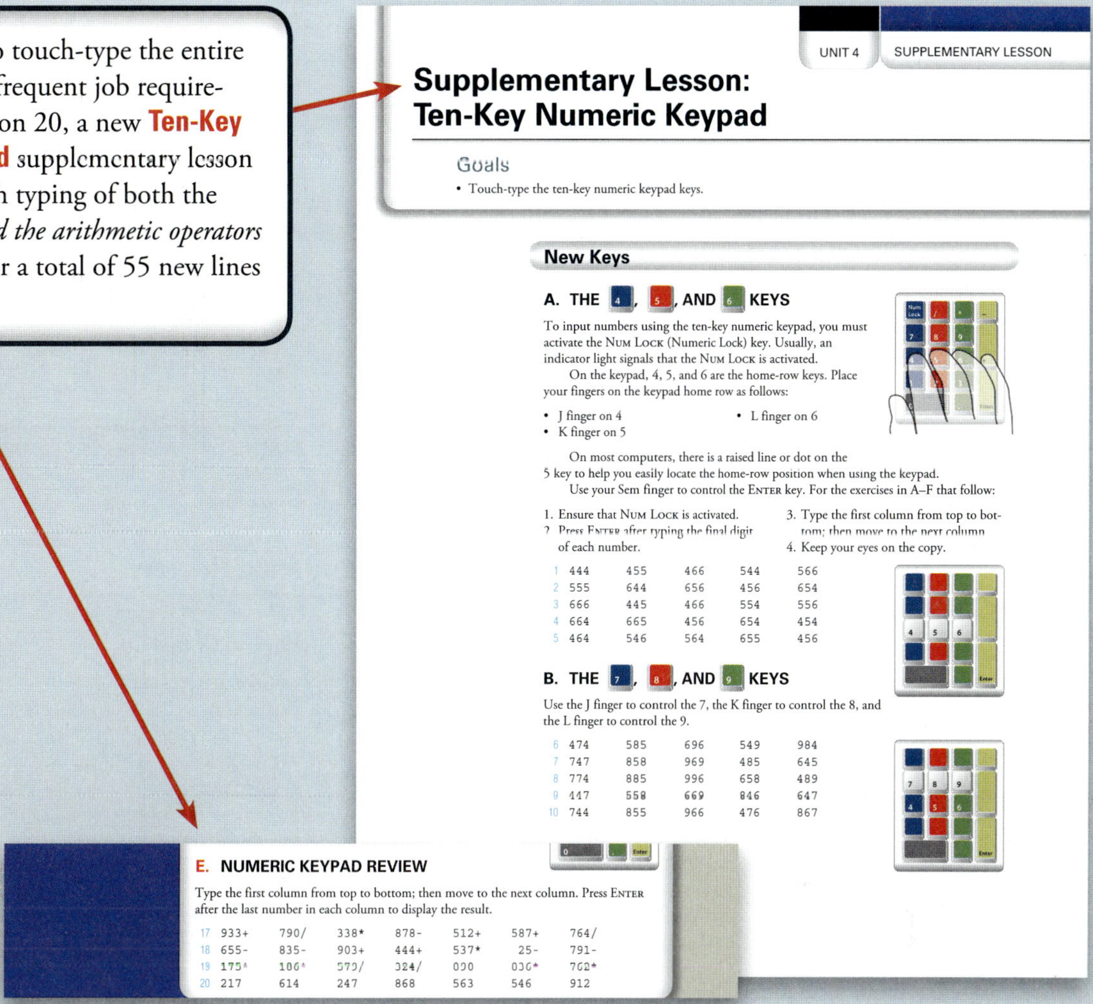

UNIT 4 SUPPLEMENTARY LESSON

Supplementary Lesson: Ten-Key Numeric Keypad

Goals

- Touch-type the ten-key numeric keypad keys.

New Keys

A. THE 4, 5, AND 6 KEYS

To input numbers using the ten-key numeric keypad, you must activate the Num Lock (Numeric Lock) key. Usually, an indicator light signals that the Num Lock is activated.

On the keypad, 4, 5, and 6 are the home-row keys. Place your fingers on the keypad home row as follows:

- J finger on 4
- K finger on 5
- L finger on 6

On most computers, there is a raised line or dot on the 5 key to help you easily locate the home-row position when using the keypad.

Use your Sem finger to control the Enter key. For the exercises in A–F that follow:

1. Ensure that Num Lock is activated.
2. Press Enter after typing the final digit of each number.
3. Type the first column from top to bottom; then move to the next column.
4. Keep your eyes on the copy.

1	444	455	466	544	566
2	555	644	656	456	654
3	666	445	466	554	556
4	664	665	456	654	454
5	464	546	564	655	456

B. THE 7, 8, AND 9 KEYS

Use the J finger to control the 7, the K finger to control the 8, and the L finger to control the 9.

6	474	585	696	549	984
7	747	858	969	485	645
8	774	885	996	658	489
9	447	558	669	846	647
10	744	855	966	476	867

E. NUMERIC KEYPAD REVIEW

Type the first column from top to bottom; then move to the next column. Press Enter after the last number in each column to display the result.

17	933+	790/	338*	878-	512+	587+	764/
18	655-	835-	903+	444+	537*	25-	791-
19	175*	106*	579/	324/	090	036*	762*
20	217	614	247	868	563	546	912

Word Processing Commands
Introduced on a *need-to-know* basis

Word processing commands are introduced when they are needed to format a particular job (in this lesson, students need to learn the Italic and Underline commands).

Students are referred to the corresponding lesson in the *Word Manual*, which contains step-by-step directions, with screen shots and practice exercises so that students don't get lost.

When students finish the practice exercises in the *Word Manual*, they are referred back to the text.

Formatting

GO TO Word Manual

E. WORD PROCESSING: ITALIC AND UNDERLINE

Study Lesson 30 in your Word Manual. Complete all of the shaded steps while at your computer. Then format the documents that follow.

Document Processing

Correspondence 30-17 Memo

Underline the text to be emphasized.

Italicize the book title.

MEMO TO: All Executive Assistants | **FROM:** Robbie Holt, Staff Development Coordinator | **DATE:** March 25, 20-- | **SUBJECT:** Standardizing Document Formats

¶ Last month we received our final shipment of new laser printers. The installation of these printers in your offices marked the final phaseout of all ink-jet printers.

¶ Because all of us can now use a variety of standardized fonts in our correspondence, please note the following change: <u>From now on, all titles in tables, correspondence, and reports should be set in Calibri 14</u>. This new formatting change will help us to standardize our communications.

¶ The latest edition of the book *Quick Reference for the Automated Office* has two pages of helpful information on laser printers. I have attached my comments. Please read these pages carefully, and we will discuss them at our next meeting.

urs | Attachment

Correspondence Review

LESSON 30

Italic and Underline

To italicize or underline text as you type:

Italic button

Underline button

1. From the **Home** tab, **Font** group, click the **Italic** or **Underline** button.

   Or: Press CTRL + I (italic) or CTRL + U (underline).

2. Type the text you want italicized or underlined; then click the **Italic** or **Underline** button again to turn off italic or underline.

To italicize or underline existing text:

plain text

italic text

<u>underlined</u> text

1. Select the text to be italicized or underlined; or for a single word, simply click inside the word.
2. Click the **Italic** or **Underline** button.

   Or: Press CTRL + I or CTRL + U.

Italic and **Underline** are toggle buttons. Click the button once to activate the feature and again to deactivate it. To undo this formatting, select the text and then click the desired button.

PRACTICE

1. Type the first line—underline "not" and italicize the book title, *To Kill a Mockingbird*; press ENTER 1 time, and type the second sentence exactly as shown:

```
I will not have time to read To Kill a Mockingbird
before Friday.
I will have time to read This Old House.
```

REFER TO Word Manual

L. 21: Choose a Command, From the Quick Access Toolbar

Use **Quick Print** to immediately print a copy of the entire document on your default printer: from the **Microsoft Office** button, click the list arrow to the right of the **Print** button, and click **Quick Print**. See Lesson 21 for steps to add Quick Print to the toolbar.

3. Click the desired print options from the **Print** window.

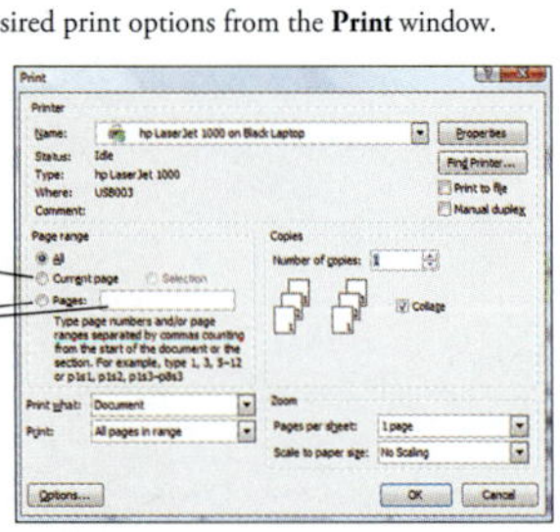

Click Current page to print just the page containing the insertion point.

Click Pages, and type the page range if you want to print only certain pages (for example, typing "2-4" would cause pages 2 through 4 of a document to print).

To print only a part of a document, select the desired text. Click the **Microsoft Office** button, point to the **Print** button, and click **Print** or press CTRL + P. Under **Page range**, click **Selection**.

PRACTICE (continued)

1. Print 2 copies of *practice-24*.
2. Save changes to *practice-24*, and return to GDP.

Check with your instructor before printing anything!

GO TO Textbook

GDP Instructor Help
Right where you need it!

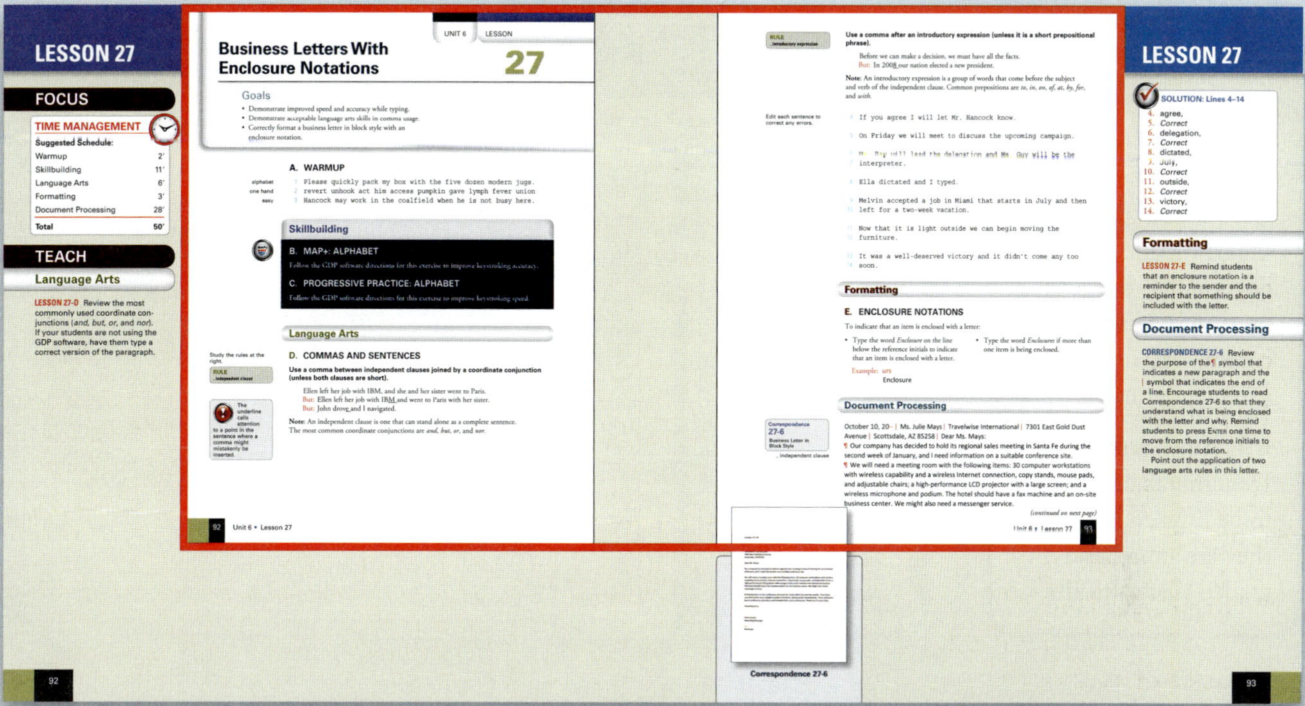

The ***Instructor Wraparound Edition (IWE)*** offers lesson plans and reduced-size student pages (shown in the red border above) to enhance classroom instruction. In addition to a mini-methods section at the front of the *IWE*, the side and bottom panels on each lesson page contain:

- Suggested times for each lesson part
- Miniature copies of the solutions for the documents students type in that lesson
- Solutions to language arts activities
- Marginal teaching notes—right where they are needed

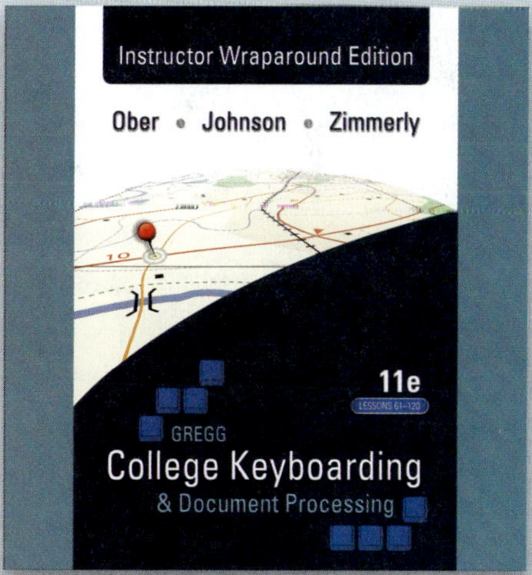

No More Grading Papers!
New! GDP now scores both keystroking and *formatting* errors

Instructors decide whether to have GDP automatically assign a grade to each document—based on parameters they choose—or to assign a grade manually.

GDP goes green. Documents don't need to be printed because they are stored and graded electronically.

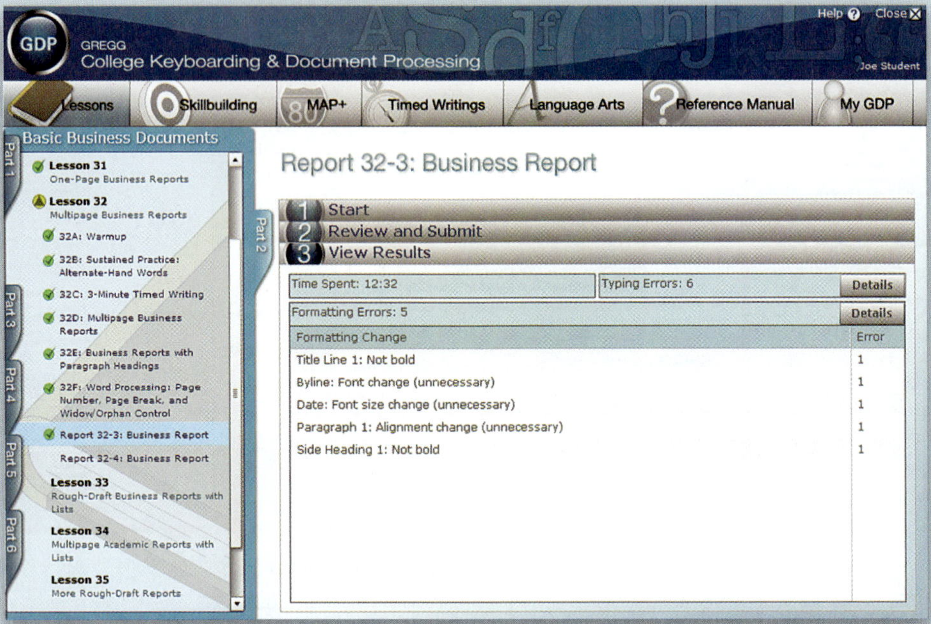

New! The customizable **GPS (Grade Posting System)** gradebook allows complete flexibility in setting up grades—with an easy-to-use, intuitive interface. Students can check their current average at any point in the school term, and instructors can save the gradebook in a comma-delimited format for uploading to Excel or to learning management systems (LMS) such as Blackboard or Angel.

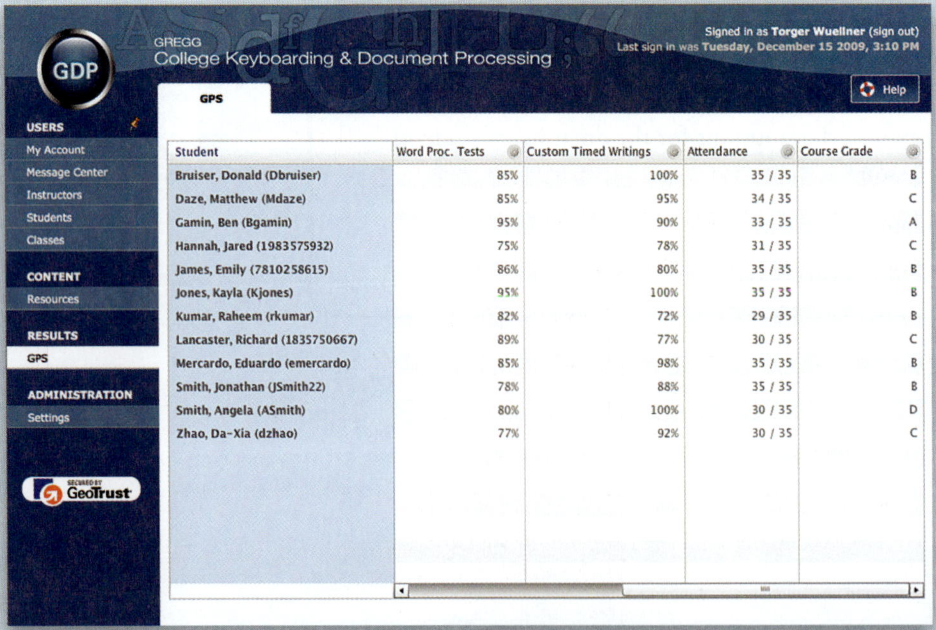

Contents

PART 5
Specialized Applications

PART 6
Using and Designing Business Documents

Preface

Gregg College Keyboarding & Document Processing is a multicomponent instructional program designed to give the student and the instructor a high degree of flexibility and a high degree of success in meeting their respective goals. The textbook is offered in several volumes: *Lessons 1–20, Lessons 1–60, Lessons 61–120,* and *Lessons 1–120.* The GDP software is a Web-delivered, PC-compatible program providing complete lesson-by-lesson instruction for each of the 120 text lessons. The document processing *Word Manual,* used in conjunction with the textbook for Lessons 21–120, teaches the document processing skills needed to create efficient business documents using Microsoft Word.

The Kit Format

For student and instructor convenience, the core components of this instructional system—the textbook, the *Word Manual,* and the Gregg College Keyboarding & Document Processing (GDP) software—are available in a variety of kit formats.

Kit 1: Lessons 1–60 This kit, designed for the first keyboarding course, provides the Lessons 1–60 textbook, the *Word Manual,* and an access card to the GDP software. Since this kit is designed for the beginning student, its major objectives are to develop touch control of the keyboard and proper keyboarding techniques, to build basic speed and accuracy, and to provide practice in applying those basic skills to the formatting of e-mails, reports, letters, memos, tables, and other kinds of personal and business communications.

Kit 2: Lessons 61–120 This kit, designed for the second course, provides the Lessons 61–120 textbook, the *Word Manual,* and an access card to the GDP software. This course continues the development of basic keyboarding skills and emphasizes the formatting of various kinds of business correspondence, reports, tables, electronic forms, and desktop publishing projects from arranged, unarranged, handwritten, and rough-draft sources.

Kit 3: Lessons 1–120 This kit, designed for both the first and second course, provides the Lessons 1–120 textbook, the *Word Manual,* and an access card to the GDP software.

Kit 4: Lessons 1–20 This kit, designed for shorter keyboarding courses, provides the Lessons 1–20 text and an access card to the GDP software.

Supporting Materials

Gregg College Keyboarding & Document Processing offers the following instructional materials:

- The special ***Instructor Wraparound Edition (IWE)*** offers lesson plans and reduced-size student pages to enhance classroom instruction. Distance-learning tips, instructional methodology, adult learner strategies, and special needs features also are included in this wraparound edition. New to this edition are miniature solutions for each document the students type; they are shown in the margins of the IWE.
- The ***Tests and Solutions Manual*** provides solution keys for all of the formatting in Lessons 25–120 in addition to objective tests and alternative document processing tests for each part.

What's New in the 11th Edition Text?

New-Key Introduction (Lessons 1–20)

- A new Enrichment page has been added to each of the first 20 lessons—for additional practice and faster development of touch-typing skills.
- MAP+ (Misstroke Analysis and Prescription) can now be used beginning with Lesson 1, thus providing unlimited new practice drills for each of the new-key lessons.
- A new supplementary lesson, Ten-Key Numeric Keypad, follows Lesson 20; it teaches the touch typing of both the number keys and arithmetic operators (+, -, /, and *), with 55 new drill lines.
- Only 3 new keys are introduced in each lesson (instead of 4)—to provide more intensive practice on each new key; all keys are still introduced in Lessons 1–20.
- The order in which new keys are introduced has been refined to balance the workload between each hand and to take into consideration how frequently keys are used. For example, in previous editions, the hyphen key was introduced early (in Lesson 6) because students used it for manual word division. With Word's automatic hyphenation feature, students don't use this key as much anymore, and the hyphen is now introduced in Lesson 11.

Skillbuilding

- MAP+ now provides an analysis and prescription of the number and symbol keys (previously, only alphabetic reaches were included). Because of this, (a) Diagnostic Practice: Symbols and Punctuation and (b) Diagnostic Practice: Numbers have been removed.
- Every Warmup exercise has been revised. Line 1 of each Warmup is now an alphabetic sentence to review all reaches, Line 2 practices a particular type of reach, and Line 3 contains easy words to build speed.

Document Processing

- Formatting correspondence (new Unit 6) is now introduced before formatting reports (new Unit 7).
- The formatting of bulleted/numbered lists in Lesson 33 and table column headings in Lesson 38 has been simplified.
- More e-mail messages are included with added coverage of formatting, such as bulleted lists, tables, and attachments.
- Eleven new Word commands are introduced: Zoom (L. 24), Widow/Orphan Control (L. 32), Table—Align Bottom (L. 38), AutoCorrect—Hyperlink (L. 49), Bookmarks and Hyperlinks (L. 89), Cover Page—Insert (L. 90), Table—Tab (L. 92), Page Color (L. 107), Mail Merge (L. 113–115), Style Set—Word 2007 (Appendix A), and PDF Format (Appendix C).
- The electronic resume in Lesson 52 (which is not being used much anymore) has been replaced by job-interviewing documents.
- The Web project in Unit 23 has been changed from creating a company home page to (a) creating an online resume and (b) introducing Mail Merge.
- Each lesson of the *Instructor's Wraparound Edition* now displays a miniature solution for each document students type in that lesson.

Introduction to the Student

Goals

- Type at least 30wpm/3′/5e by touch.
- Correctly format a business letter in block style with standard punctuation.

Starting a Lesson

Each lesson begins with the goals for that lesson. Read the goals carefully so that you understand the purpose of your practice. In the example at the left (from Lesson 26), the goals for the lesson are to type at least 30 wpm (words per minute) on a 3-minute timed writing with no more than 5 uncorrected errors and to correctly format a business letter in block style with standard punctuation.

Building Straight-Copy Skill

Warmups. Each lesson begins with a Warmup that reinforces learned alphabet, number, and/or symbol keys; practices specific reaches; and builds speed.

Skillbuilding. The Skillbuilding portion of each lesson includes a variety of drills to individualize your keyboarding speed and accuracy development. Instructions for completing the drills are always provided beside each activity.

Additional Skillbuilding drills are included in the back of the textbook and on the GDP correlated software. These drills are intended to help you meet your individual goals.

Measuring Straight-Copy Skill

Straight-copy skill is measured in wpm. All timed writings are the exact length needed to meet the speed goal for the lesson. If you finish a timed writing before time is up, you have automatically reached your speed goal for the lesson.

Counting Errors. Specific criteria are used for counting errors. The GDP software counts an error when

1. Any stroke is incorrect.
2. Any punctuation after a word is incorrect or omitted. The word before the punctuation is counted as incorrect.
3. The spacing after a word or after its punctuation is incorrect. The word is counted as incorrect.
4. A letter or word is omitted or repeated.
5. A direction about spacing, indenting, and so on, is not followed.
6. Words are transposed.

(**Note:** Only one error is counted for each word, no matter how many errors it may contain. The GDP correlated software automatically proofreads your copy and marks any errors for you.)

Determining Speed. To compute your typing speed in wpm, the GDP software counts every 5 strokes, including spaces, as 1 "word." Horizontal word scales below an activity divide lines into 5-stroke words. Vertical word scales to the right of an activity show the number of words in each line cumulatively totaled.

For example, the illustration that follows is for a 2-minute timed writing. If you complete line 30, you have typed 11 words. If you complete line 31, you have typed 22 words. Use the bottom word scale to determine the word count of a partial line. Add that number to the cumulative total for the last complete line. The GDP correlated software automatically computes your wpm speed for you.

```
     Zachary just paid for six seats and quit because he      11
could not get the views he required near the middle of the    22
field. In August he thinks he may go to the ticket office     34
to purchase tickets.                                          38
   1 | 2 | 3 | 4 | 5 | 6 | 7 | 8 | 9 | 10 | 11 | 12
```

Take two 2-minute timed writings.

Goal: At least 19wpm/2′/5e

Correcting Errors

You will make numerous errors while you are learning the keyboard; do not be overly concerned about them. Errors will decrease as you become familiar with the keyboard. Error-correction settings in the GDP software determine whether you can correct errors in timed writings and drills. Consult your instructor for error-correction guidelines.

To correct an error, press BACKSPACE (shown as ← on some keyboards) to delete the incorrect character(s). Then type the correct character(s).

If you notice an error on a different line, use the up, down, left, or right arrows to move the insertion point immediately to the left or right of the error. Press BACKSPACE to delete a character to the left of the insertion point or DELETE to delete a character to the right of the insertion point.

Typing Technique

Correct position at the keyboard enables you to type with greater speed and accuracy and with less fatigue. When typing for a long period, rest your eyes occasionally by looking away from the screen. Change position, walk around, or stretch when your muscles feel tired. Making such movements and adjustments may help prevent your body from becoming too tired. In addition, long-term bodily damage, such as carpal tunnel syndrome, can be prevented.

Follow these ergonomic principles when typing:

Workstation

1. Position your chair so that your upper and lower legs form a greater-than-90-degree angle and your lower back is supported, with your knees slightly lower than your hips.
2. Position your text on either side of the monitor as close to the monitor vertically and horizontally as possible.
3. Position the mouse on a pad next to and at the same height as your keyboard.
4. Tilt the top of the monitor slightly away from you and slightly farther than an arm's length from you.

Position at the Keyboard

5. Center your body in front of the keyboard.
6. Sit slightly reclined, with your lower back touching the back of the chair and your feet flat on the floor.
7. Keep your elbows close to your body in a relaxed position.
8. Curve your fingers naturally over the home-row position, with the back of your hands at the same angle as the keyboard.
9. Move the mouse with your whole arm—not just your wrist.

Keystroking

10. Operate all keys by touch, using the correct fingers.
11. Keep your eyes on the copy most of the time while typing.

12. Keep your forearms at a slight downward slant and raise your hands slightly when typing so that your wrists do not touch the keyboard.
13. Make quick, light strokes, returning your fingers immediately to the home-row position or moving to the next position after each stroke.

Tension-Reducing Exercises

A variety of government and health sources recommend the following exercises for computer users. Perform one exercise from each group, hold each position for three seconds, and repeat each exercise three times.

Neck

1. Look forward and slowly tilt your head as far to the left as possible. Then slowly tilt your head as far to the right as possible.
2. Slowly tilt your head forward until your chin rests on your chest. Then slowly tilt your head as far back as possible.

Shoulders

3. Roll your shoulders forward in a large circle. Then roll your shoulders backward in a large circle.
4. Extend both arms out to your side. Then slowly stretch them toward your back and squeeze your shoulder blades together. Finally, slowly bring your arms forward and touch the tops of your hands together in front of you.

Back

5. Place both hands behind your head, and slowly stretch your upper body backward. Then slowly bend all the way forward, stretching your arms toward the floor.
6. While seated, grab your left knee with both hands and slowly pull your leg in toward your body. Then repeat with your right knee.

Eyes

7. Close your eyes tightly. Then open them as wide as you can, blinking rapidly.
8. Follow the 20/20/20 rule: every 20 minutes, stare at an object 20 feet away for 20 seconds.

Reference Manual

A. MAJOR PARTS OF A COMPUTER SYSTEM

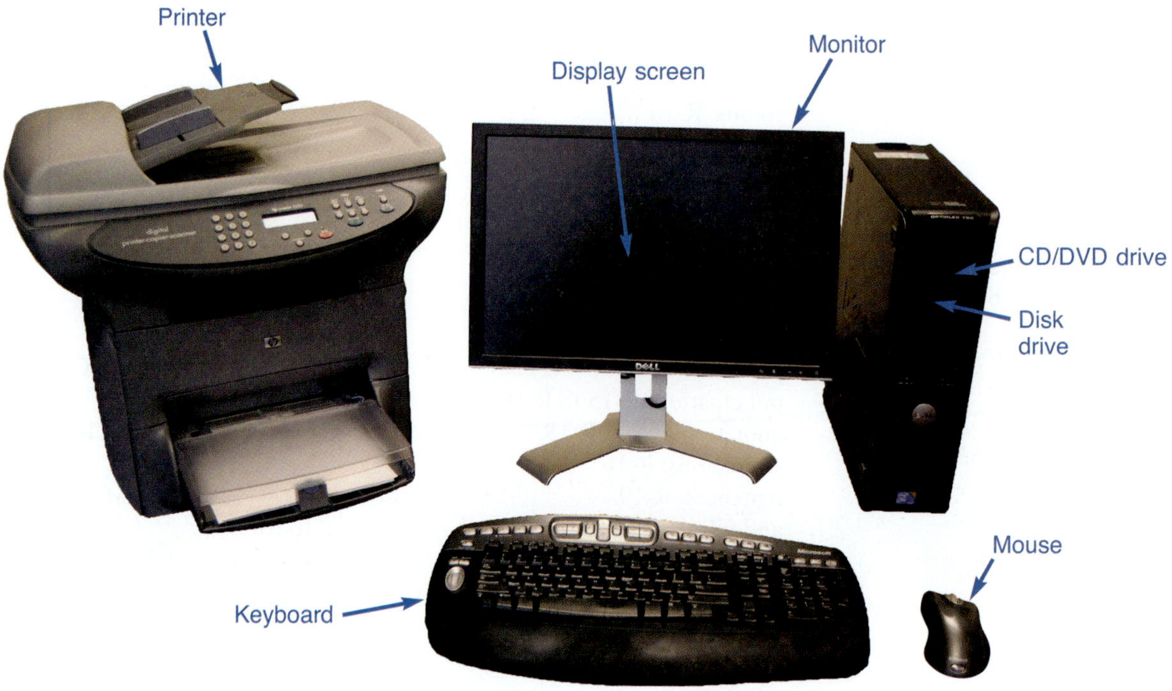

B. THE COMPUTER KEYBOARD

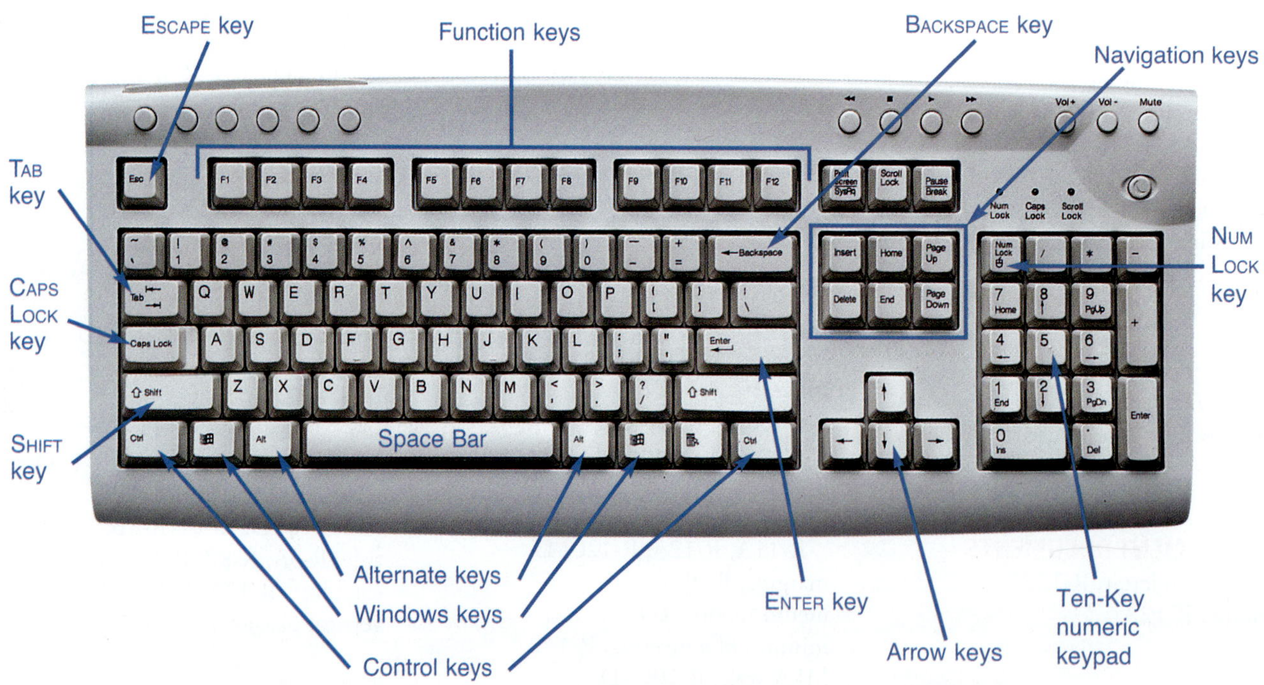

A. BUSINESS LETTER IN BLOCK STYLE

(with standard punctuation and indented display)

↓5X

Date line: September 5, 20-- ↓4X

Inside address:
Ms. Joan R. Hunter
Bolwater Associates
One Parklands Drive
Darien, CT 06820 ↓2X

Salutation: Dear Ms. Hunter: ↓2X — Standard punctuation

Body: You will soon receive the signed contract to have your organization conduct a one-day workshop for our employees on eliminating repetitive-motion injuries in the workplace. As we agreed, this workshop will apply to both our office and factory workers and you will conduct separate sessions for each group. ↓2X

We revised Paragraph 4-b shown below to require the instructor of this workshop to be a full-time employee of Bolwater Associates: ↓2X

→indent 0.5″ Paragraph 4-b of the Bolwater Associates agreement is hereby amended as follows: The instructor of the one-day workshop on eliminating repetitive-motion injuries at the workplace must be a full-time employee of Bolwater Associates. ↓2X ←indent 0.5″

Indented display

If this revision is satisfactory, please sign and return one copy of the contract for our files. We look forward to this opportunity to enhance the health of our employees. I know that all of us will enjoy this workshop. ↓2X

Complimentary closing: Sincerely, ↓4X — Standard punctuation

Signature: *Jeffrey Olszewski*

Writer's identification:
Jeffrey Olszewski
Vice President for Operations

Reference initials

B. BUSINESS LETTER IN MODIFIED-BLOCK STYLE

(with multiline list and enclosure notation)

left tab: 3.25″ (centerpoint)

↓5X

→ tab 3.25″ (centerpoint) May 15, 20-- ↓4X

Mr. Ichiro Xie
Bolwater Associates
One Parklands Drive
Darien, CT 06820 ↓2X

Dear Mr. Xie: ↓2X

I am returning a signed contract to have your organization conduct a one-day workshop for our employees on eliminating repetitive-motion injuries in the workplace. We have made the following changes to the contract: ↓2X

Multiline list

1. We revised Paragraph 4-b to require the instructor of this workshop to be a full-time employee of Bolwater Associates.
2. We made changes to Paragraph 10-c to require our prior approval of the agenda for the workshop. ↓2X

If these revisions are satisfactory, please sign and return one copy of the contract for our files. We look forward to this opportunity to enhance the health of our employees. I know that all of us will enjoy this workshop. ↓2X

→ tab 3.25″ (centerpoint) Sincerely, ↓4X

Jeffrey Olszewski

Jeffrey Olszewski
Vice President for Operations ↓2X

pec

Enclosure notation: Enclosure

C. BUSINESS LETTER IN SIMPLIFIED STYLE

(with subject line, single-line list; enclosure, delivery, and copy notations)

↓5X

October 5, 20-- ↓4X

Mr. Dale P. Griffin
Bolwater Associates
One Parklands Drive
Darien, CT 06820 ↓3X

Subject line: WORKSHOP CONTRACT ↓3X

I am returning the signed contract, Mr. Griffin, to have your organization conduct a one-day workshop for our employees on eliminating repetitive-motion injuries in the workplace. We have amended the following sections of the contract: ↓2X

Single-line list

- Paragraph 4-b
- Table 3
- Attachment 2 ↓2X

If these revisions are satisfactory, please sign and return one copy of the contract for our files. We look forward to this opportunity to enhance the health of our employees. I know that all of us will enjoy this workshop. ↓4X

Rogena Kyles

ROGENA KYLES, DIRECTOR ↓2X

iww

Enclosure notation: Enclosure

Delivery notation: By e-mail

Copy notation: c: Legal Department

D. PERSONAL-BUSINESS LETTER IN MODIFIED-BLOCK STYLE

(with international address and return address)

left tab: 3.25″ (centerpoint)

↓5X

→ tab 3.25″ (centerpoint) July 15, 20-- ↓4X

International address:
Mr. Luis Fernandez
Vice President
Arvon Industries, Inc.
21 St. Claire Avenue East
Toronto, ON M4T IL9
CANADA ↓2X

Dear Mr. Fernandez: ↓2X

As a former employee and present stockholder of Arvon Industries, I wish to protest the planned sale of the Consumer Products Division. ↓2X

According to published reports, consumer products accounted for 19 percent of last year's corporate profits, and they are expected to account for even more this year. In addition, Dun & Bradstreet predicts that consumer products nationwide will outpace the general economy for the next five years.

I am concerned about the effect that this planned sale might have on overall corporate profits, on our cash dividends for investors, and on the economy of Melbourne, where the two consumer-products plants are located. Please ask your board of directors to reconsider this matter. ↓2X

→ tab 3.25″ (centerpoint) Sincerely, ↓4X

Jeanine Ford

Return address:
Jeanine Ford
901 East Benson, Apt. 3
Fort Lauderdale, FL 33301
U.S.A.

A. BUSINESS LETTER ON EXECUTIVE STATIONERY

(7.25" × 10.5"; 1" side margins; with delivery notation)

↓5X
July 18, 20-- ↓4X

Mr. Rodney Eastwood
BBL Resources
523 Northern Ridge
Fayetteville, PA 17222 ↓2X

Dear Rodney: ↓2X

I see no reason why we should continue to consider the locality around Geraldton for our new plant. Even though the desirability of this site from an economic view is undeniable, there is not sufficient housing readily available for our workers. ↓2X

In trying to control urban growth, the city has been turning down the building permits for much new housing or placing so many restrictions on foreign investment as to make it too expensive.

Please continue to seek out other areas of exploration where we might form a joint partnership. ↓2X

Sincerely, ↓4X

Jennifer Gwatkin

Jennifer Gwatkin, Director ↓2X

mme
By fax

Delivery notation

B. BUSINESS LETTER ON HALF-PAGE STATIONERY

(5.5" × 8.5"; 0.75" side margins)

↓4 X
July 18, 20-- ↓4X

Mr. Aristeo Olivas
BBL Resources
52A Northern Ridge
Fayetteville, PA 17222 ↓2X

Dear Aristeo: ↓2X

We should discontinue considering Geraldton for our new plant. Housing is not readily available.

Please seek out other areas of exploration where we might someday form a joint partnership. ↓2X

Sincerely, ↓4X

Chimere Jones

Chimere Jones, Director ↓2X

adk

C. BUSINESS LETTER FORMATTED FOR A WINDOW ENVELOPE

(with open punctuation)

↓5X
July 18, 20-- ↓3X

Ms. Reinalda Guerrero
BBL Resources
52A Northern Ridge
Fayetteville, PA 17222 ↓3X

Dear Ms. Guerrero ↓2X *Open punctuation*

I see no reason why we should even continue to consider the locality around Geraldton for our new plant. Even though the desirability of this site from an economic view is undeniable, there is insufficient housing readily available for our workers. ↓2X

In trying to control urban growth, the city has been turning down the building permits for new housing or placing so many restrictions on foreign investment as to make it too expensive.

Please continue to seek out other areas of exploration where we might form a joint partnership. ↓2X

Sincerely ↓4X *Open punctuation*

Augustus Mays

Augustus Mays
Vice President for Operations ↓2X

woc

D. MEMO

(with ruled table, left- and right-aligned columns, and attachment notation)

↓5X →tab

MEMO TO: Nancy Price, Executive Vice President ↓2X

FROM: Arlyn J. Bunch, Operations *ajb*

DATE: July 18, 20--

SUBJECT: New Plant Site ↓2X

As you can see from the attached letter, I've informed BBL Resources that I see no reason why we should continue to consider the locality around Geraldton for our new plant. Even though the desirability of this site from an economic standpoint is undeniable, there is insufficient housing available. In fact, as of June 25, the number of appropriate single-family houses listed for sale within a 25-mile radius of Geraldton was as follows: ↓2X

Ruled table

Agent	Units
Belle Real Estate	123
Castleton Homes	11
Red Carpet	9
Geraldton Homes	5

↓1X

In addition, in trying to control urban growth, Geraldton has been either turning down building permits for new housing or placing excessive restrictions on them. Because of this deficiency of housing for our employees, we have no choice but to look elsewhere. ↓2X

woc
Attachment

Attachment notation

A. MULTIPAGE BUSINESS LETTER

(page 1; with on-arrival notation, international address, subject line, and boxed table)

↓5X
May 13, 20-- ↓2X

On-arrival notation CONFIDENTIAL ↓2X

Mr. Lester Thompson
Associate Director
British Mutual Broadcasting
24 Portland Place
International address London WIN 4BB
ENGLAND ↓2X

Dear Mr. Thompson: ↓2X

Subject line Subject: International Study Tour ↓2X

I have been invited by the Federal Communications Commission to participate in a study of television news programming in six European countries. The enclosed report explains the purpose of the study in detail. ↓2X

I have been assigned to lead a study group through six European countries to gather firsthand information on this topic. In addition to me, our group will consist of the following members: ↓2X

Boxed table 14 pt INTERNATIONAL STUDY TOUR GROUP ↓1X

12 pt ↓

Name	Organization	Location
Mrs. Katherine Grant	WPQR-TV	Los Angeles, CA
Dr. Manuél Cruz	Miami Herald	Miami, FL
Mr. Richard Logan	Cable News Network	Atlanta, GA
Ms. Barbara Brooks	Associated Press	Chicago, IL

↓1X
Our initial plans are for the team to spend at least one full day in each of these countries. That, of course, could change. Many different events have been planned. I will be organizing and facilitating meeting with the news programming

B. MULTIPAGE BUSINESS LETTER

(page 2; with page number; multiline list; company name; and enclosure, delivery, copy, postscript, and blind copy notations)

2 *Page number*

staff of one or two of the major networks, touring their facilities, viewing recent broadcasts, and, in general, getting a firsthand view of actual news operations.

Our tentative itinerary calls for a departure date of Monday, July 26. Our arrival city is London. We will spend at least two days there to be sure that all meeting participants have arrived safely.

We should arrive at Heathrow Airport at 7:10 a.m. on Tuesday, July 27. We will immediately go to our hotel and begin our tours the next morning. Would it be possible for us to do the following: ↓2X

Multiline list

1. Meet with various members of your staff sometime on July 28. We would be available from 8:30 a.m. until 1:30 p.m.
2. Receive a copy of your programming log for the week of July 26-30 and especially a minute-by-minute listing of the programming segments for your national news reporting. ↓2X

I would appreciate your contacting Barbara Jones, our liaison, at 202.555.3943 to let us know whether we may study your operations on July 28. ↓2X

Sincerely, ↓2X

Company name METRO BROADCASTING COMPANY ↓4X

Denise J. Watterson

Denise J. Watterson
General Manager ↓2X

rcp
Enclosure notation Enclosures: FCC Report, Biographical Sketches
Delivery notation By FedEx
Copy notation c: Barbara Jones, Manuél Cruz ↓2X

Postscript PS: The Federal Communications Commission will reimburse your organization for any expenses associated with our visit. ↓2X

Blind copy notation bc: Public Relations Office, FCC

C. E-MAIL MESSAGE IN MICROSOFT OUTLOOK

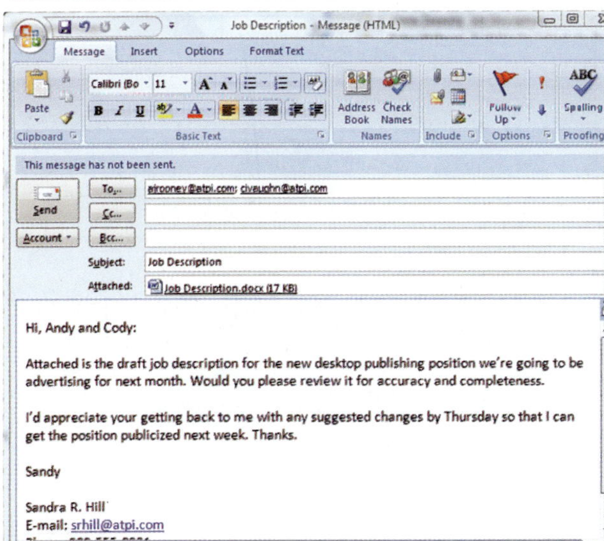

D. E-MAIL MESSAGE IN MSN HOTMAIL

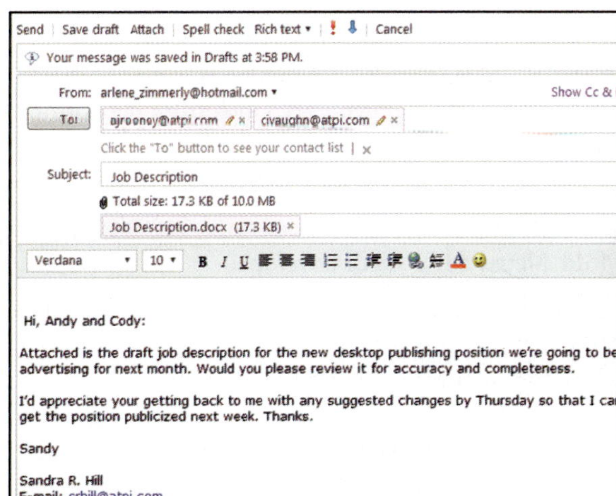

A. FORMATTING ENVELOPES

A standard large (No. 10) envelope is 9.5 by 4.125 inches. A standard small (No. 6¾) envelope is 6.5 by 3.625 inches.

A window envelope requires no formatting, since the letter is formatted and folded so that the inside address is visible through the window.

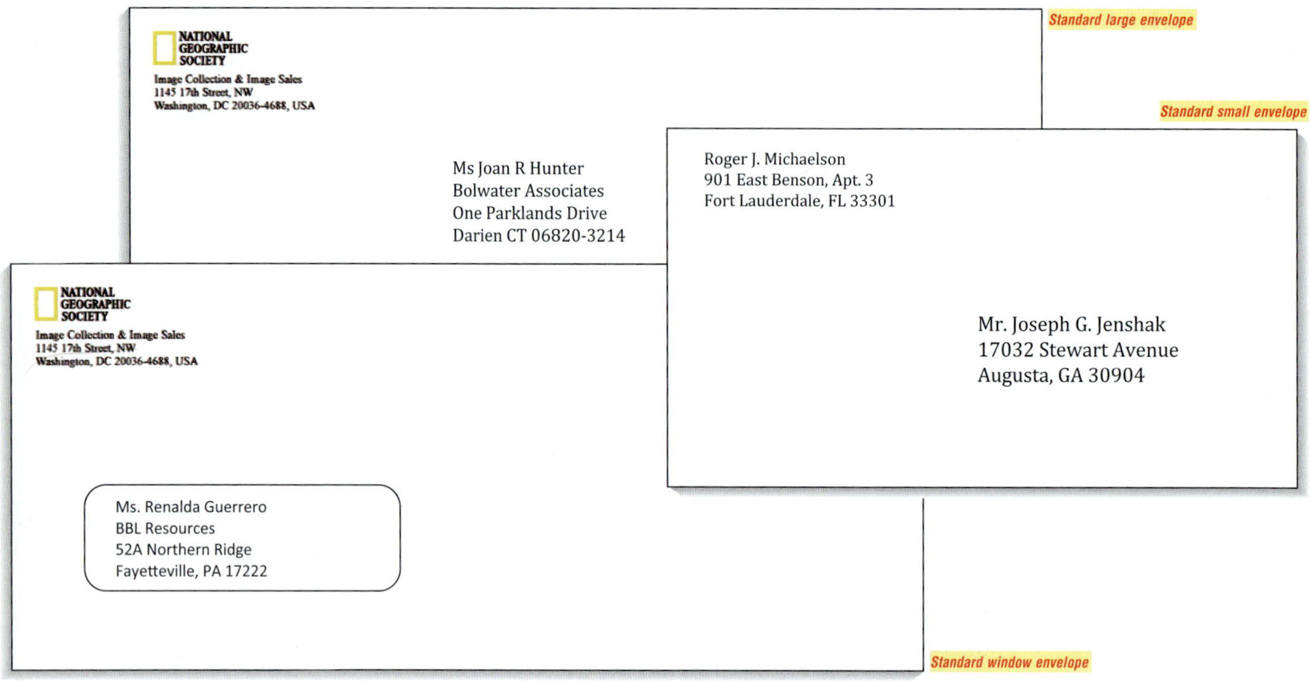

B. FOLDING LETTERS

To fold a letter for a large envelope:

1. Place the letter *face up,* and fold up the bottom third.
2. Fold the top third down to 0.5 inch from the bottom edge.
3. Insert the last crease into the envelope first, with the flap facing up.

To fold a letter for a small envelope:

1. Place the letter *face up,* and fold up the bottom half to 0.5 inch from the top.
2. Fold the right third over to the left.
3. Fold the left third over to 0.5 inch from the right edge.
4. Insert the last crease into the envelope first, with the flap facing up.

To fold a letter for a window envelope:

1. Place the letter *face down* with the letterhead at the top, and fold the bottom third of the letter up.
2. Fold the top third down so that the address shows.
3. Insert the letter into the envelope so that the address shows through the window.

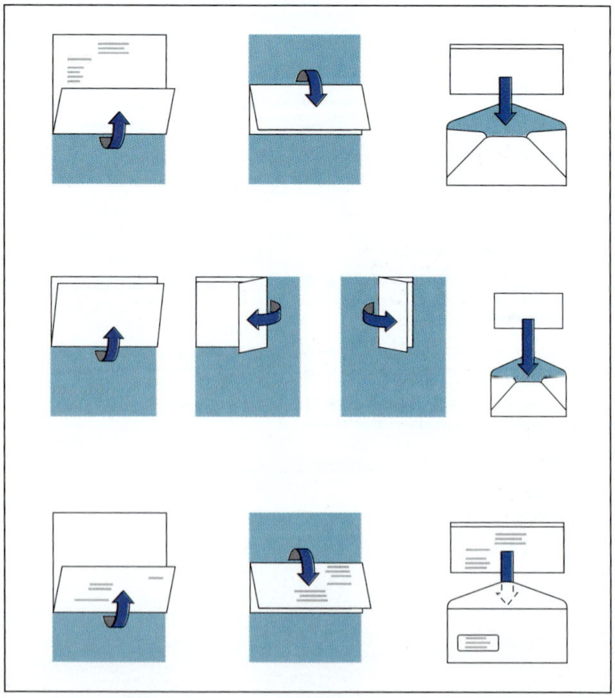

A. OUTLINE

(with 2-line title)

right tab: 0.3″
left tabs: 0.4″, 0.7″

↓5X

2-line title 14 pt **AN ANALYSIS OF THE SCOPE AND EFFECTIVENESS OF ONLINE ADVERTISING** ↓2X

12 pt ↓ **The Status of Point-and-Click Selling** ↓2X

Jonathan R. Evans ↓2X

January 19, 20-- ↓2X

→ tab 0.3″ → tab 0.4″ → tab 0.7″

I. INTRODUCTION ↓2X

II. SCOPE AND TRENDS IN INTERNET ADVERTISING
- A. Internet Advertising
- B. Major Online Advertisers
- C. Positioning and Pricing
- D. Types of Advertising ↓2X

III. ADVERTISING EFFECTIVENESS
- A. The Banner Debate
- B. Increasing Advertising Effectiveness
- C. Measuring ROI

IV. CONCLUSION

B. TITLE PAGE

(with 2-line title)

center page ↓

2-line title 14 pt **AN ANALYSIS OF THE SCOPE AND EFFECTIVENESS OF ONLINE ADVERTISING** ↓2X

12 pt ↓ **The Status of Point-and-Click Selling** ↓12X

Submitted to ↓2X

Luis Torres
General Manager
ViaWorld, International ↓12X

Prepared by ↓2X

Jonathan R. Evans
Assistant Marketing Manager
ViaWorld, International ↓2X

January 19, 20--

C. TRANSMITTAL MEMO

(with 2-line subject line and attachment notation)

↓5X →tab

MEMO TO: Luis Torres, General Manager ↓2X

FROM: Jonathan R. Evans, Assistant Marketing Manager *jre*

DATE: January 19, 20--

2-line subject line **SUBJECT:** An Analysis of the Scope and Effectiveness of Current Online →tab Advertising in Today's Marketplace ↓2X

Here is the final report analyzing the scope and effectiveness of Internet advertising that you requested on January 5. ↓2X

The report predicts that the total value of the business-to-business e-commerce market will continue to increase by geometric proportions. New technologies aimed at increasing Internet ad interactivity and the adoption of standards for advertising response measurement and tracking will contribute to this increase. Unfortunately, as discussed in this report, the use of "rich media" and interactivity in Web advertising will create its own set of problems.

I enjoyed working on this assignment, Luis, and learned quite a bit from my analysis of the situation. Please let me know if you have any questions about the report. ↓2X

plw
Attachment notation Attachment

D. TABLE OF CONTENTS

left tab: 0.5″
right dot-leader tab: 6.5″

↓5X

14 pt **CONTENTS** ↓2X

12 pt ↓

A. MULTIPAGE BUSINESS REPORT

(page 1; with side and paragraph headings, multiline list, footnote references, and footnotes)

↓5X

2-line title 14 pt **AN ANALYSIS OF THE SCOPE AND EFFECTIVENESS OF ONLINE ADVERTISING** ↓2X

Subtitle 12 pt ↓ **The Status of Point-and-Click Selling** ↓2X

Byline **Jonathan R. Evans** ↓2X

Date **January 19, 20--** ↓2X

Online advertising uses the Internet for the sole purpose of delivering marketing messages to customers. Some examples of online advertising are ads on search engine results pages, banner ads, interactive media ads, and online classified advertising. One major benefit of online advertising is the immediate publishing of content that is not limited by geography or time. Interactive advertising presents fresh challenges for advertisers.[1] ↓2X *Footnote reference*

Side heading **GROWTH FACTORS** ↓2X

Online business has grown in tandem with the expanding number of Internet users. That trend will only increase as time goes on. ↓2X

Paragraph heading **Uncertainty**. The uncertainties surrounding advertising on the Internet remain one of the major impediments to the expansion. ↓2X

Reasons for Not Advertising Online. A recent survey found two main reasons cited for not advertising online:[2] ↓2X

Multiline list

1. The difficulty of determining return on investment, especially in terms of repeat business and first-time shoppers.
2. The lack of reliable tracking and measurement data.

Footnotes

[1] Shannon Newsome, "Effective Online Advertising," *E-Mail Marketing Daily,* August 12, 2010, p. R6.

[2] "eWebStats: Online Trends in the United States," e*WebStats Home page,* August 11, 2010, <http://www.ewebstats.com/trends/ad>, accessed on September 7, 2010.

B. MULTIPAGE BUSINESS REPORT

(last page; with page number, indented display, side heading, boxed table with table number and note, and footnote)

3 *Page number*

who argue that banners have a strong potential for advertising effectiveness point out that it is not the banner format itself that presents a problem to advertising effectiveness, but rather the quality of the banner and the attention to its placement. According to Steven Mocha, president of Web Ads International: ↓2X

→indent 0.5″ ←indent 0.5″

Indented display

> A banner ad notifies visitors of the product or service and presents reasons why the consumer should choose the product in question. If the reasons are not compelling, then the banner ad has failed to achieve its purpose. If the banner ad is unattractive and obtrusive, it will alienate the consumer. When written and designed well, the banner ad is extremely effective in garnering business.[4] ↓2X

Thus, while some analysts continue to argue that the banner advertisement is passé, there is little evidence of its abandonment. Instead, ad agencies are focusing on increasing the banner's effectiveness. ↓2X

SCOPE AND TRENDS IN ONLINE ADVERTISING ↓2X

Starting from zero in 1994, analysts agree that the volume of Internet advertising spending has risen rapidly. However, as indicated in Table 3, analysts provide a wide range of the exact amount of such advertising. ↓2X

Table number title 14 pt **Table 3. INTERNET ADVERTISING**

12 pt ↓ **Current Year Estimates** ↓1X

Source	Estimate
Internet Advertising Conference	$3.92 billion
Forecaster	3.30 billion
IPC International	3.20 billion
Brown Media	980 million
Note: This information is subject to change.	

Table note

↓1X

The differences in estimates of total Web advertising spending is generally attributed to the different methodologies used by the research agencies to gather the data. Further research is pending and will be reported next month.

---

[4] Steven Mocha, "Banner Ads That Really Work," *The Online Advertising Journal,* June 17, 2010, p. D1.

C. MULTIPAGE ACADEMIC REPORT

(page 1; with 2-line title, endnote references, and multiline list)

↓5SS

2-line title 14 pt **AN ANALYSIS OF THE SCOPE AND EFFECTIVENESS** ↓1DS

OF ONLINE ADVERTISING ↓1DS

12 pt ↓ **The Status of Point-and-Click Selling** ↓1DS

Jonathan R. Evans ↓1DS

January 19, 20-- ↓1DS

One major benefit of online advertising is the immediate publishing of content that is not limited by geography or time. ↓1DS

GROWTH FACTORS ↓1DS

Online business has grown in tandem with the expanding number of Internet users, which is growing exponentially each year.[i] ↓1DS *Endnote reference*

Reasons for Not Advertising Online. A recent survey conducted by TAIR found two main reasons cited for not advertising online:[ii]

Multiline list

1. The difficulty of determining return on investment, especially in terms of repeat business and first-time shoppers.
2. The lack of reliable tracking and measurement data.

Obviously, there are many other reasons in addition to these two for not advertising online. However, with the growing number of Internet users, these

D. MULTIPAGE ACADEMIC REPORT

(last page; with page number, indented display, and endnotes)

14 *Page number*

advertising effectiveness, but rather the quality of the banner and the attention to the banner placement. According to Mike Windsor, president of Ogilvy Interactive: ↓1DS

→indent 0.5″ ←indent 0.5″

Indented display

> It's more a case of bad banner ads, just like there are bad TV ads. The space itself has huge potential. As important as using the space within the banner creatively is to aim it effectively. Unlike broadcast media, the Web offers advertisers the opportunity to reach a specific audience based on data gathered about who is surfing at a site and what their interests are.[vii] ↓2SS

From an advertiser's perspective, most effective Internet ads do more than just deliver information to the consumer and grab the consumer's attention—they also gather information about consumers (e.g., through "cookies" and other methodologies). From the consumer's perspective, this type of interactivity may represent an intrusion and an invasion of privacy.

Endnotes

[i] Shannon Newsome, "Effective Online Advertising," *E-Mail Marketing Daily,* July 12, 2010, p. R6.

[ii] "eWebStats: Online Trends in the United States," e*WebStats Home page,* August 11, 2010, <http://www.ewebstats.com/trends/ad>, accessed on September 7, 2010.

[iii] Barbara Fisher, "Net Ratings Index Predicts Rise in Web Ads," *Advertising Today,* July 19, 2010, p. 10.

[iv] Ron Heisman, "Internet Banner Ads Growth Trends," *Internet Associates Conference Home page,* November 13, 2010, <http://www.iac.net/conference>, accessed on December 8, 2010.

[v] Alexis Dirkson, "Point-and-Click Bargains for Internet Ad Surfers," *Internet Age,* March 8, 2010, p. 12.

[vi] Andrew Romero, "Gathering Statistics to Grow Your Internet Business," *The Wall Street Journal,* March 2, 2010, p. C20.

[vii] Lisa Gunderson, "Banner Banter" *The London Financial Times,* June 17, 2010, p. D1.

A. LEFT-BOUND BUSINESS REPORT

(page 1; with 2-line title, single-line list, and footnotes)

left margin: 1.5"
right margin: *default* 1"

↓5X

2-line title 14 pt **AN ANALYSIS OF THE SCOPE AND EFFECTIVENESS OF ONLINE ADVERTISING** ↓2X

12 pt ↓ **The Status of Point-and-Click Selling** ↓2X

Jonathan R. Evans ↓2X

January 19, 20-- ↓2X

Online advertising uses the Internet for the sole purpose of delivering marketing messages to customers. Some examples of online advertising are as follows: ads on search engine results pages, banner ads, interactive media ads, and e-mail marketing. One major benefit of online advertising is the immediate publishing of content that is not limited by geography or time. Interactive advertising presents new challenges for advertisers.[1] ↓2X

GROWTH FACTORS ↓2X

Online business has grown in tandem with the expanding number of Internet users. That trend will only increase as time goes on. ↓2X

Uncertainty. The uncertainties surrounding advertising on the Internet remain one of the major impediments to the expansion. All of the Internet advertising industry is today in a state of flux. ↓2X

Reasons for Not Advertising Online. A recent survey found two main reasons cited for not advertising online:[2] ↓2X

Single-line list

1. The difficulty of determining return on investment.
2. The lack of reliable tracking and measurement data.

Footnotes

[1] Shannon Newsome, "Effective Online Advertising," *E-Mail Marketing Daily*, July 12, 2010, p. R6.
[2] "eWebStats: Online Trends in the United States," *eWebStats Home page*, August 11, 2010, <http://www.ewebstats.com/trends/ad>, accessed on September 7, 2010.

B. BIBLIOGRAPHY

(for business or academic style using either endnotes or footnotes)

hanging indent ↓ ↓5X

14 pt **BIBLIOGRAPHY** ↓2X

12 pt ↓

Book—one author Adams, Ana B., *Internet Advertising*, Brunswick Press, Boston, 2009. ↓2X

Annual report AdNet Incorporated, *2010 Annual Report*, BCI, Inc., San Francisco, 2010.

Newspaper article An, Sang Jin, "Banner Ad Frenzy," *The Wall Street Journal*, July 12, 2010, p. R6.

Book—two authors Arlens, Rachel, and Seymour Schell, *E-Vertising*, New England Publishing, Cambridge, Mass., 2009.

→ hanging indent

Book—organization as author *Directory of Internet Business Services*, International Corporate Libraries Assoc., New York, 2009.

WWW page "eWebStats: Online Trends in the United States," *eWebStats Home page*, August 11, 2010, <http://www.ewebstats.com/trends/ad>, accessed on September 7, 2010.

Journal article—paged continuously Ingram, Fred, "Hiring Trends in Online Advertising," *Personnel Quarterly*, Vol. 30, September 2009, pp. 104-116.

Journal article—paged each issue Johnson, Jennifer, "WebRatings Index Shows 8% Rise in Web Ads," *Advertising Today*, July 19, 2010, p. 18.

Online database "Motivational Advertising Techniques," *Advertising Encyclopedia*, N.D., <http://www.adtech.com/motivational_advertising_techniques.html>, accessed on January 7, 2010.

Government document National Institute of Psychology, *Who Clicks? An Analysis of Internet Advertising*, TNIP Publication No. ADM 82-1195, U.S. Government Printing Office, Washington, 2009.

E-mail Williams, Dennis V., "Reaction to Analysis of Internet Ads," e-mail message, August 18, 2010.

C. MEMO REPORT

(page 1, with 2-line subject line, endnote references, and single-line list)

↓5X →tab

MEMO TO: Luis Torres, General Manager ↓2X

FROM: Jonathan R. Evans, Assistant Marketing Manager *jre*

DATE: January 19, 20--

2-line subject line **SUBJECT:** An Analysis of the Scope and Effectiveness of Current Online →tab Advertising in Today's Marketplace ↓2X

Online advertising uses the Internet and World Wide Web for the sole purpose of delivering marketing messages to customers. Some examples of online advertising are ads on search engine results pages, banner ads, interactive media ads, social network site advertising, online classified advertising, advertising networks, and e-mail marketing, including e-mail spam. ↓2X

One major benefit of online advertising is the immediate publishing of information and content that is not limited by geography or time. To that end, the emerging area of interactive advertising presents fresh challenges for advertisers.[i] Such challenges are opportunities for growth. ↓2X *Endnote reference*

GROWTH FACTORS ↓2X

Online business has grown in tandem with the expanding number of Internet users. That trend will only increase as time goes on. ↓2X

Uncertainty. The uncertainties surrounding advertising on the Internet remain one of the major impediments to the expansion. All of the Internet advertising industry is today in a state of flux.

Reasons for Not Advertising Online. A recent survey found two main reasons cited for not advertising online:[ii] ↓2X

Single-line list

1. The difficulty of determining return on investment.
2. The lack of reliable tracking and measurement data.

D. FORMATTING REPORTS

Margins, Spacing, and Indents. Begin the first page of each section (for example, the table of contents, first page of the body, and bibliography pages) 2 inches from the top of the page. Begin other pages 1 inch from the top. Use 1-inch default side and bottom margins for all pages. For a left-bound report, add 0.5 inch to the left margin. Single-space business reports. Double-space academic reports and indent paragraphs.

Titles and Headings. Center the title in 14-pt. font. Single-space multiline titles in a single-spaced report, and double-space multiline titles in a double-spaced report. Insert 1 blank line before and after all parts of a heading block (may include the title, subtitle, author, and/or date), and format all lines in bold. Format side headings in bold, at the left margin, with 1 blank line before and after them. Format paragraph headings at the left margin for single-spaced reports and indented for double-spaced reports in bold, followed by a period in bold and one space.

Citations. Format citations using Word's footnote (or endnote) feature.

Margins, Spacing, Headings, and Citations for APA- or MLA-Style Reports. See page R-10.

A. REPORT IN APA STYLE

(page 3; with header, 2-line title, byline, main heading, subheading, and citations)

top, bottom, and side margins: *default* (1")
double-space throughout

Online Advertising 3 *Header*

2-line title An Analysis of the Scope and Effectiveness

of Online Advertising

Byline Jonathan R. Evans

→ tab Online advertising uses the Internet for the sole purpose of delivering marketing messages to customers. Some examples of online advertising are ads on search engine results pages, banner ads, interactive media ads, online classifieds, advertising networks, and e-mail marketing (Gunderson, 2011, p. D1). *Citation*

One major benefit of online advertising is the immediate publishing of content that is not limited by geography or time. To that end, interactive advertising presents fresh challenges for advertisers (Newsome, 2010).

Main heading Growth Factors

Online business has grown in tandem with the expanding number of Internet users. That trend will only increase as time goes on (Arlens & Schell).

Subheading *Uncertainty* ← Italic

The uncertainties surrounding Internet advertising are impeding its expansion. A recent survey found two main reasons cited for not advertising online. The first is the difficulty of determining return on investment, especially in terms of repeat business and first-time shoppers. The second is the lack of reliable tracking and measurement data ("eWebStats," 2010).

B. REFERENCES IN APA STYLE

(page 14; with header)

top, bottom, and side margins: *default* (1")
double-space throughout

Online Advertising 14 *Header*

hanging indent ↓ References

Book—one author Adams, A. B. (2009). *Internet advertising and the upcoming electronic upheaval.*

→ hanging indent Boston: Brunswick Press.

Annual report AdNet Incoporated. (2010). *2010 annual report.* San Francisco: BCI, Inc.

Newspaper article An, S. J. (2010, July 12). Banner ad frenzy. *The Wall Street Journal,* p. R6.

Book—two authors Arlens, R., & Seymour, S. (2010). *E-vertising.* Cambridge, MA: New England Publishing.

Book—organization as author *Directory of business and financial services.* (2009). New York: International Corporate Libraries Association.

WWW page eWebStats: Advertising revenues and trends. (n.d.). New York: eMarketer. Retrieved August 11, 2010, from http://www.emarketer.com/ewebstats/2507manu.ad

Journal article—paged continuously Ingram, F. (2009). Trends in online advertising. *Personnel Quarterly, 20,* 804-816.

Journal article—paged each issue Johnson, J. (2010, July 19). WebRatings Index shows 4% rise in Web ads. *Advertising Today, 39,* 18.

Online database *Motivational advertising techniques.* (2010, January). *Advertising Encyclopedia.* Retrieved January 7, 2010, from http://www.adtech.com/ads.html

Government document National Institute of Psychology (2009). *Who clicks? An analysis of Internet advertising* (TNIP Publication No. ADM 82-1195). Washington, DC.

C. REPORT IN MLA STYLE

(page 1; with header, heading, 2-line title, and citations)

top, bottom, and side margins: *default* (1")
double-space throughout

Evans 1 *Header*

Heading Jonathan R. Evans

Professor Inman

Management 302

19 January 20--

2-line title An Analysis of the Scope and Effectiveness

of Online Advertising

→ tab Online advertising uses the Internet for the sole purpose of delivering marketing messages to customers. Some examples of online advertising are ads on search engine results pages, banner ads, interactive media ads, social network site advertising, online classifieds, and e-mail marketing (Gunderson D1). *Citation*

One major benefit of online advertising is the immediate publishing of information and content that is not limited by geography or time. To that end, interactive advertising presents fresh challenges for advertisers (Newsome 59).

Online business has grown in tandem with the expanding number of Internet users. That trend will only increase as time goes on (Arlens & Schell 376-379). The uncertainties surrounding Internet advertising remain one of the major impediments to the expansion. A recent survey found two main reasons cited for not advertising online. The first is the difficulty of determining return on investment. The second is the lack of reliable tracking and measurement data.

D. WORKS CITED IN MLA STYLE

(page 14; with header and hanging indent)

top, bottom, and side margins: *default* (1")
double-space throughout

Evans 14 *Header*

hanging indent ↓ Works Cited

Book—one author Adams, Ana. B. *Internet Advertising and the Upcoming Electronic Upheaval.*

→ hanging indent Boston: Brunswick Press, 2009.

Annual report AdNet Incoporated. *2010 Annual Report.* San Francisco: BCI, Inc., 2010.

Newspaper article An, Sang Jin. "Banner Ad Frenzy." *The Wall Street Journal,* 12 July 2010: R6.

Book—two authors Arlens, Rachel, and Seymour Schell. *E-vertising.* Cambridge, MA: New England Publishing, 2009.

Book—organization as author Corporate Libraries Association. *Directory of Business and Financial Services.* New York: Corporate Libraries Association, 2009.

WWW page "eWebStats. Advertising Revenues and Trends." 11 Aug. 2009. 7 Jan. 2010 <http://www.emarketer.com/ewebstats/ad>.

Journal article—paged continuously Ingram, Frank. "Trends in Online Advertising." *Personnel Quarterly* 20 (2010): 804-816.

Journal article—paged each issue Johnson, June. "WRI shows 4% rise in Web ads." *WebAds Today* 19 July 2010: 18.

Online database *Motivational Advertising Techniques.* 2010. Advertising Encyclopedia. 7 Jan. 2010 <http://www.adtech.com/ads.html>.

Government document National Institute of Psychology. *Who clicks?* TNIP Publication No. ADM 82-1195. Washington, DC. GPO: 2010.

E-mail Williams, Dan V. "Reaction to Internet Ads." E-mail to the author. 18 Aug. 2010.

A. MEETING AGENDA

↓5X

14 pt **MILES HARDWARE EXECUTIVE COMMITTEE** ↓2X

12 pt ↓ **Meeting Agenda** ↓2X

June 7, 20-- ↓2X

Numbered list: default format

1. Call to order
2. Approval of minutes of May 5 meeting
3. Progress report on building addition and parking lot restrictions (Norman Hodges and Anthony Pascarelli)
4. May 15 draft of Five-Year Plan
5. Review of National Hardware Association annual convention
6. Employee grievance filed by Ellen Burrows (John Landstrom)
7. New expense-report forms (Anne Richards)
8. Announcements
9. Adjournment

B. MINUTES OF A MEETING

↓5X

14 pt **RESOURCE COMMITTEE** ↓2X

12 pt ↓**Minutes of the Meeting** ↓2X

March 13, 20-- ↓1X

ATTENDANCE	The Resource Committee met on March 13, 20--, at the Airport Sheraton in Portland, Oregon, with all members present. Michael Davis, chairperson, called the meeting to order at 2:30 p.m. ↓1X
APPROVAL OF MINUTES	The minutes of the January 27 meeting were read and approved as presented.
OLD BUSINESS	The members of the committee reviewed the sales brochure on electronic copyboards and agreed to purchase one for the conference room. Cynthia Giovanni will secure quotations from at least two suppliers.
NEW BUSINESS	The committee reviewed a request from the Purchasing Department for three new computers. After extensive discussion regarding the appropriate use of the computers and software to be purchased, the committee approved the request.
ADJOURNMENT	The meeting was adjourned at 4:45 p.m. The next meeting is scheduled for April 13 in Suite B. ↓2X Respectfully submitted, ↓4X *D. S. Madsen* D. S. Madsen, Secretary

(Note: Table shown with "View Gridlines" active.)

C. ITINERARY

↓5X

14 pt **PORTLAND SALES MEETING** ↓2X

12 pt ↓ **Itinerary for Dorothy Turner** ↓2X

March 12-15, 20-- ↓1X

THURSDAY, MARCH 12	↓1X
5:10 p.m.-7:06 p.m.	Flight from Detroit to Portland; Northwest 83 (800-555-1212); e-ticket; Seat 8D; nonstop. ↓2X Jack Weatherford (Home: 503-555-8029; Office: 503-555-7631) will meet your flight on Thursday, provide transportation during your visit, and return you to the airport on Saturday morning. Airport Sheraton (503-555-4032) King-sized bed, nonsmoking room; late arrival guaranteed; Reservation No. 30ZM6-02. ↓1X
FRIDAY, MARCH 13	
9 a.m.-5:30 p.m.	Portland Sales Meeting 1931 Executive Way, Suite 10 Portland, OR 97211 (503-555-7631)
SATURDAY, MARCH 14	
7:30 a.m.-2:47 p.m.	Flight from Portland to Detroit; Northwest 360; e-ticket; Seat 9a; nonstop.

(Note: Table shown with "View Gridlines" active.)

D. LEGAL DOCUMENT

(with line numbers)

left tabs: 1″, 3.25″
right tab: 6.5″

← line numbers (court documents only)

STATE OF NEVADA → tab 6.5″ IN DISTRICT COURT ↓2X

COUNTY OF CLARK NORTHEAST JUDICIAL DISTRICT ↓2X

JOHN C. SMITH → tab 3.25″) → tab 6.5″ NO. 1 space, 20 underscores
209 East Clark Avenue)
Las Vegas, NV 89155-1603)
)
→ tab 1″ Plaintiff, → tab 3.25″)
)
vs.) → tab 6.5″ SUMMONS
)
FAITH GEORGIA)
)
Defendant.)
↓2X

THE STATE OF NEVADA TO THE ABOVE-NAMED DEFENDANT: ↓2X

→ tab 1″ You are hereby summoned and required to appear and defend against the Complaint in this action, which is hereby served upon you by serving upon the undersigned an Answer or other proper response within twenty (20) days after the service of the Summons and Complaint upon you, exclusive of the day of service. ↓2X

If you fail to do so, judgment by default will be taken against you for the relief demanded in the Complaint.

SIGNED this _____ day of July, 20--. ↓2X

1 space; 5 underscores; 1 space → tab 3.25″ underscores to the right margin

Jim Roe → tab 6.5″ Attorney at Law
229 South Civic Way
Laughlin, NV 89029-2648
Telephone: 702-555-1205
Attorney for Plaintiff

A. RESUME

↓5X

Cambria 14 pt Bold ↓ **TERRY M. MARTINA** ↓2X

Cambria 12 pt Bold ↓ **250 Maxwell Avenue, Boulder, CO 80305**
Phone: 303-555-9311; e-mail: tmartina@ecc.edu ↓1X

↓1X ↓1X Calibri 12 pt ↓

Calibri 12 pt Bold ↓

OBJECTIVE	Position in resort management anywhere in Colorado. ↓1X
EDUCATION	Edgewood Community College, Boulder, Colorado A.A. in hotel management to be awarded May 2011 → indent 0.5" Achieved grade point average of 3.1 (on 4.0 scale). Received Board of Regents tuition scholarship. ↓2X Central City High School, Denver, Colorado Graduated: May 2009 ↓1X
EXPERIENCE	*Assistant Manager, Burger King Restaurant* ← Calibri 12 pt Italic Boulder, Colorado May 2010 to Present → indent 0.5" In charge of balancing the cash register, closing the restaurant, and making night deposits. *Student Intern, Ski Valley Haven* Aspen, Colorado September to December 2009 Worked as an assistant to the manager. Gained experience in operating First-Guest software and produced daily occupancy reports. Received Outstanding Employee award.
ACTIVITIES	Activities pursued while attending college: • Volunteer tutor, Literacy Council of America • Secretary of ECC Hospitality Services Association
REFERENCES	Available upon request.

(Note: Table shown with "View Gridlines" active.)

B. APPLICATION LETTER IN BLOCK STYLE

(with return address)

↓5X
March 1, 20-- ↓4X

Mr. Lou Mansfield, Director
Human Resources Department
Rocky Resorts International
P.O. Box 1412
Denver, CO 80214 ↓2X

Dear Mr. Mansfield: ↓2X

Please consider me an applicant for the position of concierge for Suite Retreat, as advertised in last Sunday's *Denver Times*. ↓2X

I will receive my A.A. degree in hotel management from Edgewood Community College in May and will be available for full-time employment immediately. In addition to my extensive coursework in hospitality services and business, I've had experience in working for a ski lodge similar to Suite Retreats in Aspen. As a lifelong resident of Colorado and an avid skier, I would be able to provide your guests with any information they request.

After you've reviewed my enclosed resume, I would appreciate having an opportunity to discuss with you why I believe I have the right qualifications and personality to serve as your concierge. I can be reached at 303-555-9311. ↓2X

Sincerely, ↓4X

Terry M. Martina

Return address
Terry M. Martina
250 Maxwell Avenue, Apt. 8
Boulder, CO 80305 ↓2X

Enclosure

C. FORMATTING LISTS

Numbers or bullets are used in documents to call attention to items in a list and to increase readability. If the sequence of the list items is important, use numbers rather than bullets.

- Insert 1 blank line before and after the list.
- Use Word's default format for all lists in either single- or double-spaced documents, including lists in documents such as a meeting agenda. Any carryover lines will be indented automatically.
- Use the same line spacing (single or double) between lines in the list as is used in the rest of the document.

The three bulleted and numbered lists shown at the right are all formatted correctly.

D. EXAMPLES OF DIFFERENT TYPES OF LISTS

According to the Internet Advertising Bureau, the following are the most common types of advertising on the Internet:

- Banner ads that feature some type of appropriate animation to attract the viewer's attention and interest.
- Sponsorship, in which an advertiser sponsors a content-based Web site.
- Interstitials, ads that flash up while a page downloads.

There is now considerable controversy about the effectiveness of banner advertising. As previously noted, a central goal of banner advertisements is to

*****

According to the Internet Advertising Bureau, the following are the most common types of advertising on the Internet, shown in order of popularity:

1. Banner ads
2. Sponsorship
3. Interstitials

There is now considerable controversy about the effectiveness of banner advertising. As previously noted, a central goal of banner advertisements is to

*****

According to the Internet Advertising Bureau, the following are the most common types of advertising on the Internet:

- Banner ads that feature some type of appropriate animation to attract the viewer's attention and interest.
- Sponsorship, in which an advertiser sponsors a Web site.
- Interstitials, ads that flash up while a page downloads.

There is now considerable controversy about the effectiveness of banner advertising. As previously noted, a central goal of banner advertisements is to

A. BOXED TABLE

(with subtitle; bottom-aligned and braced column headings; left- and right-aligned columns; total line and table note)

center page ↓
center horizontally

Title — 14 pt **AUSTIN-REEVES PRINTER DEPOT**
Subtitle — 12 pt ↓ **Sales Trends for 20--**
(000s omitted)
↓1X

Braced column headings
align bottom ↓
↓1X

Product	**Annual Sales**		**Quarterly Sales**	
	This Year	**Last Year**	**This Quarter**	**Last Quarter**
Ink-jet: color	$ 569	$ 841	$ 120	$ 99
Ink-jet: color portable	6	24	2	6
Ink-jet: black and white	273	588	71	147
Printer/copier combination	1,622	2,054	422	509
Black-and-white laser: standard	389	507	121	129
Black-and-white laser: premium	2,368	87	592	25
Color laser	409	230	100	70
Totals	$5,636	$4,331	$1,428	$985
Note: Sales for this quarter ended at midnight, December 31.				

Total line
Table note

B. OPEN TABLE

(with 2-line title; 2-line centered, bottom-aligned column headings; left- and right-aligned columns; column entries with dollar and percent signs)

center page ↓
center horizontally

2-line title — 14 pt **SUITE HOLIDAY RETREAT**
12 pt ↓ **BOUTIQUE HOTELS**
Row 1 — **New Lodging Rates**
↓1X

Row 2 — align bottom ↓ — ↓1X — 2-line column heading
Row 3 ↓

Location	**Rack Rate**	**Discount Rate**	**Saving**
Bozeman, Montana	$ 95.75	$ 91.50	4.4%
Chicago, Illinois	159.00	139.50	12.3%
Dallas, Texas	249.50	219.00	12.2%
Las Vegas, Nevada	98.50	89.95	8.7%
Beverly Hills, California	1,179.00	950.00	19.4%
Minneapolis, Minnesota	115.00	95.00	17.4%
New York, New York	227.50	175.00	23.1%
Orlando, Florida	105.75	98.50	6.3%
Portland, Maine	93.50	93.50	0.0%
Seattle, Washington	143.75	125.75	12.5%

2 spaces for each digit
3 spaces: 2 for each digit; 1 for each comma

Column A — Column B→

(Note: Table shown with "View Gridlines" active.)

C. RULED TABLE

(with table number, title, centered column headings, and total line)

center page ↓
center horizontally

Table number and title — 14 pt **Table 2. RESCUE ONE**
COMPUTER TECHNICAL SUPPORT
↓1X

12 pt ↓ — align bottom ↓

Support Service	**Fees to Date**
Replacement parts	$ 9,200
Troubleshooting	12,850
Software support	5,095
Hardware support	8,032
Product literature	105
Technical documentation	150
Printer drivers	129
Total	$35,561

(Note: Table shown with "View Gridlines" active.)

D. FORMATTING TABLES

The three basic styles of tables are boxed, open, and ruled. Tables have vertical columns (Column A), horizontal rows (Row 1), and intersecting cells (Cell A1). Center a table vertically that appears alone on the page. Insert 1 blank line before and after a table that appears within a document. Automatically adjust column widths and horizontally center all tables.

Heading Block. Merge any cells in Row 1, and type the heading block. Center and bold throughout. Type the title in all-caps, 14-pt. font, and the subtitle in upper- and lowercase, 12-pt. font. If a table has a number, type *Table* in upper- and lowercase. Follow the table number with a period and 1 space. Insert 1 blank line below the heading block.

Column Headings. Center column headings. Type in upper- and lowercase and bold. Bottom-align all column headings if a row includes a 2-line column heading. Merge desired cells for braced headings.

Column Entries. Left-align text columns, and right-align number columns. Capitalize only the first word and proper nouns in column entries.

Column Entry Dollar and Percent Signs. Insert the dollar sign only before the amount in the first entry and before a total amount entry. Align the dollar sign with the longest amount in the column, inserting spaces after the dollar sign as needed (allowing for 2 spaces for each digit and 1 space for each comma). Repeat the percent sign for each number in each column entry (unless the column heading identifies the data as percentages).

Table Note and Total Line. For a note line, merge the cells of the last row and use "Note" followed by a colon. For a total line, add a top and bottom border, use "Total" or "Totals" as appropriate, and add a percent or dollar sign if needed.

A. FORMATTING BUSINESS FORMS

Many business forms can be created and filled in by using templates that are provided within commercial word processing software. Template forms can be used "as is" or they can be edited. Templates can also be used to create customized forms for any business.

When a template is opened, the form is displayed on screen. The user can then fill in the necessary information, including personalized company information. Data are entered into cells or fields, and you can move quickly from field to field with a single keystroke—usually by pressing TAB or ENTER.

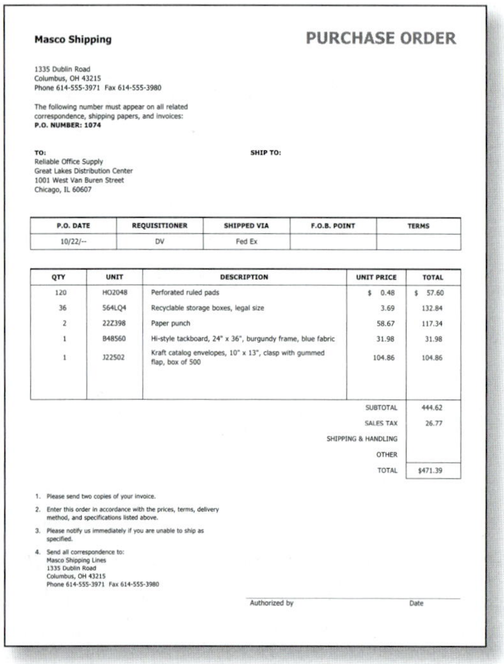

Masco Shipping PURCHASE ORDER

1335 Dublin Road
Columbus, OH 43215
Phone 614-555-3971 Fax 614-555-3980

The following number must appear on all related correspondence, shipping papers, and invoices:
P.O. NUMBER: 1074

TO:
Reliable Office Supply
Great Lakes Distribution Center
1001 West Van Buren Street
Chicago, IL 60607

SHIP TO:

P.O. DATE	REQUISITIONER	SHIPPED VIA	F.O.B. POINT	TERMS
10/22/--	DV	Fed Ex		

QTY	UNIT	DESCRIPTION	UNIT PRICE	TOTAL
120	HO2048	Perforated ruled pads	$ 0.48	$ 57.60
36	564LQ4	Recyclable storage boxes, legal size	3.69	132.84
2	22Z398	Paper punch	58.67	117.34
1	B48560	Hi-style tackboard, 24" x 36", burgundy frame, blue fabric	31.98	31.98
1	J22502	Kraft catalog envelopes, 10" x 13", clasp with gummed flap, box of 500	104.86	104.86
			SUBTOTAL	444.62
			SALES TAX	26.77
			SHIPPING & HANDLING	
			OTHER	
			TOTAL	$471.39

1. Please send two copies of your invoice.
2. Enter this order in accordance with the prices, terms, delivery method, and specifications listed above.
3. Please notify us immediately if you are unable to ship as specified.
4. Send all correspondence to:
   Masco Shipping Lines
   1335 Dublin Road
   Columbus, OH 43215
   Phone 614-555-3971 Fax 614-555-3980

Authorized by Date

B. U.S. POSTAL SERVICE ABBREVIATIONS

(for States, Territories, and Canadian Provinces)

States and Territories

Alabama	AL
Alaska	AK
Arizona	AZ
Arkansas	AR
California	CA
Colorado	CO
Connecticut	CT
Delaware	DE
District of Columbia	DC
Florida	FL
Georgia	GA
Guam	GU
Hawaii	HI
Idaho	ID
Illinois	IL
Indiana	IN
Iowa	IA
Kansas	KS
Kentucky	KY
Louisiana	LA
Maine	ME
Maryland	MD
Massachusetts	MA
Michigan	MI
Minnesota	MN
Mississippi	MS
Missouri	MO
Montana	MT
Nebraska	NE
Nevada	NV
New Hampshire	NH
New Jersey	NJ
New Mexico	NM
New York	NY
North Carolina	NC
North Dakota	ND
Ohio	OH
Oklahoma	OK
Oregon	OR
Pennsylvania	PA
Puerto Rico	PR
Rhode Island	RI
South Carolina	SC
South Dakota	SD
Tennessee	TN
Texas	TX
Utah	UT
Vermont	VT
Virgin Islands	VI
Virginia	VA
Washington	WA
West Virginia	WV
Wisconsin	WI
Wyoming	WY

Canadian Provinces

Alberta	AB
British Columbia	BC
Labrador	LB
Manitoba	MB
New Brunswick	NB
Newfoundland	NF
Northwest Territories	NT
Nova Scotia	NS
Ontario	ON
Prince Edward Island	PE
Quebec	PQ
Saskatchewan	SK
Yukon Territory	YT

C. PROOFREADERS' MARKS

Proofreaders' Marks		Draft	Final Copy
⁀	Omit space	data base	database
v or ^	Insert	if he's going (not)	if he's not going,
≡	Capitalize	Maple street	Maple Street
	Delete	a final draft	a draft
#	Insert space	allready to	all ready to
when / if	Change word	and if you (when)	and when you
/	Use lowercase letter	our President	our president
¶	Paragraph	... to use it.¶We can	... to use it. We can
•••	Don't delete	a true story	a true story
O	Spell out	the only 1	the only one
∽	Transpose	they all see	they see all

Proofreaders' Marks		Draft	Final Copy
SS	Single-space	SS first line second line	first line second line
ds	Double-space	ds first line second line	first line second line
⊐	Move right	Please send	Please send
⊏	Move left	May I	May I
∿∿	Bold	Column Heading	**Column Heading**
ital	Italic	ital Time magazine	*Time* magazine
u/l	Underline	u/l Time magazine	Time magazine
	Move as shown	readers will see	will see readers

Language Arts For Business

(50 "must-know" rules)

PUNCTUATION

Commas

RULE 1
, direct address
(L. 21)

Use commas before and after a name used in direct address.

Thank you, John, for responding to my e-mail so quickly.
Ladies and gentlemen, the program has been canceled.

RULE 2
, independent clause
(L. 27)

The underline calls attention to a point in the sentence where a comma might mistakenly be inserted.

Use a comma between independent clauses joined by a coordinate conjunction (unless both clauses are short).

Ellen left her job with IBM, and she and her sister went to Paris.
But: Ellen left her job with IBM and went to Paris with her sister.
But: John drove and I navigated.

Note: An independent clause is one that can stand alone as a complete sentence. The most common coordinate conjunctions are *and*, *but*, *or*, and *nor*.

RULE 3
, introductory expression
(L. 27)

Use a comma after an introductory expression (unless it is a short prepositional phrase).

Before we can make a decision, we must have all the facts.
But: In 2004 our nation elected a new president.

Note: An introductory expression is a group of words that come before the subject and verb of the independent clause. Common prepositions are *to*, *in*, *on*, *of*, *at*, *by*, *for*, and *with*.

RULE 4
, direct quotation
(L. 41)

Use a comma before and after a direct quotation.

James said, "I shall return," and then left.

RULE 5
, date
(L. 51)

Use a comma before and after the year in a complete date.

We will arrive on June 2, 2006, for the conference.
But: We will arrive on June 2 for the conference.

RULE 6
, place
(L. 51)

Use a comma before and after a state or country that follows a city (but not before a ZIP Code).

Joan moved to Vancouver, British Columbia, in May.
Send the package to Douglasville, GA 30135, by Express Mail.
But: Send the package to Georgia by Express Mail.

RULE 7
, series
(L. 61)

Use a comma between each item in a series of three or more.

We need to order paper, toner, and font cartridges for the printer.
They saved their work, exited their program, and turned off their computers when they finished.

Note: Do not use a comma after the last item in a series.

RULE 8
, transitional expression
(L. 61)

Use a comma before and after a transitional expression or independent comment.

It is critical, therefore, that we finish the project on time.
Our present projections, you must admit, are inadequate.
But: You must admit our present projections are inadequate.

Note: Examples of transitional expressions and independent comments are *in addition to, therefore, however, on the other hand, as a matter of fact*, and *unfortunately*.

RULE 9
, nonessential expression
(L. 71)

Use a comma before and after a nonessential expression.

Andre, who was there, can verify the statement.
But: Anyone who was there can verify the statement.
Van's first book, *Crisis of Management*, was not discussed.
Van's book *Crisis of Management* was not discussed.

Note: A nonessential expression is a group of words that may be omitted without changing the basic meaning of the sentence. Always examine the noun or pronoun that comes before the expression to determine whether the noun needs the expression to complete its meaning. If it does, the expression is *essential* and does *not* take a comma.

RULE 10
, adjacent adjectives
(L. 71)

Use a comma between two adjacent adjectives that modify the same noun.

We need an intelligent, enthusiastic individual for this job.
But: Please order a new bulletin board for our main conference room.

Note: Do not use a comma after the second adjective. Also, do not use a comma if the first adjective modifies the combined idea of the second adjective and the noun (for example, *bulletin board* and *conference room* in the second example above).

Semicolons

RULE 11
; no conjunction
(L. 97)

Use a semicolon to separate two closely related independent clauses that are not joined by a conjunction (such as *and, but, or,* or *nor*).

Management favored the vote; stockholders did not.
But: Management favored the vote, but stockholders did not.

RULE 12
; series
(L. 97)

Use a semicolon to separate three or more items in a series if any of the items already contain commas.

Staff meetings were held on Thursday, May 7; Monday, June 7; and Friday, June 12.

Note: Be sure to insert the semicolon *between* (not within) the items in a series.

Hyphens

RULE 13
- number
(L. 57)

Hyphenate compound numbers between twenty-one and ninety-nine and fractions that are expressed as words.

Twenty-nine recommendations were approved by at least three-fourths of the members.

RULE 14
- compound adjective
(L. 67)

Hyphenate compound adjectives that come before a noun (unless the first word is an adverb ending in *-ly*).

We reviewed an up-to-date report on Wednesday.
But: The report was up to date.
But: We reviewed the highly rated report.

Note: A compound adjective is two or more words that function as a unit to describe a noun.

Apostrophes

RULE 15
' singular noun
(L. 37)

Use *'s* to form the possessive of singular nouns.

The hurricane's force caused major damage to North Carolina's coastline.

RULE 16
' plural noun
(L. 37)

Use only an apostrophe to form the possessive of plural nouns that end in *s*.

The investors' goals were outlined in the stockholders' report.
But: The investors outlined their goals in the report to the stockholders.
But: The women's and children's clothing was on sale.

RULE 17
' pronoun
(L. 37)

Use *'s* to form the possessive of indefinite pronouns (such as *someone's* or *anybody's*); do not use an apostrophe with personal pronouns (such as *hers, his, its, ours, theirs,* and *yours*).

She could select anybody's paper for a sample.
It's time to put the file back into its cabinet.

Colons

RULE 18
: explanatory material
(L. 91)

Use a colon to introduce explanatory material that follows an independent clause.

The computer satisfies three criteria: speed, cost, and power.

But: The computer satisfies the three criteria of speed, cost, and power.

Remember this: only one coupon is allowed per customer.

Note: An independent clause can stand alone as a complete sentence. Do not capitalize the word following the colon.

Periods

RULE 19
. polite request
(L. 91)

Use a period to end a sentence that is a polite request.

Will you please call me if I can be of further assistance.

Note: Consider a sentence a polite request if you expect the reader to respond by doing as you ask rather than by giving a yes-or-no answer.

Quotation Marks

RULE 20
" direct quotation
(L. 41)

Use quotation marks around a direct quotation.

Harrison responded by saying, "Their decision does not affect us."

But: Harrison responded by saying that their decision does not affect us.

RULE 21
" title
(L. 41)

Use quotation marks around the title of a newspaper or magazine article, chapter in a book, report, and similar terms.

The most helpful article I found was "Multimedia for All."

Italics (or Underline)

RULE 22
title or title
(L. 41)

Italicize (or underline) the titles of books, magazines, newspapers, and other complete published works.

Grisham's *The Brethren* was reviewed in a recent *USA Today* article.

GRAMMAR

Sentences

RULE 23
fragment
(L. 21)

Avoid sentence fragments.

Not: She had always wanted to be a financial manager. But had not had the needed education.

But: She had always wanted to be a financial manager but had not had the needed education.

Note: A fragment is a part of a sentence that is incorrectly punctuated as a complete sentence. In the first example above, "but had not had the needed education" is not a complete sentence because it does not contain a subject.

RULE 24
run-on
(L. 21)

Avoid run-on sentences.

Not: Mohamed is a competent worker he has even passed the MOS exam.
Not: Mohamed is a competent worker, he has even passed the MOS exam.
But: Mohamed is a competent worker; he has even passed the MOS exam.
Or: Mohamed is a competent worker. He has even passed the MOS exam.

Note: A run-on sentence is two independent clauses that run together without any punctuation between them or with only a comma between them.

Agreement

RULE 25
agreement singular
agreement plural
(L. 67)

Use singular verbs and pronouns with singular subjects; use plural verbs and pronouns with plural subjects.

I was happy with my performance.
Janet and Phoenix were happy with their performance.
Among the items discussed were our raises and benefits.

RULE 26
agreement pronoun
(L. 81)

Some pronouns (*anybody, each, either, everybody, everyone, much, neither, no one, nobody,* and *one*) are always singular and take a singular verb. Other pronouns (*all, any, more, most, none,* and *some*) may be singular or plural, depending on the noun to which they refer.

Each of the employees has finished his or her task.
Much remains to be done.
Most of the pie was eaten, but most of the cookies were left.

RULE 27
agreement intervening words
(L. 81)

Disregard any intervening words that come between the subject and verb when establishing agreement.

That box, containing the books and pencils, has not been found.
Alex, accompanied by Tricia and Roxy, is attending the conference and taking his computer.

RULE 28
agreement nearer noun
(L. 101)

If two subjects are joined by *or, either/or, neither/nor,* or *not only/but also,* make the verb agree with the subject nearer to the verb.

Neither the coach nor the players are at home.
Not only the coach but also the referee is at home.
But: Both the coach and the referee are at home.

Pronouns

RULE 29
nominative pronoun
(L. 107)

Use nominative pronouns (such as *I, he, she, we, they,* and *who*) as subjects of a sentence or clause.

The programmer and he are reviewing the code.
Barb is a person who can do the job.

RULE 30
objective pronoun
(L. 107)

Use objective pronouns (such as *me, him, her, us, them,* and *whom*) as objects of a verb, preposition, or infinitive.

The code was reviewed by the programmer and him.
Barb is the type of person whom we can trust.

Adjectives and Adverbs

RULE 31
adjective/adverb
(L. 101)

Use comparative adjectives and adverbs (*-er, more,* and *less*) when referring to two nouns or pronouns; use superlative adjectives and adverbs (*-est, most,* and *least*) when referring to more than two.

The shorter of the two training sessions is the more helpful one.
The longest of the three training sessions is the least helpful one.

Word Usage

RULE 32
accept/except
(L. 117)

***Accept* means "to agree to"; *except* means "to leave out."**

All employees except the maintenance staff should accept the agreement.

RULE 33
affect/effect
(L. 117)

***Affect* is most often used as a verb meaning "to influence"; *effect* is most often used as a noun meaning "result."**

The ruling will affect our domestic operations but will have no effect on our Asian operations.

RULE 34
farther/further
(L. 117)

***Farther* refers to distance; *further* refers to extent or degree.**

The farther we drove, the further agitated he became.

RULE 35
personal/personnel
(L. 117)

***Personal* means "private"; *personnel* means "employees."**

All personnel agreed not to use e-mail for personal business.

RULE 36
principal/principle
(L. 117)

***Principal* means "primary"; *principle* means "rule."**

The principle of fairness is our principal means of dealing with customers.

MECHANICS

Capitalization

RULE 37
≡ sentence
(L. 31)

Capitalize the first word of a sentence.

Please prepare a summary of your activities.

RULE 38
≡ proper noun
(L. 31)

Capitalize proper nouns and adjectives derived from proper nouns.

Judy Hendrix drove to Albuquerque in her new Pontiac convertible.

Note: A proper noun is the official name of a particular person, place, or thing.

RULE 39
≡ time
(L. 31)

Capitalize the names of the days of the week, months, holidays, and religious days (but do not capitalize the names of the seasons).

On Thursday, November 25, we will celebrate Thanksgiving, the most popular holiday in the fall.

RULE 40
≡ noun #
(L. 77)

Capitalize nouns followed by a number or letter (except for the nouns *line, note, page, paragraph,* and *size*).

Please read Chapter 5, which begins on page 94.

RULE 41
≡ compass point
(L. 77)

Capitalize compass points (such as *north, south,* or *northeast*) only when they designate definite regions.

From Montana we drove south to reach the Southwest.

RULE 42
≡ organization
(L. 111)

Capitalize common organizational terms (such as *advertising department* and *finance committee*) only when they are the actual names of the units in the writer's own organization and when they are preceded by the word *the*.

The report from the Advertising Department is due today.
But: Our advertising department will submit its report today.

RULE 43
≡ course
(L. 111)

Capitalize the names of specific course titles but not the names of subjects or areas of study.

I have enrolled in Accounting 201 and will also take a marketing course.

Number Expression

RULE 44
general
(L. 47)

In general, spell out numbers zero through ten, and use figures for numbers above ten.

We rented two movies for tonight.
The decision was reached after 27 precincts sent in their results.

RULE 45
 # figure
(L. 47)

Use figures for

- **Dates. (Use *st, d,* or *th* only if the day comes before the month.)**

  The tax report is due on April 15 (not *April 15th*).
  We will drive to the camp on the 23d (or *23rd* or *23rd*) of May.

- **All numbers if two or more *related* numbers both above and below ten are used in the same sentence.**

  Mr. Carter sent in 7 receipts, and Ms. Cantrell sent in 22.
  But: The 13 accountants owned three computers each.

- **Measurements (time, money, distance, weight, and percent).**

  The $500 statue we delivered at 7 a.m. weighed 6 pounds.

- **Mixed numbers.**

  Our sales are up 9½ (or *9.5*) percent over last year.

RULE 46
 # word
(L. 57)

Spell out

- **A number used as the first word of a sentence.**

  Seventy-five people attended the conference in San Diego.

- **The shorter of two adjacent numbers.**

  We have ordered 3 two-pound cakes and one 5-pound cake for the reception.

- **The words *million* and *billion* in round numbers (do not use decimals with round numbers).**

  Not: A $5.00 ticket can win $28,000,000 in this month's lottery.
  But: A $5 ticket can win $28 million in this month's lottery.

- **Fractions.**

  Almost one-half of the audience responded to the question.

Abbreviations

RULE 47
abbreviate none
(L. 67)

In general business writing, do not abbreviate common words (such as *dept.* or *pkg.*), compass points, units of measure, or the names of months, days of the week, cities, or states (except in addresses).

Almost one-half of the audience indicated they were at least 5 feet 8 inches tall.

Note: Do not insert a comma between the parts of a single measurement.

RULE 48
abbreviate measure
(L. 87)

In technical writing, on forms, and in tables, abbreviate units of measure when they occur frequently. Do not use periods.

14 oz   5 ft 10 in   50 mph   2 yrs 10 mo

RULE 49
abbreviate lowercase
(L. 87)

In most lowercase abbreviations made up of single initials, use a period after each initial but no internal spaces.

a.m.   p.m.   i.e.   e.g.   e.o.m.
Exceptions: mph   mpg   wpm

RULE 50
abbreviate ≡
(L. 87)

In most all-capital abbreviations made up of single initials, do not use periods or internal spaces.

OSHA   PBS   NBEA   WWW   VCR   MBA
Exceptions: U.S.A.   A.A.   B.S.   Ph.D.   P.O.   B.C.   A.D.

Advanced Formatting

PART 4

Keyboarding in Health Services

Within the health services job cluster, there is an enormous range of opportunities in the medical and health care job market. Hundreds of different occupations exist in health care practice, including business-oriented positions. In fact, career opportunities within this cluster are among the fastest growing in the national marketplace.

The current job outlook is quite positive because the growth in managed care has significantly increased opportunities for doctors and other health professionals, particularly in the area of preventive care. In addition, the aging population requires more highly skilled medical workers.

Consider health care jobs, medical careers, health care management, and medical management. Various job possibilities exist in positions such as a medical assistant, clinical technician, nurse, medical analyst, surgical technician or surgeon, physical therapist, orderly, pharmacist, or medical researcher. Keyboarding skill is important for all of these positions.

Goals

Keyboarding

- Demonstrate improved speed and accuracy when operating the keyboard by touch.
- Type at least 43 words per minute on a 5-minute timed writing with no more than 5 errors.

Language Arts

- Demonstrate acceptable proofreading skills, including using proofreaders' marks correctly.
- Demonstrate acceptable language arts skills in punctuation, grammar, and mechanics.
- Demonstrate acceptable language arts skills in composing and spelling.

Word Processing

- Use appropriate word processing commands necessary to complete document processing activities successfully.

Document Processing

- Correctly format e-mail, multipage correspondence, multipage reports, and tables.

Objective Test

- Answer questions with acceptable accuracy on an objective test.

UNIT 13

Skill Refinement

Skillbuilding and Letter Review

Goals

- Demonstrate improved speed and accuracy while typing by touch.
- Demonstrate acceptable language arts skills in comma usage.
- Correctly format a rough-draft document and apply proofreaders' marks.
- Correctly format a business letter and personal-business letter in block style and in modified-block style.

A. WARMUP

alphabet	1	`Six women quietly got the prizes back from the five judges.`
concentration	2	`electromagnetically pseudointellectuals overdiversification`
easy	3	`Di may work as a tutor for the six girls who asked for one.`

Skillbuilding

B. MAP+: ALPHABET

Follow the GDP software directions for this exercise to improve keystroking accuracy.

C. PROGRESSIVE PRACTICE: ALPHABET

Follow the GDP software directions for this exercise to improve keystroking speed.

Language Arts

D. COMMAS

Study the rules at the right.

Note: The callout signals in the left margin indicate which language arts rule from this lesson has been applied.

RULE
, series

Use a comma between each item in a series of three or more.

> We need to order paper, toner, and font cartridges for the printer.
> They saved their work, exited their program, and turned off their computers when they finished.

The underlines call attention to a point in the sentence where a comma might mistakenly be inserted.

Note: Do not use a comma after the last item in a series.

RULE
, transitional expression

Use a comma before and after a transitional expression or independent comment.

It is critical, therefore, that we finish the project on time.
Our present projections, you must admit, are inadequate.
But: You must admit our present projections are inadequate.

Note: Examples of transitional expressions and independent comments are *in addition to, therefore, however, on the other hand, as a matter of fact,* and *unfortunately.*

Edit each sentence to correct any errors.

4 The lawyer the bank and the courthouse received copies.

5 The closing was delayed therefore for more than an hour.

6 The contract power of attorney and deed were in order.

7 Ms. Sperry's flight was delayed however for two hours.

8 Happily the drinks snacks and napkins arrived on time.

9 This offer I think will be unacceptable to the board.

10 Please read their report make whatever comments you feel
11 are appropriate and then route it to the others.

Formatting

E. ADVANCED FORMATTING

The document processing jobs in this unit review basic formatting for correspondence, reports, tables, and employment documents. Before beginning these jobs, review the introductory lessons in the Word Manual and the pages in the Reference Manual listed next. The fundamental information in these pages will prepare you to format and type the jobs in this unit and those that follow.

In the Word Manual, review Getting Started, Lessons 21–25, and Lesson 28. In the Reference Manual, review R-5C–D, R-14C, R-9D, R-13D, and R-12C–D.

As you format document processing jobs, note the following:

- Whenever you see "20--," type the current year in black.
- The | symbol indicates the end of a line. Press ENTER whenever you see it.
- The ¶ symbol indicates a new, blocked paragraph.
- In Word, lines wrap automatically as you approach the right margin. Your line endings in Word may not match those in the book.
- Type your own reference initials in lowercase (no periods or spaces) in black whenever you see urs in letters or memos.
- Lines are shown with extra spacing for proofreaders' marks. Use standard spacing in all jobs.
- Center tables that appear alone on a page horizontally and vertically, and automatically adjust the column widths.
- Tables with borders removed are shown with "View Gridlines" active.

REFER TO
Word Manual
L. 45

Document Processing

Correspondence 61-55
Business Letter in Block Style

REFER TO
Reference Manual
R-3A: Business Letter in Block Style

June 3, 20-- | Mr. Andres Macias | Director of Product Development | Hampton Associates Inc. | 830 Market Street | San Francisco, CA 94102-1925 | Dear Mr. Macias:

¶ Have you had customer groups assist you or provide you with advice related to pending business decisions regarding computer design? Such design standards would include industrywide interfaces and computer hardware and software.

, series

¶ I recently read an article discussing the influence consumer opinion can have on the design of various computer components. This very interesting article concluded that if customers demand standardization in computer hardware, participate in focus groups, and band together with other customers, they will see results reflected in the marketplace.

, transitional expression

¶ I am considering organizing several focus groups and, therefore, would appreciate any advice you might have. I know your expertise will prove to be invaluable, and I thank you in advance for your time and consideration.

Sincerely yours, | Alice Karns | Product Development Manager | urs

Correspondence 61-56
Personal-Business Letter in Block Style

REFER TO
Reference Manual
R-3D: Personal-Business Letter in Modified-Block Style
R-14C: Proofreaders' Marks

september 1, 20--

Dr. David L. Grant | 3329 Market Street | Salem, OR 97301 | Dear Dr. Grant:

¶ Thank you for your letter of August ~~27~~ 25 inquiring about my trip to New York city. Your letter brought back a lot of memories of those days when I was your student at Portland State University. We spent many weekends discussing all matters of importance and I'm sure we must have solved the worlds problems many times over. ¶ I will leave on Oct. 15th for a 2-week business trip where I will be conducting a workshop at Columbia University on the utilization of voice-activated ~~hardware~~ equipment. When I complete my work on October 22, I would love to have you and your wife join me in New York City. I plan to attend a number of plays, visit the Metropolitan Museum of Art and take one of the sightseeing tours. I would be happy to make hotel reservations and purchase theatre tickets.

, series

¶ I hope you'll consider joining me in the "Big Apple"! It would be great to see you and your wife again. However, I do need to know soon so that I can proceed with our plans. I look forward to hearing from you.

, transitional expression

Sincerely, | Rodney Dorey | 1329 BroadwayStreet | Eureka, ~~California~~ CA 95501

Correspondence 61-57
Business Letter in Modified-Block Style

REFER TO
Reference Manual
R-3B: Business Letter in Modified-Block Style

Open the file for Correspondence 61-55 and make the following changes:

1. Change the letter format to modified-block style.
2. Change the addressee name to this:
   `Mr. Peng Lim`
3. Change the salutation to this:
   `Dear Mr. Lim:`
4. Delete the last paragraph and replace it with this:

```
I would certainly appreciate
meeting you and discussing
this in person. Your advice
is very valuable, and your
reputation in this industry
is stellar. I will contact
you soon.
```

Skillbuilding, Memo, and E-Mail Review

Goals

- Type at least 40wpm/5′/5e.
- Correctly format a memo and an e-mail message.
- Correctly format a rough-draft document and apply proofreaders' marks.

A. WARMUP

alphabet	Very few phlox grew or bloomed just back of my zinc quarry.
one hand	tracer uplink tax lip regard plumply date phony waste polio
easy	The goal of their amendment is to make the city proficient.

Skillbuilding

B. SUSTAINED PRACTICE: ALTERNATE-HAND WORDS

Take a 1-minute timed writing on the boxed paragraph to establish your base speed. Then take a 1-minute timed writing on the following paragraph. As soon as you equal or exceed your base speed on this paragraph, move to the next, more difficult paragraph.

```
     The town council decided to shape its destiny when a      11
rich landowner lent a hand by proposing to chair the audit     23
committee. He will be a good chairman, and eight civic         34
club members will work to amend some troublesome policies.     46

     One problem relates to the change in profit for many      11
of the firms in the city. As giant property taxes do not       22
relate to income, they wish to make those taxes go down.       33
The result means increases in their sales or income taxes.     45

     All eight members of the town council now agree that      11
it is time to join with other cities throughout the state      12
in lobbying with the state legislature to bring about the      35
needed change. The right balance in taxes is the goal.         46

     The mayor pointed out that it is not only business        10
property owners who would be affected. Homeowners should       22
see a decrease in property taxes, and renters might see        33
lower rents, as taxes on rental property would be lowered.     45
  1 | 2 | 3 | 4 | 5 | 6 | 7 | 8 | 9 | 10 | 11 | 12
```

Take two 5-minute timed writings. Review your speed and errors.

Goal: At least 40wpm/5'/5e

C. 5-MINUTE TIMED WRITING

Digital photography has revolutionized the way we take 11
pictures. A digital camera puts our photos in a format that 23
makes them easy to print and share with others. Using a 34
digital camera also has the advantage that we can quickly 46
print out our photos and see the result of our efforts. 57
We can also insert our photos into word processing 68
documents, send them by e-mail to our friends, or post them 80
on the Web where they can be viewed by all. We can even 91
connect our camera to a television set and have our images 103
displayed in a slide show presentation. 111
Another advantage of digital photography is that the 121
expense of developing your own photos is much less because 133
you do not have to purchase rolls of film, nor do you have 145
to have your photos developed by others. Also, your photos 157
can be edited if you do not like what you see. You can crop 169
the photo, adjust its color or contrast, take out red-eye 180
imperfections, and even add or delete elements from the 192
photo or from other photos you have taken. 200

1 | 2 | 3 | 4 | 5 | 6 | 7 | 8 | 9 | 10 | 11 | 12

Document Processing

REFER TO Word Manual L. 23 & L. 25

Correspondence 62-58 Memo

REFER TO Reference Manual R-4D: Memo

MEMO TO: Min-Hong Dai, Theater Manager | **FROM:** Barbara Cornell, Executive Director | **DATE:** March 1, 20-- | **SUBJECT:** Season Ticket Price Schedule for Orchestra Hall

¶ We have tentatively scheduled 114 concerts for Orchestra Hall for the calendar year beginning September 1. The attached list shows the new season ticket prices for the main floor, mezzanine, balcony, and gallery.

¶ These prices are grouped in 11 different concert categories, which reflect the varied classical tastes of our patrons. These groupings also consider preferences for day of the week, time of day, and season of the year.

¶ Please see me in my office at 3 p.m. on March 10 so that we can review our ticket sales campaign. Last year's season ticket holders have had ample time to renew their subscriptions; we must now concentrate on attracting new season subscribers. I shall look forward to reviewing your plans.

urs | Attachment

Correspondence 62-59 E-Mail Message

Mr. Phillips:

¶ We are interested in implementing a new security program for the personal computers in our main office and would like to study the specifications and features your system provides.

(continued on next page)

In Word, when you type an e-mail address and then a space, an e-mail hyperlink is inserted automatically.

¶ Please send information and prices on your state-of-the-art security software. The ready availability of the Internet to the general public and others has made the prevention of identity theft, phishing, and other types of related scams a top security priority in our firm.
¶ Thank you for your assistance.
Charles | Charles Cox | E-mail: chcox@mailserver.net | Phone: 770-555-2843

Correspondence 62-60
Memo

MEMO TO: Eduardo Bocelli Cabaret pops Conductor

FROM: Marcia Greene, Executive Director

Date: March 2, 20--

SUBJECT: Erving Berlin Concert

Our Patron Advisory Program Committeee has included several recommendations in ~~it's~~ its attached letter. They would like the Irving Berlin concert to begin with some pre-World War I hits, followed by ~~music~~ songs from the 1920s and 1930s. The first part of the ~~program~~ evening will focus on favorite hit songs from the 1920s and 1930s. After the intermission, the program will focus on hit songs from the 1940s and 1950s. A planning meeting has been scheduled for you, Dolly Carpenter (the Rehearsals Coordinator), and me on Mar. 9 at 10 A.M. at Orchestra Hall. I look forward to seeing you then.

urs

Attachments

c:Dolly Carpenter

Correspondence 62-61
Memo

MEMO TO: Dolly Carpenter, Rehearsals Coordinator
FROM: Sam Steele, Executive Director
DATE: March 3, 20--
SUBJECT: Summer Cabaret Pops Concerts

¶ We are pleased that you will be our rehearsals coordinator for this summer's Cabaret Pops concerts. The five biweekly concerts will run from June 13 through August 8.

¶ As the concert schedule is much lighter during the summer months, I am quite confident that you will be able to use the Orchestra Hall stage for all rehearsals. This is the preference of Eduardo Bocelli, who will be the conductor for this summer's Cabaret Pops concerts.

¶ I look forward to seeing you on June 1.

¶ urs

Skillbuilding and Report Review

Goals

- Demonstrate improved speed and accuracy while typing.
- Demonstrate acceptable proofreading skills by comparing lines.
- Correctly format a business report and an academic report.

A. WARMUP

alphabet	1	Just keep examining every low bid quoted for zinc etchings.
practice: *u* and *y*	2	yum buy duly yuck fury your guy July busy yuk quay you jury
easy	3	Pam blames all her problems on the rituals of the sorority.

Skillbuilding

B. MAP+: NUMBERS

Follow the GDP software directions for this exercise to improve keystroking accuracy.

PPP PRETEST » PRACTICE » POSTTEST

C. PRETEST: Discrimination Practice

PRETEST

Take a 1-minute timed writing. Review your speed and errors.

```
4      Lois said the rear of the long train was right next   11
5  to the column of poplar trees. A robber had entered a red  22
6  car and stolen a case of grapefruit juice and ten cases of 34
7  soda pop. The officer quickly arrested him on the street.  45
     1 | 2 | 3 | 4 | 5 | 6 | 7 | 8 | 9 | 10 | 11 | 12
```

D. PRACTICE: Left Hand

PRACTICE

Speed Emphasis: If you made no more than 1 error on the Pretest, type each *individual* line 2 times.

Accuracy Emphasis: If you made 2 or more errors, type each *group* of lines (as though it were a paragraph) 2 times.

```
8  rtr trip trot sport train alert courts assert tragic truest
9  asa mass salt usage cased cease astute dashed masked castle
10 sds sad used suds said pods based drips curds stride guards
11 rer rear rest overt rerun older before entire surest better
```

E. PRACTICE: Right Hand

```
12 mnm menu numb hymns unmet manly mental namely manner number
13 pop post coop opera pools opens polite proper police oppose
14 olo tool yolk loon spoil lodge color stroll lottery rolling
15 iui unit quit fruit suits built medium guided helium podium
```

POSTTEST

Repeat the Pretest timed writing and compare performance.

F. POSTTEST: Discrimination Practice

Language Arts

Compare this paragraph with the last paragraph of the timed writing on page 239. Edit the paragraph to correct any errors.

G. PROOFREADING

Another advantage of digital photography is that the the expense of developing your own photos is less because you do not have to buy any rolls of film, nor do you have to have your photos developed by others. Also, your photos can be edited if you do not like what you see. You can crop the photo, adjust it's color or contrast, take out red-eye imperfections and even add or delete elements from the photo or from other photographs you have taken.

Document Processing

REFER TO Word Manual

L. 31, L. 32, L. 34 & L. 46

Report 63-34 Business Report

VIDEO-BASED TRAINING PROGRAMS

Rodolfo Madison, Training Consultant

¶ Video-based training programs are being implemented at an ever-increasing rate across the country. While this type of training should certainly not be the only method that is used to train your employees, it is very effective and can offer significant advantages over other training methods.

ADVANTAGES

¶ There are many advantages to video-based training. However, only the most significant ones are discussed here.

Save Development Time. You can shorten your training cycle because you will have the ability to deliver "just-in-time" training where and when you need it. Facilitation materials with activities and discussion points can be used in whole or in part to create training events that run anywhere from one to four hours.

Add Variety to the Delivery Mix. Workshops and lectures can become routine and boring. Video provides a change of pace and can add an entertainment factor that is not possible in a live presentation. Videos can also be used to supplement a face-to-face workshop to stimulate discussion, demonstrate concepts that could not otherwise be presented, and provide meaningful examples of the topic at hand. The more the senses are engaged in the content, the more the participants will learn.

Build a Resource Library. Building a video and/or DVD library allows you to offer a broader range of training. You will no longer be limited to custom in-house development or scheduled classroom events. Trainees can check out a DVD or access video training online.

(continued on next page)

RECOMMENDATION

¶ Video-based training materials save your organization time and money, and they make your business look progressive. Because they help build learning retention, they can also improve the return on your training investment. The next step should be a formal review of your training needs and an evaluation report to be completed by a professional video-based training firm with a proven track record.

Report
63-35
Academic Report

REFER TO Reference Manual

R-8C–D: Multipage Academic Report

BECOMING A FITNESS WORKER

Cal Jordan

According to the U.S. Department of Labor's Bureau of Labor Statistics, "Jobs for fitness workers are expected to increase much faster than the average for all occupations."[1] Fitness workers should have good job prospects due to rapid job growth in health clubs, fitness facilities, and other settings where fitness workers are concentrated.

NATURE OF THE WORK

Fitness workers primarily instruct and motivate individuals or groups in a variety of exercise activities. A rising trend is providing fitness trainers in the workplace as an employee benefit. There are several categories of fitness workers.

Personal Trainers. Personal trainers work one-on-one with individuals to help them assess their level of physical fitness and set and reach fitness goals. Trainers can also demonstrate exercises to help clients improve their exercise techniques. They may keep records of exercise sessions for monitoring progress and offer advice regarding lifestyles outside of the gym to improve fitness. They often work in a variety of places—health clubs, hospitals, fitness studios, resorts, and private homes are typical.

When you type text followed by two hyphens (--), followed by more text and then a space, a formatted em dash (—) will automatically be inserted.

Group Exercise Instructors. Group exercise instructors conduct group exercise sessions, including aerobic exercise, stretching, and muscle conditioning. Classes are often set to music, and Pilates and yoga are often incorporated. Exercise classes should be motivating, safe, and challenging. Louise Byron says that classes that incorporate Pilates and yoga can be more effective than weight training for overall strength and toning.[2]

Fitness Directors. Fitness directors oversee health club or fitness center activities. They might create programs for member orientations, fitness assessments, and workout incentive programs. They also select fitness equipment; coordinate training programs; hire, train, and supervise fitness staff; and carry out other administrative duties.

RELATED OCCUPATIONS

Other workers that focus on physical fitness include athletes, coaches, and physical therapists. For example, a physical therapist is often required to create exercise plans to improve their patients' flexibility, strength, and endurance. Dietitians and nutritionists also have related careers because they offer advice on improving and maintaining good health.

Remove any automatic hyperlinks for electronic references enclosed by angle brackets immediately after they appear, and replace the angle brackets as needed.

[1] U.S. Department of Labor, *Occupational Outlook Handbook*, <http://www.bls.gov/oco/ocos296.htm>, accessed on April 22, 2010.

[2] Louise Byron, *Pilates and Yoga for Strength and Fitness*, 2nd ed., Midwest Publishing, Chicago, 2010, p. 20.

Report 63-36
Left-Bound Business Report

REFER TO Reference Manual

R-9A: Left-Bound Business Report

Open the file for Report 63-34 and make the following changes:

1. Change the report from a business report to a left-bound business report.
2. Add this new paragraph heading and paragraph as the last paragraph in the ADVANTAGES section of the report:

   Supplement Existing Training Resources. Videos can often be used to support more than one of your training initiatives. For example, you can use a video like *Leadership for the New Millennium* to enhance workshops on decision making, leadership, teamwork, or communication.
3. Add a page number to display on the second page only.

Strategies for Career Success

Looking for a Job

Don't waste time! Start your job search early. Scan the Help Wanted sections in major Sunday newspapers or their Web sites for job descriptions and salaries. The Internet provides access to worldwide job listings at sites like Monster.com, Dice.com, Craigslist.com, and on company and government Web sites, such as the federal government's jobs site (http://www.usajobs.gov/).

Consult references such as the U.S. Department of Labor's *Occupational Outlook Handbook* (http://www.bls.gov/oco/) to research types of jobs in various fields and the requirements for those jobs. Visit your college placement office. Sign up for interviews with companies that visit your campus.

Talk with people in your field to get advice. Look for an internship or join a professional organization in your field. Attend local chapter meetings to network with people in your chosen profession.

Taking the initiative in your job search will pay off!

Your Turn: Visit the Internet site for the *National Business Employment Weekly* at http://www.employmentguide.com, which provides more than 45,000 national and international job listings online.

UNIT 13 LESSON

Skillbuilding and Table Review

64

Goals

- Type at least 40wpm/5′/5e.
- Correctly format a boxed table, an open table, and a ruled table.

A. WARMUP

alphabet 1 George W. Bush quickly fixed prize jam cakes on television.
frequent digraphs 2 ti tie anti tic site tilt tin tithe stir tide tick tip tint
easy 3 I may make a quantity of maps to aid me when I visit Japan.

Skillbuilding

B. PROGRESSIVE PRACTICE: NUMBERS

Follow the GDP software directions for this exercise to improve keystroking speed.

C. TECHNIQUE PRACTICE: SHIFT KEY

Type each line 2 times. After striking the capitalized letter, return the Shift Key finger immediately to home-row position.

4 Aldo Bonilla skied. Clara Duarte typed. Ellen Fuller filed.
5 Guy Hayes ate dinner. Isabella Jayne hid. Kevin Lee sobbed.
6 Megan Newsome sat. Otis Petrov tried. Quincy Rogers hummed.
7 Syd Tia wed Ursula Vivian. Willie Xin and Yvonne Zola lied.

Take two 5-minute timed writings. Review your speed and errors.

Goal: At least 40wpm/5'/5e

D. 5-MINUTE TIMED WRITING

The computer has changed the way you do things in the 11
office today. Jobs that used to take many hours to complete 23
now can be done in less time. A quick review of ways in 34
which the computer can help you streamline your work may 46
be in order. 48
Most software programs include helpful wizards that 59
can guide you through any project. You can use a stored 70
template, or you can create your own style. You do not need 82
to write your thoughts in longhand on paper before you type 94
them. Composing and revising documents as you type them 105
will save you lots of time. 111
Your computer is valuable for more than just writing 122
letters. Using different software applications, you can 133
create dazzling presentations for all to see. You can also 145
build databases for sorting and storing all types of data, 156
format spreadsheets, create your own calendar and colorful 169
charts, and perform calculations. You can even publish your 180
own newsletter and make business cards. It is exciting to 192
consider the ways you can use a computer. 200

1 | 2 | 3 | 4 | 5 | 6 | 7 | 8 | 9 | 10 | 11 | 12

REFER TO Word Manual
L. 28 & L. 36–39

Document Processing

Table 64-23
Boxed Table

REFER TO Reference Manual
R-13A: Boxed Table

$700 COMPOUNDED ANNUALLY
FOR 7 YEARS AT 7 PERCENT

Beginning of Year	Interest	Value
First	$00.00	$ 700.00
Second	49.00	749.00
Third	52.43	801.43
Fourth	56.10	857.53
Fifth	60.03	917.56
Sixth	64.23	981.79
Seventh	68.72	1,050.51
Eighth	78.68	1,129.19

Table
64-24
Open Table

REFER TO Reference Manual

R-13B: Open Table

SALES CONFERENCES All Sessions at Regional Offices		
Date	**City**	**Leader**
October 7	Boston	D. G. Gorham
October 17	Baltimore	James B. Brunner
October 24	Miami	Becky Taylor
November 3	Dallas	Rodney R. Nordstein
November 10	Minneapolis	Joanne Miles-Tyrell
November 17	Denver	Becky Taylor
November 26	Los Angeles	Rodney R. Nordstein

Table
64-25
Ruled Table

REFER TO Reference Manual

R-13C: Ruled Table

COMPARISON OF SALES QUOTAS AND ACTUAL SALES
July to December

Month	Sales Quotas	Actual Sales
July	$ 935,400	$ 950,620
August	970,750	896,230
September	974,510	725,110
October	990,270	990,110
November	975,890	968,290
December	1,960,470	1,978,690
Totals	$6,807,290	$6,509,050

Keyboarding Connection

Finding Business Information on the Internet

Finding information about businesses on the Internet is easy. If you want to research a company, you can go to its Web site, or you can use a search engine to find out what resources and information are available. Sites like Bloomberg.com and Yahoo! have articles about business trends and companies. Professional organizations like the American Management Association and the Chamber of Commerce also have Web sites where you can learn about their member businesses.

Start by using a search engine like Google, and you'll find plenty of business information available on the Internet. Company Web sites often have an About Us link, where you can learn more about specific companies.

Your Turn: Access the *Selected Business Resources on the Web* site at http://www.bls.gov and explore its offerings.

Skillbuilding and Employment Document Review

UNIT 13 LESSON **65**

Goals

- Demonstrate improved speed and accuracy while typing.
- Demonstrate acceptable language arts skills in composing.
- Correctly format a resume, an application letter, and a follow-up letter.
- Successfully complete a Progress and Proofreading Check with zero errors on the first scored attempt.

A. WARMUP

alphabet 1 Crazy Fredrick bought Jane many very exquisite opal jewels.

number/symbol 2 wroe@gmail.com 82% Dye & Cox (5/7) Oh! ($6.90) *8:45 #12-63

easy 3 Did a firm fix the problem of the worn element with a disk?

Skillbuilding

B. 12-SECOND SPEED SPRINTS

Take three 12-second timed writings on each line. The scale below the last line shows your wpm speed for a 12-second timed writing.

4 Jan owns a pair of old gowns and a new hat she got from me.

5 He may go with us to the giant dock down by the handy lake.

6 His civic goal for the city is for them to endow the chair.

7 If she works at home, she may make a visit to the old farm.

' ' ' ' 5 ' ' ' ' 10 ' ' ' ' 15 ' ' ' ' 20 ' ' ' ' 25 ' ' ' ' 30 ' ' ' ' 35 ' ' ' ' 40 ' ' ' ' 45 ' ' ' ' 50 ' ' ' ' 55 ' ' ' ' 60

C. PACED PRACTICE

Follow the GDP software directions for this exercise to improve keystroking speed and accuracy.

Language Arts

D. COMPOSING PARAGRAPHS

What advice can you give students who tend to get nervous when they take timed writings? Compose a paragraph of at least three to four sentences answering this question.

REFER TO
Word Manual
L. 33 & L. 51

Report
65-37
Resume

REFER TO
Reference Manual
R-12A: Resume
R-12D: Examples of Different Kinds of Lists

Document Processing

STEPHEN K. HAMILTON

6183 Nicollet Avenue South, Minneapolis, MN 55404
Phone: 612-555-9009; e-mail: shamilton@fastmail.com

OBJECTIVE	To obtain a position as a technology support specialist in a corporate environment or government agency.
EDUCATION	Minneapolis Community College, Minneapolis, Minnesota A.A. degree in information technology Graduated: December 2009 Specialize in analysis, design, and security of modern computer networks. Concentration courses emphasize local area networks, wireless local area networks, wide area networks, and network security South Minneapolis High School, Minneapolis, Minnesota Graduated: May 2008
EXPERIENCE	*Computer Systems Technician, Selkirk & Associates* Minneapolis, Minnesota September 2009 to Present Duties include installing and updating computer software programs throughout the firm. *Administrative Assistant, Kittredge Insurance Agency* Circle Pines, Minnesota August 2008 to August 2009 (part-time) Duties included coordinating office communications and setting up international videoconferences.
ACTIVITIES	Activities pursued: • College Choir, 2008 to 2009 • Business Students Club, 2006 to 2008 • Varsity Basketball, 2007 to 2008
REFERENCES	Available upon request.

Table shown with "View Gridlines" active.

Correspondence 65-62
Application Letter in Block Style

REFER TO Reference Manual
R-12B: Application Letter in Block Style

Mar. 10, 20-- | Denise Klenzman | Director of Human Resources | Cole Enterprises | 3714 Crestmont Ave. | Minneapolis, Mn 55405 | Dear Mrs. Klenzman:

¶ Please consider me an applicant for the position of technology systems specialist with your firm. I becameaware of the position through a friend who is an employee at Cole Enterprises.

¶ I am currently employed at Selkirk & Associates as a computer systems technician and have earned an A.A. degree at Minneapolis Community College in information technology. The resume and transcript enclosed will provide you with details on courses completed. I am confident that my educationl background and my Computer Systems experience make me qualified for this position. I would very much appreciate an opportunity for an interview. Plaese contact me at your convenience at 612-555-9039, or send me an e-mail message at shamilton@fastmail.com.

Sincerely yours | Stephen K. Hamilton | 6183 Nicollet Avenue South | Minneapolis, MN 55404 | Enclosure

Correspondence 65-63
Follow-Up Letter in Block Style

Progress and Proofreading Check
Documents designated as Proofreading Checks serve as a check of your proofreading skill. Your goal is to have zero typographical errors when the GDP software first scores the document.

March 19, 20-- | Mrs. Denise A. Klenzman | Director of Human Resources | Cole Enterprises | 3714 Crestmont Avenue | Minneapolis, MN 55405 | Dear Mrs. Klenzman:

¶ Thank you for the opportunity to meet with you yesterday and to learn of the exciting career opportunities at Cole Enterprises. It was inspiring for me to learn about future plans for your forward-looking company.

¶ I am confident that my education and my experience qualify me in a special way for your position of technology support specialist. I am familiar with all of your present equipment and software.

¶ I would very much like to join the professional staff at Cole Enterprises. Please let me know when you have made your decision.

Sincerely yours, | Stephen K. Hamilton | 6183 Nicollet Avenue South | Minneapolis, MN 55404

UNIT 14

Correspondence

Multipage Letters

Goals

- Type at least 41wpm/5′/5e.
- Correctly format a multipage letter.

A. WARMUP

alphabet: A puzzled woman bequeathed idiotic jerks very exotic gifts.
concentration: nonrepresentational counterinsurgencies individualistically
easy: A new toxic problem may ensue if we burn the old cornfield.

Skillbuilding

B. SUSTAINED PRACTICE: ROUGH DRAFT

Take a 1-minute timed writing on the boxed paragraph to establish your base speed. Then take a 1-minute timed writing on the following paragraph. As soon as you equal or exceed your base speed on this paragraph, move to the next, more difficult paragraph.

The possibility of aging and not being able to live as 11
independently as we want to is a prospect that no one wants 23
to recognize. One resource designed to counter some of the 35
negative realities of aging is called the Handyman Project. 47

This type of ~~project~~ program helps support elders and disabled 12
residents in their efforts to maintain the(ir) homes. As the 24
name implies, "handy" volunte(e)rs per for(m) minor home repairs 36
such as tight(e)ning leaky faucets and fixing broken windows. 48

¶ Other type(s) of work include: painting, plumbing, yard 11
work, and carpentery. The volunteers are all as divers(i)fied 23
as the wor~~d~~(k) itself. You may find a retire(e) working next too 35
an executive or a student ~~helping~~ assisting a li~~s~~(c)ensed electrician. 47

Their back gr(o)unds may vary, but ~~t~~(w)hat they share is the 11
~~hope~~ desire to put their ~~capabilities~~ abilities to good use. Volunteers ~~take~~ find 23
a high level of person~~n~~al satisfaction after ~~doing~~ finishing a job 35
~~but~~ and spending time with (an elder who really needs the help.) 47

1 | 2 | 3 | 4 | 5 | 6 | 7 | 8 | 9 | 10 | 11 | 12

Take two 5-minute timed writings.

Goal: At least 41wpm/5′/5e

C. 5-MINUTE TIMED WRITING

    Making a successful presentation to an audience is a 11
skill that is absolutely essential in your career. The art 23
of speaking before a group requires planning and hard work. 35
Although different speakers prepare in many different ways, 47
a speaker should try to adhere to certain rules. 56
    As the speaker, you are quite visible to people in the 68
audience. Therefore, you should always try to make a good 79
first impression. When you walk to the podium to speak, you 91
give the audience a chance to notice your neat appearance, 103
good posture, and confident manner. You will improve the 114
quality of your voice if you stand up straight and hold 126
your shoulders back and stomach in. 133
    As you talk, use your eyes, face, and hands to help 143
you connect with your listeners. Maintain eye contact by 155
just moving your eyes over the group without focusing on 166
any one person. Use hand movements and facial expressions 178
to convey meanings to your audience. By utilizing these 189
techniques, you will improve your speaking skills, and your 201
effort may be noted. 205

1 | 2 | 3 | 4 | 5 | 6 | 7 | 8 | 9 | 10 | 11 | 12

Formatting

D. MULTIPAGE LETTERS

To format a multipage letter:

1. Type the first page on letterhead stationery, and type continuation pages on plain paper that matches the letterhead.
2. Insert a page number in the top right-hand corner of the page header of all continuing pages, and remove the page number from the first page.

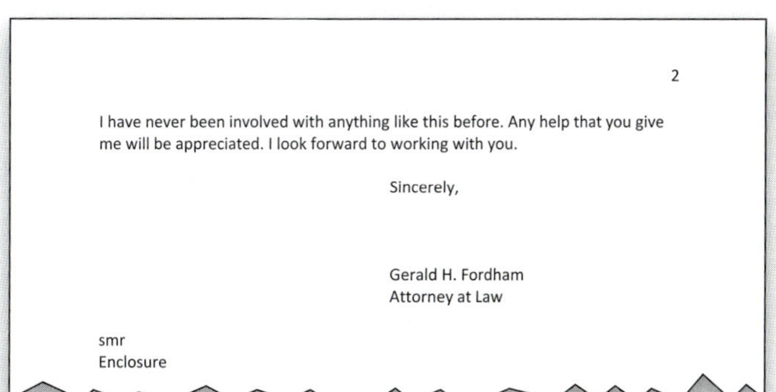
2

I have never been involved with anything like this before. Any help that you give me will be appreciated. I look forward to working with you.

Sincerely,

Gerald H. Fordham
Attorney at Law

smr
Enclosure

Document Processing

Correspondence 66-64
Business Letter in Modified-Block Style

REFER TO Reference Manual

R-5A–B: Multipage Business Letter

July 13, 20-- | Miss Florence B. Glashan | Attorney at Law | 2932 Point Street | Providence, RI 02903 | Dear Miss Glashan:

¶ It was a pleasure to meet you at the convention for trial attorneys in New York last week. In addition to the interesting program highlights of the regular sessions, the informal discussions with people like you are an added plus at these meetings. Your contribution to the program was very beneficial and highly informative.

¶ You may recall that I had just been appointed by the court to defend a woman here in Providence who has been charged with embezzling large sums of money from her previous employer. The defendant had been employed at a large department store for more than 25 years. Because of her valuable years of experience in accounting with the store, she was in charge of accounts receivable at the store. Her previous employer, the plaintiff in the case, claims that she embezzled $18,634 three years ago, $39,072 two years ago, and $27,045 last year.

¶ You mentioned that you had represented defendants in similar cases in previous years. Your assistance would be invaluable as I prepare for this defense. If you are willing to lend your professional expertise in this case, here is what is needed:

1. Within the next week, send the appropriate citations for all similar trials in which you participated.
2. Provide any other case citations that you think might be helpful in this case.
3. Meet with me in approximately two weeks for a case consultation. At that time we can discuss compensation for your work on this matter.

¶ A copy of the formal complaint is enclosed for your review. I will call you in about a week to arrange a time and place for our meeting. Please let me know if there is additional information that would be helpful in preparing for this case.

¶ This type of case will present unique challenges, but I know your guidance and years of experience will be invaluable. I look forward to working with you.

Sincerely, | Gerald H. Fordham | Attorney at Law | urs | Enclosure

Correspondence 66-65
Business Letter in Block Style

April 3, 20--

Mr. ~~Tom~~ Thomas Crawford | District Product Manager | Office Supplies of America | 2101 Pennsylvania Avenue, ~~N.W.~~ NW | Washington, dc 20006 | Dear Tom:

¶ The Sales Conference in Atlanta last week was out standing. Your winning the "Gold Key award for the most sales for the year was well deserved indeed.

¶ When you first became part of our salesteam, you showed great enthusiasm for your job immediately. There is no doubt in my mind that Office Supplies of America is well represented in the Washington Metro area.

¶ I particularly want to commend you for obtaining the McKinley account. Acquiring this account ~~have~~ has been a major objective for a number of years. None of our other sales representatives ~~has~~ have been able to accomplish this feat. What approach did you take, Tom? Did you:

(continued on next page)

1. Spend consider able time with the president, Mr. Arch Davis or one of his associates? If so, who were the individuals involved?

2. Conduct a series of presentations for key personel?

SS

3. Develop a special marketing campaign for McKinley itself?

4. Use regular campaign model and customize it for McKinley?

5. Combine various strategies in your efforts to obtain this important account?

¶ Please let me know what approaches you used to make this sale. Successes of this nature do not happen without a lot of hard work. You to are be commended for putting forth your best efforts to sign the account.

¶ If we can arrange a time at our annual sales meeting we would like to have you make a presentation to our Sales Representatives. They would benefit greatly from having you share your success story. Our annual meeting will be held in late September in Richmond, VA.

¶ Again, congratulations on receiving this very prestigious award. All of us here in the home office are very pleased with the performance of our entire sales team. Indications that are this will be a year when our sales records will be broken and we will again be in the media spotlight.

Sincerely, | Leonard d. Manchester | President | urs | bc: Maria Olson, Director of Sales

Correspondence
66-66
Business Letter in Modified-Block Style

Open the file for Correspondence 66-64 and make the following changes:

1. Change the inside address to this:

```
2632 East Main Road
Portsmouth, RI 02871
```

2. Replace the last sentence in the first paragraph with these:

```
Networking with colleagues
like you is always
enlightening and beneficial.
I value your input greatly.
```

3. Add this sentence after the last sentence in the letter:

```
I will call you in a few
days to discuss this matter
further.
```

UNIT 14 LESSON

Special Correspondence Features

67

Goals

- Demonstrate improved speed and accuracy while typing.
- Demonstrate acceptable language arts skills in using hyphens, in subject and verb agreement, and in using abbreviations.
- Correctly use Word's sort feature.
- Correctly format correspondence with multiple addresses, on-arrival notations, and subject lines.

A. WARMUP

alphabet	1	`How quickly the daft jumping zebras were vexed by the boys.`
one hand	2	`career uphill gas pin awards homonym read yummy grade lumpy`
easy	3	`He has on a tux and she has on a tan gown for their social.`

Skillbuilding

B. MAP+: ALPHABET

Follow the GDP software directions for this exercise to improve keystroking accuracy.

C. PROGRESSIVE PRACTICE: ALPHABET

Follow the GDP software directions for this exercise to improve keystroking speed.

Language Arts

Study the rules at the right.

RULE
- compound adjective

D. HYPHENS

Hyphenate compound adjectives that come before a noun (unless the first word is an adverb ending in *-ly*).

We reviewed an up-to-date report on Wednesday.
But: The report was up to date.
But: We reviewed the highly rated report.

Note: A compound adjective is two or more words that function as a unit to describe a noun.

E. AGREEMENT

RULE
agreement singular
agreement plural

Use singular verbs and pronouns with singular subjects; use plural verbs and pronouns with plural subjects.

I was happy with my performance.
Janet and Phoenix were happy with their performance.
Among the items discussed were our raises and benefits.

F. ABBREVIATIONS

RULE
abbreviate none

In general business writing, do not abbreviate common words (such as *dept.* or *pkg.*), compass points, units of measure, or the names of months, days of the week, cities, or states (except in addresses).

Almost one-half of the audience indicated they were at least 5 feet 8 inches tall.

Note: Do not insert a comma between the parts of a single measurement.

Edit each sentence to correct any errors.

```
The Sabins visited Hickory to look at four bedroom homes.

Cindy Wallace has a part time job after school.

The accountants was extremely busy from March through April.

Lydia and Margaret were invited to present their report.

The portfolio include several technology stocks.

The planning committee will meet on Tue., Sept. 26.

Please credit the acct. for the amt. of $55.48.

The mgr. said the org. will move its headquarters to NC.

Appearing last on the agenda was the reports about the urgently needed parts.
```

Formatting

G. MULTIPLE ADDRESSES

Often a letter may be sent to two or more people at the same address or to different addresses:

1. If a letter is addressed to two people at the same address, type each name on a separate line above the same inside address.
2. If a letter is addressed to two people at different addresses, type each name and address, one under the other. Press ENTER 2 times between the addresses.
3. If a letter is addressed to three or more people, type the names and addresses side by side, with one at the left margin and another beginning at the centerpoint. Press ENTER 2 times before typing the third name and address at the left margin.

↓5X
November 19, 20-- ↓4X

Dr. Albert Russell, Professor
Department of English
Appalachian State University
Boone, NC 28608 ↓2X

Dr. Kay Smith, Professor
Director of Business
Grove City College
Grove City, PA 16127 ↓2X

Dear Dr. Russell and Dr. Smith: ↓2X

It is with great pleasure that I announce the scholarship winners for this year's awards banquet to be held in the next month. The awardees' names are listed below. ↓2X

H. ON-ARRIVAL NOTATIONS

On-arrival notations (such as *CONFIDENTIAL*) should be typed on the second line below the date, at the left margin. Type the notation in all-caps. Press ENTER 2 times to begin the inside address.

↓5X
November 19, 20-- ↓2X

CONFIDENTIAL ↓2X

Mr. and Mrs. Earl Walters
3408 Washington Boulevard
New Tripoli, PA 18066 ↓2X

Dear Mr. and Mrs. Walters: ↓2X

We are very pleased to tell you that your daughter will be the recipient of a prestigious scholarship this semester. She will be recognized at a banquet to be held next month. ↓2X

I. SUBJECT LINES

A *subject line* indicates what a letter is about. Type the subject line below the salutation at the left margin, preceded and followed by 1 blank line. (The term *Re* or *In re* may be used in place of *Subject*.)

↓5X
November 19, 20-- ↓4X

Mr. and Mrs. Earl Walters
3408 Washington Boulevard
New Tripoli, PA 18066 ↓2X

Dear Mr. and Mrs. Walters: ↓2X

Subject: Scholarship Awarded ↓2X

We are very pleased to tell you that your daughter will be the recipient of a very prestigious scholarship this semester. She will be recognized at a banquet to be held next month. ↓2X

J. WORD PROCESSING: SORT

GO TO Word Manual

Study Lesson 67 in your Word Manual. Complete all of the shaded steps while at your computer. Then format the documents that follow.

Document Processing

Correspondence 67-67
Business Letter in Block Style

November 8, 20-- / CONFIDENTIAL / Mrs. Katie Hollister / 11426 Prairie View Road / Kearney, NE 68847 / Dear Mrs. Hollister: / Subject: Site for New Elementary School

¶ As you are aware, your farm, located in the northeast quarter of Section 26 in Tyro township, is a part of Independent School District 17. Each of our three elementary schools occupies 11 acres and is adjoined by an 18-acre park. We are now in the early planning stages for a fourth elementary school. Because your farm is centrally located, the District 17 Board has directed me to initiate discussions with you on the following topics regarding 11 acres of your land:

- compound adjective

Sort the bulleted list in ascending alphabetical order.

- Purchasing options
- Time frames for purchasing
- Alternative sites

¶ Please call me to arrange a meeting with you and your attorneys, Jonathan Beck and Myra Colter, no later than November 13. They informed me that they will coordinate their schedules around yours. I look forward to our discussions.

abbreviate none

Yours truly, / Irvin J. Hagg / Superintendent / urs / c: District 17 Board

Correspondence
67-68
Business Letter in Block Style

agreement plural

Sort each bulleted list in ascending alphabetical order.

October 4, 20-- | Ms. Deborah Campbell Wallace | 7835 Virginia Avenue, NW | Washington, DC 20037 | Mr. Thomas E. Campbell | 3725 Stevens Road, SE | Washington, DC 20020 | Dear Ms. Wallace and Mr. Campbell:
¶ We received your letter requesting instructions for transferring stock. The most common stock transfer situations are provided below. Determine which type of transfer you require, and select the instructions that apply to your stock transfer.

- Transferring shares to another individual
- Transferring shares to a minor
- Transferring shares from a deceased shareholder (multiple owners)
- Transferring shares from a deceased shareholder (individual ownership)
- Transfers involving a trust
- Transfers involving a power of attorney
- Changing a name

agreement singular

¶ Every transfer requires a letter of instruction specifying how you want your shares transferred. The following items are required for all types of transfers:

- Name and address of new owner
- Social security number or taxpayer identification number
- Dated and signed form
- Preferred form of ownership (that is, joint tenants or tenants in common)
- Total number of shares being transferred

abbreviate none

¶ Please be sure to submit all required documentation no later than November 1, and note that all documents submitted become part of the permanent record of transfer and will not be returned. All transfers must have your signature guaranteed by a financial institution participating in the Medallion Signature Guarantee Program.

- compound adjective

¶ If you need additional information, you may visit our Web site for step-by-step instructions, or you may call one of our customer service representatives at our toll-free number.
Sincerely, | William J. Shawley | Shareholder Services | urs

Correspondence
67-69
Personal-Business Letter in Block Style

Nov. 17, 20--
~~Doctor~~ Dr. Francesca Tuscany | 953 Foster Street | Durham, NC 27701 | Dear Dr.Tuscany: |
SUBJECT: January Meeting Book Selection

agreement plural

agreement plural

¶ Your new book, The Iron Hand (ital), has gotten excellent reviews across the nation. The citizens of durham are pleased that a respected member of one of their local colleges is receiving national attention. ¶ Our book discussion group in ~~Morehead~~ Durham, composed of members of the AAUW (American Association of University Women), is going to select 1 of your books below for discussion at our January meeting. All the topics we agreed to discuss were related to your books. We would like you very much to recommend one of these books:

Sort the bulleted list in ascending alphabetical order.

Format book titles in italic.

- *The Iron Hand*
- *Peace in Troubled Times*

SS

- *A House Divided*

I will call you next week. Your ~~presence~~ attendance at our meeting would be a real highlight.
Sincerely | TheresaMayfield | 2901 Garfield Court | Durham, NC 27701

More Special Correspondence Features

Goals

- Type at least 41wpm/5′/5e.
- Correctly use Word's table shading and e-mail blind copy features.
- Correctly format a table within a document.
- Correctly format correspondence with a company name, delivery notation, blind copy notation and postscript.

A. WARMUP

alphabet	`My folks proved his expert eloquence was just a big hazard.`
practice: *f* and *d*	`fad fold fodder fed doff defy find fled deaf fund deft fade`
easy	`Sign the forms to pay for the ivory bowl she got in Durham.`

Skillbuilding

B. PACED PRACTICE

Follow the GDP software directions for this exercise to improve keystroking speed and accuracy.

C. 5-MINUTE TIMED WRITING

Take two 5-minute timed writings.

Goal: At least 41wpm/5′/5e

```
     Taking photos with a digital camera is a process that   11
is somewhat unique and different from taking photos with     22
film. Most digital cameras store images on a device such as  34
a memory card or a memory stick. The number of photos you    46
can store on a card or stick depends on how many megabytes   58
it can hold. Once you reach the limit of the memory device,  70
you can store no new images until you either transfer or     81
delete the old ones to make room for new ones.               91
     The advantages of using a memory device are many. For  102
example, the card or stick can be used over and over; or,   113
when the device is full, just simply remove it and put in a 125
new device. You can also move the images to the computer,   137
where they can reside on the hard drive for as long as you  149
want. If the memory card or stick you have does not have    160
enough memory, you can upgrade the size.                    168
     Finally, you will see instantly any images you have    179
taken with the camera. If you decide not to keep an image   190
in the camera, you can delete it to make space for other    202
exciting images.                                            205
  1 | 2 | 3 | 4 | 5 | 6 | 7 | 8 | 9 | 10 | 11 | 12
```

D. TABLES WITHIN DOCUMENTS

To format a table that is part of a letter, e-mail message, memo, or report:

1. In a single-spaced document, press ENTER 2 times before and 1 time after the table. Be sure you are outside the table structure before pressing ENTER 1 time.
2. In a double-spaced document, press ENTER 1 time before and after the table.
3. Single-space the body of the table.
4. Adjust the column widths, and center the table within the margins of the document.
5. Never split a table between two pages if it will fit on one page. If a table will not fit at the bottom of the page on which it is first mentioned, place it at the top of the next page.

MEMO TO: Leo Guthrie

FROM: Paul Forester

DATE: January 10, 20--

SUBJECT: Sales Comparison

Listed below are the sales totals for the last two quarters. Please review the information before our staff meeting on Friday. ↓2X

SALES SUMMARY December 31, 20--		
Region	**Third Quarter**	**Fourth Quarter**
Northeast	$ 956,321	$912,980
Southeast	735,765	775,112
Northwest	825,666	857,034
Southwest	1,081,546	995,478

↓1X

Come to the meeting prepared to discuss plans for the upcoming sales promotions that will take place in our district.

mjd

E. COMPANY NAMES IN CLOSING LINES

Some business firms show the company name in the closing lines of a letter. Type the company name in all-caps on the second line below the complimentary closing. Then press ENTER 4 times and type the writer's name.

Thank you for inviting me to participate in the discussion concerning this issue. It has been very informative and helpful. ↓2X

Sincerely, ↓2X

HENDERSON AND SONS, INC. ↓4X

Mark Henderson, President ↓2X

mjd

F. DELIVERY NOTATIONS

Type a delivery notation (such as *By fax*, *By e-mail*, *By FedEx*, or *By messenger*) on the line below the enclosure notation (if used) or on the line below the reference initials. A delivery notation comes before a copy notation.

Thank you for inviting me to participate in the discussion concerning this issue. It has been very informative and helpful. ↓2X

Sincerely, ↓4X

Mark Henderson
President ↓2X

imz
Enclosure
By e-mail
c: Mary Stevenson

G. BLIND COPY NOTATIONS

Use the blind copy (*bc:*) notation when the addressee is *not* intended to know that someone else is receiving a copy of the letter. Type the *bc* notation on the file copy at the left margin on the second line after the last item in the letter.

When preparing a letter with a blind copy, print one copy of the letter; then add the blind copy notation and print another.

Thank you for inviting me to participate in the discussion concerning this issue. It has been very informative and helpful. ↓2X

Sincerely, ↓4X

Mark Henderson
President ↓2X

imz ↓2X

bc: Mary Stevenson

H. POSTSCRIPTS

If a postscript (*PS:*) is added to a letter, it is typed as the last item in the letter, preceded by 1 blank line. If a blind copy notation and postscript are used, the blind copy notation follows the postscript.

Thank you for inviting me to participate in the discussion concerning this issue. It has been very informative and helpful. ↓2X

Sincerely, ↓4X

Mark Henderson
President ↓2X

imz
Enclosure ↓2X

PS: You will be reimbursed for all expenses. Complete an expense report and submit it to your supervisor. ↓2X

bc: Mary Stevenson

I. E-MAIL WITH BLIND COPIES

Use the blind copy (*bcc:*) feature when the addressee in the To box is *not* intended to know that someone else is receiving a copy of the e-mail.

To format an e-mail message with a blind copy:

- Format the e-mail message as usual.
- No special formatting steps are needed when a blind copy is sent. Therefore, do *not* type a blind copy notation at the bottom of the e-mail message.
- Type e-mail addresses for recipients as desired in the Bcc box.

J. WORD PROCESSING: TABLE—SHADING AND E-MAIL—BLIND COPIES

GO TO Word Manual

Study Lesson 68 in your Word Manual. Complete all of the shaded steps while at your computer. Then format the documents that follow.

Document Processing

Correspondence 68-70
Business Letter in Block Style

March 1, 20-- | Ms. Ramona Gutierrez | Austin Communications | 5 Gulf Street | Concord, NH 03301 | Dear Ms. Gutierrez:

¶ We are indeed interested in designing a new corporate logo and the corresponding stationery for your fine company. As I indicated in our recent telephone conversation, we have a design staff that has won many national awards for letterhead form design.

¶ Within a couple of weeks, we will submit several basic designs to you and your committee for consideration. Here is a modified price list for the printed stationery:

Use 25 percent shading for Row 1.

Stationery	Cost
Letterhead (500 sheets)	$ 80.00
Business cards (1,000 cards)	39.50
Coated brochures (1,000 sheets)	219.30
Envelopes (1,500)	92.00

¶ In the meantime, please call me if we can be of further service.

Sincerely yours, | Samantha A. Steele | General Manager | urs | By fax | bc: Design Department

Correspondence 68-71
E-Mail Message

Hi, Renee:

¶ Samantha Steele of Imperial Graphic Design sent me a modified price list for our printed stationery. I added our own budget to the last column in the table below.

Use 100 percent shading for Row 1.

Stationery	Cost	Budget
Letterhead (500 sheets)	$ 80.00	$120.00
Business cards (1,000 cards)	39.50	25.00
Coated brochures (1,000 sheets)	219.30	300.00
Envelopes (1,500)	92.00	85.50

¶ Let me know your reaction to her proposed price list after reviewing our budget.

Ramona | Ramona Gutierrez | E-mail: gutierrez@acmail.com | Phone: 603-555-3363

Correspondence 68-72
Business Letter in Modified-Block Style

November 5, 20-- | Burlington Fitness Center | 31 Battery Street | Burlington, VT 05401 | Ladies and Gentlemen:

¶ We have 494 apartments at Fountain Ridge. As the recreation coordinator, I have concerns not only about the leisure-time activities of our residents but also about the health and physical fitness of the more than 1,100 people who call Fountain Ridge home.

¶ Our recreation facilities are excellent. In addition to our two outdoor tennis courts, putting green, and swimming pool, we have the following indoor facilities: two racquetball courts, swimming pool, whirlpool bath, sauna, steam room, and two billiard tables. However, we have no workout equipment.

¶ During the next few months we will be equipping a new gymnasium. The dimensions of the gym and schematics are enclosed. We would like to provide our residents with classes that will incorporate the equipment below:

Use 100 percent shading for Row 1 and 25 percent shading for Row 2.

CLASS SCHEDULE Fountain Ridge Sports Complex	
Equipment	**Proposed Classes**
Exercise bicycles	Spinning
Treadmills	Aerobics
Rowing machines	Toning and conditioning

(continued on next page)

¶ The needs and interests of our residents are varied. Some residents will take full advantage of the gymnasium equipment. However, many of our residents have expressed interest in an indoor track for walking; others would like to add a track for running. We hope to accommodate as many of the suggestions as we feel are feasible.
¶ The population of the residents in the Fountain Ridge complex consists of a mixture of young and middle-age adult couples as well as single residents. Some of the couples have children who would be old enough to enjoy the facilities. Therefore, safety and durability of the equipment are very important considerations. In addition, we would like to continue to develop our complex in a way that would invite family participation in our recreational activities.
¶Do you have a sales representative serving this area who could meet with me to discuss this proposal? In the meantime, please send any related information and prices.
Sincerely yours, | FOUNTAIN RIDGE | Rosa Bailey-Judd | Recreation Coordinator | urs | Enclosure | By fax | PS: Please contact me no later than November 10. | bc: Ramona Garcia

Keyboarding Connection

Creating an E-Mail Signature File

Creating a signature file saves you time and adds a personal touch to your e-mail messages. A signature file is a tag of information that is automatically included at the end of your e-mail messages. It may include your signature, a small graphic, your address, your phone number, or a quotation. Use the following guidelines to create a signature file.

Open your e-mail software. Open the menu item that allows you to create a signature file. Type the information you want to include in your signature, and then save and close the file.

Some companies don't allow graphics or quotations in e-mail signature files. E-mailing graphics uses extra bandwidth, which can slow down the network. For this reason, some e-mail software doesn't display graphics at all, instead displaying e-mail in plain text. Quotations may not align with the corporate culture or mission. Check to find out whether your company has corporate guidelines on e-mail signatures before you create your own signature file. When sending e-mail to potential employers, it's useful to add a professional signature to your e-mail that contains your contact information.

Your Turn: Create a signature file, then address an e-mail to yourself. Type "Test" in the Subject box. In the body, type "This is a test of the signature file." Send the e-mail; then open it to see how your signature file looks.

Multipage Memos With Tables

Goals

- Demonstrate improved speed and accuracy while typing.
- Demonstrate acceptable language arts skills in spelling.
- Correctly use Word's find and replace feature.
- Correctly format a multipage memo with a table.

A. WARMUP

alphabet	The lazy judge was very quick to pay tax money for the bar.
frequent digraphs	or orb for door fort more boor nor odor port orator ore ort
easy	The neighbor will do the fieldwork when she is in the glen.

Skillbuilding

B. MAP+: SYMBOL

Follow the GDP software directions for this exercise to improve keystroking accuracy.

PPP PRETEST » PRACTICE » POSTTEST

C. PRETEST: Horizontal Reaches

PRETEST

Take a 1-minute timed writing.

```
     The legal facts gave our lawyers a sense that we could 11
be ready to wrap up this case quickly. Until a written copy 23
of our testimony is given to us, we shall all be extremely  35
anxious. We added every ounce of our energy to your case.   46
  1 | 2 | 3 | 4 | 5 | 6 | 7 | 8 | 9 | 10 | 11 | 12
```

D. PRACTICE: In Reaches

PRACTICE

Speed Emphasis:
If you made no more than 1 error on the Pretest, type each *individual* line 2 times.

Accuracy Emphasis:
If you made 2 or more errors, type each *group* of lines (as though it were a paragraph) 2 times.

```
wr wrap wren wreak wrist wrote writer unwrap writhe wreaths
ou pout ours ounce cough fouls output detour ousted coupons
ad adds dead adult ready blade advice fading admits adheres
py pyre copy pygmy pylon happy pyrene choppy pyrite pyramid
```

E. PRACTICE: Out Reaches

```
yo yoga your youth yodel yowls yogurt joyous yonder younger
fa fact farm faith sofas fakes faulty unfair famous defames
up upon soup upset group upper upturn supply uplift upsurge
ga gate gave cigar gains legal gazing legacy gawked garbage
```

POSTTEST

Repeat the Pretest timed writing and compare performance.

F. POSTTEST: Horizontal Reaches

Language Arts

G. SPELLING

Type these frequently misspelled words, paying special attention to any spelling problems in each word.

16 personnel information its procedures their committee system
17 receive employees which education services opportunity area
18 financial appropriate interest received production contract
19 important through necessary customer employee further there
20 property account approximately general control division our

Edit the sentences to correct any misspellings.

21 The revised systom was adopted by the finantial division.

22 Four employes want to serve on the new property commitee.

23 Approximatly ten proceedures were included in the contract.

24 Further informasion will be recieved from the customers.

25 Their was much interest shown by the production personal.

26 The services in that aria are necesary for needed control.

Formatting

H. WORD PROCESSING: FIND AND REPLACE

GO TO Word Manual

Study Lesson 69 in your Word Manual. Complete all of the shaded steps while at your computer. Then format the documents that follow.

Document Processing

Correspondence
69-73
Memo

Highlighted words are spelling words from the language arts activities; do *not* highlight them when you type.

MEMO TO: L. B. Chinn, Station Manager | **FROM:** Mitzi Grenell, News Director | **DATE:** May 5, 20-- | **SUBJECT:** FCC European Trip

¶ This memo and others to follow will keep you informed about my upcoming trip to Europe. I have been invited by the Federal Communications Commission to lead a committee that will study television news in European countries. This opportunity came about because Jill Andrews received advance notice about the study and made the necessary arrangements so that I would be invited to participate. I am delighted to take part in this important project, which should be of great interest to all of our employees.

(continued on next page)

¶ A major focus of this study will be to compare the types of technologies used in different European countries to report and broadcast the news. Our study group will visit six European countries to gather further information. We will be visiting England, France, Denmark, Germany, Spain, and Portugal from August 24 through September 23. Four other members will offer their services to this committee:

Sandra Holton	News Director, WSVN	Miami, Florida
Manuel Cruz	News Director, National Public Radio	Boise, Idaho
Jason Chan	Station Manager, WLBZ	Bangor, Maine
Richard Logan	Operations Manager, Cable News System	Provo, Utah

Our initial plans are to spend approximately five full days in each country, meet with the news personnel of one or two of the major networks, tour their facilities, view recent broadcasts, and observe their general operations and various divisions. It should be quite an education.

¶ If you need to contact me during my absence, Barbara Brooks, our liaison at the Federal Communications Commission, is the appropriate contact. She, or any employee on her staff, will be able to provide a location and phone number.

¶ An amendment has been made to my contract that will allow production to continue as usual here at Channel 5 while I am gone. Dave Gelson will assume financial control of the department and will also supervise its day-to-day activities. Further procedures are being finalized so that Dave can make a smooth transition during my absence.

¶ As you can imagine, this is an exciting time for me. Thank you for supporting the project and for taking into account the long-term implications of this important study.

urs | PS: Thank you also for suggesting that I visit John Jacobs, one of our most valued customers. I understand that he owns property in England and France and will be at his estate in France at a time that coincides with my schedule. I will be sure to give him your best wishes.

Correspondence 69-74
Memo

Open the file for Correspondence 69-73 and make the following changes:

1. Address the memo to "All Employees."
2. Change each occurrence of the words "News Director" to "News Analyst." A total of three replacements should be made.
3. Change each occurrence of the word "France" to "Switzerland." A total of three replacements should be made.
4. Delete the fourth paragraph.
5. Add this as the second-to-the-last paragraph:

   When I return from this trip, my committee will compile a comprehensive report and analysis that will be distributed to all personnel. I will then organize some internal focus groups so that we can discuss the implications of the study on our day-to-day operations.

6. Delete the postscript at the end of the memo.

Correspondence
69-75
Memo

MEMO TO: Terri Hackworth Property Manager

FROM: Rosa Bailey-Judd, recreation coordinator

DATE: Apr. 14, 20--

Subject: Fitness Center

¶ The new fitness center will be ready for our residents to use in approximately one month, and interest continues to grow. Your leadership in constructing a fitness center on this property is sincerely appreciated. As soon as appropriate research is completed I will be requesting further financial support to purchase the following equipment in the quantity specified:

Single-space the table.

No.	Equipment
20	Exercise Bicycles
10	Treadmills
8	rowing machines

¶ Three types of other equipment were seriously considered, but the ones listed above are the most important in terms of what is necesary to schedule our proposed fitness classes. I am not quite ready to sign a contract with a specific supplier. We expect that there will be heavy usage ofthe specified equipment and are requesting inforamtion from vendors regarding durability, warranties, and the support of service personnel. I will receive that information within the week and will read through it carefully before signing a final contract.

¶ Thank you again for your full support and cooperation with this project. The general

contractor you hired has received rave reviews The new gym is a golden opportunity for all our residents to vastly improve their quality of life.

urs

Memo Reports

Goals

- Type at least 41wpm/5′/5e.
- Correctly format a memo report with report headings and a bibliography.
- Successfully complete a Progress and Proofreading Check with zero errors on the first scored attempt.

A. WARMUP

alphabet	1	Those five lazy movers quit packing the hard jewelry boxes.
number/symbol	2	(fay237@yahoo.com) 33% Coe & Tan 6/8 Hi! $2.41 *Oct. #95-01
easy	3	One half of the endowments may be paid by the town members.

Skillbuilding

B. 12-SECOND SPEED SPRINTS

Take three 12-second timed writings on each line. The scale below the last line shows your wpm speed for a 12-second timed writing.

```
4 That new city law may help us to fish for cod on the docks.
5 He may sign over the title to his autos when he is in town.
6 She may go with me to the city to visit my son and his pal.
7 The doe and buck by the old bush may dig up the giant oaks.
  ''''5''''10''''15''''20''''25''''30''''35''''40''''45''''50''''55''''60
```

C. TECHNIQUE PRACTICE: BACKSPACE KEY

Type each line 2 times, using your Sem finger to strike the BACKSPACE key when you see the ← symbol. For example, type *bud*, backspace, and type *m,* thus changing *bud* to *bum.*

```
8  bud←m gig←n dew←n rag←m tad←n own←l get←m tie←n toe←n
9  car←p hoe←g yea←n pie←n vat←n hug←m rug←m pod←i per←p
10 job←y yaw←m bus←y pad←l lad←p the←y nag←p fur←n nub←n
11 fad←n max←y jag←m fig←n ice←y oaf←k add←o mow←p log←o
```

Take two 5-minute timed writings.

Goal: At least 41wpm/5′/5e

D. 5-MINUTE TIMED WRITING

In most offices, many products that are used each day 11
are made of materials that can now be recycled. Amazingly, 23
items made of glass, steel, aluminum, plastics, and paper 34
can be recycled to make many products that we need. Also, 46
the recycling process can help the environment. 56

Some unique examples of the process of recycling the 66
items we often throw away are listed here. Those old coffee 78
filters can be used to make soles for new shoes. Pieces of 90
paper that are thrown away each day can be used to make 101
tissue paper or paper towels. Most plastics that are used 113
in soda bottles can be recycled for insulation for jackets 125
and auto interiors. Used lightbulbs and some glass products 137
can also be used to replace the surface on our streets. 148

Look around the room in which you are working. If you 159
are not already taking part in a recycling program, you may 171
want to recycle some items that you no longer need. Items 183
such as used paper, file folders, and aluminum cans can be 194
collected very quickly. What other items can you add? 205

1 | 2 | 3 | 4 | 5 | 6 | 7 | 8 | 9 | 10 | 11 | 12

Formatting

E. REPORT HEADINGS IN MEMOS

REFER TO Reference Manual

R-9C: Memo Report

There are times when a memo report is used rather than a cover memo to accompany a report. The memo and the report are combined into one, and headings are formatted as they are in a report. If a table is included in the body of the report, it should be formatted as it would be in a report. Use reference initials at the end of a memo report.

Document Processing

Report **70-38** Memo Report

MEMO TO: All Employees | **FROM:** Frank Reynolds, Director | **DATE:** February 24, 20-- | **SUBJECT:** New Security System

¶ Beginning April 1, we will be using a new security access system. Various security system options were researched thoroughly before a final decision was made to implement a fingerprint access system. Complete installation should occur by the end of March, but the system will not be activated until April 1. The system includes digital surveillance cameras and a fingerprint access system at all entrances. This will provide a more secure working environment, especially in the evenings and on weekends. Please carefully read the specifications below and follow the detailed instructions for using the new system:

(continued on next page)

FINGERPRINT ACCESS SYSTEM

Description	Specifications
Fingerprint memory capacity	78 people
Password capacity	78 people
False identification rate	Less than 0.0001%
Password length	8 bytes
Unlock methods	Fingerprint or keypad code

FINGERPRINT AND KEYPAD CODES

¶ Once the new system is installed, you simply touch the fingerprint keypad lock with your index finger for access during nonworking hours. You will also receive a keypad code for alternate access. Although mechanical keys can be used, they will not be created or distributed. Human Resources will begin programming fingerprint codes during the week of March 20. Further instructions will be issued at that time.

ENTRANCE AND EXIT PROCEDURES

¶ Entrances will unlock automatically each day at 8 a.m. and lock automatically at 5 p.m. To enter, touch the fingerprint keypad lock with your index finger. When the green light comes on, open the door. Do not hold the door open longer than 30 seconds when you enter or exit, or the alarm will sound. When you exit the building, do not use the special latch handle to open the door, or the alarm will sound. Instead, use the push bar. Sign in and sign out at the front desk each time you enter and exit.

¶ If you have questions about our new security access system and procedures, send an e-mail message to me at freynolds@infotech.com.

urs

Report
70-39
Bibliography

REFER TO Reference Manual

R-9B: Bibliography

BIBLIOGRAPHY

"Biometric Fingerprint Keypad Locks," *OfficeSecuritySystems,* January 11, 2010, <http://www.officesecuritysystems.com/fingerprint>, accessed on January 15, 2010.

"Business Alarm Monitoring," *SecurityZone,* December 11, 2009, <http://www.securityzone.com/securitymonitoring>, accessed on January 16, 2010.

De La Cruz, Stacey, "Digital Surveillance Systems," *Security Systems Today,* November 19, 2009, p. 18.

Paisley, Robert, "What's New in Business Security Systems," *The Daily Sentinel,* January 12, 2010, p. D6.

Report
70-40
Memo Report

Progress and Proofreading Check

Documents designated as Proofreading Checks serve as a check of your proofreading skill. Your goal is to have zero typographical errors when the GDP software first scores the document.

MEMO TO: All Employees
FROM: Won Chul Lee, President
DATE: March 2, 20--
SUBJECT: New Administrative Center

¶ You will all be very pleased to know that after extensive consultation with several architectural firms, I have finalized plans for a new administrative center to be constructed at 3900 Rockefeller Plaza. This memo will

(continued on next page)

provide you with general information about the exciting plans for the center's exterior and interior development.

ARCHITECTURE AND LANDSCAPING

¶ Exterior plans will maintain the historical integrity and beauty of the surrounding area and reflect the architecture of other buildings in the office park. Landscaping plans include a park area, a picnic area, and a small pond. Paseos (winding walkways) will connect the various businesses within the complex and include both bike paths and foot paths.

DEPARTMENTAL LOCATIONS

¶ Staff will be located within the new facility as follows:

1. Accounting will be located on the first floor in the west wing.
2. Sales and marketing will be located on the first floor in the east wing. All staff will be grouped according to product line.
3. Technical support will be located in the basement level of the east wing. All staff will be grouped according to product support.
4. All other staff will be located on the second floor. Exact locations will be determined at a later date.

SPECIAL FACILITIES

¶ Conference rooms will be located in the center of the building on the first floor to provide easy access for everyone. All rooms will be equipped with state-of-the-art technology. Our new center will also include a full-service cafeteria, a copy center, a library, an athletic center, and an on-site day-care center.

¶ Construction of the new center will begin when the necessary permits have been obtained. I hope you are looking forward to our new location as much as I am. More information will be forthcoming as plans are finalized.

urs

UNIT 15

Reports

Itineraries 71

Goals

- Demonstrate improved speed and accuracy while typing.
- Demonstrate acceptable language arts skills in using commas.
- Correctly format an itinerary.

A. WARMUP

alphabet	1	My faxed jokes won me a pager from the cable TV quiz shows.
concentration	2	electromagnetically antirevolutionaries overdiversification
easy	3	The big dog down by the lake may bury the eighty fishbowls.

Skillbuilding

B. MAP+: ALPHABET

Follow the GDP software directions for this exercise to improve keystroking accuracy.

C. PROGRESSIVE PRACTICE: ALPHABET

Follow the GDP software directions for this exercise to improve keystroking speed.

Language Arts

Study the rules at the right.

RULE
, nonessential expression

D. COMMAS

Use a comma before and after a nonessential expression.

Andre, who was there, can verify the statement.
But: Anyone who was there can verify the statement.
Van's first book, *Crisis of Management,* was not discussed.
Van's book *Crisis of Management* was not discussed.

Note: A nonessential expression is a group of words that may be omitted without changing the basic meaning of the sentence. Always examine the noun or pronoun that comes before the expression to determine whether the noun needs the expression to complete its meaning. If it does, the expression is *essential* and does *not* take a comma.

RULE
, adjacent adjectives

Use a comma between two adjacent adjectives that modify the same noun.

We need an intelligent, enthusiastic individual for this job.
But: Please order a new bulletin board for our main conference room.

Note: Do not use a comma after the second adjective. Also, do not use a comma if the first adjective modifies the combined idea of the second adjective and the noun (for example, *bulletin board* and *conference room* in the second example).

Edit each sentence to correct any errors.

```
The school president Mr. Roberts will address the students.

The fall planning meeting which is held in Charlotte has been canceled.

Students planning to take the certification test must register for the orientation class.

The sleek luxury car is scheduled for delivery next week.

Margaret brought her fast reliable laptop to the meeting.

A stamped addressed envelope should be included with the survey.
```

Formatting

E. ITINERARIES

REFER TO Reference Manual
R-11C: Itinerary

An itinerary is a proposed outline of a trip that provides a traveler with information, such as flight times and numbers, meeting times, travel dates, and room reservations. An itinerary may also include notes of special interest to the traveler.

To format an itinerary:

1. Press ENTER 5 times to begin the first line of the itinerary 2 inches from the top of the page.
2. Insert an open table with 2 columns and enough rows to accommodate the completed itinerary.
3. Insert 1 blank line between each part of the heading block in Row 1.
4. Type the date in Row 2, Column A, in all-caps and bold; press ENTER 1 time.
5. Type the time in Column A and the corresponding information in Column B; press ENTER 1 time as shown after each group of lines in Column B.
6. Repeat these steps until the itinerary is finished, and adjust the column widths as needed.

Report
71-41
Itinerary

↓5X

14 pt **RESOURCE CONSULTANTS SALES MEETING** ↓2X

12 pt↓ **Itinerary for Linda Padilla** ↓2X

March 12-14, 20-- ↓2X

THURSDAY, MARCH 12 ↓1X	
9:39 a.m.-10:07 a.m.	Flight from Atlanta to New Orleans; Delta 1585 (800-555-1222); e-ticket; Seat 8D; nonstop. ↓2X Sharon Lee (Cell: 504-555-8029; Office: 504-555-7631) will meet your flight on Thursday, provide transportation during your visit, and return you to the airport on Saturday morning. Airport Embassy Suites (504-555-4032) King-sized bed, nonsmoking room; late arrival guaranteed; Reservation No. 0312010-AZ. ↓1X
FRIDAY, MARCH 13	
9 a.m.	Resource Consultants Sales Meeting Royal New Orleans Hotel 730 Rue Bienville, Bourbon Street Suite New Orleans, LA 70130 (503-555-7631)
7 p.m.	Dinner at the Royal New Orleans Hotel—The French Quarter Bistro.
SATURDAY, MARCH 14	
6:30 a.m.	Meet Sharon Lee, who will accompany you on the return flight, in the lobby of the Airport Embassy Suites for transportation to the airport.
8:30 a.m.-10:50 a.m.	Flight from New Orleans to Atlanta; Delta 5995; e-ticket; Seat 10D; nonstop.

, nonessential expression

(Note: Table shown with "View Gridlines" active.)

Report 71-42
Itinerary

, nonessential expression

, adjacent adjectives

RSA TECHNOLOGY CONFERENCE | **Itinerary for Mrs. Norma McKinley** | **September 25-29, 20--** | **WEDNESDAY, SEPTEMBER 25** | 1:50 p.m.-4:10 p.m. | Flight from Columbus to Boston; US Airways 2053; Seat 13F; nonstop. | Boston Inn (617-555-3982) | King-sized bed, nonsmoking room; late arrival guaranteed. | Judith Greenburg, who will be at the same conference, will meet you in the lobby at 6 p.m. for dinner. | **THURSDAY, SEPTEMBER 26** | 8:30 a.m.-5 p.m. | RSA Technology Conference, Suite 201 | A compact, full-featured presentations projector will be ready in the suite no later than 8 a.m. | **FRIDAY, SEPTEMBER 27** | 9 a.m.-10:17 a.m. | Flight from Boston to New York City; US Airways 454; Seat 10D; nonstop. | **SUNDAY, SEPTEMBER 29** | 2:07 p.m.-4:18 p.m. | Flight from New York City to Columbus; US Airways 324; Seat 9A; nonstop.

Report 71-43
Itinerary

, adjacent adjectives

, nonessential expression

HEALTH EFFECTS INSTITUTE CONFERENCE | **Itinerary for Dr. Ron Jacobs** | **July 8-10, 20--** | **MONDAY, JULY 8** | 2:45 p.m.-4:05 p.m. | Flight from Houston to Los Angeles; United 834; Seat 10C; nonstop. | Marriott (310-555-1014) | King-sized bed; nonsmoking room; late arrival guaranteed; Reservation No. 45STX78. | **TUESDAY, JULY 9** | 6 a.m.-7:15 a.m. | Flight from Los Angeles to Sacramento; American 206; Seat 4A; nonstop. | Sacramento Garden Inn (916-555-7373) | King-sized bed; nonsmoking room; late arrival guaranteed; Reservation No. QRR6H. | A spacious, well-equipped welcome booth, including computers with Internet access, will be available in the Executive Center, Room 12B. | 10 a.m.-4:30 p.m. | Health Effects Institute Conference, Executive Center, Room 12A. | **WEDNESDAY, JULY 10** | 7 a.m.-11:15 a.m. | Flight from Sacramento to Houston; United 307; Seat 7B; nonstop.

Strategies for Career Success

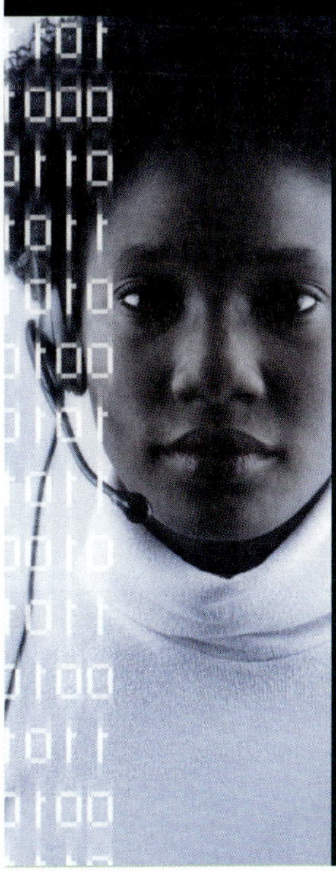

Successful Interviewing Techniques

The Interview is a useful tool for gathering more information about a company. Here are some steps to effective interviewing.

Conduct preliminary research so you can ask intelligent questions and make efficient use of the interview time. Prepare a list of questions to use in the interview. Make sure questions are open-ended, unbiased, and geared toward gathering insights you can't gain through reading about the company. Be prepared to take notes, listen actively, and ask follow-up questions, as needed.

Remember that an interview, whether for a job or for information gathering, is also your opportunity to find out if a company or career would be a good fit for you. It is in everyone's best interest to find out during a job interview if you will be happy at the company, so ask questions about things that are important to you. These might be things like potential for advancement, various career paths within a specialty, and corporate culture (e.g., does the company promote a work-life balance, or is it a place where overtime is routine and can lead to better opportunities?).

Greet the interviewer by name, and thank him or her for taking time to talk to you. If it's not a job interview, explain why you are interested in interviewing him or her. Stay within the scheduled time. In closing the interview, thank the person again, and ask if you can get in touch if other questions come to mind.

Your Turn: Prepare a list of questions you might use in interviewing someone concerning what his or her company does.

Agendas and Minutes of Meetings

Goals

- Type at least 42wpm/5′/5e.
- Correctly format an agenda and the minutes of a meeting.

A. WARMUP

alphabet	Quick brown foxes jumped over the lazy dog who was resting.
one hand	adverb hookup was ply target minimum beat knoll acted kinky
easy	The quantity of profits for the coalfield is a big problem.

Skillbuilding

B. SUSTAINED PRACTICE: SYLLABIC INTENSITY

Take a 1-minute timed writing on the boxed paragraph to establish your base speed. Then take a 1-minute timed writing on the following paragraph. As soon as you equal or exceed your base speed on this paragraph, move to the next, more difficult paragraph.

```
     Each of us has several bills to be paid on a monthly    11
basis. For most of us, a checkbook is the tool that we use   23
to take care of this chore. However, in this electronic      34
age, other ways of doing this have received rave reviews.    45

     You will likely be surprised to learn that the most     11
basic way and the cheapest way to pay bills electronically   22
involves the use of a Touch-Tone phone. The time required    34
is approximately a third of that used when writing checks.   46

     Several banking institutions offer or plan to offer     11
screen phones as a method for paying bills. It is possible   22
to buy securities, make transfers, and determine account     34
balances. You will save time by using a Touch-Tone phone.    45

     A third type of electronic bill processing involves     11
using a microcomputer and a modem. Software programs have    22
on-screen checkbooks linked to bill-paying applications.     34
Other microcomputers use online services through a modem.    45
   1 | 2 | 3 | 4 | 5 | 6 | 7 | 8 | 9 | 10 | 11 | 12
```

Take two 5-minute timed writings.

Goal: At least 42wpm/5′/5e

C. 5-MINUTE TIMED WRITING

Whether you are searching for your first job or are 11
looking to change jobs, your networking skills may play a 22
crucial role in how successful you are in that endeavor. 34
Networking can be defined in some respects as a group of 45
people who are linked closely together for the purpose of 57
achieving some sort of end result. In this case, the end 68
result will be to establish new contacts who might be able 80
to assist you in your job search. 87
Your network is made up of dozens of people you have 97
met. You can never be sure who has the potential of helping 109
you the most in your job search. Therefore, it is important 121
that you consider all acquaintances. You should certainly 133
network with business associates, and especially those you 145
have met at various meetings or conferences. And don't 158
forget former teachers in whose classes you were enrolled. 168
Former classmates provide an excellent base on which 178
to build your network, and friends and family should also 190
be included. Also, use the Internet to nurture any online 202
contacts you may have made over the years. 210

1 | 2 | 3 | 4 | 5 | 6 | 7 | 8 | 9 | 10 | 11 | 12

Formatting

D. AGENDAS

REFER TO Reference Manual

R-11A: Meeting Agenda

An agenda is a list of topics to be discussed at a meeting. It may also include a formal program of a meeting and consist of times, rooms, speakers, and other related information.

To format an agenda:

1. Press ENTER 5 times to begin the first line of the agenda 2 inches from the top of the page.
2. Center and type the name of the company or committee in all-caps, bold, and 14-point font.
3. Press ENTER 2 times; then center and type `Meeting Agenda` in upper- and lowercase, bold, and 12-point font.
4. Press ENTER 2 times; then center and type the date in upper- and lowercase, bold, and 12-point font.
5. Press ENTER 2 times and turn off bold.
6. Type all agenda items as a numbered list using Word's default format.

↓5X

14 pt **BECKER CORPORATION STAFF MEETING** ↓2X

12 pt↓ **Meeting Agenda** ↓2X

February 17, 20-- ↓2X

default format

1. Call to order
2. Approval of minutes of January 15 meeting
3. Progress report on the remodeling of the staff lounge, copy center, and reception area (Roger Wilcox)
4. Discussion of plans for group presentations at the National Advanced Technology Institute meeting
5. Annual company picnic (Rachel Morris)
6. Announcements
7. Adjournment

E. MINUTES OF MEETINGS

REFER TO Reference Manual

R-11B: Minutes of a Meeting

Items discussed during a meeting are officially recorded as the minutes of a meeting.

To format the minutes of a meeting:

1. Press ENTER 5 times to begin the first line of the minutes 2 inches from the top of the page.
2. Insert an open table with 2 columns and enough rows to accommodate the completed meeting minutes.
3. Insert 1 blank line between each part of the heading block in Row 1.
4. Type the first section heading in Row 2, Column A, in all-caps and bold.
5. Type the corresponding information in Column B; press ENTER 1 time after the final line in Column B.
6. Move to the next row and repeat steps 4 and 5 until all remaining sections have been completed.
7. Type the closing and signature lines in Column B of the final row; press ENTER 4 times to allow room for the signature.
8. Adjust the width of Column A to accommodate the longest heading as shown in the illustration that follows.

↓5X

14 pt **PLANNING COMMITTEE** ↓2X

12 pt↓ **Minutes of the Meeting** ↓2X

February 10, 20-- ↓1X

ATTENDANCE	The Planning Committee meeting was called to order at 1 p.m. on February 10, 20--, by Michelle North, chairperson. Members present were Cal Anderson, L. T. Braddock, Lisa Samson, Sharon Owens, and J. R. Stern. ↓1X
APPROVAL OF MINUTES	The minutes of the January 10 meeting were read and approved as presented.
OLD BUSINESS	The committee reviewed bids for the purchase of a new computer for the Cheyenne office. The committee will accept the lower of two bids that have been submitted.
NEW BUSINESS	The committee reviewed a proposal for a new complex in Helena. After much discussion, the committee agreed to contact the Helena county clerk's office to get information on zoning ordinances.
ADJOURNMENT	The meeting was adjourned at 2:45 p.m. The next meeting is scheduled for March 22 in Room 26 at 1 p.m. ↓2X Respectfully submitted, ↓4X *Barbara Cheng* Barbara Cheng, Secretary

(Note: Table shown with "View Gridlines" active.)

Document Processing

Report
72-44
Agenda

Use Word's default numbering format.

FOX ASSOCIATES STAFF MEETING

Meeting Agenda

April 15, 20--

1. Call to order
2. Approval of minutes of March 15 meeting
3. Progress reports for the construction of new media center
4. Discussion of the upcoming time management seminar (F. Pryor and J. Harrington)
5. Discussion of Internet security and antivirus software (T. Rashid)
6. Annual charity event (J. Simpatico)
7. Announcements
8. Adjournment

Report
72-45
Agenda

GREENWAY SECURITY CORPORATION

Meeting Agenda

October 13, 20--

1. Call to order
2. Approval of minutes of September 10 meeting
3. Progress reports on biometric access control technology (Marie Newsome)
4. Upgrading of 8.0 presentation media
5. Handheld scanners and readers product development (Andrew Slovinsky)
6. Visitor registration and tracking (Juan Mendoza)
7. Announcements
8. Adjournment

Report
72-46
Minutes of a Meeting

ADVISORY COMMITTEE

Minutes of the Meeting

June 10, 20--

ATTENDANCE	The Advisory Committee meeting was called to order at 1 p.m. on June 10, 20--, by Suzanne Higgins-North, chairperson. Members present were Georgia Holton, James Duncan, Mary Benavidez, Pete Bergstrom, Quan Ying Zhao, and Sharon Rose.
APPROVAL OF MINUTES	The minutes of the May 10 meeting were read and approved as presented.
OLD BUSINESS	The committee reviewed recommendations for new hardware and software and new ergonomically sound workstations, lighting, and seating.
NEW BUSINESS	The committee reviewed a proposal for a new classroom complex in Helena. After much discussion, the committee agreed to contact the Helena county clerk's office to get information on zoning ordinances.
ADJOURNMENT	The meeting was adjourned at 2:45 p.m. The next meeting is scheduled for July 10 in Room 16. Respectfully submitted, Nancy Jacobs, Secretary

(Note: Table shown with "View Gridlines" active.)

Report
72-47
Minutes of a Meeting

HUMAN RESOURCES DEPT.

Minutes of The Meeting

May 20, 20--

ATTENDING On May 14, 20--, A meeting of the Human Resources Department was held in the office of Mr. Choi. Members were present except Donald Clark, who was representedby Monica Cruz. The meeting was called to order at 10 A.M.

APPROVAL OF MINUTES The minutes of the Apr. 14 meeting were read and approved as presented.

OLD BUSINESS Andrea Fields was in charge of a staff-development survey. Ninetyseven questionnaires were returned, and a copy of the staff-development survey was discussed. The committee will

consider the findings and be prepared to make recomendations for up dated job descriptions at the next monthly meeting.

NEW BUSINESS Mr. Choi discussed plans to disseminate information about vaacncies that occur within the company to prospective job applicants. Monica Cruz will draft a flyer to be sent to the Lakeview Sentinel. Programs for the N P A convention to be held in Los Angeles were distributed to all members. Each committee member was asked to distribute copies to employees all in his or her department.

ADJOURNMENT The meetingwas ended at 11:45 a.m. The meeting has been scheduled for July 10 in the Conference Center.

Respectfully submitted,

Brandon Scher Secretary

Procedures Manual

Goals

- Demonstrate improved speed and accuracy while typing.
- Demonstrate acceptable proofreading skills by editing a paragraph.
- Correctly use Word's footer feature.
- Correctly format a procedures manual.

A. WARMUP

alphabet / practice *u* and *y* / easy

```
The jobs of waxing linoleum frequently peeved chintzy kids.
yum buy duly yuck fury your guy July busy yuk quay you your
Laurie may dismantle her tan bicycle and put it in the van.
```

Skillbuilding

B. MAP+: NUMBERS

Follow the GDP software directions for this exercise to improve keystroking accuracy.

PPP PRETEST » PRACTICE » POSTTEST

C. PRETEST: Vertical Reaches

PRETEST
Take a 1-minute timed writing.

```
     Janice and her escort were late for a dance at the      10
resort. The drummers in the band had just started to play    22
as they came in. It seems Janice injured the back of her     33
knee on the bank of the river during a cruise that morning.  45
   1 | 2 | 3 | 4 | 5 | 6 | 7 | 8 | 9 | 10 | 11 | 12
```

D. PRACTICE: Up Reaches

PRACTICE
Speed Emphasis:
If you made no more than 1 error on the Pretest, type each *individual* line 2 times.
Accuracy Emphasis:
If you made 2 or more errors, type each *group* of lines (as though it were a paragraph) 2 times.

```
at late flatly rebate atomic rather repeat attest atom what
dr draft drank dryer drew drain drama dread dream drag drug
ju judge juice jumpy junks juror judo julep jumbo jump just
es essay nests tests less dress acres makes uses best rests
```

E. PRACTICE: Down Reaches

```
ca cable caddy cargo scare decay yucca pecan cage calm case
nk ankle blank crank blink junk think trunk brink bank sink
ba tuba ballot cabana bakery abates global basket balk band
sc scar scale scalp scene scent scold scoop scope scan disc
```

POSTTEST

Repeat the Pretest timed writing and compare performance.

F. POSTTEST: Vertical Reaches

Language Arts

Edit the paragraph to correct any errors.

G. PROOFREADING

Many home computer user like the challenge of haveing the latest in both hardware and software technology. Their are those however, who's needs likely can be satisfied at a very low costs. A used Pentium personnel computer with color monitor and keyboard might be your's for under $ 300. Check out th Yellow Page, or visit a used-computer store.

Formatting

H. PROCEDURES MANUAL

Organizations often prepare procedures manuals to assist employees in identifying the steps or methods they must follow to accomplish particular tasks. The illustration depicts a continuation page in a procedures manual for American Bistro. The title of the manual is "Employee Manual" and the report section name is "Training Program."

To format a procedures manual:

1. Type the manual using standard formatting for the body of a business report.
2. Insert a header (suppressed on the first page) with the company name followed by a comma and the manual title at the left margin.
3. Move to the right margin, and type the name of the report section in italics.
4. Insert a footer with the word "Page" followed by a page number field centered in the footer.

Strategies for Career Success

Corrective Feedback

Sometime in your career, you will give someone corrective feedback. You can use positive communication to do this and not appear to criticize the person.

Here are some things you should not do. Do not correct the person in front of others. Avoid giving feedback when you are angry. Stay away from derogatory or dismissive comments (for example, "That's a useless idea!"). Do not dismiss a person's enthusiasm with comments like "We've never done that before" or "It won't work."

Here are some things you should do. Listen to the other person's side of the situation. Ask for ideas on how to fix the situation. Express yourself in a positive way, such as saying, "You're getting much closer" or "That's an interesting idea." Be specific about what the person can do to correct the situation. Follow up within a short time and identify all progress.

Your Turn: Think about the last time you received corrective feedback. Did the person giving you feedback use techniques to create a positive outcome?

American Bistro, Employee Manual *Training Program* Header italic

A high-quality dining experience doesn't happen without preparation. A careful, systematic plan for training and then mentoring must occur. Our training program includes a structured plan for training for the following positions: ↓2X

- Server
- Dishwasher
- Line Cook
- Prep Cook
- Bus Person
- Host or Hostess
- Bartender ↓2X

Each of these positions is discussed in detail and many constructive suggestions are outlined. ↓2X

SERVER ↓2X

The functions and the responsibilities of the server are many and varied. General guidelines and specific responsibilities and opening and closing procedures are critical. Guest service is the goal for all restaurant employees but is particularly important for those who deal with the customer directly. ↓2X

Quality Control and Ordering. A server must be aware of quality control in terms of the food being served. Is it fresh, properly prepared, and promptly served? Ordering procedures must be in place so that the guest feels confident that the order will arrive promptly, accurately, and as expected.

Personal Appearance. Guests will make a direct correlation between a server's personal appearance and the overall quality of the dining experience. If the server is not dressed appropriately, the guest will begin the dining experience with a negative impression. If the server creates a good first impression in appearance and attitude, the guest will anticipate a wonderful and very pleasant dining experience.

Suggestive Selling. Suggestive selling as a guest is ordering and reviewing the menu is a fine art that must be practiced and rehearsed. The specials and features

Page 8 Footer

I. WORD PROCESSING: FOOTERS

GO TO Word Manual

Study Lesson 73 in your Word Manual. Complete all of the shaded steps while at your computer. Then format the documents that follow.

Document Processing

Report 73-48
Procedures Manual

Abbott Industries, Employee Training Manual *Introduction*

¶ Managers are responsible for developing training programs for new employees who have been hired in any of the seven regional branches of Abbott Industries. The basic content of this employee training program is outlined next.

EMPLOYEE TRAINING MANUAL OUTLINE

¶ Abbott Industries will distribute this manual to all new managers to help familiarize them with the day-to-day procedures of the company. Also, answers are provided to the following questions with specific details included in each section:

- Where does the training manual fit within the training program?
- For whom is the manual designed, and what does it contain?
- How should the manual be used?
- Can the manual be used in a classroom setting?
- Can the manual be used as self-paced instructional material?
- Can study guides accompany the manual?

(continued on next page)

EMPLOYEE TRAINING PROGRAM PHILOSOPHY AND GOALS

¶ Well-trained employees are the key to the continued success of Abbott Industries. Studies have shown that the most successful, productive employees are those who have received extensive training. One of the positive results of a training program is that employees often feel they have a strong stake in the company's future. That internalized sense of ownership is highly motivational. The next section in this training manual explains the program guidelines.

Page 2

Report
73-49
Procedures Manual

Studio One Photography, Presentation Software Guide *Presentation Overview*

PRESENTATION ACTION PLAN

¶ An effective presentation does not happen by accident. It must be designed and formatted in a way that is appropriate to the audience and the topic. It must focus carefully on the subject at hand and include the right amount of text and graphics on each slide without appearing busy. Artwork, tables, and charts should be used purposefully to convey information clearly.

¶ Sound and video must be used with discretion as they can become a distraction rather than an enhancement. The same holds true for animation. It can quickly become annoying unless it is used sparingly. A good presentation should include a closing that provides the audience with an opportunity for questions, answers, and discussion.

PRESENTATION SOFTWARE

¶ There are several different computer-assisted presentation methods. However, Studio One Photography is using PowerPresentation software exclusively at this time. Any presentation can be delivered directly from a computer by connecting to a large external monitor or to a projection system.

¶ The software also allows presentations to be saved in a format for publishing on the Internet. Self-running presentations can be created specifically for the Internet; however, some of the special effects and animation may be lost in the process. Presentations can also be saved to a CD that will start automatically when the CD is inserted into a computer. Because the CD contains both the presentation and special viewer software, distributing the presentation is seamless.

Page 7

Report
73-50
Procedures Manual

1. Open Report 73-49.
2. Edit the header, and type `Clip Art Overview` as the section name.
3. Edit the footer so the page number starts at page 8.
4. Delete the entire content of the report body, and replace it with this:

ADDING **Clip Art**

Clip art can enhance the appearance of aslide, and it can be easily added to selected slides or to every slide in your presentation. Several clip art images are included in this presentation package and any 1 of them can be used in slides that you prepare. If you choose, therefore, you can insert clip art images from other packages. To insert a clip art image from your Presentation software package, follow these steps:

1. Click the icon for adding a clip art image.
2. Select the image from the software clip art library and size and move it to its new location.
3. Size and move the image to its correct location on the presentation slide.
4. Copy the image to the slide master if it is to appear on all slides.

You can also change the appearance of a clip art image by changing the colors used or by changing the contrast or brightness. A mirror image is created by flipping the image so that its horizontal or vertical position are reversed. To eliminate un wanted sections of an image, crop the unwanted sections. This process is similar to what happens you when take a printed picture and use scissors to cut off portions of picture except that it happens electronically.

Keyboarding Connection

Observing Netiquette

Netiquette is proper conduct for e-mail users. It shows courtesy and professionalism and conveys a good impression of you and your company. Since e-mail is close to speech, it is the most informal of business documents.

Check your e-mail daily. Try to answer it the same day it arrives. Don't let it accumulate in your mailbox; you risk offending the sender. Use regular capitalization. All-caps indicate SHOUTING; all-lowercase text conveys immaturity. Most readers tolerate an infrequent typo, but if your message is filled with errors, you appear unprofessional. Use your spell checker, and don't overwhelm people with unnecessary e-mail. Use discretion. Don't automatically reply all; make sure the information is relevant to each e-mail recipient.

Be considerate. Be professional. Don't forward jokes or nonwork-related e-mail at work. Anything you write can wind up in your personnel file. E-mail that criticizes another person can be forwarded to him or her without your knowledge.

Your Turn: Review your next e-mail message for the use of netiquette.

UNIT 15 LESSON 74

Reports Formatted in Columns

Goals

- Type at least 42wpm/5′/5e.
- Correctly use Word's column and hyphenation features.
- Correctly format a magazine article.

A. WARMUP

alphabet 1 Amusing quips galvanized a few of the mock jury in the box.

frequent digraphs 2 th that bath them both math then moth the myth theft thirty

easy 3 The doe and buck by the old bush may dig up the giant oaks.

Skillbuilding

B. PROGRESSIVE PRACTICE: NUMBERS

Follow the GDP software directions for this exercise to improve keystroking speed.

C. TECHNIQUE PRACTICE: SPACE BAR

Type each line 2 times, using your right thumb to strike the SPACE BAR in the center.

4 Mr. Li may ask an arm and a leg for the new car on the lot.
5 The hot sun in the sky led Ann to ask him for a cup of tea.
6 Bo may use an old key to the gym for the new job if he can.
7 One ton of wet tar on the dam may be a bit too hot for him.

Take two 5-minute timed writings.

Goal: At least 42wpm/5′/5e

D. 5-MINUTE TIMED WRITING

Have you ever given any thought to starting your own 11
business? Obviously, there is some risk in starting out in 23
a venture such as this. However, if you realize there are 34
some issues to starting up a business, it may not seem to 46
be such a daunting undertaking. Let's quickly look at just 58
some of the issues that are involved in this task. 68

First of all, you need to think about whether you want 79
to do so badly enough to work long hours without knowing if 91
you will make any money at the end of the month. It would 103
be advantageous if you had worked previously for another 114
company as a manager or have managerial experience. 124

You have to have some sense for just how much money 135
you will need to start your business. It will take some 146
working capital to get you started. If you have put money 158
aside to invest in the company, there is a good possibility 170
you will succeed. If you don't have enough put aside, can 181
you get credit from a lending institution to assist you 193
through the first few months? And, of course, you'll need 204
to get credit from suppliers. 210

1 | 2 | 3 | 4 | 5 | 6 | 7 | 8 | 9 | 10 | 11 | 12

Formatting

E. MAGAZINE ARTICLES

Magazine articles can be formatted as a newspaper-style column in which text flows from the bottom of one column to the top of the next column. Magazine articles are generally formatted as 2-column reports.

To format a magazine article with two columns:

1. Turn hyphenation on.
2. Press ENTER 5 times to begin the first line of the magazine article 2 inches from the top of the page.
3. Center and type the title in all-caps, bold, and 14-point.
4. Press ENTER 2 times; then center and type the byline in upper- and lowercase, bold, and 12-point.
5. Press ENTER 2 times and change to left alignment.
6. Type the article single-spaced; insert 1 blank line before and after all side headings.
7. Select the body of the report, and change to justified alignment.
8. For a multipage article, insert a header (suppressed on the first page) with the author's last name, a space, and the page number aligned at the right.
9. Carefully select text beginning just before the first character in the first paragraph through the last typed character of the document excluding the paragraph formatting following the last character.
10. Format the body into 2 columns.
11. If any heading appears as a one-liner at the bottom of the first page, keep it with the text on the next page.
12. Balance the columns if necessary.
13. Fix any large gaps that might appear between the words of the last line of the body.

↓5X

14 pt **TIME AND PERCEPTION** ↓2X

12 pt ↓ **Shannon Jones** ↓2X

Time is a method human beings use to measure and sequence events, to compare the durations of events, and to measure the intervals between events. Time is a hot topic in terms of religion, philosophy, and science. However, defining time in an objective, accepted way has been nearly impossible among scholarly types. How, in fact, do you compare one moment to the next?

As human beings, our perception of time has grown out of a natural series of rhythms that are linked to daily, monthly, and yearly cycles. No matter how much we live by our wristwatches, our bodies and our lives will always be somewhat influenced by an internal clock. What is of even greater interest, though, are the many uses and perceptions of time based on individuals and their cultures.

RHYTHM AND TEMPO

Rhythm and tempo are ways we relate to time and are discerning features of a culture. In some cultures, people move very slowly; in others, moving quickly is the norm. Mixing the two types may create feelings of discomfort. People may have trouble relating to each other because they are not synchronized. To be synchronized is to subtly move in union with another person; it is vital to a strong partnership.

In general, Americans move at a fast tempo, although there are regional departures. In meetings, Americans tend to be impatient and want to "get down to business" right away. They have been taught that it is best to come to the point quickly and avoid vagueness. Because American business operates in a short time frame, prompt results are often of more interest than the building of long-term relationships.

PERCEPTION AND MEMORY

Picture yourself in a room watching someone enter, walk across the room, and sit down. By the time the person sits down, your brain must remember the actions that happened previous to the act of sitting down. All these memories and perceptions are filed as bits of data in the brain. The perception of the passing of time from the first event of entering the room to the last event of sitting down occurs only if the observer is aware and comparing the events.

What would happen if the observer could not remember one or more of the events from the time the person entered the room to the time that person was seated? The brain might interpret the scene and assign a time frame, but unless the observer remembers, the perception of time passing would not exist.

LIVING IN THE MOMENT

If a human being perceives himself to be of a certain age, this is because he has accumulated data, remembers that data, and has a basis for a comparison. If a person cannot remember his past, such as a person with dementia, then he would not be aware of the existence of such a past. He would only be experiencing the single "moment" he was living in.

F. WORD PROCESSING: COLUMNS AND HYPHENATION

GO TO Word Manual

Study Lesson 74 in your Word Manual. Complete all of the shaded steps while at your computer. Then format the documents that follow.

Document Processing

Report
74-51
Magazine Article

INTERVIEW TECHNIQUES
Sandra Dolan

¶ The interview process enables a company to gather information about you that was not provided on your resume or application form. This information may include such items as your career goals, appearance, personality, poise, and ability to express yourself verbally.

¶ Regardless of where you went to school or how much experience you have, if you aren't able to interview successfully, you won't get the job. Take note of the information in this article to help you interview successfully and get the job you want.

APPEARANCE

¶ Plan your wardrobe carefully because first impressions are lasting ones when you walk into the interviewer's office. If you are not quite certain about what you should wear, dress conservatively.

¶ Whatever you choose, be sure that your clothing is clean, neat, and comfortable. You should also pay attention to details such as personal hygiene, clean hair, shined shoes, well-groomed nails, and appropriate jewelry and other accessories.

MEETING THE INTERVIEWER

¶ Be sure to arrive at the interview site a few minutes early. Stand when you meet the interviewer for the first time. If the interviewer offers to shake hands, shake hands in a confident, firm manner. A great deal of nonverbal communication occurs even in a simple handshake.

THE INTERVIEW PROCESS

¶ Maintain direct eye contact with the interviewer when you respond to his or her questions. Listen intently to everything that is said. Be aware of any movements you make with your eyes, your hands, and other parts of your body during the interview. Too much movement may be a signal to the interviewer that you are nervous, that you lack confidence, or that you are not certain of your answers.

¶ During the interview, the interviewer will judge not only what you say but also how you say it. As you answer questions, you will be judged on grammar, articulation, vocabulary, and tone of voice. The nonverbal skills that the interviewer may judge are your attitude, enthusiasm, listening ability, and promptness in responding to questions.

ENDING THE INTERVIEW

¶ Let the interviewer determine when it is time to close the interview. When this time arrives, ask the interviewer when he or she expects to make a decision on hiring for this position and when you may expect to hear about the job. Thank the interviewer for taking the time to meet with you, and make a graceful, prompt exit.

¶ After the interview, send a follow-up letter to remind the interviewer of your name and your continued interest in the company. This follow-up letter will set you apart from the competition and provide another example of your communication skills. Let the interviewer know how to contact you by providing a telephone number where you can be reached. A cell phone number is preferable to a home phone number. Make it easy for the interviewer to contact you.

Report
74-52
Magazine Article

PACIFIC INSURANCE DISCOUNTS

Sharon Brooks

¶ Policyholders of Pacific Insurance (and their dependents) are eligible for a wide range of discount services. These services provide you with a variety of items you can purchase, from automobiles to computers to jewelry. Here are some examples of the merchandise and services that are available to all Pacific Insurance members.

AUTO PRICING

¶ You can order the most sophisticated auto information guide on the market. The guide will give you information on retail prices, vehicle specifications, safety equipment, and factory-option packages.

¶ When you are ready to place your order for an automobile, a team of company experts will work with you and with the prospective dealer to ensure that you are getting the best possible price through a network of nationwide dealers. You are guaranteed to get the best price for the automobile you have chosen.

¶ Once you have purchased your automobile, Pacific Insurance will provide all your insurance needs. Discounts on policy rates are provided for completion of a driver-training program, for installed antitheft devices, and for installed passive restraint systems, such as air bags.

¶ Finally, Pacific Insurance can make your purchase decision an easy one by always providing a low-rate finance plan for you. You can be certain that you are getting the most competitive interest rate for the purchase of your automobile when you finance with Pacific Insurance.

CAR RENTAL DISCOUNTS

¶ When you need to rent an automobile while traveling, take advantage of special rates available to you from five of the largest car rental agencies. Send us an e-mail message at pacificinsurance@mail.com to receive all details regarding car rental rates and participating agencies.

(continued on next page)

ROAD AND TRAVEL SERVICES

¶ You can enjoy the security of specialized coverage for both towing and roadside emergency through the Pacific Insurance Road and Travel Plan. If you're locked out of your car or need a jump start, a tire changed, or a tow, Pacific Insurance is there.

¶ As a Pacific Insurance traveler, you can take advantage of our exclusive discounts and bonuses on cruises and tours. Our travel plan provides daily and weekend trips to over 100 destinations.

MERCHANDISE BUYING

¶ Each quarter a buying services catalog will be mailed to you. This catalog includes a variety of items that can be purchased through Pacific Insurance, and you'll never find better prices! Through the catalog you can purchase jewelry, furniture, sports equipment, electronics, appliances, computers, and much more. To place an order, simply call Pacific Insurance free at 1-800-555-3838 or visit our Web site.

Report 74-53
Magazine Article

Open the file for Report 74-51 and make the following changes:

1. Change the author's name to "Debra Winger."
2. Add the following section just before the section entitled "ENDING THE INTERVIEW."

```
INTERVIEW QUESTIONS
¶ Be prepared for common
interview questions, and be
prepared to ask some of your
own. You might ask about the
company's mission statement,
about the typical career
path for this position, or
about a typical workday at
that organization. Ask some
questions that show you are
interested in learning more
about the company and want
to make a commitment to its
success as a future employee.
```

Report Review

75

Goals

- Demonstrate improved speed and accuracy while typing.
- Demonstrate acceptable language arts skills in composing paragraphs.
- Correctly format an agenda, the minutes of a meeting, and a magazine article.
- Successfully complete a Progress and Proofreading Check with zero errors on the first scored attempt.

A. WARMUP

alphabet	1	I quickly explained that many big jobs involve few hazards.
number/symbol	2	rlow@juno.com 294% (Dix & Wu) 8/9 Yes! $1.34 *Fri. #1257-60
easy	3	Jane did not blame the busy auditor for her usual problems.

Skillbuilding

B. 12-SECOND SPEED SPRINTS

Take three 12-second timed writings on each line.

4 I may make us one set of maps to aid us when we visit them.
5 I hid a big car in my new lot, but I may not get to it by two.
6 It is a shame she works such odd anthems into her busy art.
7 It is the duty of the busy worker to take apart the panels.

' ' ' ' 5 ' ' ' ' 10 ' ' ' ' 15 ' ' ' ' 20 ' ' ' ' 25 ' ' ' ' 30 ' ' ' ' 35 ' ' ' ' 40 ' ' ' ' 45 ' ' ' ' 50 ' ' ' ' 55 ' ' ' ' 60

C. PACED PRACTICE

Follow the GDP software directions for this exercise to improve keystroking speed and accuracy.

Language Arts

D. COMPOSING PARAGRAPHS

Do you think it is safe to make and pay for purchases online? Compose a paragraph of at least three to four sentences answering this question.

Report 75-54
Agenda

UNITED BANK OF THE WEST

Meeting Agenda

May 15, 20--

1. Call to order
2. Approval of minutes of April 15 meeting
3. Installment loans (Gerald Hagen)
4. Mortgage loans (William McKay)
5. Series EE bonds (Francis Montoya)
6. Club memberships (Louise Abbey)
7. Certificates of deposit (Robert Hunt)
8. Closing remarks
9. Adjournment

Report 75-55
Minutes of a Meeting

ART SOCIETY OF MENDO CINO

Minutes of the Meeting

Nov. 19, 20--

ATTENDANCE Linda Scher called the meeting to order at 8 p.m. in the Mendocino Fine arts Center.

APPROVAL OF MINUTES The minutes of the ~~May~~ October 10~~th~~ meeting were read ~~and approved~~ with 1 correction—the spring arts fair will be held in April rather than in May of next year.

OLDBUSINESS Susan Firtz furnished each member with a list of artists and the names of the watercolor paintings by each artist.

NEW BUSINESS Martha Steward informed members taht a new supply of canvas and oil paint arrived. Members can check out any items they need to begin their winter projects. She reminded everyone that The Winter Arts Fair will be held December 14 at the Centennial Convention Center.

ADJOURNMENT The Meeting was adjourned at 9:45 p.m. The ~~November~~ December meeting will be ~~skipped~~ canceled and the next meeting will be held ~~December~~ January 12.

Respectfully submitted

Carole Little

Report
75-56
Magazine Article

Progress and Proofreading Check

Documents designated as Proofreading Checks serve as a check of your proofreading skill. Your goal is to have zero typographical errors when the GDP software first scores the document.

PUBLIC SPEAKING TIPS

Donna Barnes

¶ We have all been giving performances since our very early years. The most terrifying part of each performance was probably the fear that we would "freeze" when it came our turn to perform. Whenever we find ourselves in this predicament, we should accept that fear and learn to let it work for us, not against us. We need to recognize that nervousness or fear may set in during our performance. Then, when it does happen (if it does), we will be ready to cope with it and overcome it.

¶ If you forget some lines in a recitation, try to remember other lines and recite them. Doing so may help those forgotten lines to "pop back" into your memory so that you put them in at a later time.

¶ You always want to leave your audience with the idea that you have given them something worthwhile that they can use or apply to their own lives. For maximum impact on your audience and to make sure that they remember what you say, use audiovisual aids to reinforce your message. Remember, however, that audiovisual aids are nothing more than aids. The real message should come in the words you choose when giving your presentation.

¶ Study your speech well; even rehearse it, if necessary. However, do not practice it to the extent that it appears that you are merely reading what is written down on the paper in front of you. Much of your personality should be exhibited while you are giving your speech. If you are an enthusiastic, friendly person who converses well with people face-to-face, then those same qualities should be evident during your speech. A good piece of advice is to just go out there and be yourself—you will be much more comfortable by doing so, and your audience will relate to you better than if you try to exhibit a different personality when at the podium.

¶ No matter how rapidly you speak, slow down when you are in front of a group. The fact that you are nervous can cause your speech rate to increase. The best way to slow down your speaking is to breathe deeply. Doing so also causes your nervous system to relax, allowing you to proceed with your speech calmly.

¶ Finally, the best advice for giving a successful speech is to be prepared. You will be more confident if you are thoroughly prepared. Do your research, rehearse your speech, and make notes about any points you want to emphasize.

Strategies for Career Success

Audience Analysis

Knowing your audience is fundamental to the success of any message. Ask the following questions to help identify your audience.

What is your relationship with your audience? Are they familiar—people with whom you work—or people unknown to you? The latter will prompt you to conduct some research to better communicate your purpose. What is the attitude of your audience? Are they hostile or receptive to your message? How will your message benefit them? What is your anticipated response? Asking these questions first can help prevent message mishaps later.

When writing to a diverse audience, direct your message to the primary audience. These key decision makers will make a decision or act on the basis of your message. Determine the level of detail, organization, formality, and use of technical terms and theory.

Your Turn: Compose a thank-you e-mail to a friend. How would it differ from an interview thank-you letter?

UNIT

16

Tables

Tables With Footnotes or Source Notes

Goals

- Type at least 43wpm/5′/5e.
- Correctly use Word's table features to change text direction and insert or delete rows or columns.
- Correctly format a table with source notes or footnotes.

A. WARMUP

alphabet — My wife wove six dozen plaid jackets before the girls quit.
concentration — disenfranchisements unconstitutionality contemporaneousness
easy — The girl may make a formal gown of fur to go with her hair.

Skillbuilding

B. SUSTAINED PRACTICE: NUMBERS AND SYMBOLS

Take a 1-minute timed writing on the boxed paragraph to establish your base speed. Then take a 1-minute timed writing on the following paragraph. As soon as you equal or exceed your base speed on this paragraph, move to the next, more difficult paragraph.

```
     There is a need at this time to communicate our new       11
pricing guidelines to our franchise outlets. In addition,      22
they must be made aware of inventory implications. They        33
will then be in a position to have a successful operation.     45

     Franchise operators could be requested to use either      11
a 20% or a 30% markup. A $50 item would be marked to sell      22
for either $60 or $65. Depending on future prospects for       34
sales, half of the articles would be priced at each level.     45

     Ms. Aagard's suggestion is to assign items in Groups      11
#1470, #2830, and #4560 to the 20% category. The Series 77     23
items* would be in the 30% markup category except for the      34
items with a base rate under $100. What is your reaction?      48

     Mr. Chavez's recommendation is to assign a 30% markup     11
to Groups #3890, #5290, #6480, and #7180. About 1/4 of the     23
remainder (except for soft goods) would also be in the 30%     35
category. Groups #8340 and #9560 would have a 20% markup.      46
  1 | 2 | 3 | 4 | 5 | 6 | 7 | 8 | 9 | 10 | 11 | 12
```

Take two 5-minute timed writings.

Goal: At least 43wpm/5'/5e

C. 5-MINUTE TIMED WRITING

```
     Starting up your own business may mean that you are      11
thinking about acquiring an existing business. If so, is     22
that business doing well in the community? If you are going  34
to buy out an established business, you need to know the     45
reason the current owner wishes to sell the company. If      57
there are other businesses in the area, you should first     68
find out what reputation that business has built up in the   80
community. Do other businesses think highly of the company?  92
     You must also consider what type of advertising you     102
plan to use to get your business off to a good start. You    114
might use ads in newspapers, on television, in magazines,    128
or on the Internet. When you start your ad campaigns, you    137
should consider hiring an ad agency to put out the right     149
message for your company and its products. You should also   160
consider the types of ads being used by your competitors to  172
determine what has worked well for them.                     181
     Yes, there are major issues that need to be addressed   192
when starting up your own business; and all of the issues    203
should be dealt with before you decide to take such a step.  215
  1 | 2 | 3 | 4 | 5 | 6 | 7 | 8 | 9 | 10 | 11 | 12
```

Formatting

REFER TO Reference Manual

R-8B: Multipage Business Report
R-13A: Boxed Table

D. TABLES WITH SOURCE NOTES OR FOOTNOTES

To format tables with source notes or footnotes:

1. When you insert a table, include an additional row at the bottom of the table for the source note or footnote.
2. Merge the cells in the bottom row.
3. For a source note, type `Note:` or `Source:` as applicable in the bottom row; then type the corresponding information for the source note.
4. For a footnote, type an asterisk (or another symbol) at the relevant point within the table; then in the bottom row, type an asterisk and the corresponding information for the footnote.

GO TO Word Manual

E. WORD PROCESSING: TABLE—TEXT DIRECTION AND TABLE—INSERT, DELETE, AND MOVE ROWS OR COLUMNS

Study Lesson 76 in your Word Manual. Complete all of the shaded steps while at your computer. Then format the documents that follow.

Document Processing

Table
76-26
Boxed Table

1. In Row 1, set the text direction to display vertically from bottom to top, and change the alignment to bottom center.
2. Adjust the row height so that none of the column heading lines wrap to a second line.
3. In the merged cells in the bottom row, type the table note as shown.

Portfolio Counselor	Years of Experience	Fund Title Code	MSC World Index	Maxim Global Funds Index	Class A Management Fees	Class B Management Fees	Class C Management Fees
Steven Burgess	16	529-A	40.33%	38.78%	.37%	.37%	.37%
Jean Carol	5	529-B	38.78%	5.65%	.23%	1.00%	.25%
Mark Denning	12	361-A	21.42%	1.23%	.15%	.15%	.14%
Rex Humber	3	361-B	38.29%	3.99%	.75%	1.52%	.76%
Note: This information is subject to change.							

Table
76-27
Boxed Table

Open the file for Table 76-26 and make the following changes:

1. Delete the table note row.
2. Delete Column H.
3. Insert a row above Row 3. Type this:

   `Marie Alexander | 20 | 436-C | 26.17% | 24.39% | .52% | 1.25%`

4. Insert a column to the left of Column F. Type this:

   `United Fund Index | 31.29% | 19.07% | 9.73% | 2.75% | 5.41%`

5. Adjust the alignment of the new column heading to bottom center.
6. Move Column D to the right one column so it will become Column E.
7. Move Row 3 up one row so it becomes Row 2.
8. Insert a row at the bottom of the table, merge the cells, and type this left-aligned note: `Note: This information will be updated next quarter.`
9. Apply a 25 percent shading to Row 1.

Table
76-28
Boxed Table

1. In Row 1, set the text direction to display vertically from bottom to top, and change the alignment to bottom center.
2. Adjust the row height so that none of the column heading lines wrap to a second line.
3. In the merged cells in the bottom row, type the table footnote as shown.

Office Supply Account*	LED Laser Printer	Internal Fax Modem	Cash Management System	Plain-Paper Laser Fax
OE-9	$405	$181	$199	$249
DD-7	395	150	205	234
US-2	410	125	183	252
OB-1	420	167	179	245
*Codes are subject to change.				

Keyboarding Connection

Virus and Spam Prevention

Use caution when opening e-mail attachments or downloading files from the Internet. Download files only from reliable Web sites. Do not open files attached to an e-mail from an unknown source. Also question files attached to e-mail from a known source. Some viruses replicate themselves and are sent through e-mail without users' knowledge.

Delete any e-mail with an odd subject, a chain e-mail, or electronic junk mail, commonly known as spam. If you're given the opportunity to unsubscribe from a spammer's list, think twice. Your reply will stop the messages from a reputable mailing list, but replying to e-mail spam lets the spammers know your e-mail address is legitimate and can actually increase the amount of spam you receive.

To protect against lost data, back up your files on a regular basis. Then you will be prepared if a virus infects your computer. New viruses are discovered daily, so update your antivirus software regularly.

Your Turn: How do you handle junk mail via snail mail? Do you notice similarities when dealing with spam?

Tables With Braced Column Headings

Goals

- Demonstrate improved speed and accuracy while typing.
- Demonstrate acceptable language arts skills in capitalization.
- Correctly format a table with braced column headings.

A. WARMUP

alphabet	1	Grumpy wizards made toxic brew for Jack and the evil queen.
one hand	2	assets linkup bat kin tested phonily wave imply refer puppy
easy	3	Kent may fish with me for cod at the docks on their island.

Skillbuilding

MAP+

B. MAP+: ALPHABET

Follow the GDP software directions for this exercise to improve keystroking accuracy.

C. PROGRESSIVE PRACTICE: ALPHABET

Follow the GDP software directions for this exercise to improve keystroking speed.

Language Arts

Study the rules at the right.

D. CAPITALIZATION

RULE
≡ noun #

Capitalize nouns followed by a number or letter (except for the nouns *line, note, page, paragraph,* and *size*).

Please read Chapter 5, which begins on page 94.

RULE
≡ compass point

Capitalize compass points (such as *north, south,* or *northeast*) only when they designate definite regions.

From Montana we drove south to reach the Southwest.

Edit each sentence to correct any errors.

The marketing manager had a reservation on flight 505 to Atlanta.

Please order two model 6M printers.

The desktop publishing seminar will be held in Room 101.

Study pages 120-230 for the unit test.

Please contact all representatives in the northern states.

Didn't line 9 of the directions say to drive south?

The population of the south continues to increase.

Formatting

E. TABLES WITH BRACED COLUMN HEADINGS

A braced column heading is a heading that applies to more than one column (for example, *Explore Chicago Pass* and *Chicago City Pass* in the table shown below). To create a braced column heading:

1. Position the insertion point where you want the braced heading to appear.
2. Merge the cells that will hold the braced heading.
3. Center the braced column heading over the appropriate columns.

Document Processing

Table 77-29
Boxed Table

≡ noun #

CHICAGO ATTRACTION DISCOUNT CARDS Spring Rates*					
Explore Chicago Pass			**Chicago City Pass**		
Month	**Adult**	**Child**	**Month**	**Adult**	**Child**
March	$60	$45	March	$55	$40
April	70	55	April	65	50
May	90	75	May	85	70
*Read page 2 of "Big City on a Budget" for details.					

Table 77-30
Boxed Table

≡ compass point

CHICAGO TRAVEL BOOKS Sales Trends			
Midwest Publishing		**Total Sales**	
Region	**Sales Representative**	**Last Year**	**This Year**
Illinois	Jeff Meyer	$1,956,250	$2,135,433
Wisconsin*	Marjorie Matheson	859,435	1,231,332
Indiana	Valerie Harper	737,498	831,352
*Includes only eastern Wisconsin.			

Table
77-31
Boxed Table

Single-space the table.

AMERICA DISCOVERY TOURS			
Illinois Tour Highlights		**San Francisco tour Highlights**	
Attraction	**Location**	**Attraction**	**Location**
Land Of Lincoln	Springfield	Golden Gate Park	Central Richmond
Adler Planet arium	South Shore of Chicago	Exploratorium	Presidio
Lincoln Park	North Side ofChicago	Yerba Buena Gardens	South Beach
The Navy Pier	Downtown Chicago	Coit Tower	The Embarcadero
Aquarium Shedd	South Shore of Chicago	Fishermans Wharf	North Beach
Wrigley Building	North Side of Chicago	Palace of Fine Arts	Persidio

UNIT 16 LESSON **78**

Tables in Landscape Orientation

Goals

- Type at least 43wpm/5′/5e.
- Correctly use Word's page orientation feature.
- Correctly format a table in landscape orientation.

A. WARMUP

alphabet: Those heavy boxers performed quick waltzes and lively jigs.
practice *r* and *t*: rat try rotate trust tort tutor treat Trent trite trot hurt
easy: His body of work may disorient the visitors in the chapels.

Skillbuilding

B. PACED PRACTICE

Follow the GDP software directions for this exercise to improve keystroking speed and accuracy.

C. 5-MINUTE TIMED WRITING

Take two 5-minute timed writings.

Goal: At least 43wpm/5′/5e

This is the third in a series of timed writings on 10
starting up a new business. In this presentation, you will 22
consider some expense and merchandise issues as well as 33
some thoughts on the building you will move into or build. 45
There are several expenses that you will have to look 56
at for your new business. For example, do you realize how 68
much construction costs will be, or, if you are going to 79
rent a building, how much that expense will amount to? You 91
must also project expenses for insurance on the building 102
and its contents, utilities costs for running the business, 114
interest expense on any loans you secure to purchase or 128
renovate the building, and any new advertising expenses. 137
You must also consider the amount of merchandise you 148
will have on hand when you first open your store. If you 159
have several lines of merchandise, you need to determine 171
how many products and how much of each product you will 182
keep on the shelves and how much you will keep in inventory 194
in your warehouse. To acquire this merchandise, you must 205
locate suppliers who will sell you what you need. 215

1 | 2 | 3 | 4 | 5 | 6 | 7 | 8 | 9 | 10 | 11 | 12

Formatting

D. TABLES IN LANDSCAPE ORIENTATION

The default page orientation for 8.5- by 11-inch paper is vertical (also known as *portrait*). Sometimes, however, the content of a document would fit better or appear more attractive in horizontal orientation (called *landscape*). Format all tables in this lesson in landscape orientation.

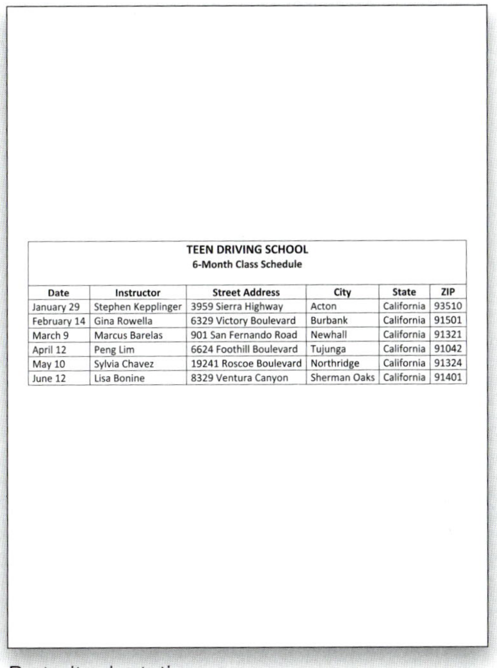

TEEN DRIVING SCHOOL
6-Month Class Schedule

Date	Instructor	Street Address	City	State	ZIP
January 29	Stephen Kepplinger	3959 Sierra Highway	Acton	California	93510
February 14	Gina Rowella	6329 Victory Boulevard	Burbank	California	91501
March 9	Marcus Barelas	901 San Fernando Road	Newhall	California	91321
April 12	Peng Lim	6624 Foothill Boulevard	Tujunga	California	91042
May 10	Sylvia Chavez	19241 Roscoe Boulevard	Northridge	California	91324
June 12	Lisa Bonine	8329 Ventura Canyon	Sherman Oaks	California	91401

Portrait orientation.

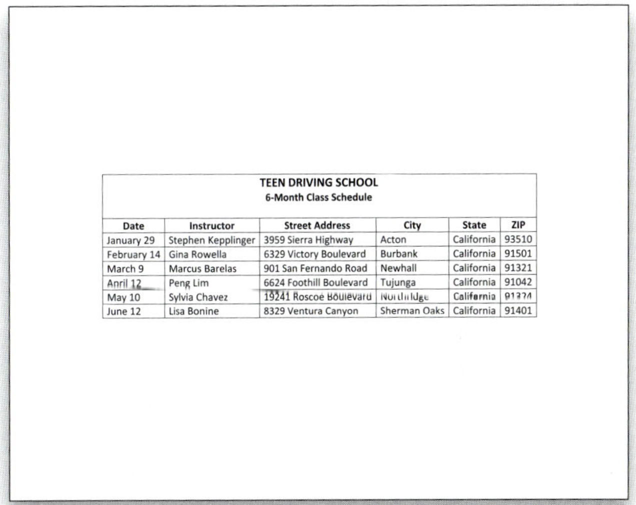

TEEN DRIVING SCHOOL
6-Month Class Schedule

Date	Instructor	Street Address	City	State	ZIP
January 29	Stephen Kepplinger	3959 Sierra Highway	Acton	California	93510
February 14	Gina Rowella	6329 Victory Boulevard	Burbank	California	91501
March 9	Marcus Barelas	901 San Fernando Road	Newhall	California	91321
April 12	Peng Lim	6624 Foothill Boulevard	Tujunga	California	91042
May 10	Sylvia Chavez	19241 Roscoe Boulevard	Northridge	California	91324
June 12	Lisa Bonine	8329 Ventura Canyon	Sherman Oaks	California	91401

Landscape orientation.

E. WORD PROCESSING: PAGE ORIENTATION

GO TO Word Manual

Study Lesson 78 in your Word Manual. Complete all of the shaded steps while at your computer. Then format the documents that follow.

Strategies for Career Success

Developing Confidence as a Presenter

Public speaking anxiety is quite common. As many as 77 percent of experienced speakers admit to having some anxiety on each speaking occasion. Normally, stage fright decreases with experience.

Even if there are no physical expressions of anxiety, speakers often assume others can see through their smiles to their fears. However, listeners are actually poor judges of the amount of anxiety that speakers experience.

A little anxiety can actually stimulate a better presentation. The best way to control your anxiety is to be well prepared for the presentation. Carefully analyze your audience, research your topic, organize the speech, practice your delivery, and believe in the ideas. Being well prepared puts you in an excellent position to control your anxiety.

Your Turn: "I'm glad I'm here. I'm glad you're here. I know that I know." What are the benefits of repeating this to yourself before each presentation?

Table
78-32
Boxed Table

THE TRAVEL SHOP
Travel Agent Contact Information*

Name	Street Address	City	State	ZIP	Telephone	E-Mail
Ronald Dahl	8787 Orion Place	Columbus	OH	43240	614-555-4951	rdahl@tts.com
Ming Dai	1415 Elbridge Payne Road	Chesterfield	MO	63017	636-555-9940	mdai@tts.com
Amber Palmer	3100 Breckinridge Boulevard	Duluth	GA	30096	770-555-7007	apalmer@tts.com
Anita Mills	21600 Oxnard Street	Woodland Hills	CA	91367	818-555-2675	amills@tts.com

*Contact information was last updated on July 1.

Table
78-33
Boxed Table

Open the file for Table 78-32 and make the following changes:

1. Change Ronald Dahl's address to this:

   `376 West Lane Avenue`

2. Add this information for another travel agent in a new row just above the table note:

   `Mike Cassidy | 2739 Idaho Avenue | Kenner | LA | 70062 | 504-555-0089 | mcassidy@tts.com`

3. Change the table note to read as follows:

   `*For a complete listing of all travel agents, visit http://www.thetravelshop.com and click "Contact Us."`

Table
78-34
Boxed Table

Ohio CUSTOMER SURVEY RESULTS

Office Products Un limited

July 1 20--

Customer | **Address** | **City** | **Zip** | **Telephone No** | **Most Recent Purchase**

Becker, Steve | 121 North Summit ~~Avenue~~ Street | Toledo | 44426 | 419-555-2384 | Label maker

Cross Mario | 20604 Lucile Rd. South | Columbus | 43230 | 614-555-2074 | Book case and Shelving

Dusenberry, Rich | 322 West Lyons Road | Cleve land | 44902 | 261-555-2002 | Portable hard drive

Ferrer, Marie | 5914 Bay Oaks Place | Chillicothe | 45601 | 614-555-1399 | Portable DVD player

Goodrich, Mike | 10386 Drive Power | Stuebenville | 43952 | 614-555-7821 | Digital camera

Juarez, Ismael | 231 East Front Street | Youngstown | ~~54401~~ 44502 | 216-555-3885 | Postal scale

Lancaster, Robert | 6823 Creekwood Dr. | Columbus | 43085 | 614-555-2934 | Wireless router

Pastor, Sandra | 26044 Manzano Court | ~~Columbus~~ Youngstown | 44505 | 216-555-1777 | Cordless keyboard

Wee, Ju Jong | 936 East Wind Drive | Cleveland | 44121 | 216-555-8239 | Industrialshredder

Multipage Tables

Goals

- Demonstrate improved speed and accuracy while typing.
- Demonstrate acceptable language arts skills in spelling.
- Correctly use Word's table feature to repeat a heading row.
- Correctly format a multipage table with a heading row.

A. WARMUP

alphabet
1 A large fawn jumped quickly over seven white boxes of zinc.

frequent digraphs
2 or orb for door fort more boor nor odor port orator ore ort

easy
3 Did the naughty lapdog put my pajama top down on the chair?

Skillbuilding

B. MAP+: SYMBOL

Follow the GDP software directions for this exercise to improve keystroking accuracy.

PPP PRETEST » PRACTICE » POSTTEST

C. PRETEST: Alternate- and One-Hand Words

PRETEST
Take a 1-minute timed writing.

```
4      The usual visitors to the rocky island are from either 11
5  the city of Lakeland or Honolulu. They like to visit hilly 23
6  areas and taste the giant fruit. The eight signs that girl 35
7  made gave us an extra boost and some added revenue as well. 47
     1 | 2 | 3 | 4 | 5 | 6 | 7 | 8 | 9 | 10 | 11 | 12
```

D. PRACTICE: Alternate-Hand Words

PRACTICE
Speed Emphasis:
If you made no more than 1 error on the Pretest, type each *individual* line 2 times.
Accuracy Emphasis:
If you made 2 or more errors, type each *group* of lines (as though it were a paragraph) 2 times.

```
8  also angle field bushel ancient emblem panel sight fish big
9  both blame fight formal element handle proxy signs girl and
10 city chair giant island visitor profit right their laid cut
11 down eight laugh theory chaotic visual shape usual work she
```

E. PRACTICE: One-Hand Words

```
12 acts hilly award uphill average poplin refer jolly adds him
13 area jumpy based homily baggage you'll serve union beat ink
14 case onion extra limply greater unholy wages imply draw you
15 gave pupil extra unhook wastage lumpy swears pylon star you
```

POSTTEST

Repeat the Pretest timed writing and compare performance.

F. POSTTEST: Alternate- and One-Hand Words

Language Arts

Type these frequently misspelled words, paying special attention to any spelling problems in each word.

G. SPELLING

16 assistance compliance initial limited corporation technical
17 operating sufficient operation incorporated writing current
18 advice together prepared recommend appreciated cannot based
19 benefit completing analysis probably projects before annual
20 issue attention location association participation proposed

Edit the sentences to correct any misspellings.

21 The complience by the corporation was sufficient to pass.

22 I cannot reccomend the project based on the expert advise.

23 The location of the proposed annual meeting was an issue.

24 Your assistance in completeing the project is appreciated.

25 Together we prepared an analysis of their current operation.

26 The writing was incorporated in the initial asociation bid.

Formatting

H. MULTIPAGE TABLES

Tables should generally be formatted to fit on one page. However, if a table extends to another page, follow these formatting rules:

1. Repeat the column headings at the top of each new page.
2. Insert a page number in the top right-hand corner of the page header of all continuing pages, and remove the page number from the first page.
3. Do not center a multipage table vertically.

50 LONGEST RIVERS OF THE WORLD
(Miles rounded to nearest 10)

River	Outflow	Miles
Nile	Mediterranean	4,160
Amazon	Atlantic Ocean	4,000
Chang	East China Sea	3,960
Huang	Yellow Sea	3,400
Ob-Irtysh	Gulf of Ob	3,360
Amur	Tatar Strait	2,740
Lena	Laptev Sea	2,730
Congo	Atlantic Ocean	2,720
Mekong	South China Sea	2,600
Niger	Gulf of Guinea	2,590
Yenisey	Kara Sea	2,540
Parana	Rio de la Plata	2,490
Mississippi	Gulf of Mexico	2,340
Missouri	Mississippi River	2,320
Murray-Darling	Indian Ocean	2,310
Volga	Caspian Sea	2,290
Purus	Amazon River	2,100
Medeira	Amazon River	2,010
Sao Francisco	Atlantic Ocean	1,990
Yukon	Bering Sea	1,980
Rio Grande	Gulf of Mexico	1,900
Brahmaputra	Bay of Bengal	1,800
Indus	Arabian Sea	1,800
Danube	Black Sea	1,780
Japura	Amazon River	1,750
Euphrates	Shatt al Arab	1,700
Zambezi	Indian Ocean	1,700
Tocantins	Para River	1,680
Orinoco	Atlantic Ocean	1,600
Amu	Aral Sea	1,580
Paraguay	Parana River	1,580
Ural	Caspian Sea	1,580

2

50 LONGEST RIVERS OF THE WORLD
(Miles rounded to nearest 10)

River	Outflow	Miles
Ganges	Bay of Bengal	1,560
Salween	Andaman Sea	1,500
Arkansas	Mississippi River	1,460
Colorado	Gulf of California	1,450
Dnieper	Black Sea	1,420
Negro	Amazon	1,400
Syr	Aral Sea	1,370
Irrawaddy	Bay of Bengal	1,340
Orange	Atlantic Ocean	1,300
Red	Atchafalaya River	1,290
Columbia	Pacific Ocean	1,240
Don	Sea of Azov	1,220
Peace	Slave River	1,210
Xi	South China Sea	1,200
Tigris	Shatt al Arab	1,180
Angara	Yenisey River	1,150
Songhua	Amur River	1,150
Snake	Columbia River	1,040

I. WORD PROCESSING: TABLE—REPEATING TABLE HEADING ROWS

GO TO Word Manual

Study Lesson 79 in your Word Manual. Complete all of the shaded steps while at your computer. Then format the documents that follow.

Table 79-35 Boxed Table

Document Processing

Follow these steps to create a boxed table:

1. Apply a 100 percent shading to Row 1.
2. Apply a 25 percent shading to Row 2. Your completed table may look different from the table shown.

FIFTY FREQUENTLY MISSPELLED WORDS	
Word	**Common Business Meaning**
Accommodate	House or contain
Advice	Guidance
Apparently	Evidently
Analysis	Examination
Annual	Yearly
Apparent	Obvious or clear
Appreciated	Valued
Argument	Quarrel or squabble
Assistance	Help
Association	Friendship or relationship
Attention	Notice or interest
Believe	Think or accept as true
Based	Found or established
Before	Previous to
Benefit	Advantage; help
Calendar	Datebook or schedule
Category	Group or class
Changeable	Variable or unpredictable
Committed	Dedicated or steadfast
Completing	Finishing
Consensus	Agreement
Compliance	Conformity
Corporation	Company
Current	Present
Definite	Exact or distinct
Exceed	Go beyond
Guarantee	Assurance or promise
Incorporated	Included
Independent	Self-governing or free

FIFTY FREQUENTLY MISSPELLED WORDS	
Word	**Common Business Meaning**
Initial	First
Issue	Subject or concern
Judgment	Ruling or decision
Limited	Incomplete or restricted
Location	Site or place
Occasionally	Infrequently
Occurrence	Event or incident
Operating	In service or working
Operation	Process or procedure
Participation	Contribution or involvement
Personnel	Employees
Precede	Come first or go before
Prepared	Ready or arranged
Probably	Most likely
Projects	Assignments or tasks
Proposed	Planned or anticipated
Recommend	Advise or suggest
Sufficient	Enough or adequate
Technical	Scientific or procedural
Together	Jointly or collectively
Writing	Script

Table 79-36
Ruled Table

Open the file for Table 79-35 and make the following changes:

1. Change the shading in Row 1 to clear.
2. Change the table format to a ruled table.
3. Insert these new rows of information in alphabetical order within the table:

Noticeable	Visible
Principal	Main or most important
Principle	Belief or theory
Schedule	Timetable or plan

Table 79-37
Boxed Table

Follow these steps to create a boxed table:

1. Format the table in landscape orientation.
2. Apply a 100 percent shading to the title row.
3. Apply a 25 percent shading to the column heading row.

INVESTMENT SUMMARY				
Limited Partnership	**Date of Issue**	**Initial Cost**	**Dividend***	**Owner**
HS Properties	January 2010	$ 50,000	$ 6,066	Alpha Association
Northern Lumber	May 2009	50,000	4,750	CXT Corporation
United Western Real Estate	February 2010	50,000	7,500	Smith & Sons Incorporated
United Inland Real Estate	December 2010	100,000	12,250	Q and S Company
*Annual dividends based on current market analysis.				

Tables With Predesigned Formats

Goals

- Type at least 43wpm/5'/5e.
- Correctly use Word's table styles feature.
- Correctly format a predesigned table.

A. WARMUP

alphabet	1	Judge Hank Powell quickly gave six embezzlers a stiff fine.
number/symbol	2	(ali41@cs.com) (10%) Guy & Lee 7/8 In! $5.40 *f.o.b. #26-39
easy	3	Claudia may sign the title to her auto when she is in town.

Skillbuilding

B. 12-SECOND SPEED SPRINTS

Take three 12-second timed writings on each line.

4 Jake moved to amend the law to let the worker take the job.
5 Jan and her son may make a bowl of fish and a cup of cocoa.
6 Jane can buy fuel for the old blue auto at the nearby lots.
7 Kay and she may both visit us in May when they are in town.

' ' ' ' 5 ' ' ' ' 10 ' ' ' ' 15 ' ' ' ' 20 ' ' ' ' 25 ' ' ' ' 30 ' ' ' ' 35 ' ' ' ' 40 ' ' ' ' 45 ' ' ' ' 50 ' ' ' ' 55 ' ' ' ' 60

C. TECHNIQUE PRACTICE: TAB KEY

Press Tab 1 time between words. Type each line 2 times.

Press Tab where you see the → symbol.

8	are→	Mag→	Uzi→	Lew→	Mel→	adz→	ace→	ale→	Jew→	air→	Poe
9	axe→	Job→	Leo→	Mia→	Jon→	Peg→	arc→	ago→	ate→	Pia→	Una
10	aha→	Ott→	Ivy→	zag→	ape→	Obi→	Ike→	Hsu→	and→	asp→	zip
11	May→	Liz→	Lou→	Kit→	Ned→	Kim→	Ham→	age→	aft→	zoo→	Mel

Take two 5-minute timed writings.

Goal: At least 43wpm/5'/5e

D. 5-MINUTE TIMED WRITING

```
     Finding a job is a challenge in today's job market,      11
but there are some steps you can take to remain competitive  23
in the job market. First of all, be sure you know something  35
about the company. Does it have offices in a location to     48
which you would move, and is the position in that company    58
one in which you would like to spend the next five to ten    69
years of your working life?                                  75
     To be successful during the interview, you need to      85
know yourself. What are your strengths, and what are your    97
weaknesses, if any? Be sure to emphasize your unique skills 109
both in your resume and during the interview. Let others    120
know what makes you the best candidate for the job. Some    132
excellent traits to emphasize would be enthusiasm, a high   143
motivation level, and an excellent work ethic.              153
     When you go for your interview, take into account how  164
you dress. Choose your wardrobe as you would for your first 178
day on the job. If you are uncertain as to the particular   187
dress code, always err on the side of conservatism. Also,   199
be mindful of your personal grooming. Make certain your     210
hair is trimmed and neat.                                   215
    1 | 2 | 3 | 4 | 5 | 6 | 7 | 8 | 9 | 10 | 11 | 12
```

Formatting

E. PREDESIGNED TABLES

Predesigned table styles are used to quickly refine the look and layout of a table and to format major table elements, such as title blocks and total lines, in unique ways. Bolding and varying font sizes have been used up to this point to distinguish the title, subtitle, and column headings in a table. A table style will distinguish these table elements in a more refined way through colorful, customized designs. As with any style, repeating a table style also ensures design consistency.

Table styles help comprehension by giving readers visual style cues for different content. For example, if the bottom table row includes a total line, a table style option could be used to format that row in a distinct way. Likewise, a unique treatment could be applied to the first column if the content calls for it.

F. WORD PROCESSING: TABLE—STYLES

GO TO Word Manual

Study Lesson 80 in your Word Manual. Complete all of the shaded steps while at your computer. Then format the documents that follow.

Document Processing

Table 80-38
Predesigned Table

Your completed tables may look different from the tables shown.

1. Apply a table style of your choice.
2. In Rows 1 and 2, verify that all text is bolded.
3. In Row 2, align the column headings at the bottom center.

HIGH-YIELD CD RATES **1-Year Deposits**			
Institution	**Rate**	**APY**	**Minimum Deposit**
ADSCapital.com	2.45%	2.70%	$10,000
Amber Direct	2.50%	2.50%	10,000
Arizona First National Bank	2.18%	2.20%	5,000
Chorus Bank	2.71%	2.74%	10,000
GCBank.com	2.57%	2.60%	1,000
GMBC Bank	2.71%	2.75%	500
HTSM Direct	2.27%	2.30%	10
New Mercantile	2.35%	2.38%	10,000
Nexus Bank	2.53%	2.56%	1,000
Regal Capital Bank	2.45%	2.45%	2,000
State Bank	2.51%	2.54%	500
State Bank of Indiana	2.30%	2.32%	5,000
UTCDirect.com	2.52%	2.55%	8,000
Average	2.47%	2.51%	$ 4,847

Table 80-39
Predesigned Table

1. Apply a table style of your choice.
2. In Rows 1 and 2, verify that all text is bolded.
3. In Row 2, align the column headings at the bottom center.

BUILDING DIRECTORY **National Convention Center**			
No.	**Room Name**	**Seating**	**Square Feet**
102	Alabama	35	400
104	Colorado	150	1,600
106	Delaware	25	350
108	Georgia	50	600
202	Montana	35	400
204	Nevada	50	600
206	New Jersey	300	3,200
208	Pennsylvania	350	3,600

Table 80-40
Predesigned Table

1. Apply a table style of your choice.
2. In Rows 1 and 2, verify that all text is bolded.
3. In Row 2, align the column headings at the bottom center.

ABC MEMBER VACATIONS Promotional Sailing Prices*						
	7-Day Cruises			12-Day Cruises		
Location	Interior	Ocean-View	Balcony	Interior	Ocean-View	Balcony
Alaska	$ 599	$ 699	$1,299	$1,199	$1,299	$1,899
Canada	965	1,290	1,445	1,565	1,890	2,045
Caribbean	739	839	1,239	1,139	1,239	1,839
Hawaii	699	799	1,999	1,299	1,399	2,699
Mexico	599	749	849	999	1,149	1,249
Panama Canal	1,299	1,749	2,099	1,699	2,049	2,449
*All prices are subject to change.						

Progress and Proofreading Check

Documents designated as Proofreading Checks serve as a check of your proofreading skill. Your goal is to have zero typographical errors when the GDP software first scores the document.

Strategies for Career Success

Cell Phone Manners Matter

Mind your cell phone manners! Although the cell phone allows you to keep in touch with your boss, coworkers, and clients, it also requires you to consider your communication etiquette. One of the worst violations of etiquette and safety is driving and talking at the same time. Several states now have laws restricting or forbidding cell phone use while driving. It is much safer to pull off the road to make or answer a call.

Consider others when you use a cell phone in a public place (for example, a restaurant). Don't use your cell phone at the movies or in a public restroom. If you use the phone in public, talk quietly and watch what you say. Cell phones in meetings can distract others or interrupt the meeting completely; some companies prohibit them in business meetings.

Your Turn: Observe cell phone users in a public place. Are they mindful of others when they use their phones?

Outcomes Assessment on Part 4

Test 4

5-Minute Timed Writing

Many business firms create their own special documents 11
today by using software packages that are designed to do 23
the job. These packages help people with limited design 34
skills create pages with very little effort. The challenge, 48
though, is for the person to design the pages effectively 57
so that the readers will read them. After all, the reason 69
for putting in all that time and money is to get people to 81
read the articles. 85
Designing pages that are easy to read is not quite as 98
easy as it seems. For example, a reader may be confused if 107
a page has too many headlines. Instead, a reader may want 119
to read fewer headlines that are printed in large type. 130
Desktop publishers require just a few good tools to 141
interest the reader. A good plan to use is to be sure to 152
put the most important articles at the top of the first 164
page and the less important articles on the inside pages. 175
The use of bullets or side headings is also a helpful guide 187
to help a reader zip through pages. A final suggestion is 199
to use pictures and graphics that can make the text much 210
more interesting to read. 215

1 | 2 | 3 | 4 | 5 | 6 | 7 | 8 | 9 | 10 | 11 | 12

Report Test
4-57
Memo Report

MEMO TO: All Members

FROM: Judy Greenburg

DATE: June 23, 20--

SUBJECT: Understanding Your Dental Plan

The FultonCommunity College district sent out a quarterly news letter early in July explaining the dental plan benefits offered to all of our employees. The highlights of each plan were reviewed and many of you requested further information.

Vanguard Dental PPO

If you are a Dental Vanguard Plan member, ask the dentist specifically if he or she is a Vanguard Dental provider and if he or she is in the ppo or Premiere network. Your benefits vary greatly depending upon the dentists affiliation. The table below includes examples of the costs you might pay with each types of Vanguard Dental providers.

Bottom-align column headings. Single-space the table.

VANGUARD DENTAL PPO

Charges For a Crown*

Category	PPO Dentist	**Out-of-Network Premiere Dentist**	**Out-of-Network Non-Contracted Dentis**
Dentists charge	$1,000	$1,000	$1,000
Vanguard's approved fee	640	800	800
Plan payment	512	640	640
Member payment	128	160	360
*Dentist's charges and approved fees are hypothetical.			

HEALTHGUARD DENTAL HMO

If yuo are a Healthguard Dental member remember that you may change your dentist any at time and as often as you wish as long as your dentist is a participating provider. Other covered family members do not have to choose the same dentist.

Visit www.vanguard.net and www.healthguard.net for further details and a Directory of Dentists.

urs

Correspondence Test
4-76
Business Letter in Block Style

January 10, 20-- | Mr. James F. Duncan | 229 Foster Street | Durham, NC 27701 | Dear Mr. Duncan:

¶ I am sorry that I had to end our phone call so abruptly yesterday. I would like to respond to both of your questions more specifically and give you a few more details regarding the tax consequences of hiring your daughter as an employee in your business.

1. You will need to issue her a W-2 form if you are paying her as an employee this year.
2. You cannot deduct her wages as a business expense on Schedule C because she is over the age of 19 and because you have paid her more than $600 this year.

¶ Please check with your tax attorney, and read IRS Publication 15 for further details. Sincerely yours, | Arlene R. Weiser | Attorney at Law | urs | PS: You may want to discuss this matter with your daughter before calling your tax attorney for an appointment. | bc: Peggy Jennings

Table Test
4-41
Boxed Table

Apply a 100 percent shading to Row 1 and a 25 percent shading to Row 3 and Row 11.

VALENCIA MEADOWS POOL Lesson Schedule*			
Session A		**Session B**	
Time	**Code**	**Time**	**Code**
7:10-8:10 a.m.	3508.310	7:05-8:05 a.m.	4001.910
8:20-9:20 a.m.	3509.311	8:25-9:25 a.m.	4002.911
9:30-10:30 a.m.	3510.312	9:40-10:30 a.m.	4003.912
10:45-11:15 a.m.	3511.313	10:35-11:35 a.m.	4004.913
12:05-1:05 p.m.	3512.314	12:15-1:15 p.m.	4005.914
5:40-6:40 p.m.	3513.315	5:10-6:10 p.m.	4006.915
7:15-8:15 p.m.	3514.316	7:15-8:15 p.m.	4007.931
*Session A begins June 15; Session B begins August 1.			

Specialized Applications

5 PART

Keyboarding in Information Technology (IT) Services

Work in the IT services cluster involves designing, developing, managing, and operating communication and IT systems, networks, and related hardware and software for telecommunications and computing services.

Opportunities in IT Services

People working in telecommunications design and maintain telephone, satellite, and laser communication systems. Among the numerous IT jobs are programmer, software engineer, technical support representative, information systems operator/analyst, and network administrator. Satellites above the earth receive and send signals, thus speeding up communications. Skilled engineers design systems that enhance the ways by which people communicate.

We are all globally connected by technology, and IT services support those necessary connections. Technology is spreading at an ever-increasing rate and affecting every aspect of our daily lives. This industry is full of opportunity for individuals with superior technical and mathematical skills. The ability to communicate complex ideas clearly, handle many details, and solve problems is an asset. Of course, keyboarding proficiency is critical.

Goals

Keyboarding

- Demonstrate improved speed and accuracy when operating the keyboard by touch.
- Type at least 47 words per minute on a 5-minute timed writing with no more than 5 errors.

Language Arts

- Demonstrate acceptable proofreading skills, including using proofreaders' marks correctly.
- Demonstrate acceptable language arts skills in punctuation, grammar, and mechanics.
- Demonstrate acceptable language arts skills in composing and spelling.

Word Processing

- Use appropriate word processing commands necessary to complete document processing activities successfully.

Document Processing

- Correctly format international business documents, formal report projects, medical office documents, and legal office documents.

Objective Test

- Answer questions with acceptable accuracy on an objective test.

UNIT 17

International Formatting

International Formatting—Canada

Goals

- Demonstrate improved speed and accuracy while typing.
- Demonstrate acceptable language arts skills in agreement between pronouns and verbs.
- Correctly use Word's paper size feature.
- Correctly format a letter and a table on metric paper.
- Correctly format a letter with an international address and a date line using the day/month/year format.

A. WARMUP

alphabet 1 Amazingly, a few of the discotheques now provide jukeboxes.
concentration 2 intellectualization disadvantageousness deindustrialization
easy 3 A naughty chap may ambush the fiendish cowhand if he ducks.

Skillbuilding

B. MAP+: ALPHABET

Follow the GDP software directions for this exercise to improve keystroking accuracy.

C. PROGRESSIVE PRACTICE: ALPHABET

Follow the GDP software directions for this exercise to improve keystroking speed.

Language Arts

Study the rules at the right.

D. AGREEMENT

RULE
agreement pronoun

Some pronouns (*anybody, each, either, everybody, everyone, much, neither, no one, nobody,* and *one*) are always singular and take a singular verb. Other pronouns (*all, any, more, most, none,* and *some*) may be singular or plural, depending on the noun to which they refer.

Each of the employees has finished his or her task.
Much remains to be done.
Most of the pie was eaten, but most of the cookies were left.

RULE
agreement intervening words

Disregard any intervening words that come between the subject and verb when establishing agreement.

That box, containing the books and pencils, has not been found.
Alex, accompanied by Tricia and Roxie, is attending the conference and taking his computer.

Edit each sentence to correct any errors.

Everybody who signed up for the trips are to be at Building 16.

All the tourists are sending cards to us from their hotels.

Everyone on the trip, including spouses, have been having fun.

Some of the postcards from their vacations are not arriving.

Two of the sales reps from Region 4 were given cash bonuses.

The fastest runner from all five teams are receiving a trophy.

Formatting

E. METRIC PAPER SIZE

Paper size for correspondence in the United States is typically 8.5 by 11 inches. However, correspondence in most foreign countries is often formatted on metric-sized paper. The most popular of these is called A4 paper, and it measures 210 by 297 millimeters—approximately 8.25 by 11.75 inches.

F. METRIC ENVELOPE SIZE

A standard large envelope (No. 10) measures 9.5 by 4.125 inches. A large envelope for metric size paper is called DL, and it measures 110 by 220 millimeters—approximately 4.33 by 8.67 inches. The No. 10 envelope is not as deep as the metric envelope, but it is slightly wider.

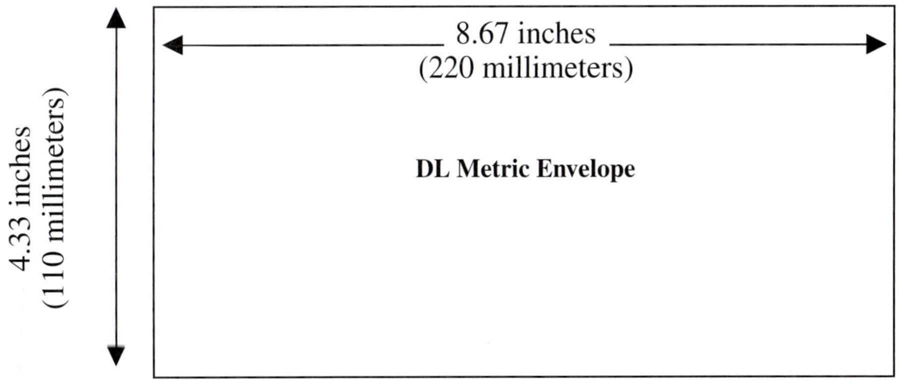

G. INTERNATIONAL ADDRESSES IN LETTERS

International addressing is becoming more common with the increased popularity of the Internet and frequently requires changes to the address lines, such as the addition of special codes, abbreviations, and capitalization. Individual organizational preferences for international address formatting will vary. Therefore, the most technologically efficient formats for international addresses will be used, including the use of all-caps and the name of the country spelled out as the last entry of the address, as shown in the examples below.

Canada Address Example:

Mr. Allen C. Woodruff	Recipient's Name
843 Portage Avenue	Street Address [street number followed by street name]
Winnipeg, MB R2B 2C8	City/Province Abbreviation/Postal Code [2 spaces after the province; 1 space between first 3 and last 3 characters]
CANADA	Country Name [typed in all-capitals]

China Address Example:

Mrs. Jiaying Chen	Recipient's Name
1382 Nanjing Road, Changsha	Street Address, City
410001 Hunan	Postal Code, Province
P.R. CHINA	Country Name [typed in all-capitals; "P.R." denotes People's Republic of China.]

France Address Example:

Madam Duval	Recipient's Name
42, Pasteur	Street Address [street number followed by a comma and street name]
14395 Cabourg	Postal Code, City
FRANCE	Country Name [typed in all-capitals]

Germany Address Example:

Mr. Herman Krantz	Recipient's Name
Beckergang 184	Street Address [street name followed by street number]
20987 Hamburg	Postal Code, City
GERMANY	Country Name [typed in all-capitals]

Mexico Address Example:

Mr. Alonzo Diaz	Recipient's Name
1184 Almendro	Street Address, Street Name
48321 Puerto Vallarta, C.P.	Postal Code/City/Province Abbreviation
MEXICO	Country Name [typed in all-capitals]

H. DAY/MONTH/YEAR FORMAT

In international correspondence, the date line is often formatted in this sequence: day, month, year. Thus, the first line of a letter to a foreign recipient may appear as shown in the illustration.

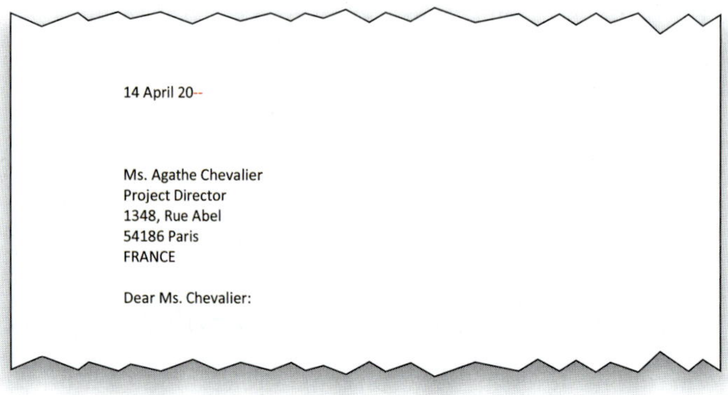
14 April 20--

Ms. Agathe Chevalier
Project Director
1348, Rue Abel
54186 Paris
FRANCE

Dear Ms. Chevalier:

I. WORD PROCESSING: PAPER SIZE

GO TO Word Manual

Study Lesson 81 in your Word Manual. Complete all of the shaded steps while at your computer. Then format the documents that follow.

Document Processing

Situation: You work for CanCom Computers, an international computer manufacturer located in Winnipeg, Canada. CanCom has a global client base. For the purposes of this simulation, your name will be Janet Osborne, and you are an executive assistant for CanCom.

For the next five days, you will prepare documents for several CanCom executives. Your firm follows formatting guidelines for metric paper and envelope size and international addresses, dates, phone numbers, and measurements.

Today is June 22, and you will spend your first day preparing documents that appear in your in-basket. All documents—with the exception of e-mail messages—will be typed on A4 paper, which has a slightly different midpoint at which to start typing the date and closing lines. However, use a left tab of 3.25″ to type these lines, as you do on a standard sheet of paper.

Correspondence 81-77
Business Letter in Modified-Block Style

22 June 20-- | Mr. David L. Brazil | Northern Electronics Inc. | 389 Boyd Avenue | Winnipeg, MB ROC 3Z8 | CANADA | Dear Mr. Brazil:
¶ Thank you for your recent computer order. We are pleased that you have decided to update your computers with our C-410 model.
agreement pronoun
¶ Each of the 50 computers you ordered has a DVD drive, as you requested. There will be no extra charge for installing the DVD drive to replace the CD drive that comes standard with the C-410 model you ordered.
agreement intervening
agreement pronoun
¶ Your order, which includes the toner cartridges you requested, is leaving our warehouse within three days. All our order processing and shipping departments are online, and you can check the progress of your order by going to www.cancom.com and clicking on Customer Orders.
agreement pronoun
¶ Everyone at CanCom looks forward to the opportunity of serving your computer needs for many years to come.
Sincerely, | Brenda T. Cahill | Sales Manager | jo | c: Bruce Snell, Lloyd Wilkes |
agreement intervening
PS: The software training manual, but not the USB connectors, is on back order. We anticipate it to be shipped on June 30.

Table
81-42
Boxed Table

Prepare Table 81-42 in landscape orientation. Apply shading of 25 percent to Row 2.

CUSTOMER SHIPPING INFORMATION				
Name	**Address**	**City/Province**	**Postal Code**	**Kilometers**
Abrams, Andrew	2218 College Avenue	Regina, SK	S0G 4C0	571
Brewer, Royce	345 Barr Road, NW	Calgary, AB	T1Y 1A8	1,208
Lazano, Gary	1084 Rue Coderre	Montreal, QC	H1A 1J2	1,821
Osborn, Connie	8701 Pine Street	Sudbury, ON	P3A 1B1	1,254
Purdy, Vickie	383 Jubilee Road	Halifax, NS	B3H 1B4	2,573
Rollins, Helene	811 Pears Avenue	Toronto, ON	M4C 1A3	2,222
Swenson, Hillary	284 Maple Avenue	Brandon, MB	R7A 0C8	199
Tetrault, Brandon	844 Ross Street	Red Deer, AB	T4N 0B6	1,192
Williams, Allen	1840 Oxford Street	Victoria, BC	V8N 1B5	2,295

Table
81-43
Boxed Table

Open the file for Table 81-42 and make the following changes:

1. Add the following entry after Royce Brewer's information:

   ```
   Collins, Steve | 816 55th
   Street, NW | Edmonton, AB |
   T5A 0C5 | 1,305
   ```

2. Sort Column E so that the kilometers are displayed in a descending order.

Keyboarding Connection

Finding People on the Internet

Remember that long-lost friend from high school? Well, he or she may not be lost for long if you use the Internet's assistance. It is easy to search for a person on the Internet.

Social networking sites such as LinkedIn, MySpace, and Facebook allow you to search for lost friends, family, and coworkers. You also can use a search engine to search for a person's name. Many schools and organizations have Web sites where you can look for old friends. When searching for someone in a search engine, it can be helpful to type the location or other identifying information along with the person's name.

Your Turn: Access a search engine, and conduct a search on your own name. Then try a search for a high school friend.

International Formatting—Mexico

82

Goals

- Type at least 44wpm/5′/5e.
- Correctly format international URLs.
- Correctly use Word's insert symbol feature.
- Correctly format an e-mail message, a business report, and a table.

A. WARMUP

alphabet	1	Jack Farmer realized that big yellow quilts were expensive.
one hand	2	barber poplin car joy feared million area hilly craft milky
easy	3	If the town signs an entitlement, the profit may go to her.

Skillbuilding

B. SUSTAINED PRACTICE: CAPITALS

Take a 1-minute timed writing on the boxed paragraph to establish your base speed. Then take a 1-minute timed writing on the following paragraph. As soon as you equal or exceed your base speed on this paragraph, move to the next, more difficult paragraph.

4 A visit to Europe is a vacation that many people dream 11
5 of doing. There are many countries to visit and hundreds of 23
6 sites to see if you can spend at least four weeks on the 34
7 continent. A trip to Europe is one you will never forget. 46

8 If you decide to visit Europe, the months of June and 11
9 July would probably be the prettiest, but they would also 23
10 be the busiest. England, France, and Germany are popular 34
11 countries to visit; Spain is popular for Americans as well. 46

12 In England you will want to visit St. Paul's Cathedral 11
13 and Big Ben. And, of course, when you are in England, you 23
14 do not want to pass up the opportunity to see Buckingham 34
15 Palace. Plan on staying a few days to see all the sites. 45

16 France certainly is a highlight of any European visit. 11
17 Paris offers many sites such as the Arc de Triomphe, the 23
18 Louvre, the Eiffel Tower, and the Gothic Cathedral of Notre 35
19 Dame. Other cities to visit are Nice, Lyon, and Versailles. 46

1 | 2 | 3 | 4 | 5 | 6 | 7 | 8 | 9 | 10 | 11 | 12

Take two 5-minute timed writings.

Goal: At least 44wpm/5'/5e

C. 5-MINUTE TIMED WRITING

Critical thinking is a skill that can be learned and 11
applied to more than a few situations. There are many ways 23
to describe critical thinking skill. The common theme that 34
runs through each of these descriptions is related to the 46
use of cognitive skill. 51

With this skill, the person thinks with a purpose in 62
mind and likely directs some of the focus toward goals. The 74
person looks at a situation and decides rationally what to 86
believe or not to believe. In critical thinking, the goal 97
is to achieve understanding, judge more than one viewpoint, 109
and then solve problems. 114

After a person thinks through all the elements of the 125
problem, a decision is made based on all of the facts and 137
exact findings. Bias, prejudice, and feelings should not 148
sway the final outcome. 153

Critical thinking is useful in reading, listening, 163
speaking, and writing. A critical thinker will ask great 175
questions. He or she listens carefully to others and gives 187
feedback. A critical thinker seeks the truth with zeal and 198
then willingly accepts change when new facts are presented. 210
Critical thinking is needed for problem solving. 220

1 | 2 | 3 | 4 | 5 | 6 | 7 | 8 | 9 | 10 | 11 | 12

Formatting

D. INTERNATIONAL URLs

Uniform resource locators (URLs) identify a site on the World Wide Web where specific information can be found. In international URLs, an abbreviation for a country is often included in the URL, as shown in red below.

Country	Uniform Resource Locator (URL)
Canada	http://www.samuels.animate.chap2.ca
Mexico	http://www.reloj.baja.mx
France	http://www.education.grad.up.fr
Germany	http://www.mercedes.de
China	http://www.peking.transportation.costs.cn

E. WORD PROCESSING: SYMBOL—INSERT

Accents and other marks are used in many languages to indicate how words should be pronounced. Some examples of commonly used symbols are shown below.

Symbol	Application
á	Yucatán
é	Quertéro
í	García
ñ	Señor
ó	Torreón
ú	Cancún
ü	Nürnberg

GO TO Word Manual

Study Lesson 82 in your Word Manual. Complete all of the shaded steps while at your computer. Then format the documents that follow.

Document Processing

Situation: Today is June 23, your second day, and you will prepare an e-mail message and a business report with a table. Begin with the e-mail. Type the e-mail greeting `Hi, Mr. Sanchez:` and the body shown below in correct format. Type your name (`Janet`) as the sender, with the following writer's identification: `Janet Osborne | E-mail: josborne@cancom.com | Phone: +1.204.555.8823`

Correspondence 82-78
E-Mail Message

REFER TO Reference Manual
R-5C–D: E-Mail Message

REFER TO Reference Manual
R-12C–D: Formatting Lists

¶ As you know, sales in our international divisions have been accelerating since the advent of our new Genesis laptop. As a result, several new manufacturing plants will open in the next eight years. All of the plants are to open in France and Germany.

¶ To market our new manufacturing plants and promote the Genesis, the Marketing Division is planning to open new Web sites on the Genesis home page. The following links will be added to advertise our plant expansion:

- Lyon, France: http://www.lyon.fr.genesis.new.html
- Reims, France: http://www.reims.fr.genesis.new.html
- Bremen, Germany: http://www.bremen.de.genesis.new.html
- Leipzig, Germany: http://www.leipzig.de.genesis.new.html
- Nürnberg, Germany: http://www.nurnberg.de.genesis.new.html

Use an umlaut in Nürnberg

(continued on next page)

agreement pronoun

agreement intervening

¶ Each of our sites, including the plants in France and Germany, is scheduled to go online in late August. Until then, plan to work with the Marketing Division personnel to implement the marketing plan we discussed at our meeting last month (the International Proposal). When the sites go online in August, we hope to maximize our exposure on the WWW. If they are as successful as we believe they will be, our promotional campaign may also be implemented at our plants in Torreón, Querétaro, and León.

Use accent marks in Torreón, Querétaro, and León.

Report
82-58
Business Report

Use A4 paper.

MEXICO TRAVEL DESTINATIONS
Popular Sites Visited
June 23, 20--

¶ Since the mid-1990s, national parks in Mexico have become popular tourist sites for visitors from the Americas, Asia, and Europe. Because of this popularity, an increasing number of requests have been made for maps and travel brochures from our Visitors' Bureau. Therefore, in the coming weeks, we will be publishing several new maps and brochures to accommodate these requests.

BROCHURES

¶ The brochures will include a detailed description of the site, providing information on beginning and ending visitation schedules, highlights of the site, and popular photography locations. Brochures will be prepared on the sites and locations shown below. The fourth column indicates how many years each site has been ranked among the top ten most popular sites in Mexico.

Use accent marks as shown in the city and state names in this table.

Site	City	State	Top 10
Bosque de la Primavera	Guadalajara	Jalisco	4 yrs.
Cancún	Quintana Roo	Cancún	10 yrs.
Chichén Itzá	Merida	Yucatán	8 yrs.
Dzibilchaltún	Merida	Yucatán	7 yrs.
El Tepozteco	Tepoztlán	Morelos	5 yrs.
Fuerte de San Miguel	Campeche	Campeche	5 yrs.
Parque Papagayo	Acapulco	Guerrero	4 yrs.
Temple Pyramid	Cholula	Puebla	3 yrs.
Uxmal	Merida	Yucatán	6 yrs.

(continued on next page)

MAPS

¶ Maps will be supplied for these sites, with detailed insets to guide visitors from the nearest cities to the tourist attractions. Walking trails and resting stations will be highlighted, and approximate walking times will be noted on the maps. Individual maps will be prepared for each site, and an area map will also be available for each city. Everyone is encouraged to send his or her advertising pieces to Señor Garcia, Public Relations Director.

International Formatting—France

Goals

- Demonstrate improved speed and accuracy while typing.
- Demonstrate acceptable proofreading skills by comparing lines of copy.
- Correctly format a letter, a table, and an e-mail message with dot-style telephone numbers and international telephone access codes.

A. WARMUP

alphabet	1	She was watching Alex Trebek's fun TV quiz game "Jeopardy!"
substitution: *m* and *n*	2	man men amen hymn unman norm name many unmet norm mine mend
easy	3	Six girls may buy a new gown for the big social in the gym.

Skillbuilding

B. MAP+: NUMBERS

Follow the GDP software directions for this exercise to improve keystroking accuracy.

PPP PRETEST » PRACTICE » POSTTEST

PRETEST
Take a 1-minute timed writing.

C. PRETEST: Common Letter Combinations

```
4      Della Daly will return to Detroit because she believes 11
5  her income will increase. She will share an apartment with 23
6  Joann to save on rent. Their rental was lowered, however,  35
7  because of the intent complaints of the outraged dwellers. 46
     1 | 2 | 3 | 4 | 5 | 6 | 7 | 8 | 9 | 10 | 11 | 12
```

PRACTICE
Speed Emphasis:
If you made no more than 1 error on the Pretest, type each *individual* line 2 times.
Accuracy Emphasis:
If you made 2 or more errors, type each *group* of lines (as though it were a paragraph) 2 times.

D. PRACTICE: Word Beginnings

```
8  re- repel renew remit relax refer ready react really reveal
9  in- inept insert inert inset input infer index incur inches
10 be- beauty bears beams beach below being began befit beside
11 de- deny decide defend design detain devise depress deforms
```

E. PRACTICE: Word Endings

```
12 -ly truly weekly madly lowly early daily apply hilly simply
13 -ed sized hired dated opened cited based acted added showed
14 -nt plant meant giant front event count agent amount fluent
15 -al Val mental cereal bridal fungal normal literal informal
```

POSTTEST

Repeat the Pretest timed writing and compare performance.

F. POSTTEST: Common Letter Combinations

Language Arts

Compare these lines with lines 35–40 on page 331. Edit the lines to correct any errors.

G. PROOFREADING

Criticle thinking is useful in reading, listenning, speaking, or writing. A critical thinker may ask great questions. He or she listens carefully to others and gives feedback. A critical tinker seeks truth with zeal and then willingly accepts changes when new facts are presented. Critical thinking is important for problem solving.

Formatting

H. DOT-STYLE TELEPHONE NUMBERS

In the United States, hyphens are used in telephone numbers. A hyphen is used after the 3-digit area code and after the first 3 digits of the telephone number; for example, 701-555-1234. Another format, used in many countries, is to replace the hyphens with periods without spaces before or after; for example, 701.555.4832 or 818.555.3424.

I. INTERNATIONAL TELEPHONE ACCESS CODES

Special access codes are needed to make a phone call from one country to another. To make an international call, dial the IDD (International Direct Dialing) code first. Then dial the country code for the country you are calling, next the area code (if any), and finally the telephone number. The IDD code in many countries changes periodically.

The United States and Canada have the same IDD (011) and country code (1). When you provide a United States (or Canadian) telephone number in a document being sent to an international address, use a plus sign (+) in front of the area code, instead of the IDD code, followed by 1 (the country code for the United States). For example, if you are writing a letter to an international address and you are giving your own telephone number in Los Angeles, you would express your number as +1.323.555.8923. Some of the more common access codes are listed on the next page.

Country	From U.S. to Foreign Country		From Foreign Country to U.S.	
	IDD Code	Country Code	IDD Code	Country Code
Canada	011	1	011	1
China	011	86	00	1
France	011	33	00	1
Germany	011	49	00	1
Italy	011	39	00	1
Japan	011	81	001	1
Mexico	011	52	98	1
Taiwan	011	886	002	1
United Kingdom	011	44	00	1
Note: The United States and Canada have the same IDD (011) and country code (1).				

Document Processing

Situation: Today is June 24, your third day, and you will prepare a letter, a table, and an e-mail message. Begin with the letter.

Correspondence 83-79
Business Letter in Block Style

Use A4 paper.

23 June 20-- | Mr. Claude R. Moreau | Human Resources Director | Walther Techtronics | 38, Rue du Caire | 75106 Paris | FRANCE | Dear Mr. Moreau:
¶ I am pleased that we will be involved in an employee exchange this coming year. As we discussed earlier, the exchange of our 36 production employees will benefit both companies.
¶ We plan to rotate all 36 employees through the various units of our production process, starting from the raw materials division and continuing right on through our shipping operations. I have enclosed a projected rotation plan for you to review. Included in the plan are all the employee rotations we discussed at our last meeting. Please review the plan and e-mail me if you have any changes. You can e-mail me at tlambeer@cancom.com; or, if you wish to speak to me directly, you can call +00.1.204.555.9090.
¶ I look forward to working with you this coming year. As soon as we have agreed on the rotation plan, we can make copies for all affected employees. I know that everyone from our end is eagerly anticipating this collaborative effort.
Sincerely, | Tom R. Lambeer | Human Resources Manager | jo | Enclosure | c: Sheila Southern, Geraldine Gouet

Table
83-44
Boxed Table

Add 25 percent shading to Row 2.

Type the body of the table single-spaced.

PROJECTED ROTATION PLAN CanCom Group and Walther Tech tronics		
Department	**Rotation Start Date**	**Rotation End Date**
[Raw] Materials	3 May 20--	11 June 20--
Board Assembly	~~12~~ [14] June 20--	22 ~~June~~ [July] 20--
Drive As[s]embly	25 July 20--	3 (Sept.) 20--
Power Unit	6 (Sept.) 20--	15 October 20--
Testing (&) Evaluation	October 15 20--	2 November 20--

Type the e-mail greeting, `Hi, Mr. Moreau:`, and the body shown below in correct format. Type `Janet` as the sender's name, and use the following as the writer's identification: `Janet Osborne | E-mail: josborne@cancom.com | Phone: +1.204.555.8823`

Correspondence
83-80
E-Mail Message

¶ *I am sending you this e-mail to alert you to a change we must make in the rotation plan I sent you last week. We will have to refit several of our board assembly production unit relay systems during the week of 14 June through 18 June. To avoid significantly altering the remaining rotation plan, I would like to suggest that we use one-half of the drive assembly rotation period to complete the board assembly rotation.*

¶ *Please respond to my e-mail as soon as possible so that we can make whatever changes are necessary.*

International Formatting—Germany

84

Goals

- Type at least 44wpm/5'/5e.
- Correctly format an e-mail message, a business letter, and a business report that include metric units of measure content.

A. WARMUP

alphabet 1 The foxy General Schwarzkopf jumbled his words on Iraqi TV.
frequent digraphs 2 he heed ache hem heel herb her chef she here shed head hear
easy 3 The proficient sleuth may own both the giant bowl and dish.

Skillbuilding

B. PROGRESSIVE PRACTICE: NUMBERS

Follow the GDP software directions for this exercise to improve keystroking speed.

C. TECHNIQUE PRACTICE: ENTER KEY

Type each line 2 times. Type each sentence on a separate line by pressing ENTER after each sentence.

4 Ah. What? We do. Speak. Stop. Ed saw her. Go. Ah. Begin it.
5 Stop. Why not? See? Get it? Why me? Who, me? Well? She can.
6 Who? See me. Read it. What? Really! Who is? So soon? Do it.
7 Who knew? Enough? What is it? Go slow. She did. How so? So?

Strategies for Career Success

Letter of Complaint

Is a poor product or bad service getting you down? By writing a concise, rational letter of complaint, you have the possibility of the reader honoring your request.

In the first paragraph, give a precise description of the product or service (for example, model and serial number). Include a general statement of the problem (for example, "It does not work properly."). In the middle section, provide the details of what went wrong (for example, when it happened or what failed). Refer to copies of invoices, checks, and so on. Describe how you were inconvenienced, with details about time and money lost. State what you want (for example, a refund, a repair, or a replacement). In the closing paragraph, ask for a timely response to the complaint (for example, "Please resolve this problem within the next two weeks.").

Your Turn: Think about the last time you experienced a poor product or service. Did you write a letter of complaint? If so, what was the response?

Take two 5-minute timed writings.

Goal: At least 44wpm/5'/5e

D. 5-MINUTE TIMED WRITING

Proofreading skill is developed with practice. You may 11
want to master several techniques that will help develop 23
and improve your proofreading skills. 30
In order to be a successful proofreader, you will want 41
to schedule time to read through the completed job several 53
times. At the first reading, check your work to see if the 65
margins are correct and the page numbers are in the right 76
places. Determine if the spacing and the font styles are 88
correct. With each reading, zoom in on a specific type of 99
error. If possible, read your work out loud and read only 111
one word at a time. 115
You may find that placing a ruler under each line as 126
you read it will give your eyes a manageable amount of text 138
to read. 140
At the next reading, be sure that the content of the 150
document follows a logical order. If any cited works are 162
included, be sure the citations are in the proper format 173
with complete and accurate data. Check to be sure that all 185
the basic rules of grammar, spelling, and punctuation have 197
been followed. Proofread your document when you are fresh 208
and alert. Remember, proofreading takes time and patience. 220

1 | 2 | 3 | 4 | 5 | 6 | 7 | 8 | 9 | 10 | 11 | 12

Formatting

E. METRIC UNITS OF MEASUREMENT

The metric system of measurement was devised in 1670. It is based on units of 10 and is used by almost every nation in the world. The five common measurements in the metric system are length, area, volume, capacity, and weight and mass. The table below gives the basic units of measure used in the metric and U.S. systems.

Quantity	Metric Units of Measure	U.S. Units of Measure
Length	millimeter, centimeter, meter, kilometer	inch, foot, yard, mile
Area	square centimeter, square meter, hectare	square inch, square foot, square yard
Volume	cubic centimeter, cubic decimeter, cubic meter, liter, hectoliter	cubic inch, cubic foot, fluid ounce, pint, gallon
Weight	milligram, gram, kilogram, tonne	ounce, pound, ton

Document Processing

Situation: Today is June 25, your fourth day, and you will prepare an e-mail message, a business letter, and a multipage business report with tables. Begin with the e-mail. Type the e-mail greeting, `Hi, Mr. Kaufmann:`, and the body shown below in correct format. Type `Janet` as the sender's name, and use the following as the writer's identification: `Janet Osborne | E-mail: josborne@cancom.net | Phone: +1.204.555.8823`

Correspondence 84-81
E-Mail Message

Use an umlaut in Düsseldorf.

¶ The total conversion of our manufacturing plants to the metric system, which was discussed previously, is six months away. Ms. Eisenberg has asked for your continuing support and cooperation as you prepare employees who are presently transferring to the Düsseldorf plant in accordance with the provisions of our policies. Please send me the summary report used when you were monitoring the conversion last year.

¶ The metric system will be quite foreign to many employees, especially the younger ones, who were not involved in the planning stages. The summary report will give them a head start on metrication, as indicated in the assessment.

Use an umlaut in Düsseldorf.

¶ Call Ms. Eisenberg Thursday morning (+1.204.555.8823) to discuss the Frankfurt plant closing. Plant operations will be transferred to Düsseldorf in May. She has asked that you use your judgment to monitor the quality of the operation closely until the transfer has been fully implemented.

Correspondence 84-82
Business Letter in Block Style

Use A4 paper.

28 June 20-- | Ms. Faye Fruehauf | Marketing Department | Melitta Bentz Inc. | Hohe Weide 5 | 22753 Hamburg | GERMANY | Dear Ms. Fruehauf:

¶ Frank Sparks has asked that I send a copy of the summary report on metrics that we completed in the last quarter. As you recall, I sent you that report previously to share with the new employees at our Bremen plant.

¶ As many of the employees in the Production Division were transferred to your plant last April, it is likely that they are not yet aware of the actual impact of our metric conversion that we completed late last year. Feel free to share the summary report with all those employees.

¶ If you wish for copies of the report to be mailed directly from our office, e-mail me a list of all employees to whom the report should be sent.

Sincerely, | Sigfried Krause | Human Resources Manager | jo | Enclosure

Report 84-59
Business Report

SUMMARY REPORT ON METRICS

April 7, 20--

¶ The metric system was devised by Gabriel Mouton, a French man, in 1607. It is a system based on units of 10 and is considered by ~~some~~ *many* to be more accurate and easier to use than the Imperial system of measure used in the U.S.

¶ When it was first defined, a meter was considered to be 1/10,000,000 of the distance from the pole to the equator. This is the basis for all *metric* measurements; it is a system that is used by an overwhelming majority of nations *around the globe*.

(continued on next page)

Use an umlaut in Düsseldorf.

¶ The most common metric measurements are for length, area, volume, and weight and mass. For our Düsseldorf plant, the most crucial measurements for new employees from the U.S. will be volume. Table 1 shows metric and U.S. comparisons for weight.

Table 1. METRIC/U.S. COMPARISONS For Volume		
Metric Unit	**Metric Example**	**U.S. Equivalent**
Cubic centimeter	1 cubic centimeter	0.061 cubic inch
Cubic meter	1,000 cubic centimeters	0.035 cubic feet
Cubic meter	100 cubic decimeters	1.31 cubic yards
liter	1 cubic decimeter	2.21 pints
Hectoliter	100 liters	26.42 gallons

Use an umlaut in Düsseldorf.

The Düsseldorf plant will be impacted by wiegeht measurements, though not as prominently as the volume measurement as noted in table 1. The metric and United States comparisons for weight are displayed in Table 2 below.

Table 2. METRIC/U.S. COMPARISONS For Weight		
Metric Unit	**Metric Example**	**U.S. Equivalent**
Miligram	1 milligram	0.015 grain
Gram	1,000 miligrams	0.035 ounce
Kilogram	1,000 grams	2.205 pounds
tonne	1,000 kilograms	1.01 tons

(continued on next page)

¶ We are convinced that our employees will adapt quickly to the Metric System when they use it on a daily basis. Although we encourage all employees to make calculations in the metric system, it may be helpful for the first few days if they are aware of the conversion factors involved in comparing the measurement systems. The following conversions may therefore be helpful to them:

- Multiply inches by 2.45 to get centimeters
- Multiply feet by 0.305 to get meters
- Multiply miles by 1.6 to get kilometers
- Divide lbs. by 2.2 to get kilograms
- Multiply ounces by 28 to get grams
- Multiply fluid ounces by 30 to get mililiters
- Multiply gallons by 3.8 to get litters

¶ More detailed conversions and metric information can be obtained by visiting the web site for the U.S. Metric Association at http://lamar.colostate.edu/metric.html.

International Formatting—China

Goals

- Demonstrate improved speed and accuracy while typing.
- Demonstrate acceptable language arts skills in composing an e-mail message.
- Correctly format a business letter, an e-mail message, and a table containing international content.
- Successfully complete a Progress and Proofreading Check with zero errors on the first scored attempt.

A. WARMUP

alphabet
```
1 Four quick brown foxes jumped lazily over the resting dogs.
```
number/symbol
```
2 eck@hotmail.com 92% Cho & Orr 9/13 (Shh!) $4.57 *2010 #86-3
```
easy
```
3 Jake's amendment may also entitle the prodigy to a new job.
```

Skillbuilding

B. 12-SECOND SPEED SPRINTS

Take three 12-second timed writings on each line.

```
4 I will lend a hand to anyone if he or she signals for help.
5 A bushel of corn was thrown under the elm tree by the boys.
6 The giant wiry dog put half of the bones down on the chair.
7 A pair of cozy socks and a cup of soup may fix me right up.
  ''''5''''10'''15'''20'''25'''30'''35'''40'''45'''50'''55'''60
```

C. PACED PRACTICE

Follow the GDP software directions for this exercise to improve keystroking speed and accuracy.

Language Arts

D. COMPOSING AN E-MAIL MESSAGE

Compose an e-mail message to your keyboarding instructor. Use an appropriate greeting. Your instructor has a strict policy that cell phones must be turned off during class. In the first paragraph, explain that your sister is expecting her first child any day and that you would like to keep your cell phone on in case your family calls with any news. Explain that you will keep your phone on vibrate and that you will go out into the hallway to accept the call. End the e-mail with an appropriate note of appreciation.

Document Processing

Situation: Today is June 26, your fifth day, and you will prepare a letter, an e-mail message, and a table. Begin with the letter.

Correspondence
85-83
Business Letter in Block Style

Use A4 paper.

26 June 20-- | Mr. Chao Chang | Chief Technology Officer | Tian Hao Technology | 47 Renmin Road, Zhengzhou | 450347 Henan | P.R. CHINA | Dear Mr. Chang:

¶ You are one of six technology executives from various countries with whom we will be working to develop the technology alliance strategic venture. Your company has long been known for its excellence in developing green technology in a global community, and CanCom Computers is pleased to play a collaborative part with you in this venture.

¶ Our development teams have been working with their counterparts from all six participating venture companies over the past several weeks, and we look forward to this continued, cooperative spirit.

¶ Because the strategic venture includes participants from various countries, we believe it would be helpful if you could share with us any particular ideas you have for our upcoming meeting in Hefei that are unique to your country's promotion of green technology. If you could send those ideas to me, we will gladly include them in our agenda.

Sincerely, | Donna T. Parsons | Project Coordinator | jo | c: Chan Huang, Jia Wang, Charlotte Chrisler

Correspondence
85-84
E-Mail Message

Type the e-mail greeting, `Hi, Ms. Parsons:`, and the body shown below in correct format. Type `Janet` as the sender's name, and use the following as the writer's identification: `Janet Osborne` | `E-mail: josborne@cancom.com` | `Phone: +1.204.555.8823`.

¶ It is my pleasure to inform you that Jia Wang will be forwarding to your office a summary of Tian Hao Technology's ideas for the promotion of green technology. Ms. Wang's report presents a very aggressive approach to this technology, and I know many of the venture members will benefit appreciably from her ideas. She has asked that you call her at +00.1.204.555.7788 when her report arrives at CanCom.

¶ After you receive Ms. Wang's report, please forward it immediately to the other committee members. By this time next week, we should have received all six reports and will be able to set our next agenda for the Hefei meeting.

Table
85-45
Boxed Table

Use 25 percent shading for Row 2.

Progress and Proofreading Check

Documents designated as Proofreading Checks serve as a check of your proofreading skill. Your goal is to have zero typographical errors when the GDP software first scores the document.

TECHNOLOGY ALLIANCE STRATEGIC VENTURE **Committee Members**		
Name	**City/Country**	**Affiliation**
Bachmann, Alexis	Frankfurt, Germany	Volkert Technology
Chang, Chao	Zhengzhou, China	Tian Hao Technology
Chernov, Vasily	Saratov, Russia	Kinetic Technologies
Kapoor, Deepak	Mumbai, India	Kolkata Pradish
Parsons, Donna	Winnipeg, Canada	CanCom Computers
Uda, Yoshifumi	Osaka, Japan	Tadashi Corporation

Keyboarding Connection

Effective Teleconferencing for Meetings

Teleconferencing is a useful way to conduct meetings with businesspeople across the globe. To make the best use of teleconferences, follow these guidelines.

Decide whether you will have a teleconference (audio only) or a videoconference (video and audio). Since sound quality varies greatly, use the best equipment available. Your company may already have the necessary equipment, or you might need to rent it from an audiovisual company. If you have a teleconference, there is software such as NetMeeting or WebEx to allow a presentation to be viewed in all locations via the Internet or company intranet. Make sure you test the equipment in advance and that each location has someone who has tested and knows how to use the equipment there.

Allow individual participants enough time to participate in the meeting. Distribute agendas to everyone in advance. Be sensitive to time zone differences. Since it is possible the meetings will be at an inconvenient time for some attendees, especially for international meetings, consider rotating the times of the meetings. Assign someone to prepare and e-mail to the participants a brief summary covering the main discussion topics, decisions, and action items of the meeting.

Your Turn: List what you think are the advantages and disadvantages of conducting meetings via teleconference or videoconference.

UNIT 18

Formal Report Project

Formal Report Project—A

86

Goals

- Type at least 45wpm/5′/5e.
- Correctly use Word's styles feature.
- Correctly format a multipage business report.

A. WARMUP

alphabet A zoo quickly bought a jinxed mauve dog with pink fur ears.
concentration superstitiousnesses comprehensibilities incomprehensibility
easy Dudley may then dismantle the tan bicycle out on the lanai.

Skillbuilding

B. SUSTAINED PRACTICE: PUNCTUATION

Take a 1-minute timed writing on the boxed paragraph to establish your base speed. Then take a 1-minute timed writing on the following paragraph. As soon as you equal or exceed your base speed on this paragraph, move to the next, more difficult paragraph.

One of the strengths you must have if you are going to 11
be a success in business is good writing skills. You must 23
practice your writing skills every day if you want them to 35
improve. Perfection of writing skills takes much practice. 46

You must always strive to write clearly, concisely, 11
and accurately. Remember always that your writing can be 22
examined by more people than just the one to whom you have 34
written. It's often looked at by other readers as well. 45

You want to be sure that your letters always convey a 11
positive, helpful attitude. Don't forget, you represent 22
more than yourself when you write--you also represent your 34
company! This is an important, useful rule to remember. 45

Try to stay away from negative words like "can't" or 11
"won't." Readers also do not like phrases such as "because 23
of company policies" or "due to unforeseen circumstances." 34
Using these words and phrases never helps resolve problems. 46

1 | 2 | 3 | 4 | 5 | 6 | 7 | 8 | 9 | 10 | 11 | 12

Take two 5-minute timed writings.

Goal: At least 45wpm/5'/5e

C. 5-MINUTE TIMED WRITING

During upbeat economic times, businesses have trouble 11
finding and keeping their skilled workers. As a result, 22
some places may offer great benefits to the workers. These 34
could include such things as sick leave, life insurance, 45
profit sharing, paid time off each year, and flextime. 56
The concept of flextime was brought to the workforce 67
quite a few years ago. Companies implemented this concept 78
for a lot of reasons. Among the top reasons for flexible 90
work schedules at that time were to reduce the number of 101
cars on the road, to help workers to meet their families' 113
needs and demands, and also to attract more women back to 124
the workforce. 127
Businesses can manage such a schedule in a few ways. 138
Employees may have a chance to choose when to arrive and 150
leave for the day. This policy allows people who like to 161
work early in the day to start early and end early and vice 173
versa. Other companies may allow their employees to work 184
extended hours for four days and then enjoy three days off. 196
This type of benefit has assisted both workers and 206
companies. Companies recognize that their workers are more 218
productive and absences are lower. 225

1 | 2 | 3 | 4 | 5 | 6 | 7 | 8 | 9 | 10 | 11 | 12

Formatting

D. WORD PROCESSING—STYLES

GO TO Word Manual

Study Lesson 86 in your Word Manual. Complete all of the shaded steps while at your computer. Then format the document that follows.

Document Processing

You will begin typing Report 86-60, a formal business report project, in this lesson and will continue adding pages and features to the report in Lessons 87, 88, and 89.

- In Report 86-60, you will apply a Title style and Subtitle style to the title block and a Heading 2 style to the side headings. You will also insert a header and lists.
- In Report 87-61, you will apply styles, insert a list and two tables, format a displayed paragraph, and insert footnotes.
- In Report 88-62, you will apply styles, format a displayed paragraph, and insert clip art and footnotes.
- In Report 89-63, you will apply styles, insert a table, format a displayed paragraph, insert clip art and a footnote, and create bookmarks and hyperlinks.

Follow these steps to create the first two pages of the business report. Do not apply any styles until directed to do so:

1. Press ENTER 5 times, type the title in all-caps, and press ENTER 1 time.
2. Type the byline information in upper- and lowercase letters, and press ENTER 1 time after each line; then type the date, and press ENTER 2 times.
3. Type the first paragraph; then press ENTER 1 time.
4. Type the side heading in all-caps, and press ENTER 1 time. (Additional spacing will be added above the side heading later when the Heading 2 style is applied.)
5. Continue in like manner until all paragraph and side headings have been typed.
6. Insert a header that will display on all pages except the first page; type `Human Resources Department` at the left margin, and type `Page` followed by a space and an automatic page number at the right margin.
7. Select all header text and format it using Cambria 10 pt. Italic.
8. Add a bottom border; then close the header.

After you finish typing the part of the report shown in Lesson 86, do this:

1. Apply the Title style to the report title. (The title style automatically bolds the text.)
2. Apply the Subtitle style to the byline information and date line; then bold these lines.
3. Apply the Heading 2 style to the side headings. (The Heading 2 style automatically applies italic and bold and inserts blank space above the heading.)

Report
86-60
Business Report

Title style ↓5X

INTERCULTURAL SEMINARS ↓1X

Subtitle style

Heath R. Watkins, Director ↓1X

Human resources department ↓1X

March 10, 20-- ↓2X

Calibri 12 pt

¶ The Marketing department has been conducting surveys of our world wide offices, foreign customers, and prospective foreign customers over the last several months. Information received through the use of ~~our~~ mailed questionnaires has made us aware of an urgent need to improve our communication skills at the international level. Therefore, weare going to conduct a series of Seminars to focus on intercultural awareness issues. This ~~The~~ report addresses the process involved in developing the seminars, the ~~instructional~~ approach to be used, the seminar content that will be provided, and the schedule for conducting the seminars. ↓1X

Heading 2 style

PROBLEM

¶ Some incidents have been reported to us in which we have failed to negotiate contracts with foreign customers and foreign prospective customers because of ~~serious~~ breakdowns in communication. Some of these setbacks have been the result of conscious negative acts on the part of our employees. However, the main culprit seems to be lack of awareness of cultural differences and lack of appreciation for the nuances that reflect these cultural differences. Indeed, there are unlimited possibilities almost for misunderstandings, insults, miscues, and avenues for people of good intent to miscommunicate. These issues must be addressed immediately to preclude any future breakdowns in communications.

Heading 2 style

INTERCULTURAL SEMINARS

¶ Three-day seminars designed to improve intercultural communication skills will be held at regional sites in the United States and in selected forieqn cities where we have offices: ↓2X

- Beijing
- Hamburg
- Madrid
- Melbourne
- Oslo
- Rio de Janeiro
- Tokyo
- Warsaw ↓2X

¶ It will be our intent that all employees who have direct contact with people from other countries will participate in these seminars over a four-month period. Depending on

(continued on next page)

the success of these seminars, the programs will be made available in the company to others who express an interest in acuiring or enhancing there cultural awareness. Any future seminars will always be scheduled on an as-needed basis during the up coming calendar year.

¶ It would be unreasonable to assume that a small team of people from our company would have the breadth of knowledge needed to conduct these seminars in 7 foreign cities. However, Celeste Fuhrmann, Robert Driscoll, and Han Lee have agreed to work together as the co-ordinating team for this effort. Ms. Fuhrman, Mr. Driscoll, and Mr. lee will be soliciting volunteers to work with them in areas of expertise. They hope to gain representative views and opinions for the purpose of molding an impressive array of seminar topics. Please contact these individuals if you believe you have the necessary background and/or experience and would like to volunteer.

¶ Each of these individuals has worked over the past 2 months with the managers of our international offices as well as with natives in specific countries to formulate a preliminary plan for these in-service programs. There plan will use the expertise of our employees in each country who have had negotiating experience and who have knowledge of local customs as demonstrated by natives. We are confident that through this team approach, every one will gain an understanding of problems only not from the position of our company but also from the perspective of those with whom they conduct business.

Heading 2 style

BENEFITS OF ATTENDING THE SEMINARS

¶ Besides the benefits that seminars such as these provide, invited speakers will lead discussions on a variety of topics to provide answers to questions such as the following:

- How can I develop a good working relationship with other coleagues?
- How can I avoid offending people?
- Do I need to adopt to another peoples culture when I travel abroad?
- Is cultural stereo typing harmful or helpful?
- How do people from different cultures approach the decision-making process?
- How can we improve international cooperation?

¶ It is our hope that the Seminars will help all participants gain a much greater awareness and understanding of the environment in which they work. We believe the Seminars will assist all participants in avoiding cultural mistakes that might be costly to the company. Finally, for those employees who frequently work in one of our foreign branches, the Seminars will enable these people to adapt much more quickly to the cultures of the country in which they work.

Save this unfinished report. You will resume work on it in Lesson 87.

Formal Report Project—B

87

Goals

- Demonstrate improved speed and accuracy while typing.
- Demonstrate acceptable language arts skills in using abbreviations.
- Correctly format a multipage business report.

A. WARMUP

alphabet	1	Freight to me sixty dozen quart jars and twelve black pans.
one hand	2	career uphill gas pin awards homonym read yummy grade lumpy
easy	3	The Auburn sorority may dock in England for a formal visit.

Skillbuilding

MAP+

B. MAP+: ALPHABET

Follow the GDP software directions for this exercise to improve keystroking accuracy.

C. PROGRESSIVE PRACTICE: ALPHABET

Follow the GDP software directions for this exercise to improve keystroking speed.

Language Arts

Study the rules at the right.

D. ABBREVIATIONS

RULE
abbreviate measures

In technical writing, on forms, and in tables, abbreviate units of measure when they occur frequently. Do not use periods.

14 oz   5 ft 10 in   50 mph   2 yrs 10 mo

RULE
abbreviate lowercase

In most lowercase abbreviations made up of single initials, use a period after each initial but no internal spaces.

a.m.   p.m.   i.e.   e.g.   e.o.m.
Exceptions: mph   mpg   wpm

RULE
abbreviate =

In most all-capital abbreviations made up of single initials, do not use periods or internal spaces.

OSHA   PBS   NBEA   WWW   VCR   MBA
Exceptions: U.S.A.   A.A.   B.S.   Ph.D.   P.O.   B.C.   A.D.

Edit each sentence to correct any errors.

```
A mixture of 25 lb of cement and 100 lb of gravel was used.

The desk height must be reduced from 2 ft. 6 in. to 2 ft 4 in.

The 11 a. m. meeting was changed to 1 p. m. because of a conflict.

The eom statement was published over the Internet on the W.W.W.

She enlisted in the U.S.M.C. after she received her MBA degree.

His Ph. D. dissertation deals with the early history of NATO.
```

Document Processing

When you type the remaining report pages in Lessons 87, 88, and 89, do this:

1. Type all lists, tables, displayed paragraphs, and footnotes in standard format.
2. Apply styles as the last step in each lesson.

Report 87-61
Business Report (Continued)

INSTRUCTIONAL APPROACH

¶ Fruehauf and Chang suggest a framework of instruction that was recognized by several international groups, and has been used by seminar groups around the globe. This approach includes the following 3 components:

1. The Cognitive component
2. The Affective component
3. The Experiential component

¶ The cognitive component includes information about comunicating with people of other cultures. The effective component is the area in which attention is given to attitudes, emotions, and resulting behaviors as they are affected by human interaction in a multicultural environment. The experiential component is the "hands-on" element that suggests several possibilities. Others who have used this instructional approach have found that the use of simulations is a natural. Writing letters, memos, e-mails, and reports to persons in other cultures also provides beneficial learning experiences. In addition, the use of tutors can be very helpful to workers unfamiliar with a particular culture.[1]

---

[1] Faye Fruehauf and Chao Chang, "Communication Across Cultures," *International Business World*, April 2010, pp. 33-47.

(continued on next page)

SEMINAR CONTENT

abbreviate ≡

¶ The cognitive, affective, and experiential components would be applied as appropriate for each of the topics included. The coordinating team members have used the resources available to them at our three local universities.

The co ordinating team has found that most colleges and universities now provide instruction in international communication. Many offer separate degrees in international Communication, and the number of majors and minors in this disipline have been growing rapidly for the past several years. While the content of international communication is integrated into several Business Administration and Psychology courses, there has been a trend in recent years to provide a course specifically designed for business interaction in an intercultural setting. The very nature of this type of study makes it very difficult to segment the broad topical areas, as all elements are so closely intertwined.

¶ The seminars must reflect the broad involvement of our international operations. There is a need for many workers in our domestic offices to develop an appreciation of the inter cultural challenge. This is true not only for those in the marketing and sales areas. Those in our finance department and our legal department are increasingly involved only not with foreign companies but also with huge multinational corporations that, at times, are as large as or larger than the biggest companies in the U.S. Table 1, page 4, provides a summary of the largest multinational corporations with whom we have worked on numerous projects since the early 1980s.

REFER TO Reference Manual

R-8B. Tables in Reports

Table 1. Largest International Companies

(Doing Business With CanCom, Inc.)

Company Name	Location	Global Rank
HSBC Holdings	United Kingdom	1
Royal Shell Dutch	Netherlands	6
Toyota Motor	Japan	7
BNP Paribas	France	13
Allianz	Germany	14
Gaz Prom	russia	19
Banco Santander	Spain	24
ENI	Italy	28
China Petro	China	30
Nokia	Finland	69

(continued on next page)

¶ Several seminar topics have been suggested to the coordinating team members and the literature reviewed by the team suggests that there might be possibly more than a dozen from which to choose. Because of time constraints, however, we have decided to include 8 topics that are recommended by Chernov, Uda, and Kapoor. The topics and presentation times are displayed in Table 2 below.[2]

abbreviate measures

Table 3. SEMINAR TOPICS

Instructional Topic	Time
Body positions and movements	2 hrs
Concept of Culture	3 hrs
Conflict Resolution	2 hrs
Intimacy in Relationships	3 hrs
Language	2 hrs
Male and Female roles	2 hrs
Space & Time	2 hrs
Religion, Values, and Ethics	4 hrs

¶ **Body Positions and Movements.** Body language—that is, facial expressions, gestures, and body movements—convey messages about attitude and may be interpreted by people in different cultures. For example, firm handshakes are the normal in the U.S.; loose handshakes are the custom in some other countries. The way we stand, sit, and hold our arms may convey different messages in different cultural settings.

¶ **concept of culture.** This session will be an over view of the various cultures in which we conduct business, including ecommerce. Clooney identifies the needs for varied marketing strategies within the different economic, political, and cultural environments:

Indent the long quotation ½ inch from each margin.

> International web use and access are growing exponentially, and many businesses are wanting to capitalize on this trend and grab their share of this global market. English-speaking audiences are not expected to continue to dominate this market. Certainly, more than a literal translation will be required to reach this culturally diverse audience.[3]

¶ Case studies will be reviewed that are considered classics in the field of international communication. In addition, summaries of some of our own sucesses and failures will be reported.

---

[2] Vasily Chernov, Yoshifumi Uda, and Deepak Kapoor, *The Dynamics of Intercultural Seminars*, Gateway Publishing, St. Louis, 2009.

[3] Sandra Boucher, "Cultural Comparisons in E-Commerce," January 17, 2010, <http://www.ecommerce.com/news.htm>, accessed on February 23, 2010.

Save this unfinished report. You will resume work on it in Lesson 88.

Formal Report Project—C

Goals

- Type at least 45wpm/5′/5e.
- Correctly use Word's clip art feature.
- Correctly format a multipage business report.

A. WARMUP

alphabet
1 Jeff had his size to help him quickly win over Gene Baxter.

practice: *a* and *s*
2 ask has say sales bases areas scans seams sodas visas tasks

easy
3 Duane may try to fix the auditory problems in the city gym.

Skillbuilding

B. PACED PRACTICE

Follow the GDP software directions for this exercise to improve keystroking speed and accuracy.

C. 5-MINUTE TIMED WRITING

Take two 5-minute timed writings.

Goal: At least 45wpm/5′/5e

4 Technology surrounds us. It is everywhere you look. 11
5 People use cellular phones to speak to one another just 22
6 about anywhere. They carry their pagers so that they can be 34
7 reached at any time. Everyone, from the busy executive to 45
8 the college student, is now quite used to being available 57
9 at all hours of the day or night. 64
10 In recent years, busy travelers have become used to 74
11 using their laptops everywhere. They use computer ports in 86
12 airports, hotel rooms and lobbies, and even taxis. This 97
13 technology allows the busy traveler to have access to the 109
14 Internet while on the go. Using the laptop, the user can 120
15 access the latest weather report, sports scores, and news, 132
16 almost as soon as they happen. 138
17 Using the latest technology, you can keep up with your 150
18 work and maintain contact with your office. You can even 161
19 access your bank accounts and pay bills while waiting in 172
20 traffic. Also, if you are in a new place, you can find a 184
21 restaurant or call for directions as needed. The technology 196
22 options that have become available to almost everyone are 207
23 quite amazing. We are living in a small world that seems to 219
24 be getting smaller each day. 225

1 | 2 | 3 | 4 | 5 | 6 | 7 | 8 | 9 | 10 | 11 | 12

Formatting

D. WORD PROCESSING: CLIP ART—INSERT

GO TO Word Manual

Study Lesson 88 in your Word Manual. Complete all of the shaded steps while at your computer. Then format the document that follows.

Document Processing

Report 88-62
Business Report (Continued)

¶ **Conflict Resolution.** Whether people are involved in negotiating a contract, working together to remedy product quality issues, or resolving contract interpretations, the need for tact and skill is particularly important in the foreign setting. Many of the seminar topics have implications in the area of conflict resolution. While every effort should be made to prevent conflict, there is a need for guidance in resolving disagreements in foreign cultures.

¶ **Intimacy in Relationships.** The degree of physical contact that is acceptable varies considerably. Hugs and kisses are the standard, even in the business office, in some countries. By contrast, the act of touching a person is considered an extreme invasion of privacy in other places. The use of first names may or may not be acceptable. To ask a personal question is extremely offensive in some cultures. While socializing with business clients is to be expected in some countries, it would be highly inappropriate in others. These are only a few of the relationship concerns that will be explored.

Insert clip art related to communication, similar to the above example. Set the clip art width to 1 inch, set the wrap style to square, and align the clip art at the right margin, even with the first line of the Language paragraph.

¶ **Language.** It is obvious that language differences play a major part in business miscommunication. Whenever there is an interpreter or a written translation involved, the chances for error are increased. There are over 3,000 languages used worldwide. Just as with English, there are not only grammar rules but also varied meanings as words are both spoken and written. Even with the English language, there are differences in usage between the English used in the United States and that used in England.

¶ Although English is the language usually used in international communication, the topics identified in Table 2 illustrate the complexity of communicating accurately; and the problem continues to grow. For example, literal translations of American advertising and labeling have sometimes resulted in negative feelings toward products. As world trade increases, so does the need for American businesses to understand the complexities of cultural differences. Matthews offers this example:

> A businessperson must change his or her expectations and assumptions away from what is customary and acceptable in the United States in terms of personal and social conduct to what is customary and acceptable within the culture of the country where he or she is conducting business. Any other assumption can have serious consequences and undesirable results. In the other person's mind, you are the foreigner, and therefore you will be the one who might look out of place or act in a way that is considered socially unacceptable.[4]

---

[4] Craig Matthews, *Comparing Cultural Differences*, Grant Publishing Company, Los Angeles, 2010, p. 37.

(continued on next page)

Insert clip art related to shaking hands, similar to the above example.
Set the clip art width to 1 inch, set the wrap style to square, and align the clip art at the right margin, even with the first line in the Male and Female Roles paragraph.

¶ A good sense of humor is an asset not only in our personal lives but also in the business environment. However, it probably should be avoided in multicultural settings because the possibilities for misinterpretation are compounded. Do not use humor that makes fun of a particular individual, group, or culture. Remember that what may appear to be humorous to you may have a negative connotation in another culture.

¶ **Male and Female Roles.** There are major contrasts in the ways male and female roles are perceived in different cultures. The right to vote is still withheld from women in countries all over the world. Opportunities for female employment in the business environment vary considerably. Pay differentials for men and women continue to exist. Opportunities for advancement for men and women often are not the same.

¶ **Space and Time.** The distance one stands from someone when engaged in conversation is very important. If a person stands farther away than usual, this may signal a feeling of indifference or even a negative feeling. Standing too close is a sign of inappropriate familiarity. However, it should be recognized that different cultures require a variety of space for business exchanges to take place. In the United States, that space is typically from three to five feet, but in the Middle East and in Latin American countries, this distance is considered too far.

abbreviate lowercase

abbreviate lowercase

¶ There is also the element of time—a meeting that is scheduled for 9 a.m. likely will start on time in the United States, but in other cultures the meeting may not start until 9:30 a.m. or even 10 a.m. Punctuality and time concepts vary with the customs and practices of each country. Patience really can be a virtue.

Save this unfinished report. You will work on it again in Lesson 89.

Keyboarding Connection

Protecting Your Files With Antivirus Programs

A virus is a computer program intentionally written to contaminate your computer system. Viruses can enter your system from files downloaded from the Internet or can be acquired from infected files sent to you via e-mail, instant message or chat, or other storage media.

You can protect your computer by purchasing an antivirus program. These programs periodically scan your computer system for viruses. They also scan files that you bring into the system. Some antivirus manufacturers allow you to download a trial copy of their software from their Web site. You can try the software for a few days before you decide if you want to buy it.

Your Turn: If you want to visit antivirus sites to find out what they have to offer, search for *antivirus software* in your search engine.

Formal Report Project—D

Goals

- Demonstrate improved speed and accuracy while typing.
- Demonstrate acceptable language arts skills in spelling.
- Correctly use Word's features to insert a file, add bookmarks, and add hyperlinks.
- Correctly format a boxed table and a multipage business report.

A. WARMUP

alphabet	1	Quick goblins jumped over a lazy dwarf with the onyx rings.
frequent digraphs	2	in ink nine chin pin kind main sin mind tin skinny win inns
easy	3	The right bicycle may fix the problems of the ban on autos.

Skillbuilding

B. MAP+: SYMBOL

Follow the GDP software directions for this exercise to improve keystroking accuracy.

PPP PRETEST » PRACTICE » POSTTEST

C. PRETEST: Close

PRETEST
Take a 1-minute timed writing.

```
4      Old Uncle Bert lived northeast of the swamp, opposite   11
5  a dirty old shop. Last week we asked him to agree to allow   23
6  Aunt Gretel to purchase a jeweled sword for her birthday.   34
7  He fooled all of us by getting her a new topaz necklace.    46
     1 | 2 | 3 | 4 | 5 | 6 | 7 | 8 | 9 | 10 | 11 | 12
```

D. PRACTICE: Adjacent Keys

PRACTICE
Speed Emphasis:
If you made no more than 1 error on the Pretest, type each *individual* line 2 times.
Accuracy Emphasis:
If you made 2 or more errors, type each *group* of lines (as though it were a paragraph) 2 times.

```
8  as asked asset based basis class least visas ease fast mass
9  op opera roped topaz adopt scope troop shops open hope drop
10 we weary wedge weigh towed jewel fewer dwell wear weed week
11 rt birth dirty earth heart north alert worth dart port tort
```

E. PRACTICE: Consecutive Fingers

```
12 sw swamp swift swoop sweet swear swank swirl swap sway swim
13 un uncle under undue unfit bunch begun funny unit aunt junk
14 gr grade grace angry agree group gross gripe grow gram grab
15 ol older olive solid extol spool fools stole bolt cold cool
```

POSTTEST

Repeat the Pretest timed writing and compare performance.

F. POSTTEST: Close Reaches

Language Arts

G. SPELLING

Type these frequently misspelled words, paying special attention to any spelling problems in each word.

16 means valve entry patient officer similar expenses industry
17 quality judgment academic provisions previously cooperation
18 foreign closing indicated secretary especially construction
19 monitoring assessment continuing registration manufacturing
20 products policies capacity presently accordance implemented

Edit the sentences to correct any misspellings.

21 Every company offiser will have simaler expenses next week.

22 In my judgement, we must insist on co-operation from all.

23 My secertary said that she traveled to a foriegn country.

24 We must continue monitering the progress for assesment.

25 The new policeis must be implimented for all products.

26 We must implement continuing registeration during the
27 closeing weeks.

Formatting

H. WORD PROCESSING: FILE—INSERT AND BOOKMARKS AND HYPERLINKS

GO TO Word Manual

Study Lesson 89 in your Word Manual. Complete all of the shaded steps while at your computer. Then format the documents that follow.

Table
89-46
Boxed Table

This table will later be inserted into Report 89-63.

Table 3. FOREIGN-CITY SEMINARS		
City	First Seminar	Second Seminar
Melbourne	May 2-4	July 5-7
Rio de Janeiro	May 9-11	July 11-13
Beijing	May 16-18	July 18-20
Hamburg	May 23-25	July 25-27
Tokyo	June 6-8	August 1-3
Warsaw	June 13-15	August 8-10
Oslo	June 20-22	August 15-17
Madrid	June 27-29	August 22-24

Report
89-63
Business Report (Continued)

¶ **Religion, Values, and Ethics.** While we can recognize the difficult challenge presented by language differences, this category (religion, values, and ethics) is in some ways the area that can bring about the most serious breakdowns in relations with those from other cultures.

¶ The very nature of religious beliefs suggests that this is a delicate area, especially for those involved in business transactions in foreign countries. Also, religious beliefs affect the consumption of certain products throughout the world. Examples are tobacco, liquor, pork, and coffee.

¶ Values are a reflection of religious beliefs for most people. We have previously heard of references to right and wrong as applied to the ideals and customs of a society. Values relate to a range of similar topics, and they may pertain to areas such as cleanliness, education, health care, and criminal justice. Such values are often very personal and as such can have a variety of interpretations. The more interpretations there are, the more likely it is that miscommunication will occur.

¶ Ethics can be considered as standards of conduct that reflect moral beliefs as applied to both one's personal life and one's business life.

¶ Delaney suggests that now more than ever, a code of ethics is essential within the business environment. When this code of ethics is missing or if it is not enforced, chaos and financial ruin for everyone associated are often the result.

(continued on next page)

Insert clip art related to world travel, similar to the above example.
Set the clip art width to 1 inch, set the wrap style to square, and align the clip art at the right margin, even with the first line of the first paragraph in the TENTATIVE SEMINAR SCHEDULE section.

A quality code of ethics is presently being recognized as an intrinsic and critical component in any business environment. Newspapers are filled with reports of scandalous, unconscionable, unethical behavior that has led to the downfall of otherwise successful businesses.[5]

TENTATIVE SEMINAR SCHEDULE

¶ As indicated earlier, all employees who have direct contact with people in other cultures will participate in these continuing seminars. That means that we need to have two identical three-day seminars scheduled at each site. These seminars will be conducted in the cities shown in Table 3.

(Insert Table 89-46 here)

¶ The Marketing Department is to be commended for calling our attention to the seriousness of our international communication problem. Celeste Fuhrmann, Robert Driscoll, and Han Lee also deserve our sincere thanks for their planning efforts for implementing the intercultural communication seminars. Through their efforts, we have experienced a high level of cooperation from all departments.

¶ As can be seen, special attention is being given to the seminar topics for these in-service programs. Efforts are also being made to identify instructors and resource persons who will develop instructional strategies that will be effective, interesting, and well received by the participants. These seminars will help significantly in increasing our market share in the international market.

---

[5] Denise C. Delaney, *Business Ethics and Workplace Compliance,* Empire Publishing Company, San Francisco, 2009, p. 35.

After completing Report 89-63, add three bookmarks and three hyperlinks by following these directions:

1. Add the first bookmark to Table 1 in the table title on page 4 of the report. Add a text hyperlink to the words "Table 1" found on page 3, last paragraph, to link to this bookmark.
2. Add the second bookmark to Table 2 in the table title on page 4 of the report. Add a text hyperlink to the word "topics" found on page 8, last paragraph, to link to this bookmark.
3. Add the third bookmark to Table 3 in the table title on page 7 of the report. Add a text hyperlink to "seminars," found on page 2, second paragraph, to link to this bookmark.

Formal Report Project—E

90

Goals

- Type at least 45wpm/5′/5e.
- Correctly use Word's feature to insert a cover page.
- Correctly format a cover page, a table of contents, and a bibliography.
- Successfully complete a Progress and Proofreading Check with zero errors on the first scored attempt.

A. WARMUP

alphabet	1	The wizard's main job was to vex the chimps quickly in fog.
number/symbol	2	jjoy@aol.com 66% (Ott & Poe) 5/8 Out! $2.16 *et al. #73-490
easy	3	Did the fiendish old men fight a duel down by the lakeside?

Skillbuilding

B. 12-SECOND SPEED SPRINTS

Take three 12-second timed writings on each line.

4 We may take a number of maps to aid us when we visit there.
5 Alan may then take apart both of the toys out on the lanai.
6 The eight old books are to be thrown into the fields today.
7 Andy will use eight hand signals if he is able to see them.
' ' ' ' 5 ' ' ' ' 10 ' ' ' ' 15 ' ' ' ' 20 ' ' ' ' 25 ' ' ' ' 30 ' ' ' ' 35 ' ' ' ' 40 ' ' ' ' 45 ' ' ' ' 50 ' ' ' ' 55 ' ' ' ' 60

C. TECHNIQUE PRACTICE: SHIFT KEY

Type each line 2 times. After striking the capitalized letter, return the Shift Key finger immediately to home-row position.

8 Ann Bonn asked for lunch. Colin Dix and Elaine Fochs moved.
9 Glen Hans filed as Iris James typed. Kay Lee talked loudly.
10 Maya Nevins and Orin Parks tried. Quinn Roberts lost a bet.
11 Skye Tynch sat. Uriah Vin and Winn Xung ate. Yates Zyd hid.

Take two 5-minute timed writings.

Goal: At least 45wpm/5'/5e

D. 5-MINUTE TIMED WRITING

Anyone with a supervisory position will occasionally 11
have to deal with a problem employee. If you learn to deal 23
with this type of worker in a good way, it will benefit 34
everyone within the organization. 41

As a manager, you should address the problem as soon 51
as you are made aware of it. However, if you are extremely 63
upset, it may be best to wait until you calm down and have 75
time to plan what you will say. Avoid using an approach 86
based on reaction, which can often be ineffective and too 98
emotional. Speaking up too quickly might bring you some 109
unwanted results. 113

When you talk to an employee, be sure you get to the 123
real issue. Present the facts and tell the employee exactly 135
what he or she is doing wrong on the job. Do not express 147
your own personal opinion. You need to present a positive 158
and mutually fair solution to the employee in question to 170
solve a problem. 173

At the end of the meeting, ask the person to explain 184
his or her problems to you and the changes that are needed. 196
By following this procedure, you know everyone understands 208
what is happening. Set up a time to meet in a few days to 220
follow up with this person. 225

1 | 2 | 3 | 4 | 5 | 6 | 7 | 8 | 9 | 10 | 11 | 12

Formatting

E. WORD PROCESSING: COVER PAGE—INSERT

GO TO Word Manual

Study Lesson 90 in your Word Manual. Complete all of the shaded steps while at your computer. Then format the documents that follow.

Document Processing

Report 90-64 Cover Page

Create a cover page for Report 89-63 using the Insert Cover Page feature in Word. Use the following information to complete the cover page:

- Select a suitable cover page from the Word gallery that includes (1) company name, (2) report title, (3) author, and (4) name. Delete any extra elements on the page.
- Type `CanCom Inc.` as the company name.
- Type `INTERCULTURAL SEMINARS` as the document title.
- Delete the document subtitle.
- Type `Heath R. Watkins` as the author name.
- Use the current year.
- Delete the company address.

Report
90-65
Table of Contents

Create a table of contents for Report 89-63 as a separate document. Use the illustration that follows as an example. The table of contents shown is incomplete. You must refer to Report 89-63 to compose and complete all of the entries for the table of contents. Make these changes:

1. Type the title in Calibri 14 pt. Bold. A title style will be applied later to conform with the title in your report.
2. Refer to Report 89-63 to compose and type the table of contents. The entries should include all side headings and paragraph headings from the report, as well as the appropriate page numbers for each heading.
3. Type the side headings in all-caps at the left margin.
4. Type the paragraph headings in upper- and lowercase, indented 0.5 inch from the left margin.
5. When you are finished typing the table of contents, apply the Title style to "CONTENTS."

Use a Title style for CONTENTS.

CONTENTS

REFER TO Reference Manual

R-7D: Table of Contents

Report
90-66
Bibliography

Type the bibliography for Report 89-63, shown on page 367, as a separate document using standard format. Follow these steps:

1. Type the title in Calibri 14-pt. Bold. A title style will be applied later to conform with the title in your report.
2. Type the bibliography in standard format.
3. When you are finished typing the bibliography, apply the Title style to "BIBLIOGRAPHY."

Use a Title style for BIBLIOGRAPHY.

REFER TO Reference Manual

R-9B: Bibliography

Progress and Proofreading Check

Documents designated as Proofreading Checks serve as a check of your proofreading skill. Your goal is to have zero typographical errors when the GDP software first scores the document.

BIBLIOGRAPHY

Boucher, Sandra, "Cultural Comparisons in E-Commerce," January 17, 2010, <http://www.ecommerce.com/news.htm>, accessed on February 23, 2010.

Chernov, Vasily, Yoshifumi Uda, and Deepak Kapoor, *The Dynamics of Intercultural Seminars,* Gateway Publishing, St. Louis, 2009.

Delaney, Denise C., *Business Ethics and Workplace Compliance*, Empire Publishing Company, New York, 2009, p. 35.

Fruehauf, Faye, and Chao Chang, "Communication Across Cultures," *International Business World,* April 2010, pp. 33-47.

Matthews, Craig, *Comparing Cultural Differences*, Grant Publishing Company, Los Angeles, 2010, p. 37.

Finalize the report project:

- Proofread all the pages for format and typing errors.
- Assemble the pages in this order: cover page, table of contents, body, bibliography, and a blank page for a back cover sheet.
- Staple the report pages in the upper-left corner.

Strategies for Career Success

Business Communication

There are five components to the communication process, whether written or oral. The sender is the person who initiates the communication process. The message is the information that needs to be communicated (for example, "There will be a meeting at . . ."). The channel is the method for transmitting the message (for example, e-mail, letter, memo, or orally). The audience is the person(s) who receives the message. Feedback is the response given to the sender by the audience that enables the sender to determine if the message was received as intended.

The most effective communication within companies must flow not only downward but also upward.

Your Turn: Suppose you send an e-mail to 20 people in your department announcing a meeting to discuss your company's new policy on flextime. Who is the sender? What is the message? What is the channel you use to transmit the message? Who is the audience? What is the ultimate feedback?

UNIT 19

Medical Office Documents

Medical Office Documents—A

91

Goals

- Demonstrate improved speed and accuracy while typing.
- Demonstrate acceptable language arts skills in colon and period usage.
- Correctly format a business letter, a boxed table, and a memo.

A. WARMUP

alphabet	1	`Back in June we delivered oxygen equipment of the odd size.`
concentration	2	`counterinsurgencies distinguishableness nonrepresentational`
easy	3	`A problem with the old chapel at the lake is its odd shape.`

Skillbuilding

B. MAP+: ALPHABET

Follow the GDP software directions for this exercise to improve keystroking accuracy.

C. PROGRESSIVE PRACTICE: ALPHABET

Follow the GDP software directions for this exercise to improve keystroking speed.

Language Arts

Study the rules at the right.

D. PUNCTUATION

RULE
: explanatory material

Use a colon to introduce explanatory material that follows an independent clause.

The computer satisfies three criteria: speed, cost, and power.
But: The computer satisfies the three criteria of speed, cost, and power.
Remember this: only one coupon is allowed per customer.

Note: An independent clause can stand alone as a complete sentence. Do not capitalize the word following the colon.

RULE
. polite request

Use a period to end a sentence that is a polite request.

Will you please call me if I can be of further assistance.

Note: Consider a sentence a polite request if you expect the reader to respond by doing as you ask rather than by giving a yes-or-no answer.

Edit each sentence to correct any errors.

4 We need the following items, pens, pencils, and paper.

5 May I suggest that you send the report by Tuesday?

6 These are some of your colleagues: Bill, Mary, and Ann.

7 Would you please pay my bills when I am on vacation?

8 Our flag is these three colors; red, white, and blue.

9 Would you please start my car to warm it up for me.

10 One thing is certain: We will be busy that day.

Document Processing

Situation: Today is September 1. You work for Bayfield Hospital in Eugene, Oregon. For the purposes of this simulation, your name will be Carrie N. Garrison. Your e-mail address is cgarrison@bayfield.org, and you use *cg* as your reference initials in correspondence.

For the next five days, you will prepare documents for several units within the hospital—Admissions, Billing, Dermatology, Oncology, and Surgery. You will also format various documents, such as correspondence and medical reports, for these units.

You will spend your first day working for Brenda T. Atwood in the Admissions Office, preparing documents that appear in your in-basket. Proofread your work carefully, and check for spelling, punctuation, grammar, and formatting errors so that your documents are mailable.

Correspondence 91-85
Business Letter in Block Style

September 1, 20-- | Ms. Diane R. Williamson | 3727 Rambling Drive | Springfield, OR 97477 | Dear Ms. Williamson:

¶ Thank you for contacting us and considering us as your primary care provider. We are confident that you will be pleased with our services and our patient care, and we look forward to many years of serving your health needs.

¶ Now that you have made your final selection, we would like you to complete the enclosed Patient Information form. As you can see, the form asks mostly for personal information so that we can contact you or your employer if necessary. In addition, the form requests the following information: the name, address, and telephone number of your insurance company and your insurance policy number. Could you please return the form by Wednesday of next week.

: explanatory material

. polite request

¶ Again, welcome to Bayfield Hospital! If there is any additional information we can provide about our services, do not hesitate to call us at 541-555-4400 or e-mail me at batwood@bayfield.org.

Sincerely, | Brenda T. Atwood | Admissions Manager | cg | Enclosure

Table
91-47
Boxed Table

Create a patient information form using the illustration below and these steps:

1. Insert a table with 1 column and 15 rows.
2. Split cells as shown to provide room for individual entries.
3. Type the information as shown.
4. Type the headings in Cambria 14 pt., and the remaining text in Calibri 12 pt.
5. Bold the information in Rows 1, 7, 11, and 15.
6. Apply 25 percent shading to Rows 1, 7, 11, and 15.
7. Manually adjust the width of the cells so that they appear similar to those shown in the illustration.

↓1X

Cambria 14 pt

↓1X

↓1X

Calibri 12 pt

PATIENT INFORMATION		
Date:		
Name (last, first):		Birth Date:
Street Address:		Phone:
City:	State:	ZIP:
E-Mail:		
EMPLOYER INFORMATION		
Employer:		
Street Address:		Phone:
City:	State:	ZIP:
INSURANCE INFORMATION		
Name of Company:		
Address:		
Phone:	Policy Number:	
Signature:	**Date:**	

Correspondence
91-86
Memo

MEMO TO: All Employees / FROM: Lucille R. Medford / DATE: September 1, 20-- / SUBJECT: Flu Shot

¶ Next week Bayfield Hospital will make flu shots available for all employees. If you would like to schedule a flu shot, call one of these nurses: R.N. Tim Bradford at Extension 224 or R.N. Karen Fishburn at Extension 228.

: explanatory material

¶ The clinic will be open from 10 a.m. to 2 p.m., Monday through Friday, for company employees. If you cannot schedule a flu shot during these times, they will also be available during the week of October 10. During that week, shots will be administered on an appointment basis only.

¶ If you would like to schedule flu shots for any of your dependents, the charge will be $10 per person. Flu shots for your dependents will be scheduled only during the October 10 session. Could you please have any of your dependents schedule their flu shots no later than October 5.

. polite request

cg

Keyboarding Connection

Capturing an Image from the Internet

Would you like to copy an image or graphic from the Internet? It's easy!

Point the mouse pointer to the image or graphic and press the right mouse button. When the shortcut menu appears, choose Save Picture As (or Save Image As). The Save Picture dialog box appears. Select the appropriate drive and name the file if necessary. Click Save. The image is usually saved with a .gif, .jpg, or .bmp file extension. To insert the image into a Word document, select the Insert tab, choose Picture, locate the file, and click Insert. You also could right-click the image, choose Copy, and then click the Paste button in Word.

Remember that images on the Internet are copyrighted and cannot be used without permission and possibly payment. This is especially important for business communication. Be sure to check the Web site for information about copyright and usage before you copy images or graphics.

Your Turn: Conduct a Web search, and locate an image or graphic to save. Right-click the image, choose Save Picture As, name the file, and save the image. Insert the image into a word processing document.

Medical Office Documents—B

92

Goals

- Type at least 46wpm/5′/5e.
- Correctly use Word's tab set feature to set and use tabs within a table.
- Correctly format a business report and a predesigned table.

A. WARMUP

alphabet	Jay visited back home and gazed upon a brown fox and quail.
one hand	exceed kimono ads mop geared opinion cast onion weave plump
easy	Jan and her son may make a bowl of fish and a cup of cocoa.

Skillbuilding

B. SUSTAINED PRACTICE: ALTERNATE-HAND WORDS

Take a 1-minute timed writing on the boxed paragraph to establish your base speed. Then take a 1-minute timed writing on the following paragraph. As soon as you equal or exceed your base speed on this paragraph, move to the next, more difficult paragraph.

A downturn in world fuel prices signals a lower profit 11
for giant oil firms. In fact, most downtown firms might 22
see the usual sign of tight credit and other problems. The 34
city must get down to business and make plans in the fall. 46

The hungry turkeys ate eight bushels of corn that were 11
given to them by our next-door neighbors. They also drank 23
the eight bowls of water that were left in the yard. All in 35
all, the birds caused quite a bit of chaos early that day. 46

A debate on what to do about that extra acreage in the 10
desert dragged on for four hours. One problem is what the 22
effect may be of moving the ancient ruins to a much safer 34
place. City officials must always protect our environment. 45

Molly was dressed in a plain pink dress at the annual 11
meeting that was taking place at the hotel in Tempe later 23
that last week in September. The agenda included four very 34
controversial topics that have often generated much debate. 46

1 | 2 | 3 | 4 | 5 | 6 | 7 | 8 | 9 | 10 | 11 | 12

Take two 5-minute timed writings.

Goal: At least 46wpm/5'/5e

C. 5-MINUTE TIMED WRITING

```
     The first impression you make on a job interview will  11
be a lasting one, and you will want it to be favorable. A   23
safe choice is to dress conservatively. If you have time,   34
find out what people who are currently employed at this     45
company wear to work. You can acquire this information by   57
simply calling the human resources office. Or, you could    68
observe what the current employees are wearing when you     80
pick up a job application from a company.                   88
     As you plan the details of your appearance before your 99
job interview, be cognizant of all the details. You will   110
want to present a neat and clean appearance. Your clothing 122
should be clean and very neatly pressed. Your hair and your 134
nails should be neatly groomed, and your shoes should be   146
clean and polished. You should use only a small amount of  157
perfume or cologne and wear only basic jewelry.            167
     Next, plan to arrive for the appointment in time to   177
make a check of your appearance before the interview.      188
     Your appearance may not be the sole factor that will  199
secure the job, but it will help you make a positive first 211
impression. Remember to dress for the position you would   222
like rather than the position you have.                    230
    1 | 2 | 3 | 4 | 5 | 6 | 7 | 8 | 9 | 10 | 11 | 12
```

Formatting

D. WORD PROCESSING: TABLE—TAB

GO TO Word Manual

Study Lesson 92 in your Word Manual. Complete all of the shaded steps while at your computer. Then format the documents that follow.

Document Processing

Situation: Today is September 2, the second day of your assignment at Bayfield Hospital. Today you are assigned to the Billing Office, where you will complete documents related to the activities in that office. Your first assignment is to prepare a report describing the billing procedure at Bayfield Hospital.

Report
92-67
Business Report

BAYFIELD BILLING PROCESS

September 2, 20--

¶ The billing process at Bayfield hospital will be under going a review during *the month of* October. Our last billing review was conducted 3 years ago. This report ~~will explain~~ *explains* how fees are determined, how transactions are ~~being~~ recorded, how payments are made, and how overdue accounts are collected.

(continued on next page)

Determining Fees

¶ Fees that a physician charges for service should be fair both to the patients that are under his or her care and to the Medical Profession. A doctors' fees should be based on the following criteria:

- The amount of time involved in providing the service
- The level of skill required in providing the service
- The degree of expertise required to interpret the results of the service provided

¶ Fees should be identified in a schedule fee that lists doctor's and patient's names, procedures performed, and the charges assessed for those procedures. The patient's fee schedule should be made available us if it is requested. If patients inquire about the amount of the fee, an estimate should be given to the patient. In all instances, this estimate should not be made available to the patient before treatment has begun. An example of a fee schedule currently used by bayfield is shown in Table 1.

Apply a 25 percent shading to Row 2.

Bayfield Heart Clinic **1061 N. 3rd Place** **Eugene, OR 97477**				
Date	**Doctor**	**Patient**	**Procedure**	**Fee**
02/02/--	Crispman	Diane Crowley	Place stent	1,875
02/04/--	Sanchez	Diane Crowley	Ultrasound intracoronary	2,911
02/04/--	Crispman	Diane Crowley	Catheterize left heart	540
06/02/--	Crispman	Diane Crowley	Imaging, pulmonary angio	105
02/07/--	Sanchez	Diane Crowley	Electrocardiogram	165
Total Fees				$5,596

RECORDING TRANSACTIONS

¶ A record of all patient visits must be maintained. A charge slip should be used to record procedures. The charge slip includes information such as a check list of all procedures; a checklist of all diagnosis; space for additional information; and an area for all charges, payments, and balances. As the doctor performs procedures annotations and changes are made to the charge slip so that it is kept current. The

(continued on next page)

charge slip should be attached to the patients' chart. When all procedures have been completed, a copy of the charge slip is sent to the patient to indicate the charges incurred during the patient's visit.

MAKING PAYMENT ARRANGEMENTS

¶ A patient's bill can be paid by one of the following methods:

- a patient can pay the bill by cash or check at the conclusion of the visit.
- A patient can pay amounts of the bill at designated times, weekly or monthly.
- A bill (statement) can be sent to the patient at the conclusion of the visit.
- A bill can be sent to the Health Insurance Carrier.

Regardless of which method of payment is used, the patient will not be assessed any overdue charges prior to 30 days after service has been rendered.

COLLECTING OVERDUE Accounts

¶ There are a number of reasons why a patient might not pay a bill. Whatever the reason, however steps must be taken to collect accounts delinquent. If you find that an account is overdue, here are some steps you can take to resolve the issue:

1. Attach a reminder when the bill is sent if payment is thirty days or more over due.
2. Call the patient if payment is received after the reminder is sent.
3. Attach a personal note to a statement that is over due, possibly as long as sixty days.
4. Make one further attempt to telephone the patient for payment.
5. Send a collection letter for payment. the letter should be firm but friendly.
6. Establish a payment plan to assist the patient in making payments on a schedule.
7. Go to court for legal action, or turn the account over to a collection agency.

We certainly do not wish to take legal action to collect any of our overdue accounts. Please make every attempt to collect overdue accounts so that we can avoid this step.

Table
92-48
Predesigned Table

Create a boxed table using a predesigned style. Use the following guidelines to create the table:

1. Apply a table style of your choice.
2. After the style has been applied, verify that the bolding shown in the illustration is used.
3. Remove any automatic hyperlink that might appear for the e-mail address in Row 1.

18 pt **BILLING STATEMENT** 14 pt **Allison Price, M.D.** 12 pt ↓ **Bayfield Hospital** **254 Carmel Avenue** **Eugene, OR 97440** ↓2X **Telephone: 541-555-3434** →tab **E-Mail: billing@bayfield.org** ↓1X				
↓1X **Patient:** →tab Karen S. Fairchild **Address:** 701 Maple Street **City, State, and ZIP:** Eugene, OR 97438 ↓1X				
Date	**Description**	**Charge**	**Payment**	**Balance**
7/18/--	EKG	$235.00	$125.00	$110.00
7/21/--	Laboratory work	175.00	50.00	125.00
7/28/--	X-ray	110.00	0.00	110.00
8/04/--	Laboratory work	80.00	50.00	30.00
8/18/--	Office medical	135.00	100.00	35.00
Total Due →right tab **$410.00**				

Strategies for Career Success

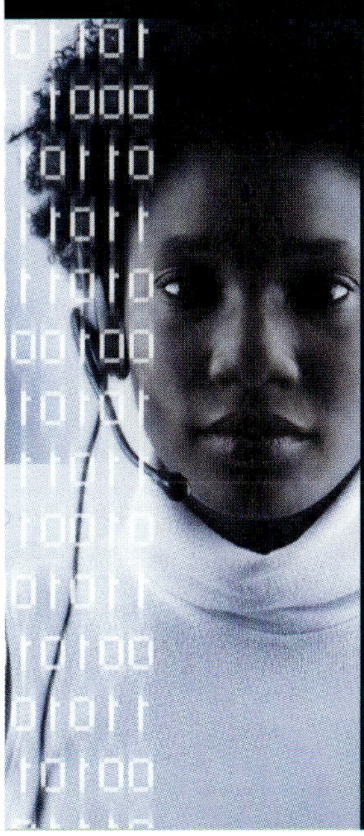

Enhancing Your Presentation With Visual Aids

Visual aids capture people's attention while increasing their retention. Use visual aids to present an outline of your presentation, explain detailed technical or numerical information, and summarize your key points.

Be selective. Don't bombard your audience with visuals. Your visual aids should support and clarify your verbal presentation. Consider the size of your audience and the size of the room before selecting your visuals. Audiences have little patience for visuals that are too small to read or too busy. Types of visual aids are slides, photographs, flip charts, maps, flowcharts, handouts, and computer graphics including tables, graphs, and charts. You can have printed visual aids if the room is small, or you can use a multimedia projector that attaches to a laptop computer to project your presentation. This is also useful for Web conferencing, so that people in different locations also can see your visual aids.

Limit the amount of information on a visual. Use simple graphics. Continue displaying the current visual until you are ready to discuss the next one. Always keep the projector on during your presentation.

Your Turn: In what ways would your visual aids differ if your audience had 10 people or 110?

UNIT 19 LESSON

Medical Office Documents—C

93

Goals

- Demonstrate improved speed and accuracy while typing.
- Demonstrate acceptable proofreading skills by editing copy.
- Correctly format a business letter and a business report.

A. WARMUP

alphabet
1 The quixotic knights' wives were found on jumpy old zebras.

practice: *s* and *d*
2 sad Sid deeds desks dosed dudes dusts sheds sides soda suds

easy
3 The ivory tusk may be a key to their ancient rogue rituals.

Skillbuilding

B. MAP+: NUMBERS

Follow the GDP software directions for this exercise to improve keystroking accuracy.

PPP PRETEST » PRACTICE » POSTTEST

PRETEST

Take a 1-minute timed writing.

C. PRETEST: Discrimination Practice

4 Did the new clerk join the golf team? James indicated 11
5 to me that Beverly invited her prior to last Wednesday. He 23
6 believes she must give you a verbal commitment at once. We 35
7 should convince her to join because she is a gifted golfer. 46

1 | 2 | 3 | 4 | 5 | 6 | 7 | 8 | 9 | 10 | 11 | 12

PRACTICE

Speed Emphasis:
If you made no more than 1 error on the Pretest, type each *individual* line 2 times.

Accuracy Emphasis:
If you made 2 or more errors, type each *group* of lines (as though it were a paragraph) 2 times.

D. PRACTICE: Left Hand

8 vbv bevy verb bevel vibes breve viable braves verbal beaver
9 wew went week weans weigh weave wedges thawed weaker beware
10 ded dent need deals moved ceded heeded debate edging define
11 fgf guff gift flags foggy gaffe forget gifted guffaw fights

E. PRACTICE: Right Hand

12 klk kale look kilts lakes knoll likely kettle kernel lacked
13 uyu buys your gummy dusty young unduly tryout uneasy jaunty
14 oio oils roil toils onion point oriole soiled ration joined
15 jhj jell heed eject wheat joked halved jalopy heckle jigsaw

POSTTEST

Repeat the Pretest timed writing and compare performance.

F. POSTTEST: Discrimination Practice

Language Arts

Edit the paragraph to correct any errors.

G. PROOFREADING

Suprising as it may seem, thcir has been a good deal of interest in comunicating with a computer through the human voice for about fourty years. Researchers haev spent millions ofdollars in hteir efforts to improve voice input tecknology. It is likly that in the next decade we will see many use ful applications in busness and in education.

Document Processing

Situation: Today is September 3, the third day of your assignment. You will work in a specialty area—the Dermatology Unit. Dermatology is a branch of science dealing with the skin and its structure, functions, and diseases.

Correspondence 93-87

Business Letter in Modified-Block Style

September 3, 20-- | Dr. Avery R. Childress | Professor of Medical Science | Kingswood General Hospital | 2832 Lincoln Street | Eugene, OR 97403-2512 | Dear Dr. Childress:

¶ We would like to invite you as one of six dermatology specialists to address the students in our medical science class on the topic of dermatology. We have the following dates open for your presentation: November 5, November 12, and December 10. The time frame we have scheduled is from 10 a.m. to noon or 2:30 p.m. to 4:30 p.m. on these three dates.

¶ Would it be possible for you to speak on the topic of skin rashes and their causes and treatments? Naturally, we would appreciate any comments based on the release of your latest article in the August 15 edition of the *Journal of Marketing Research.*

¶ We would be honored to include you in our program. If you agree to one of the above dates for your presentation, I will send you further information on how to reach the auditorium where your presentation will be held. I am enclosing a speaker's form that you can fill out to designate any presentation needs you have (Internet connection, computer, handouts, etc.).

Sincerely yours, | Stephanie Hill, M.D. | cg | Enclosure | PS: Please let me know no later than September 15 if you will be able to participate in our professional seminar.

Report
93-68
Business Report

COMMON SKIN RASHES
Their Causes and Cures
Dr. Stephanie Hill

¶ Skin rashes are caused by many different things. They are frequently recognized by symptoms of blistering, dryness, itching, reddening, or scabbing of the skin. Some of the more common ailments that fall into the category of skin rashes are eczema, dermatitis, and psoriasis. This paper discusses these three common types of skin rashes.

ECZEMA

¶ Eczema, also known as atopic dermatitis, causes the skin to appear red and blotchy. The disease can occur at any age, from infants to adults, but it typically occurs from infancy to childhood. It affects about 3 percent of the United States population. There are two types of eczema—atopic eczema and hand eczema.

¶ **Atopic Eczema.** Atopic eczema is caused by contact with woolen clothing, by heat, by detergents, by the house dust mite, and by stress.

¶ **Hand Eczema.** Hand eczema is caused by detergents, grease, oils, sensitive skin, and too much exposure to wet work.

DERMATITIS

¶ Dermatitis is often referred to as contact dermatitis. Some of the more common substances that cause dermatitis are cosmetics, jewelry, household and industrial chemicals, perfumes, plants, rubber, and soaps. Contact dermatitis is further classified as either allergic contact dermatitis or irritant contact dermatitis.

¶ **Allergic Contact Dermatitis.** This skin rash occurs after contact is made with certain substances, called allergens. The rash occurs as a reaction of the body's immune system to expel the allergen from the skin. Common allergens are often found in jewelry and cosmetics metals.

¶ **Irritant Contact Dermatitis.** This skin rash does not require exposure to an allergen but can develop when you come in contact with substances such as detergents, oils, skin cleansers, and solvents.

PSORIASIS

¶ Psoriasis is a chronic skin disease characterized by skin scaling and inflammation. This disease affects about 5.5 million people in the United States. It occurs in all age groups and affects both men and women. When psoriasis develops, patches of skin redden and become covered with scales. The skin then cracks and may cause severe irritation in places like the face, scalp, elbows, knees, and lower back.

¶ It is believed that psoriasis is a disorder of the immune system in which there are not enough white blood cells to help protect the body against infection and diseases of this type.

UNIT 19 LESSON

Medical Office Documents—D

94

Goals

- Type at least 46wpm/5'/5e.
- Correctly format a ruled table, a business letter, and a predesigned table.

A. WARMUP

alphabet	1	Jeb quickly drove a few extra miles on the glazed pavement.
frequent digraphs	2	on bon con none noon don ion one son ton won onto moon font
easy	3	When did the busy men fix the two fishbowls for the busman?

Skillbuilding

B. PROGRESSIVE PRACTICE: NUMBERS

Follow the GDP software directions for this exercise to improve keystroking speed.

C. TECHNIQUE PRACTICE: BACKSPACE KEY

Type each line 2 times, using your Sem finger to strike the BACKSPACE key.

The ← symbol means to backspace. For example, type *mar*, backspace, and type *p*, thus changing *mar* to *map*.

```
4 mar←p hex←y woe←k wow←n cot←p wag←n fro←y tea←n tar←p
5 has←y mad←n rid←p tot←p egg←o dug←n his←p gag←y box←y
6 cow←y tie←n nub←n via←m par←n has←y dab←y hot←p pie←n
7 ton←e why←o pot←p gee←l the←y job←y pub←n she←y bat←y
```

Take two 5-minute timed writings.

Goal: At least 46wpm/5'/5e

D. 5-MINUTE TIMED WRITING

Innovative technology may bring new problems for our 11
homes and businesses. A rising shift to use a cell phone is 23
causing many people to look at the etiquette of cell phone 35
usage. Are there times and places where a cell phone should 47
not be used? 49
People want to be able to stay in touch, no matter 60
where they are or what they are doing. However, in some 71
places, cell phone usage is inappropriate or not allowed. 82
For example, you would not want a ringing cell call to 94
disrupt the entire production if you are enjoying a concert 106
or play. As a consideration to everyone in the audience, 117
the management may make an announcement asking audience 128
members to turn off their cell phones or pagers before the 140
production begins. Making this request gives everyone the 152
chance to enjoy the show. 157
Often you see someone driving a car while talking on 168
cell phone. Talking on the phone while you are driving is 179
not a good idea. When you are talking on the phone and not 191
concentrating on driving, you may cause an accident. If you 203
are driving a vehicle in traffic, your full focus should be 215
on the road. Be cognizant of this. Do not use your cell 226
phone when driving. 230

1 | 2 | 3 | 4 | 5 | 6 | 7 | 8 | 9 | 10 | 11 | 12

Keyboarding Connection

Coping With Spam

Have you received those heaps of unsolicited e-mail, commonly known as spam? Everyone wants to get rid of those irritating online sales pitches. Unfortunately, there is not much you can do about them. You can make use of various filters, but they aren't foolproof.

If you end up on a spammer's list and receive a courteous e-mail asking you to reply if you wish to be removed from the list, *do not reply.* The spammer may interpret your reply to mean that you read e-mail, and you may be put on the hot list. The best action is to try to avoid divulging your e-mail address to spammers. Most importantly, use an alternate account if posting in any kind of online forum.

Your Turn: Other than relying on spam filters, are there any other actions you have taken to reduce the number of unsolicited e-mails you receive?

Document Processing

Situation: Today is September 4, the fourth day of your assignment. Today you are working in the Oncology Unit. Oncology is a branch of science dealing with the study of tumors. You will begin by typing this ruled table.

Table
94-49
Ruled Table

Proofread the medical terms very carefully.

DESCRIPTIONS AND TREATMENTS OF ADULT BRAIN TUMORS ↓1X

Types of Tumors	Description and Treatment
Astrocytomas	Tumors that start in brain cells. Treatment includes surgery, chemotherapy, and radiation. ↓1X
Brain stem gliomas	Tumors located in the bottom part of the brain, which connects to the spinal cord. Treatment includes radiation and biological therapy.
Cerebellar astrocytomas	Tumors that occur in the area of the brain called the cerebellum. Treatment is similar to that for astrocytomas.
Craniopharyngiomas	Tumors that occur near the pituitary gland. Treatment includes surgery and radiation.
Oligodendrogliomas	Tumors that begin in brain cells that provide support and nourishment for the cells that transmit nerve impulses. Treatment includes surgery, chemotherapy, and radiation.

Correspondence
94-88
Business Letter in Block Style

September 4, 20-- | Dr. Victor D. Samuels | Oregon Medical Center | 782 Olive Street | Eugene, OR 97404-1410 | Dear Vic: | Subject: George M. Collins

¶ On August 21 I examined Mr. Collins and discovered a Stage 1A, Cleaved B cell follicular lymphoma in the right inguinal region. I conducted a surgical excision and recommended radiation therapy. Mr. Collins completed his radiation therapy three weeks ago and feels well at this time. He has no complaints, his appetite and energy are normal, and he looks good. His weight is down seven pounds upon my recommendation three weeks ago that he lose some excess weight.

¶ There are no abdominal or inguinal lymph nodes to his scrotal sac exam. There are, however, three- to four-millimeter nodes in the left inguinal region that appear totally unchanged from his original exam on August 21. His lungs are clear, his heartbeat is regular, the liver and spleen are not enlarged, and there are no palpable masses.

¶ It appears to me that Mr. Collins has recovered satisfactorily from his radiation therapy. He has requested a second opinion, and I am therefore recommending that he make an appointment with you at his earliest convenience. We will prepare a referral for Mr. Collins and forward it to your office by Friday of this week.

Sincerely, | Joan T. Rashid, M.D. | cg

Table
94-50
Predesigned Table

Open the file for Table 94-49 and make the following changes:

1. Add the following two entries to the table so that they appear in alphabetical order:
   - `Gliomas`
     `The general name for tumors that come from the supportive tissue of the brain; for example, astrocytomas or oligodendrogliomas. They may be benign or malignant. Treatment includes surgery and radiation.`
   - `Plasmacytoma`
     `Under a microscope these tumors are round in shape; thus, they are called round cell tumors. They can appear as one single tumor or as multiple tumors and are usually located on the thoracic or lumbar areas of the spine. Treatment includes radiotherapy.`
2. Apply a table style of your choice.
3. After the style has been applied, verify that the text in Rows 1 and 2 is bolded.

Strategies for Career Success

Letter of Resignation

When you plan to leave a job, you should write a resignation letter, memo, or e-mail to your supervisor and send a copy to Human Resources. Follow these guidelines to write an effective resignation.

Start a resignation letter positively, regardless of why you are leaving. Include how you benefited from working for the company, or compliment your coworkers.

In the middle section, state why you are leaving. Provide an objective, factual explanation and avoid accusations. Your resignation becomes part of your permanent company record. If it is hostile, it could backfire on you when you need references. Stipulate the date your resignation becomes effective (providing at least a two-week notice).

End the letter of resignation with a closing of goodwill (for example, "I wish all of you the best in the future").

Your Turn: List the benefits of *not* burning your bridges (showing anger or bitterness) in your letter of resignation.

Medical Office Documents—E

95

Goals

- Demonstrate improved speed and accuracy while typing.
- Demonstrate acceptable language arts skills by composing an e-mail message.
- Correctly format an open table, a business report, and an e-mail message.
- Successfully complete a Progress and Proofreading Check with zero errors on the first scored attempt.

A. WARMUP

alphabet	1	Four European jackdaws loved my big sphinx of quartz glass.
number/symbol	2	edow@msn.com 38% Ely & May (6/9) Wow! $4.12 *ibid. #573-012
easy	3	He may go with us to the giant dock down by the handy lake.

Skillbuilding

B. 12-SECOND SPEED SPRINTS

Take three 12-second timed writings on each line.

```
4 Glen may take apart the old robots when he comes into town.
5 Blanch may go with me to town to visit my son and his pals.
6 Due to the big quake, the city may start to move all autos.
7 Bob owns a pair of old bikes and a new car he got from dad.
  ''''5''''10'''15'''20'''25'''30'''35'''40'''45'''50'''55'''60
```

C. PACED PRACTICE

Follow the GDP software directions for this exercise to improve keystroking speed and accuracy.

Language Arts

D. COMPOSING AN E-MAIL MESSAGE

Compose an e-mail message to Dr. Natalie Benson, whose e-mail address is nbenson@bayfield.org, informing Dr. Benson of the appointments you have scheduled for Tuesday, September 29. The first appointment is with James Mitchell, who is coming for his annual physical—make this appointment at 9 a.m.

The second appointment is with Karen McDaniels, who is going to have her blood pressure and cholesterol checked. She will see Dr. Benson at 10 a.m. The final appointment is with Mary Ann Bradley, who will see the doctor about flu symptoms. Make her appointment at 2:30 p.m. Be sure you use an appropriate greeting, closing, and signature.

Save but do not send this e-mail message.

Document Processing

Situation: Today is September 5, the final day of your assignment, and you are working in the Surgery Unit. The specialty within this unit is knee surgery. Your first assignment is to create a table listing various medical terms and their definitions. Insert 1 blank line after each entry in Column B of the table.

Table
95-51
OpenTable

MEDICAL TERM & THEIR DEFINITIONS	
September 5, 20--	
Adenopathy	Swelling or enlargement of the lymph nodes
Auscultation	The act of listening to sounds made by the various structures as a diagnostic procedure
Cholcystectomy	Surgical removal of the gall bladder
Fibroperitonal	Related to the tissue that borders the abdominal cavity which covers most of the viscera
Enterstomy	An incision into the intestines that produces a hole in the abdoman through which the intestines are emptied
Femur	The extremely long bone of the thigh
Laparoscopy	A minimally evasive surgical technique that uses a fiber-optic instrument
Hemostasis	The arrest of bleeding
Laparotomy	Incision in to the abdominal wall
Trocar	An instrument for withdrawing fluid from a cavity

Correspondence
95-89
E-Mail Message

Hi, Dr. Sanchez:

¶ Mr. Shipman came in today with a lesion crusted in his back. Lesion was removed using 1% xylocaine with epinephrin loc. Wound was closed with 4.0 nylon suteres. stitches should be removed in aproximately 10 days. Suture should remain dry for 3 days. Mr. Walden is to call if he has questions or if problems arise.

Carrie

Carrie n. Garrison

E-mail: cgarrison@bayfield.org

phone: 541-555-3829

Report
95-69
Business Report

Progress and Proofreading Check

Documents designated as Proofreading Checks serve as a check of your proofreading skill. Your goal is to have zero typographical errors when the GDP software first scores the document.

RECOVERING FROM KNEE SURGERY

Dr. Paige Freidman

September 5, 20--

¶ Specific procedures should be followed by patients who are recovering from knee surgery. Depending on the particular surgery that was performed, postoperative needs of patients with knee replacements vary greatly. Healthy, young individuals may require only a few therapy sessions to recover from their surgery completely. Older individuals with no family or friends to help them at home may need special assistance or equipment to aid their mobility. Some patients may benefit from a short stay in a rehabilitation facility. To enhance the rate of recovery, patients should identify and address any special needs that may require attention before their operation.

¶ To promote full recovery, Bayfield Hospital has developed a coordinated pathway of physical and occupational therapy for patients' use. Patient Rehabilitation and Therapy Service (PRTS) and Bayfield Hospital have collaborated on recommending a specific sequence of procedures to follow.

¶ Prior to surgery, we recommend that patients determine any special equipment that will be required to promote recovery. Also, correct techniques should be learned for performing day-to-day activities such as getting in and out of bed, driving an automobile, taking showers, getting up from a seat, and going up and down stairs. Finally, patients need to be aware of what exercises will help facilitate their recovery.

¶ After surgery, patients must participate in physical therapy to ensure that they can:

1. Extend the knee straight or bend it past 90 degrees.
2. Place weight on the knee to test for strength and stability.
3. Use the knee without discomfort.

¶ If you have any questions regarding these procedures, do not hesitate to contact my administrative assistant, Carrie Garrison, at Extension 4400.

UNIT 20

Legal Office Documents

Legal Office Documents—A

Goals

- Type at least 47wpm/5′/5e.
- Correctly format a warranty deed, a boxed table, and an e-mail message.

A. WARMUP

alphabet — Ban all foul toxic smog which can quickly jeopardize lives.
concentration — counterinsurgencies individualistically interchangeableness
easy — Bob can use eight hand signals if he is proficient in them.

Skillbuilding

B. SUSTAINED PRACTICE: ROUGH-DRAFT

Take a 1-minute timed writing on the boxed paragraph to establish your base speed. Then take a 1-minute timed writing on the following paragraph. As soon as you equal or exceed your base speed on this paragraph, move to the next, more difficult paragraph.

Are you eating wisely? If you're like most Americans, 11
you have never been hungrier for information about food and 23
health. As medical research transforms yesterday's beliefs 35
into today's fallacies, many folks are changing their ways. 47

For example, many currant discussions have focussed on 11
the value of fiber in our deits, but did you know there are 23
two types of fiber? Oatmeal is high in soluble fiber, and 35
bran is known for it's high amount of insoluble fiber. 46

What are their diferences? Insoluble fiber adds bulk to 11
the content of the intestines, which might may ward off colon 23
cancer. Soluble fiber adds bulk to the stomachs' contents, 35
making diets feel stuffed and help reduce cholstrol. 46

Americans typicaly eat half the amount daily of fiber 11
recomended by the national cancer institute. A serving of 23
some sereals can supply up to one third of the daily quote. 35
Other first rate sources are certain fruits and vegetables. 47

1 | 2 | 3 | 4 | 5 | 6 | 7 | 8 | 9 | 10 | 11 | 12

Take two 5-minute timed writings.

Goal: At least 47wpm/5'/5e

C. 5-MINUTE TIMED WRITING

Many businesses across the country are adopting a new 11
dress code called business casual. Depending on the type of 23
place for which you work, business casual can have various 35
meanings. Most places allow their workers to dress down a 46
notch from what was expected in the past. 55
If people wore suits and ties in the past, then the 65
business casual code would allow them to stop wearing ties 77
and suit jackets. It is quite necessary for a company to 89
formulate dress code guidelines for workers to follow when 100
business casual goes into effect at the firm. 110
Surveys from a range of firms show mixed results when 121
employees were given a choice of dressing more casually. 132
Some firms feel business casual is a perk that works for 143
employees. But other firms report that job productivity 155
rates zoom down when workers are allowed to dress down. 166
More research is needed. 171
When you feel good about the way you look, you will 181
show this attitude in your performance. If your company has 193
adopted a business casual dress code, you must keep in mind 205
that business casual does not mean that you can dress in a 217
sloppy manner. A neat appearance and good grooming always 229
enhance a business casual look. 235

1 | 2 | 3 | 4 | 5 | 6 | 7 | 8 | 9 | 10 | 11 | 12

Formatting

D. LEGAL DOCUMENTS

Legal documents can be classified as either noncourt documents or court documents. Examples of noncourt documents are a warranty deed and a last will and testament. Examples of court documents are an affidavit, a summons, a complaint, and a judgment. Line numbers are added to all court documents so that any part of a document can be easily referenced.

State statutes, court rules (federal, state, appellate, and so on), and law office preferences determine the format of legal documents, including margins, line numbering, line spacing, line lengths, page numbering, indents, alignment, and bolding. Therefore, the legal documents and formatting guidelines in this unit have been designed to serve as simplified examples of acceptable legal formats.

Follow these guidelines to format the legal documents in this unit:

- Type a legal document on 8.5- by 11-inch paper.
- Use default margins on all sides.
- Use single spacing and no bold.
- Indent paragraphs 1 inch; press ENTER 2 times between paragraphs.
- For multipage legal documents, insert a centered page number at the bottom of each page, including page 1.
- For all signature lines, set a 3.25-inch left tab. Then type a continuous underscore from the 3.25-inch tab to the right margin.

Document Processing

Report
96-70
Warranty Deed

A seller who provides a warranty deed warrants (or guarantees) that he or she has full ownership of a property and has the right to sell it. The seller also guarantees all rights of the property to the buyer.

Insert a space before and after the underscore representing the date.

WARRANTY DEED ↓2X

5 underscores

→tab 1″ THIS INDENTURE, made this ____↓____ day of February, 20--, between Alicia R. Carpenter, Grantor, and Karen T. Draper, Grantee, whose post office address is 3214 Benton Blvd., Kansas City, KS 66105-2843. ↓2X

WITNESS, for and in consideration of the sum of EIGHTY-SEVEN THOUSAND and 00/100 DOLLARS ($87,000), Grantor does hereby GRANT to Grantee, all of the following real property lying in the County of Wyandotte, State of Kansas, and described as follows, to wit:

Lots Fifteen (15) and Sixteen (16), Block Sixty-three (63), Original Townsite of Kansas City, Kansas, SUBJECT TO mineral conveyances, easements, special or improvement taxes and assessment, rights-of-way, and reservations of record.

(THIS DEED IS IN FULFILLMENT OF THAT CERTAIN CONTRACT FOR DEED ENTERED INTO BY AND BETWEEN THE SAME PARTIES ON THE DATE HEREOF.)

And the said Grantor for herself, her heirs, executors and administrators, does covenant with the Grantee that she is well seized in fee of the land and premises aforesaid and has the right to sell and convey the same in manner and form aforesaid: that the same are free from all encumbrances, except assessments for special improvements which have not been certified to the County Treasurer for collection or installments of special assessments, and the above lands and premises in the possession of said Grantee, against all persons lawfully claiming or to claim the whole or any part thereof, the said Grantor will warrant and defend.

WITNESS, the hand of the Grantor. ↓2X

→ tab 3.25″ ______________________________ underscores to the right margin
Alicia R. Carpenter ↓2X

STATE OF KANSAS ↓2X

County of Wyandotte ↓2X

On this _____ day of October, 20--, before me, a notary public for said County and State, personally appeared Alicia R. Carpenter, to me known to be the person described in and who executed the foregoing instrument and acknowledged to me that she executed the same as her free act and deed.

____
Boyd H. Fraser → 6.5″ right tab Notary Public
Wyandotte County, Kansas
My Commission Expires August 21, 2015

Table
96-52
Boxed Table

Apply 25 percent shading to Row 2.

Press ENTER 1 time after each entry in Column B.

Your finished table will have different line endings for Column B when you resize the column widths to fit the contents.

WARRANTY DEED TERMINOLOGY State of Kansas	
Term	**Definition**
Appurtenance	Something attached to the land
Consideration	The value of the property
Escrow	A system of document transfer in which the document is given to a third party to hold until the conditions of the agreement have been met
Grantee	The person who is buying the property
Grantor	The person who owns the property
Mortgage	The pledge of property as security for a loan
Quitclaim	A document that transfers a property title to another
Warranty deed	A deed in which the seller forever guarantees clear title to the land

Keyboarding Connection

Transferring Text From a Web Page

Have you ever wished you could copy the text from a Web page? You can!

To select the desired text to copy, click at the beginning of the text and drag your cursor to the end of it, so all the text you want to copy is highlighted. On the Edit menu in your browser, click Copy. (Or you can right-click the selected text and click Copy.) Open your word processing document and position the cursor where you want to paste the text. In the Clipboard section of the Home tab, select Paste. The text will appear in your word processing document.

When you copy text information from the Web, you must cite the source in your document by giving information such as the URL (Web page address), Web page name, and author, if given.

Your Turn: Open a Web page. Copy some text, and paste it in a word processing document.

Correspondence
96-90
E-Mail Message

Type the e-mail below in correct format. Type Chao as the sender's name, and use the following as the writer's identification: Chao Chang | E-mail: cchang@webmail.net | Phone: 913-555-9962.

Hi, Daniel:

¶ You might recall last week that I indicated there might be a foreclosure property available and that it would be auctioned at the Wyandotte Courthouse. On January 19, 3 properties in Southern Wyandotte county will be auctioned as fore closures. These properties are located adjacent to the lots you purchased last year; I know that you would be interested in expanding your lot size with this purchase. Specifically they are located in 4 counties surrounding Wyandotte County, as follows:

1. Douglas County, Lot 9.
2. Jefferson County, Lot 15.
3. Johnson County, Lot 17.
4. Lot 23, Leavenworth County.

¶ I expect these properties will sell for $52,000 each; their excellent location may force the bidding into the $60,000 or $70,000 range. If you cannot be present for the auction but would like to place your bid on the properties, please let me know so that I can act as your agent. If you elect to do this, send me the bidding you wish to present for each of the properties. I need confirmation from you no later than January 8 so that I can register as your agent to present your bid.

Legal Office Documents—B

97

Goals

- Demonstrate improved speed and accuracy while typing.
- Demonstrate acceptable language arts skills in using semicolons.
- Correctly format a last will and testament and a business letter in block style.

A. WARMUP

alphabet	1	`I quizzed five wine experts jokingly on samples of Chablis.`
one hand	2	`garage homily sea oil seated Honolulu ever jump eager plunk`
easy	3	`Do not blame their firms for the low quantity of auto fuel.`

Skillbuilding

B. MAP+: ALPHABET

Follow the GDP software directions for this exercise to improve keystroking accuracy.

C. PROGRESSIVE PRACTICE: ALPHABET

Follow the GDP software directions for this exercise to improve keystroking speed.

Language Arts

D. SEMICOLONS

Study the rules at the right.

RULE
; no conjunction

Use a semicolon to separate two closely related independent clauses that are not connected by a conjunction (such as *and, but,* or *nor*).

Management favored the vote; stockholders did not.

But: Management favored the vote, but stockholders did not.

RULE
; series

Use a semicolon to separate three or more items in a series if any of the items already contain commas.

Staff meetings were held on Thursday, May 7; Monday, June 7; and Friday, June 12.

Note: Be sure to insert the semicolon between (not within) the items in a series.

Edit each sentence to correct any errors.

Paul will travel to Madrid, Spain; Lisbon, Portugal, and Nice, France.

Mary's gift arrived yesterday, Margie's did not.

Bring your textbook to class: I'll return it tomorrow.

The best days for the visit are Monday, May 10, Tuesday, May 18, and Wednesday, May 26.

Jan is the president; and Peter is the vice president.

Document Processing

Report 97-71
Last Will and Testament

A last will and testament is a legal document stating how a person wants his or her property distributed after death.

LAST WILL AND TESTAMENT
OF
EDUARDO D. HERNANDEZ ↓2X

I, EDUARDO D. HERNANDEZ, residing in Portales, New Mexico, do hereby make and declare this to be my Last Will and Testament, hereby revoking any and all former Wills and Codicils by me at any time heretofore made. ↓2X

ARTICLE I ↓2X

This will is made in New Mexico and shall be governed and administered according to New Mexico law, even though subject to probate or administered elsewhere. The New Mexico laws applied shall not include any principles or laws relating to conflicts of laws.

ARTICLE II

Whenever used herein, words using the singular shall include the plural, and words using the masculine shall include the feminine and neuter, and vice versa, unless the context requires otherwise.

ARTICLE III

; no conjunction

I am married, and my wife's name is Maria R. Hernandez. All references hereinafter made to "wife" or "spouse" shall refer to her and no other; if she is not my legal wife at the time of my death, then she shall be deemed for the purpose of this, my last Will and Testament, to have predeceased me. I was formerly married to Angela Sanchez, who is now deceased. There were three (3) children born of my marriage to Angela Sanchez. The names of those children are as follows: Rita Calderon, Timothy Sanchez, and Brian Sanchez.

1

(continued on next page)

ARTICLE IV

; series

If My Spouse Survives. Except as may be provided hereunder in this Article IV, if my spouse survives me, I give to my spouse all my interest in household furniture and furnishings, books, apparel, and similar personal effects; art objects, gun collections, and jewelry; sporting and recreational equipment; all other tangible property for personal use; all other like contents of my home and any vacation property that I may own or reside in on the date of my death; all animals; any motor vehicles that I may own on the date of my death; and any unexpired insurance on all such property.

ARTICLE V

If My Spouse Does Not Survive. Except as may be otherwise provided in this Article IV, if my spouse does not survive me, I give the property described above in this Article (except motor vehicles) to my children who survive me, to be divided among them as they shall agree, or in the absence of such agreement, as my Personal Representative shall determine, which determination shall be conclusive.

ARTICLE VI

If any beneficiary named or described in this Will fails to survive me for 120 hours, all the provisions in this Will shall lapse, and this Will shall be construed as though the fact were that he or she predeceased me.

ARTICLE VII

All estate, inheritance, transfer, succession, and any other taxes plus interest and penalties thereon that become payable by reason of my death upon property passing under this instrument shall be paid out of the residue of my estate without reimbursement from the recipient and without apportionment. All death taxes upon property not passing under this instrument shall be apportioned in the manner provided by law.

Insert a space before and after the underscores representing the day and the month.

IN WITNESS WHEREOF, I have hereunto affixed my hand and seal this _____ day of ____________________, 20--. ↓2X

↑ 5 underscores

20 underscores

→ tab 3.25" ______________________________ underscores to the right margin

EDUARDO D. HERNANDEZ Testator

↑ 6.5" right tab

The foregoing instrument, consisting of TWO (2) pages (this page included), was on this _____ day of ____________________, 20--, subscribed on each page and at the end thereof by Eduardo D. Hernandez, the above-named Testator and by him signed, sealed, published, and declared to be his Last Will, in the presence of us, and each of us, who thereupon, at his request, in his presence, and in the presence of each other, have hereunto subscribed our names as attesting witnesses thereto. ↓2X

34 underscores

__________________________________ residing at ______________________________ ↓2X

__________________________________ residing at ______________________________

2

Correspondence 97-91
Business Letter in Block Style

; no conjunction

April 10, 20-- | Mr. Eduardo Hernandez | 248 Oklahoma Dr. | Portales, NM 88123-3342 | Dear Mr. Hernandez: | Subject: Will provisions

¶ Your last will and testament has been drafted; it is enclosed for your review. Please review it carefully for any omissions or deletions.

Although your will has been drafted as you indicated, there are still a couple of alternative inclusions that I would ~~suggest~~ recommend:

- Do you wish to include a fiduciary summary power in the will?
- What division of estate do you wish to include for your family?

¶ These inclusions could be rather comprehensive. Therefore could we schedule a meeting for next ~~Monday~~ Tuesday to accomodate these changes? Please call my Administrative Assistant so she can put you on my calendar.

Sincerly, | Paula T. Tisdale | Attorney at Law | urs | Enclosure | c: T. Bailey, Roland, B. Wells

Strategies for Career Success

Designing a Page for Readability

A well-designed document is appealing to the eye, is easy to read, and shows you are professional and competent. Follow these simple guidelines to increase the readability of your documents.

Use white space (that is, empty space) to make material easier to read by separating it from other text. Side margins should be equal. Create white space by varying paragraph length. The first and last paragraphs should be short—three to five typed lines.

Use bulleted or numbered lists to emphasize material. Make sure all items in the list are grammatically parallel in structure. Use headings to introduce new material. Use full caps sparingly. Consider desktop publishing software to visually enhance your document. Remember to balance graphics, lists, and text.

Your Turn: Review a document you have recently written. What page design and format techniques did you use to make the document more readable?

Legal Office Documents—C

Goals

- Type at least 47wpm/5′/5e.
- Correctly use Word's line numbering feature.
- Correctly format an affidavit and a business letter in block style.

A. WARMUP

alphabet — My woven silk pajamas can be exchanged for the blue quartz.

practice: *f* and *d* — fad fold fed Fido doffs defy find fled deaf fund deft faded

easy — Sue and I may fish for cod and smelt when I am at the lake.

Skillbuilding

B. PACED PRACTICE

Follow the GDP software directions for this exercise to improve keystroking speed and accuracy.

C. 5-MINUTE TIMED WRITING

Take two 5-minute timed writings.

Goal: At least 47wpm/5′/5e

```
     From the time you start attending school, you begin to  11
develop new skills in making friends and getting along with  23
people. These skills are used throughout your life journey.  35
If you want to be successful in any business or career, you  47
can't be a loner. You must learn skills for working with     59
people from all cultures.                                    64
     In a corporation, people use their unique skills to     74
work as a team in order to accomplish their goals. Like a    86
finely tuned orchestra or a football team, all members must  98
work together to achieve a desired objective. If a person   110
does not work efficiently within the group, then other team 122
members may have to work harder to compensate so that the   133
effort of the team will not fall short.                     141
     Working with others allows you the chance to learn     152
from other people. You may also learn some things about     163
yourself. To get along with your coworkers, you may have to 175
overlook the personal faults of others. Everyone has some   186
faults, and your faults may be just as disconcerting to     198
other people as their faults are to you.                    206
     The ability to work with people will also enhance      216
your quest for career advancement. You can expect amazing   228
results when you work with your team.                       235
  1 | 2 | 3 | 4 | 5 | 6 | 7 | 8 | 9 | 10 | 11 | 12
```

Formatting

D. WORD PROCESSING: LINE NUMBERING

GO TO Word Manual

Study Lesson 98 in your Word Manual. Complete all of the shaded steps while at your computer. Then format the documents that follow.

Document Processing

Report 98-72
Affidavit of Possession

Add line numbers to all lines in this court document. When your document is typed, the line that appears next to the line number will vary from some of those shown here.

An affidavit is a sworn written statement made under oath. It is a court document.

←Line numbers for a court document

AFFIDAVIT OF POSSESSION ↓2X

STATE OF SOUTH CAROLINA ↓2X

COUNTY OF CHARLESTON ↓2X

Travis Bradley, being first duly sworn, deposes and says: ↓2X

That he is an adult person and is a resident of Charleston County, South Carolina, and that his mailing address is 105 Livingston Lane, Rockville, SC 29487.

That he knows the ownership, occupancy, and history of the following property located in Charleston County, South Carolina, to wit:

All that part of the Southwest Quarter of the Northwest Quarter of Section Ten (10), Township Sixty-two (62), further described as follows: Beginning at the Northeast corner of said Southwest Quarter of the Northwest Quarter; thence South along the East line of said quarter 2000.00 feet; thence West 425.00 feet; thence North 150.00 feet; thence West 315.00 feet; thence North 600.00 feet; thence East 882.00 feet.

That the record title holder in fee simple of the above property is Travis Bradley, a single person; that he is presently in possession of the above-described premises;

That ownership of the aforesaid property is based upon an unbroken chain of title through immediate and remote grantors by deed of conveyance which has been recorded for a period of more than twenty-five (25) years, to wit: Since August 21, 1985; at 4 a.m.;

(continued on next page)

That the purpose of this Affidavit of Possession is to show proof of ownership by providing and recording evidence of possession for marketable title as required by the Marketable Record Title Act of the State of South Carolina.

DATED this _____ day of May, 20--, at Rockville, South Carolina.

____
James Cates Attorney at Law

Subscribed and sworn to before me this _____ day of May, 20--.

____
Denise Crocker Notary Public
Charleston County, South Carolina
My Commission Expires April 18, 2015

Correspondence
98-92
Business Letter in Block Style

June 15, 20-- | Mr. Douglas Stengel | 1338 Phobe Street | Mt. Pleasant, SC 29464 | Dear Mr. Stengel:

¶ Enclosed is a copy of an Affidavit of Possession that was filed on your behalf with the Charleston County Courthouse. After checking with the County Recorder's Office, we have determined that your affidavit was filed on November 17, 1985. To your knowledge, have there been any legal transactions that have not been recorded that would reveal a change of ownership since your affidavit was filed?

¶ If you are aware of any unrecorded transactions that might change the ownership status of your property, please contact our office immediately to update your property records.

¶ If you have any questions, you can contact my office at 843-555-3838.

Sincerely yours, | Brandon Whitfield | Attorney at Law | urs | Enclosure | c: Sharon Steeley, Cameron Estrada

Keyboarding Connection

Searching the Yellow Pages

Do you find the Yellow Pages of your phone directory handy? Try the Internet as an alternate source. Many of the Web's search engines allow you to search for phone numbers, addresses, and e-mail addresses.

You can use the Yellow Pages feature to search for mailing addresses and phone numbers of businesses and organizations. Access your search engine and type "yellow pages." You'll see a list of links for a variety of sites where you can search for location and contact information of businesses. The site http://www.yellowpages.com is the online equivalent of the Yellow Pages books. Search engines also might provide you with a map of the location of the business or organization.

Using the Yellow Pages online is like having all of the phone directories in the United States at your fingertips.

Your Turn: Access the Yellow Pages online via your favorite search engine. Search for a business in your city by name and then by category. Did you retrieve the address and phone number of the business using both search methods?

Legal Office Documents—D

99

Goals

- Demonstrate improved speed and accuracy while typing.
- Demonstrate acceptable language arts skills in spelling.
- Correctly format a summons, a memo, and a predesigned table.

A. WARMUP

alphabet	1	The wolves exited quickly as the fanged zoo chimp jabbered.
frequent digraphs	2	en end den deny gene hen men lend menu pen ten oven yen Ben
easy	3	Vivian may risk a penalty if she is privy to the right bid.

Skillbuilding

B. MAP+: SYMBOL

Follow the GDP software directions for this exercise to improve keystroking accuracy.

PPP PRETEST » PRACTICE » POSTTEST

C. PRETEST: Horizontal Reaches

PRETEST

Take a 1-minute timed writing.

```
4      Art enjoyed his royal blue race car. He bragged about  11
5  how he learned to push for those spurts of speed which made 23
6  him win races. The car had a lot of get-up-and-go. He had  35
7  daily meetings with his mechanics when a race date was set. 46
      1 | 2 | 3 | 4 | 5 | 6 | 7 | 8 | 9 | 10 | 11 | 12
```

D. PRACTICE: In Reaches

PRACTICE

Speed Emphasis:
If you made no more than 1 error on the Pretest, type each *individual* line 2 times.

Accuracy Emphasis:
If you made 2 or more errors, type each *group* of lines (as though it were a paragraph) 2 times.

```
8  oy ahoy ploy toys loyal coyly royal enjoy decoy Lloyd annoy
9  ar fare arch mart march farms scars spear barns learn radar
10 pu pull push puts pulse spurt purge spuds pushy spurs pupil
11 lu luck blue lure lucid glued lumps value lulls bluff lunge
```

E. PRACTICE: Out Reaches

```
12 ge gear gets ages getup raged geese lunge pages cagey forge
13 da dare date data dance adage dazed sedan daubs cedar daily
14 hi high hick hill hinge chief hires ethic hiked chili hitch
15 ra rate rare brag ranch brace ratio bravo rayon prawn races
```

POSTTEST

Repeat the Pretest timed writing and compare performance.

F. POSTTEST: Horizontal Reaches

Language Arts

Type these frequently misspelled words, paying special attention to any spelling problems in each word.

G. SPELLING

16 distribution executive extension requested specific carried
17 recommended alternative programs access budget issued seize
18 objectives indicated calendar family could these until your
19 administrative accommodate possibility students fiscal past
20 transportation employee's categories summary offered estate

Edit the sentences to correct any misspellings.

21 The executive requested an extention on spicific programs.

22 I have recomended alternitive programs for early next week.

23 These objectives were indacated for the new calender year.

24 These passed administrative goals will accomodate the team.

25 These categories could be included in the employee summery.

26 I offerred early access to the estate's budjet distributions.

Document Processing

Report
99-73
Summons

A summons is a court document that notifies a defendant that a lawsuit has been filed and that an appearance must be made before the court, at a specified time, to answer the charges.

Type the title (SUMMONS) on the same line as *vs.*

Add line numbers to all lines in this court document. When your document is typed, the line that appears next to the line number will vary from some of those shown here.

STATE OF TEXAS → 6.5″ right tab IN DISTRICT COURT ↓2X

COUNTY OF HUNT NORTHEAST JUDICIAL DISTRICT ↓2X

FIRST NATIONAL BANK → tab 3.25″) → 6.5″ right tab NO. ____________________ (20 underscores)
105 Royal Lane)
Commerce, TX 75428-2230)
)
→ tab 1″ Plaintiff,)
)
vs.) → 6.5″ right tab SUMMONS
)
JAMES MCFEELEY)
)
Defendant.)

THE STATE OF TEXAS TO THE ABOVE-NAMED DEFENDANT:

→ tab 1″ You are hereby summoned and required to appear and defend against the Complaint in this action, which is hereby served upon you by serving upon the undersigned an Answer or other proper response within twenty (20) days after the service of the Summons and Complaint upon you, exclusive of the day of service.

If you fail to do so, judgment by default will be taken against you for the relief demanded in the Complaint.

SIGNED this _____ day of July, 20--.

→ tab 3.25″ ________________________________
Rachel Simmons Attorney at Law (↑ 6.5″ right tab)
334 Alamo Street
Commerce, TX 75428-3110
Telephone: 903-555-1130
Attorney for Plaintiff

Correspondence
99-93
Memo

MEMO TO: Christopher Redding

FROM: Darlene Ruzi

DATE: October 13, 20--

SUBJECT: Client listing

¶ As you requested, I am enclosing an up-to-date new client summary for our Dallas area clients. This list is current as of this week and it shows the distribution of clients in the counties of Dallas, Ellis, hunt, Kaufman, and Rockwall. Please note that the billing hours total are also indicated in this list. Dallas and Kaufman counties represents the greatest number of clients per county. Just in the past quarter, these 2 counties represented nearly 70% of our client base. Rockwall County clients do not represent a sizable percentage of our client base but the opening of two new family law offices in that county will certainly generate considerable new business in the next calendar year.

¶ We will send you an updated list bi weekly. The next list could show the possibility of client gains in Rockwall county, and we expect business in Ellis and Hunt counties to continue growing to accommodate the population growth in those specific areas.

urs | Enclosure | c: Blake Zachry

Table
99-53
Predesigned Table

Your completed table may look different from the table shown.

1. Apply a table style of your choice.
2. In Rows 1 and 2, verify that all text is bolded.
3. In Row 2, align the column headings at the bottom center.

CLIENT LIST **October 15, 20--**			
Name	**Address**	**County**	**Billing Hours**
Carroll Azteca	423 North Avenue	Hunt	25
Thomas Bryan	302 Bradley Lane	Rockwall	30
Maria Calhoun	1204 Park Street	Kaufman	23
Raymond Cooper	144 Cypress Circle	Rockwall	14
Denise Johnson	3076 Burns Avenue	Hunt	18
Vickie Nichols	483 Laurel Trace	Ellis	7
Margie Rambert	291 Shelby Drive	Kaufman	9
Pearl Sibley	402 Waverly Way	Dallas	32
Heather Wong	2421 Hope Road	Ellis	12
Ray Zhen	2232 Alvin Lane	Dallas	28

Legal Office Documents—E

100

Goals

- Type at least 47wpm/5'/5e.
- Correctly format a complaint, a warranty deed, and a judgment.
- Successfully complete a Progress and Proofreading Check with zero errors on the first scored attempt.

A. WARMUP

alphabet	1	Brown jars prevented the mixture from freezing too quickly.
number/symbol	2	coy20@cox.net 70% Hsu & Van 5/7 Win! ($4.93) *op. cit #16-8
easy	3	Jay may ask if my own neighbor is proficient in such a job.

Skillbuilding

B. 12-SECOND SPEED SPRINTS

Take three 12-second timed writings on each line.

```
4  Keith must work with a tutor when he has need of more help.
5  Chris may clap his hands when they chant the songs at camp.
6  Do not blame my firm for the low level of fuel in the tank.
7  The new city law may allow us to fish for cod on the docks.
   ''''5''''10''''15''''20''''25''''30''''35''''40''''45''''50''''55''''60
```

C. TECHNIQUE PRACTICE: SPACE BAR

Type each line 2 times, using your right thumb to strike the SPACE BAR in the center.

```
8  A toy dog in the pen is apt to be a big hit at the new gym.
9  We may go to the zoo for the day if the sun is not too hot.
10 Eli and Max may use a map to see how to get to the new pub.
11 If it is to be, it is up to you and Ben to do it for a fee.
```

Take two 5-minute timed writings.

Goal: At least 47wpm/5'/5e

D. 5-MINUTE TIMED WRITING

```
     Company loyalty may be a thing of the past. A worker          11
who stayed and worked in one place for thirty or more years      23
is rare these days. People are moving to different jobs at       35
a faster pace than in the past. Changing jobs many times         46
over a career no longer carries the stigma of the past.          57
Some workers are just looking for new challenges.                67
     Those who change jobs are able to market their skills       78
and to get a salary increase. Hopping from job to job can        90
pay amazing returns for some careers. Firms may be quite        101
willing to offer higher pay and more perks to attract the       113
best and most skilled people. People who change jobs a lot      125
have the experience and knowledge that other firms may be       136
eager to get.                                                   139
     The chance to change jobs is there not only for the        150
younger worker but also for older workers who are well into     162
their careers. For example, computer technology has been        173
experiencing a boom. The Internet industry has a big demand     185
for computer programmers. People with knowledge in this         196
field can request higher salaries.                              203
     A firm may even offer additional benefits in order to      214
attract experienced workers with great credentials. It is       226
really up to each person to decide what to do.                  235
   1 | 2 | 3 | 4 | 5 | 6 | 7 | 8 | 9 | 10 | 11 | 12
```

Document Processing

Report 100-74
Complaint

Add line numbers for all lines in this court document, and restart line numbers on each page. When your document is typed, the line that appears next to the line number will vary.

A complaint is the initial document filed with a court by a plaintiff to initiate a lawsuit by establishing the facts or legal claims. A complaint is a court document.

STATE OF IOWA		IN DISTRICT COURT
COUNTY OF DES MOINES		CENTRAL JUDICIAL DISTRICT
PEOPLE'S COUNTY BANK	)	NO. ____________________
215 Grand Avenue	)	
Des Moines, IA 50304	)	
	)	
Plaintiff,	)	
	)	
vs.	)	COMPLAINT
	)	
COLEMAN FARMS, INC.	)	
STEVEN R. COLEMAN	)	
	)	
Defendant.	)	

(continued on next page)

Press ENTER 2 times before each roman numeral. Center all roman numerals between the margins.

PLAINTIFF FOR ITS CAUSE OF ACTION AND COMPLAINT AGAINST THE DEFENDANT, COMPLAINS, ALLEGES, AND SHOWS TO THE COURT:

I.

That defendant owes plaintiff $10,885.00, plus interest and charges, under the terms of a promissory note executed April 18, 20--, a copy of which is attached hereto and incorporated by reference as "Exhibit A."

II.

That defendant has not, upon due demand, satisfied his obligation under the terms of the promissory note.

III.

That Coleman Farms is an Iowa for-profit corporation duly organized under the corporate laws of the State of Iowa.

IV.

That the registered agent of Coleman Farms is Steven R. Coleman.

V.

That Steven R. Coleman executed a Commercial Guaranty for the note dated April 18, 20--, a copy of which is attached hereto and incorporated herein as "Exhibit B."

VI.

That Steven R. Coleman executed a Commercial Guaranty on the prior promissory note No. 7249, and the Commercial Guaranty provides that the guaranty extends to ". . . all renewals of, extensions of, modifications of, refinancings of, consolidations of, and substitutions for the promissory note or agreement." A copy of that Commercial Guaranty is attached hereto and incorporated hereby by reference as "Exhibit C."

VII.

That the indebtedness was the renewal of a prior promissory note executed by Coleman Farms to People's County Bank on June 28, 20--, which was in the original principal amount of $10,480, a copy of which is attached hereto and incorporated by reference as "Exhibit D."

VIII.

That Steven R. Coleman is personally liable for the amount of the debt, as is the corporation, Coleman Farms.

WHEREOF, PLAINTIFF DEMANDS JUDGMENT AGAINST THE DEFENDANT, AS FOLLOWS:

For the numbered list, press TAB 1 time, then create the numbered list.

1. For the amount of $5,780.00, plus interest on that amount from and after April 18, 20--, at the rate of 12.75% per annum; and for its costs, late charges, and disbursements in this action;

(continued on next page)

2. For such other and further relief as the Court may deem appropriate.

SIGNED this _____ day of December, 20--.

____

Barry R. Jacobs   Attorney at Law
484 Grand Avenue
Des Moines, IA 50305
Telephone: 515-555-3399
Attorney for Plaintiff

Report
100-75
Warranty Deed

WARRANTY DEED

¶ THIS DEED, is made this _____ day of August, 20--, between Edward J. Garcia, hereby called the Grantor, whose address is 937 Ludlow Street, Hamilton, OH 45012, and Samuel Ramsey, hereby called the Grantee, whose address is 1104 Buckeye Street, Hamilton, OH 45011.

¶ THE GRANTOR, in consideration of the sum of TWO HUNDRED TWENTY-FIVE THOUSAND and 00/100 DOLLARS ($225,000), does hereby grant, bargain, sell, and convey unto the Grantee, in fee simple, all of the property described in Exhibit "A" attached hereto and made a part thereof;

¶ And the remainders, rents, issues, and profits thereof and all of the estate, right, title, and interest of the Grantor, therein and thereto;

¶ TO HAVE AND TO HOLD the same, together with all structures, improvements, rights, easements, privileges, and appurtenances thereon and thereunto belonging or held and enjoyed therewith, unto the Grantee according to the tenancy hereinafter set forth.

¶ WITNESS, the hand of the Grantor.

____

Edward J. Garcia

STATE OF OHIO

County of Butler

(continued on next page)

¶ On this ______ day of August, 20--, before me, a notary public within and for said County and State, personally appeared Edward J. Garcia, to me known to be the person described in and who executed the within and foregoing instrument and acknowledged to me that he executed the same as his free act and deed.

____

Marcia H. Gates Notary Public
Butler County, Ohio
My Commission Expires May 15, 2015

Report
100-76
Judgment

Add line numbers to all lines in this court document. When your document is typed, the line that appears next to the line number will vary from some of those shown here.

Progress and Proofreading Check

Documents designated as Proofreading Checks serve as a check of your proofreading skill. Your goal is to have zero typographical errors when the GDP software first scores the document.

A judgment is a decision by a court to resolve a controversy. A judgment is a court document; it determines the rights and obligations of the parties.

STATE OF GEORGIA	IN DISTRICT COURT
COUNTY OF DOUGLAS	NORTH-CENTRAL JUDICIAL DISTRICT

James S. Crenshaw	)	
d/b/a Crenshaw Computers	)	CIVIL NO. 45-98-C-00127
6823 Creekwood Drive	)	
Douglasville, GA 30135	)	
	)	
Plaintiff,	)	
	)	
vs.	)	JUDGMENT
	)	
Peachtree Hospital Association	)	
d/b/a Peachtree Nursing Care	)	
	)	
Defendant.	)	

The defendant, Peachtree Hospital Association, d/b/a Peachtree Nursing Care, having been regularly served with process, and having failed to appear and answer the plaintiff's Complaint filed herein, and the default of said defendant having been duly entered, and it appearing by the affidavits of plaintiff that plaintiff is entitled to judgment herein.

IT IS THEREFORE ORDERED AND ADJUDGED, that the plaintiff have and recover from the defendant, Peachtree Hospital Association, d/b/a Peachtree Nursing Care, the sum of $12,000.00 plus interest thereon from and after October 10, 20--, until paid, together with costs in the sum of $343.75.

SIGNED this _____ day of ____________________, 20--.

____
Clerk of the District Court

Outcomes Assessment on Part 5

Test 5

5-Minute Timed Writing

When you submit your resume to apply for a job, you 11
want your resume to be noticed. Here are some things you 22
might do to make certain your resume receives the time and 34
focus it deserves. 38

First, be neat. Review each page to make sure that it 49
is free of typos and spelling errors. Check each page for 60
correct grammar. Remember that this document will make the 72
first impression with a potential employer. You want the 83
document to represent you in the best way. Use white paper 95
of good quality to print your resume. 103

Second, try to be creative. Make your resume unique. A 114
future employer may be looking for specific things when he 126
or she scans the pages of your resume. Be sure to provide 137
facts that explain exactly what skills you have acquired in 149
positions you have held in the past. Avoid using the same 161
buzzwords that everyone else uses. 168

Finally, state a career objective on your resume. Some 179
experts suggest that by stating a career objective, you are 191
showing a career path. Others think that stating a career 203
objective may limit many job possibilities. If you state a 215
career objective, make sure the objective is in line with 226
the specific job for which you are applying. 235

1 | 2 | 3 | 4 | 5 | 6 | 7 | 8 | 9 | 10 | 11 | 12

Correspondence Test 5-94
Business Letter in Block Style

17 March 20-- | Mr. Antoine Devereux | Manager | Technik Group | 3148, Rue Richer | 75214 | Paris | France | Dear Mr. Devereux:

¶ We have astounding news to share with you regarding our Lyon plant in Genesis. Sales at the Lyon plant during its first 3 months of operation have surpassed our Bremen and Leipzig sales over the same period. Much of this sucess is due to your marketing effort to promote the Jefy throughout France.

¶ We are going to promote the same marketing approach at our Bremen and Leipzig plants because of the success you experienced at the Lyon plant. I would like you to lead the effort in that campaign. Therefore would you please put together for me a proposal and send it to me by the end of the month.

¶ We look forward to receiving your proposal.

Sincerely, | Alex Defforey | V.P., Marketing | urs | c: Mary Kay Summers, Richard Laforgue

Table Test
5-54
Boxed Table

Add 25 percent shading to Row 2.

PATIENT MEDICAL REPORT		
Patient Name:		
Chest X-Ray (Code 410)	Normal	Abnormal
Cholesterol—HDL (Code 466)	Normal	Abnormal
Cholesterol—LDL (Code 724)	Normal	Abnormal
Cholesterol—Total (Code 682)	Normal	Abnormal
EKG (Code 562)	Normal	Abnormal
Kidney Function (Code 401)	Normal	Abnormal
Liver Function (Code 382)	Normal	Abnormal
Sugar (Code 790)	Normal	Abnormal
Thyroid Level (Code 242)	Normal	Abnormal
Triglycerides (Code 491)	Normal	Abnormal

Report Test
5-77
Summons

Add line numbers to all lines in this court document. When your document is typed, the line that appears next to the line number will vary from some of those shown here.

STATE OF MINNESOTA IN DISTRICT COURT

COUNTY OF PENNINGTON NORTHERN JUDICIAL DISTRICT

DALE E. MATTHEWS) NO. ____________________
248 Hughes Street)
Thief River Falls, MN 56701)
)
Plaintiff,)
)
vs.) SUMMONS
)
MELANIE D. HILL)
)
Defendant.)

THE STATE OF MINNESOTA TO THE DEFENDANT:

YOU ARE HEREBY SUMMONED and required to appear and defend, within the time designated in this action and in this Court. You shall appear and defend within 20 days after the service of the Complaint against you, exclusive of the day of service. Service by publication is complete 30 days after the date of first publication.

YOU ARE HEREBY NOTIFIED that in case of your failure to appear and defend within the time designated, judgment by default shall be rendered against you for the relief demanded in the Complaint.

SIGNED this _____ day of March, 20--.

____
Donna Farrington Attorney at Law
879 James Street
Thief River Falls, MN 56702
Telephone: 218-555-8844
Attorney for Plaintiff

Using and Designing Business Documents

6 PART

Keyboarding in Legal Services Careers

A career in legal services can take many forms. Lawyers, of course, are responsible for legal work, but a number of other positions in the legal services field are available. Often, lawyers assign tasks to paralegals. Paralegals—also referred to as legal assistants—have taken on a larger percentage of responsibilities in recent years. Another profession in the law field, that of court reporter, requires excellent communication skills. Court reporters must take exact notes of proceedings. Keyboarding skills are important for many job functions in legal services careers, and they can prove to give a job candidate an advantage.

Paralegals can work in many different business settings, but they are found most commonly in law firms and government offices. Court reporters are responsible for providing an accurate and detailed legal record of any proceeding. For individuals working in the legal services field, strong communication skills, written and spoken, are very important, but being able to convey ideas in a typed report in a timely manner is even more important.

Goals

Keyboarding

- Demonstrate improved speed and accuracy when operating the keyboard by touch.
- Type at least 50 words per minute on a 5-minute timed writing with no more than 5 errors.

Language Arts

- Demonstrate acceptable proofreading skills, including using proofreaders' marks correctly.
- Demonstrate acceptable language arts skills in punctuation, grammar, and mechanics.
- Demonstrate acceptable language arts skills in composing and spelling.

Word Processing

- Use appropriate word processing commands necessary to complete document processing activities successfully.

Document Processing

- Correctly format office forms, office publications, online resumes, and form letters.

Objective Test

- Answer questions with acceptable accuracy on an objective test.

UNIT

21

Using and Designing Office Forms

UNIT 21 LESSON

Using Correspondence Templates

101

Goals

- Demonstrate improved speed and accuracy while typing.
- Demonstrate acceptable language arts skills in adjective and adverb agreement.
- Correctly use Word's correspondence templates.
- Correctly format a memo using a template.

A. WARMUP

alphabet 1 Jimmy quit and packed the seventy extra bags for Liz Owens.

concentration 2 paleoanthropologist extraterritoriality oversimplifications

easy 3 Cory works with a tutor when he works with theory problems.

Skillbuilding

B. MAP+: ALPHABET

Follow the GDP software directions for this exercise to improve keystroking accuracy.

C. PROGRESSIVE PRACTICE: ALPHABET

Follow the GDP software directions for this exercise to improve keystroking speed.

Language Arts

D. ADJECTIVES AND ADVERBS AND AGREEMENT

Study the rules at the right.

RULE
adjective/adverb

Use comparative adjectives and adverbs (*-er, more,* and *less*) when referring to two nouns or pronouns; use superlative adjectives and adverbs (*-est, most,* and *least*) when referring to more than two.

The shorter of the two training sessions is the more helpful one.
The longest of the three training sessions is the least helpful one.

RULE
agreement nearer noun

If two subjects are joined by *or, either/or, neither/nor,* or *not only/but also,* make the verb agree with the subject nearer to the verb.

Neither the coach nor the players are at home.
Not only the coach but also the referee is at home.
But: Both the coach and the referee are at home.

Edit each sentence to correct any errors.

Of the three printers, the faster one was the most expensive.

Of the two phones purchased, the first one is the better model.

The quietest of the five printers is also the less expensive.

Not only the manager but also the employees wants to attend.

Neither the printer nor the monitors is in working order.

Either Mr. Cortez or his assistants have to sign the order.

Coffee or soft drinks is available for the afternoon session.

Not only the manual but also the software were mailed.

Formatting

E. FILLING IN FORMS

Business forms can be created by using templates that are provided within word processing software. When a template is opened, a generic form is displayed on the screen. Specific information that is appropriate for that form may then be added.

Template forms contain data fields that correspond to blank sections on printed forms. For example, a memo template may include the guide words *To:*, *CC:*, *From:*, *Date:*, and *Re:* for the subject. Templates are usually designed so that you can replace data in fields easily by clicking in the field or by selecting the information you want to replace and typing the needed data. You can also delete fields that you do not wish to have included in your template. Built-in styles are also readily available.

You can customize a generic template by filling in repetitive information (such as the company name and telephone number) and saving it as a new template. Then each time you open that newly created template, the customized information appears automatically.

F. WORD PROCESSING: TEMPLATES—CORRESPONDENCE

GO TO Word Manual

Study Lesson 101 in your Word Manual. Complete all of the shaded steps while at your computer. Then format the documents that follow.

Document Processing

Form
101-1
Memo Template

Note: You may want to print the information in the template before deleting it.

1. Type this memo using the preselected blank memo template that has opened automatically.
2. Type the information for the memo from the copy shown next.

To: Philip Acoosta, Senior web designer

CC: Delores Easterwood, Manager

From: Bradley Pollard, General Manager

Date: April 14, 20--

Re: Web Site Update

agreement nearer noun

¶ Neither the Arbor Station Web site nor the Chapel Hills Web site have been updated in the last 2 years. The older of the two Web sites is the one that needs the greatest number of revisions. It is essential that our web sites reflect all the choices and amenities that are available to only not our current residents but also to those interested in joining our neighborhood.

adjective/adverb

¶ Philip, could you please draft a proposal that focuses on changes you make to our Web site. Most certainly, you will want to include the new villages that have been added the last 2 years: Creekwood village and Springwood village. These 2 add a total of 42 units to our sub division, and we want to make certain all home owners are aware of these new additions when they visit our Web site. | urs

Form **101-2** Memo Template

To: Bradley Pollard, General Manager | **CC:** Delores Easterwood, Design Manager | **From:** Philip Acosta, Senior Web Designer | **Date:** April 30, 20-- | **Re:** Revising the Web Sites

agreement nearer noun

¶ Brad, I am in the process of revising subdivision Web sites. Neither the Arbor Station Web site nor the Chapel Hills Web site has updated links. As you might recall, we updated the other subdivision Web pages last February so that we could add the real estate, local resources, and classified ads links to their sites. Of these three links, the real estate link will involve the greatest amount of revision because of all the graphic images that will be displayed.

adjective/adverb

¶ I plan to complete the first draft of the Web site revisions on May 5, but this draft will not include an update for the real estate link. Because of the complexity of this link, I am planning to send you my first draft of that link on May 10.

¶ If you have any questions regarding the status of the Web sites, feel free to call me at Extension 224 or stop by my office on the 4th floor. | urs

Microsoft Word automatically formats ordinals in superscript.

Form **101-3** Memo Template

To: Delores Easterwood, Design Manager | **CC:** Bradley Pollard, General Manager | **From:** Philip Acosta, Senior Web Designer | **Date:** May 11, 20-- | **Re:** Web Site Presentation

¶ Delores, I have finished my update of the Web sites and would like to schedule Meeting Room 120 to present my finished product. Brad indicated that this update was a top priority for the Design Department; therefore, I would like all department heads to attend the presentation and provide any feedback they wish to share.

¶ Would you please make reservations for Room 120 for May 15, preferably at 1 or 2 p.m. I expect the presentation and follow-up questions will take the better part of an hour.

¶ I'm excited about the changes we have made to the Web sites, and I believe through my revisions our subdivision sites will see a tremendous surge in hits in the coming months. | urs

Using Report Templates

102

Goals

- Type at least 48wpm/5′/5e.
- Correctly use Word's report templates.
- Correctly format a report using a template.

A. WARMUP

alphabet	1	That crazy man waved a quart jug of bad milk at the sphinx.
one hand	2	rebate minion red mom desert lumpily draw imply erase jolly
easy	3	Ken had a dish of lamb and cut up a mango and ripe apricot.

Skillbuilding

B. SUSTAINED PRACTICE: SYLLABIC INTENSITY

Take a 1-minute timed writing on the boxed paragraph to establish your base speed. Then take a 1-minute timed writing on the following paragraph. As soon as you equal or exceed your base speed on this paragraph, move to the next, more difficult paragraph.

```
 4      People continue to rent autos for personal use or for  11
 5 their work, and the car-rental business continues to grow.  23
 6 When you rent a car, look carefully at the insurance cost.  35
 7 You might also have to pay a mileage charge for the car.    46

 8      It is likely that a good deal of insurance coverage is 11
 9 part of the standard rental cost. But you might be urged    23
10 to procure extra medical, property, and collision coverage. 35
11 If you accept, be ready to see your rental charge increase. 46

12      Perhaps this is not necessary, as you may already have 11
13 the kind of protection you want in a policy that you have   23
14 at the present time. By reviewing your own auto insurance   34
15 policy, you may easily save a significant amount of money.  46

16      Paying mileage charges could result in a really large  11
17 bill. This is especially evident when the trips planned     22
18 involve destinations that are many miles apart. Complete a  34
19 total review of traveling plans before making a decision.   45
     1 | 2 | 3 | 4 | 5 | 6 | 7 | 8 | 9 | 10 | 11 | 12
```

Take two 5-minute timed writings.

Goal: At least 48wpm/5'/5e

C. 5-MINUTE TIMED WRITING

```
     Job stress is not so uncommon in today's workplace.     11
There may be many causes of job stress; but the most likely  23
reasons it occurs are overwork, possible layoffs, conflicts  35
with people at work, or just simply working in a job that    46
is no longer to your liking.                                 52
     Symptoms of job stress are common to many people, and   53
they include changes in sleeping patterns, short temper,     74
upset stomach, headache, and low morale. Although many of    86
us suffer from one or more of the above symptoms, we should  98
take them seriously if the symptoms continue or if we tend  110
to experience three or four of the symptoms at the same     121
time continuously.                                          125
     Sometimes it is possible to reduce the stress in your  136
work by taking a commonsense approach to the situation. If  148
you think that you are being overworked, take a vacation or 160
avoid taking work home with you. If you are concerned about 172
layoffs, then be certain that you are prepared to make a    183
career change if it is required.                            190
     If you have conflicts with your boss or with others at 201
the office, try to work them out by discussing the issues   213
with the people involved to be certain they understand all  224
aspects of the conflict. Then, work together to minimize    236
any future conflicts.                                       240
  1 | 2 | 3 | 4 | 5 | 6 | 7 | 8 | 9 | 10 | 11 | 12
```

Formatting

D. WORD PROCESSING: TEMPLATES—REPORT

GO TO Word Manual

Study Lesson 102 in your Word Manual. Complete all of the shaded steps while at your computer. Then format the documents that follow.

Document Processing

Form
102-4
Report Template

1. Type this report using the preselected blank report template that has opened automatically.
2. Type `TopDesign` as the company name.
3. Type the following as the address:

   `3724 Woodbine Avenue`
   `Knoxville, Tennessee 37903`

4. Type `Web Page Mistakes` as the title.
5. Type `Designing a Web Page` as the subtitle.
6. Move to the second page and type the same title as you did in step 4; then type the subtitle again on the second page.
7. Type the rest of the information into the template, as indicated in the copy shown next.

¶ Look closely and you'll find that almost all Web pages have design mistakes embedded with in. There are millions of Web pages on the WWW, and most of them were created by users who have never studied the finer points of web page design. Here are a few of the more common mistakes made in Webpage design.

Top 3 Mistakes

¶ Don't use fancy fonts or multiple fonts on your Web Page. There are literally 1,000s of fonts from which to choose. If you don't have them on your computer, you can search for any font you want on the WWW. Don't use many fonts that are too small or fonts that are difficult to read, such as script fonts.

¶ Don't use music on your Site! When Web pages were in there infancy, Web designers attempted to use music to attract visitors. Guess what—it miserably failed! If you must use an audio link, let the visitor choose as to whether or not he or she wishes to use it. People are attracted to your site on a quest for information. Unless that quest involves a search for songs, music is not the key to keeping them there!

¶ Don't use blinking text or animated GIFs. Such techniques detract the visitor from the content of your Web page. In today's world of Web page design, blinking text and animated GIFs make your site look unprofessional.

Other Common Mistakes

¶ Although we're discussing Web page design mistakes, spelling and grammar play still a critical role in designing a sucessful Web page. A page that contains these errors leads the visitor to believe that if you have not taken the time to check for spelling and grammar mistakes, then the content may also be compromised.

¶ You should attempt to con struct your page with an easy-to-understand navigation structure. If a visitor clicks on one of the links on your page, it should lead him or her to the information that is being sought. If you take someone to a page that is totally irrelevant to the topic being searched there's a pretty good chance that you will loose that visitor forever.

Form
102-5
Report Template

1. Type this report using the preselected blank report template that has opened automatically.
2. Type `Home Planning Inc.` as the company name.
3. Type the following as the address:

```
580 Market Street
Lexington, Kentucky 40505
```

4. Type `Creating a Budget` as the title.
5. Type `Solutions for the Home` as the subtitle.
6. Use the same title on the second page of the report; then repeat the subtitle on the second page.
7. Type the rest of the information into the template, as indicated in the copy shown next.

¶ To begin your budget analysis, write down every time you spend money; list what your expenses are during the month. Think also about different categories that you can list under which your expenses will fall. Keep your expenses in a columnar arrangement so they can be added up easily at the end of the month.

¶ You also need to list all your sources of income. As you did with your list of expenses, arrange all your income sources in a columnar format.

Reviewing Your Budget

¶ During the month, review both your income and your expenses. Do you notice any large or unusual amounts that don't typically appear every month? If there are, you might want to exclude them or place them in a different section of your budget. Leaving them categorized as typical monthly expenses may distort your budget. Look also to see if you have expenses that don't occur on a monthly basis. Maybe you have auto insurance that renews every six months. If that is the case, set aside the monthly equivalent of that six-month expense so that you know how much will be assigned each month.

¶ After listing all your expenses and all your income, look at the grand totals for both categories. Does the expense column total exceed the income column total? If so, you are spending more than you are earning, and some adjustments need to be made. You could possibly reduce the amount you spend on items such as entertainment or cut back on the number of times you eat out in a restaurant rather than preparing your meals at home.

¶ During the month, be sure that you record every time you spend money. If it looks like you are spending too much money and that you might run out of money before the month is over, you will have to cut back on some of your expenses. You cannot spend money you do not have!

Looking Back

¶ At the end of the month, see how well you have done with your expenses. Did you record every expense? Did you have to cut back because you were spending too much? What expenses did you cut back to make certain that you did not exceed your monthly income? After analyzing your month's budget, make adjustments and start with a new budget the next month. After a few months of preparing and analyzing your budget, you will be a better caretaker of your money.

Designing Letterheads

Goals

- Demonstrate improved speed and accuracy while typing.
- Demonstrate acceptable proofreading skills by comparing lines.
- Correctly use Word's features for small caps and text boxes.
- Correctly format a letterhead form.

A. WARMUP

alphabet
1 Jackson believed that we quizzed the old sphinx from Egypt.

practice: *v* and *b*
2 verb bevel bevy above Bev livable vibe bovine brave visible

easy
3 Rodney may risk half of his profits for the old oak mantel.

Skillbuilding

B. MAP+: NUMBERS

Follow the GDP software directions for this exercise to improve keystroking accuracy.

PPP PRETEST » PRACTICE » POSTTEST

C. PRETEST: Vertical Reaches

PRETEST
Take a 1-minute timed writing.

4 The senior lawyer was able to tackle the case in June. 11
5 He knew he would be making himself available to the court 23
6 for a fourth time in a month. He said he needed to revamp 34
7 his vacation plans to guard against whatever might go awry. 45
1 | 2 | 3 | 4 | 5 | 6 | 7 | 8 | 9 | 10 | 11 | 12

D. PRACTICE: Up Reaches

PRACTICE
Speed Emphasis:
If you made no more than 1 error on the Pretest, type each *individual* line 2 times.
Accuracy Emphasis:
If you made 2 or more errors, type each *group* of lines (as though it were a paragraph) 2 times.

8 aw awry away paws drawer awakes spawns brawny awards aweigh
9 se self seen sewn bosses paused senior seller seizes itself
10 ki kiln kilt kite skirts joking kinder bikini making unkind
11 rd hard lard cord hurdle overdo lizard inward boards upward

E. PRACTICE: Down Reaches

12 ac acid ache aces jacked facial actors tacked jackal places
13 kn knot knee knob knives kneels knight knotty knocks knaves
14 ab able blab ably tables fabric babies rabbit cabana cables
15 va vase vain Vail evades revamp valley avails ravage canvas

POSTTEST

Repeat the Pretest timed writing and compare performance.

F. POSTTEST: Vertical Reaches

Language Arts

G. PROOFREADING

Compare these lines with lines 38–42 on page 419. Edit the lines to correct any errors.

```
     If you have conflicts with your boss or with others at your office, try to work them out by discusing the issue with the people involved to be curtain they understand all all aspects of the conflict. Work together to minimize any any future conflict.
```

Formatting

H. DESIGNING A FORM

Use the following guidelines to design an attractive, effective form:

1. Keep all elements of your design simple and balanced.
2. Limit the number of fonts, attributes (bold, italics, and so on), and sizes. Using no more than two fonts is a good rule of thumb.
3. Use white space liberally to separate and open up text and graphics.
4. Use different alignments (left, center, right, and full) to add interest and emphasis and to improve readability.
5. Experiment and change—Word makes both easy to do.

I. WORD PROCESSING: FONT—SMALL CAPS AND TEXT BOXES

GO TO Word Manual

Study Lesson 103 in your Word Manual. Complete all of the shaded steps while at your computer. Then format the documents that follow.

Form
103-6
Letterhead Form

REFER TO
Word Manual

L. 88: Clip Art—Insert

1. Change the top, left, and right margins to 0.3 inch.
2. Insert a text box at the top of the page that is 1.4 inches high and 7.8 inches wide.
3. Center the text box horizontally and position it relative to the top margin.
4. Click inside the text box, and change the text alignment to right.
5. Change to Calibri 24 pt. Bold, Small Caps, and type this:

   ROCKWALL REAL ESTATE

6. Press ENTER 1 time, change the font to Calibri 11 pt., and type this:

   893 Shoreview Drive
   Rockwall, TX 75032
   972-555-8900

7. Change the font to Calibri 11 pt. Italic, and type this:

   www.rockwallhomes.com

8. Click outside the text box, and then insert clip art related to real estate.
9. Set the clip art wrap style so the clip art is on top of the text box; and then size and move it so that it fits inside the text box as shown in the illustration below.
10. Change the text box and clip art shapes to appear as rounded rectangles.
11. Select a text box border and shading that complement the colors in the clip art.
12. Select all text, and change the font color to one that complements the colors in the clip art.
13. Compare your finished letterhead to the illustration that follows. Make any necessary changes, including removing any automatic hyperlink.

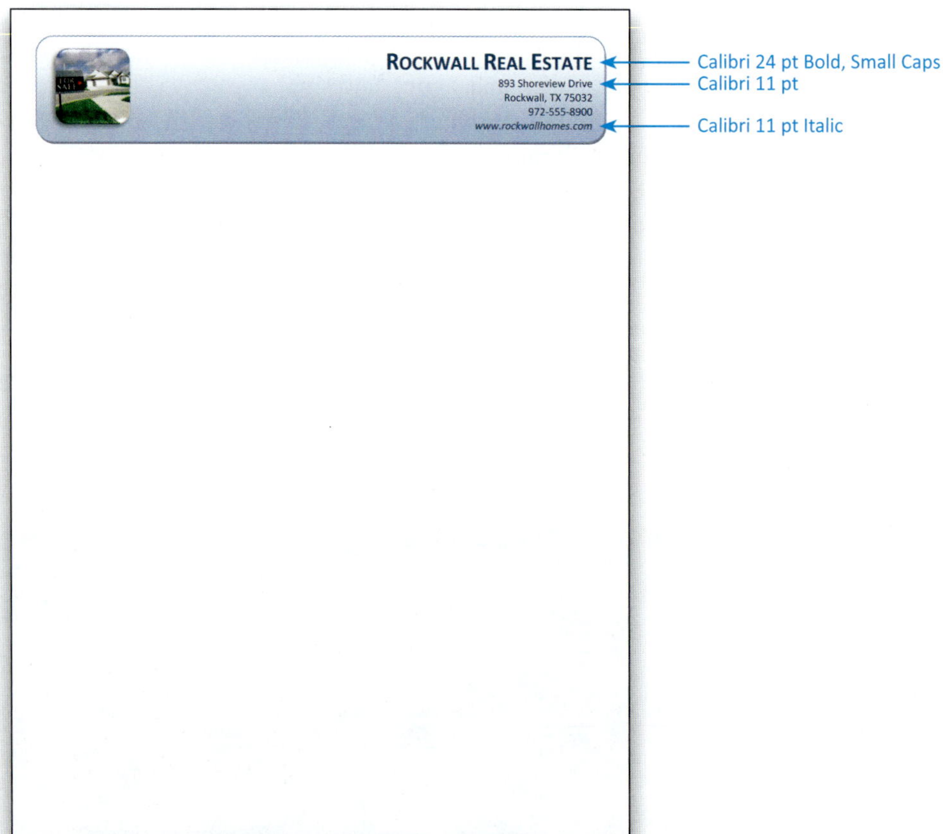

Form
103-7
Letterhead Form

1. Change the top, left, and right margins to 0.3 inch.
2. Insert a text box at the top of the page that is 1.1 inches high and 7.8 inches wide.
3. Click inside the text box, and change the text alignment to center.
4. Change to Cambria 24 pt. Bold Italic, Small Caps, and type this:

   `Jack's Matting and Framing`

5. Press Enter 1 time, and change the font to Calibri 12 pt. Bold, and type this:

   `123 Pearl Street`

6. Press the Space Bar 2 times, and then insert a square bullet symbol from the Wingdings font group.
7. Press the Space Bar 2 times and type this:

   `Boulder, CO 80306`

8. Press the Space Bar 2 times, insert a square bullet symbol, press the Space Bar 2 times, and type this:

   `303-555-9022`

9. Press Enter 1 time, then change the font to Calibri 12 pt. Bold Italic, and type this:

   `www.weframe.com`

10. Click outside the text box, and then insert clip art related to picture framing.
11. Set the clip art wrap style so the clip art is on top of the text box; and then size and move it so that it fits inside the left side of the text box as shown in the illustration below.
12. Copy the clip art; then paste it to the right side of the text box, in a position similar to the clip art on the left side of the text box as shown in the illustration below.
13. Change the text box and clip art shapes to appear as rounded rectangles.
14. Select a text box border and shading that complement the colors in the clip art.
15. Select all text, and change the font color to one that complements the colors in the clip art.
16. Compare your finished letterhead to the illustration that follows. Make any necessary changes, including removing any automatic hyperlink.

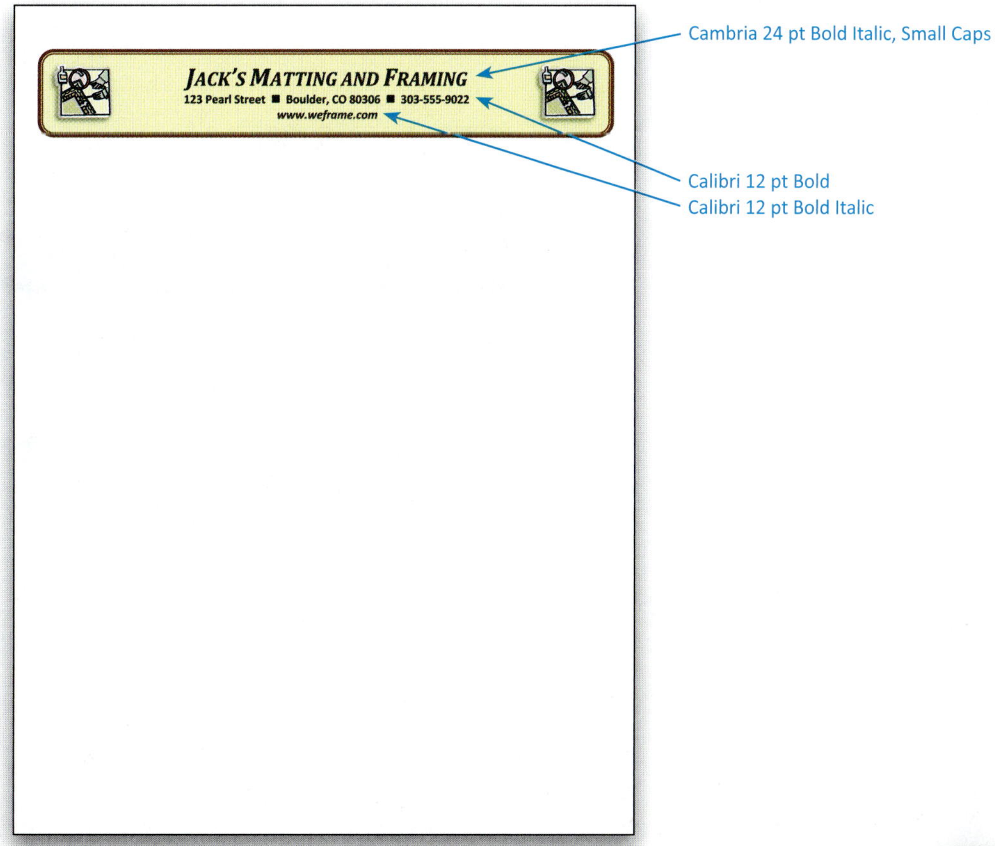

Form
103-8
Letterhead Form

1. Create a letterhead design of your own—for you personally, for your institution, or for a business.
2. Insert at least one picture that enhances the theme of the letterhead.
3. Remember to include complete information in the address block.
4. Try using fonts that you have not yet applied—experiment with point sizes and attributes.

Strategies for Career Success

Managing Business Phone Time

The average American spends an hour a day on the phone. Phone calls can be extremely distracting. Time is spent taking care of the call and following up after the call. You can take steps to reduce wasted time on the phone.

Before you make an outgoing call, organize the topics you want to discuss. Have all the materials you need: pens, paper, order forms, and so on. Consider sending an e-mail when appropriate, rather than making a phone call. E-mail is less intrusive and can be answered when the recipient has time instead of when it's sent. If you do decide to use e-mail, be prepared to follow up later if you don't get a response.

When you take an incoming call, answer it promptly. Identify yourself. It is common to answer the phone with your first and last name (for example, "Mary Smith speaking" or "Mary Smith"). Limit social conversation; it wastes time. Give concise answers to questions. At the end of the call, summarize the points made. End the conversation politely.

Your Turn: Keep a log of your time on the phone for one day. What is your average conversation time? What can you do to reduce your average phone conversation time?

Designing Notepads

104

Goals

- Type at least 48wpm/5′/5e.
- Correctly use Word's print options.
- Correctly format a notepad form.

A. WARMUP

alphabet	1	Save his quiz by fax; I jammed it in a plain brown package.
frequent digraphs	2	es ewes yes espy eves less desires west exes eyes fees mess
easy	3	The giant world map is the handiwork of the man in Langley.

Skillbuilding

B. PROGRESSIVE PRACTICE: NUMBERS

Follow the GDP software directions for this exercise to improve keystroking speed.

C. TECHNIQUE PRACTICE: TAB KEY

Press Tab 1 time between words. Type each line 2 times.

4 Kim→ apt→ Mac→ art→ Nat→ Meg→ ads→ arm→ all→ ado→ Joy
5 Orr→ awl→ Jan→ Ida→ Moe→ Lin→ zap→ Joe→ zed→ ark→ awe
6 Kai→ Lev→ add→ ask→ Mom→ Uri→ Jeb→ Nan→ aid→ Lot→ amp
7 Jay→ Hal→ Ima→ Ira→ ail→ aim→ Ian→ Max→ Pat→ Liv→ Jim

Keyboarding Connection

Effective E-Mail Management

Are you bombarded with e-mail? Take a few simple steps to manage e-mail more efficiently and reduce wasted time.

Create separate accounts, or perhaps different folders with filters for routing incoming messages, for receiving messages that require your direct attention. Keep your mailbox clean by deleting or archiving messages you no longer need. Create folders to organize messages you need to keep (for example, set up folders for separate projects).

Keep backups of important files. Be cautious of e-mail from people you do not know. Check your e-mail on a regular basis to avoid buildup of messages. Set up an automatic responder message for when you are out of the office, so people know not to expect an immediate response, and tell whom they should contact in your absence.

Your Turn: Review the current organization of your e-mail. List ways you can improve your e-mail management.

Take two 5-minute timed writings.

Goal: At least 48wpm/5'/5e

D. 5-MINUTE TIMED WRITING

Employers are always searching for people who have 10
salable skills. Having salable skills makes you unique and 22
desirable as an employee. Developing skills and qualities 34
such as a pleasing personality, a good sense of humor, a 45
positive attitude, an ability to get along with people, and 57
the ability to manage your time and prioritize your work 69
may help you find a job. 74
A tenacious person is persistent and maintains strong 85
work habits. He or she does not give up on a task easily 96
and always expects to finish the assigned task. 106
A good sense of humor and a positive attitude are two 117
traits that can help a person advance on the job. Although 128
there are times to be serious at work, sometimes you have 140
to look at things humorously. If you maintain a positive 151
attitude, other workers will like to work with you. 162
When you acquire the skills to manage your time and 172
prioritize your work, you will be successful in anything 184
you try to do. When you are given an assignment, ask for 195
guidelines so that you will know what needs to be done and 207
in what order. Then try to complete the assignment in a 218
timely fashion. The skills may be difficult to learn, but 230
you will be glad you can manage your time and work. 240

1 | 2 | 3 | 4 | 5 | 6 | 7 | 8 | 9 | 10 | 11 | 12

Formatting

GO TO Word Manual

E. WORD PROCESSING: PRINT OPTIONS

Study Lesson 104 in your Word Manual. Complete all of the shaded steps while at your computer. Then format the documents that follow.

Form
104-9
Notepad Form

Many ink-jet printers do not print beyond the bottom half inch on a sheet of paper. Keep this in mind when positioning objects at the bottom of a page.

1. Insert a picture of an appointment book or a picture related to a day planner.
2. Drag and size the picture so that it looks similar to the one in the illustration that follows.
3. Create a text box, about the same size and in the same position as the one in the illustration, to hold the words "A Note From Sheila McDaniel."
4. Remove the border around the text box.
5. Change to Calibri 36 pt. Bold, and center and type this:

   `A Note From Sheila McDaniel`

6. Create a text box at the bottom of the page, about the same size and in the same position as the one in the illustration, to hold the company name, address, and telephone number.
7. Remove the border around the text box.
8. Change to Calibri 20 pt. Bold Italic; then type this:

   `Computer Solutions Made Simple`

9. Press ENTER, change to Calibri 14 pt. Bold; then type this:

   `4829 Kramer Street, Boise, Idaho 83702`

10. Press ENTER; then type this:

    `208-555-1344`

11. Display formatting marks; then anchor all objects to the first blank line at the top of the page.
12. Change to a whole-page view, click outside any objects, and select and copy the entire document.
13. Move to the end of the document, and insert three manual page breaks to create three additional blank pages.
14. Paste the copied document, into each of the three newly created pages: click in the fourth page, and paste; click just *before* the Page Break formatting code on the third page, and paste; click just *before* the Page Break formatting code on the second page, and paste.
15. Use the print option to print four pages per sheet on 8.5- by 11-inch paper.

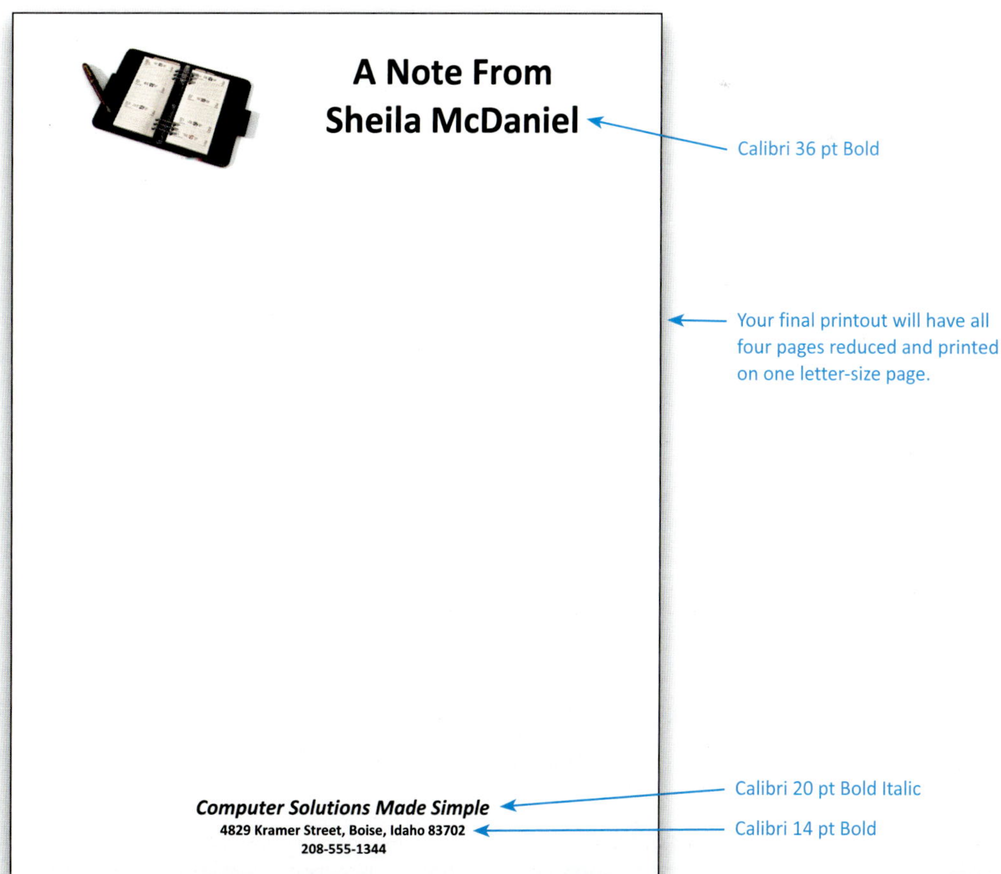

Form
104-10
Notepad Form

1. Insert a picture of a heart or a hospital.
2. Drag and size the picture so that it looks similar to the one in the illustration that follows.
3. Create a text box, about the same size and in the same position as the one in the illustration, to hold the words "The Heart Clinic."
4. Remove the border around the text box.
5. Change to Calibri 36 pt. Bold, Small Caps, and center and type this:

   `THE HEART CLINIC`

6. Apply a color to the text that complements the picture you inserted in step 1.
7. Press ENTER, change to Calibri 16 pt. Bold Italic, and type this:

   `www.heartclinic.org`

8. If necessary, remove the hyperlink from www.heartclinic.org.
9. Create a text box, about the same size and in the same position as the one in the illustration, to hold the doctors' names displayed at the bottom of the page.
10. Remove the border around the text box.
11. Change to Calibri 20 pt. Bold, and type this:

    `Appointment With`

12. Insert a check box from the Wingdings font group, using 20 pt.
13. Change to Calibri 20 pt. Bold Italic, then type `Dr. Anderson` and press ENTER.
14. Repeat steps 12 and 13 for the remaining names in the list: `Dr. Fields` and `Dr. Krachman`.
15. Display formatting marks; then anchor all objects to the first blank line at the top of the page.
16. Change to a whole-page view, click outside any objects, and select and copy the entire document.
17. Move to the end of the document and insert three manual page breaks to create three additional blank pages.
18. Paste the copied document into each of the three newly created pages: click in the fourth page, and paste; click just *before* the Page Break formatting code on the third page, and paste; click just *before* the Page Break formatting code on the second page, and paste.
19. Use the print option to print four pages per sheet on 8.5- by 11-inch paper.

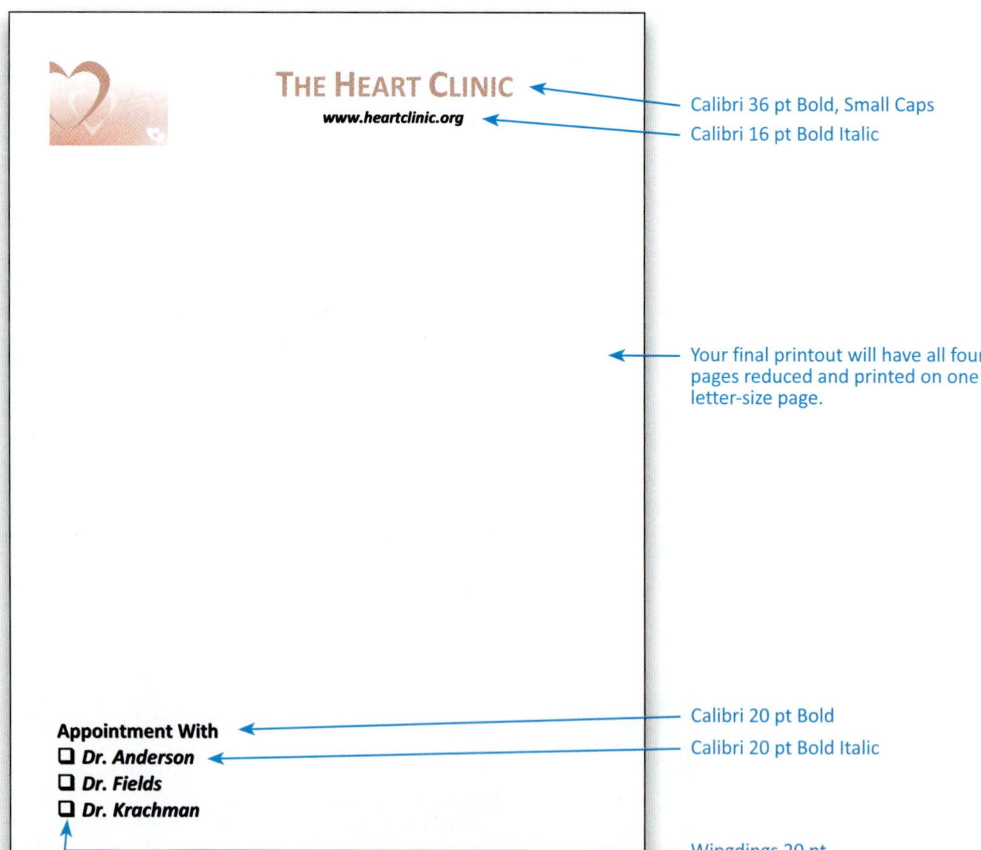

Form
104-11
Notepad Form

1. Create a notepad design of your own—for you personally, for your institution, or for a business.
2. Insert at least one picture that enhances the theme of the notepad.
3. Insert at least one text box with a fill.
4. Try using fonts that you have not yet applied. Experiment with point sizes and attributes.

Keyboarding Connection

Using Hyperlinks

Do you know how to surf the Web? It's easy! The Web contains pages, which are blocks of text, visuals, sound, or animation. Hyperlinks are certain words in the text of the Web page that are highlighted, underlined, or colored differently from the other words. These words link to other pages on the Web.

When you point your cursor at a hyperlink and click, the page connected to that word is displayed. Therefore, one page on the Web can connect to many other pages. Hyperlinked pages do not have to be read in any specific order.

Hyperlinks enable you to connect and retrieve Web pages from computer networks worldwide. With hyperlinks, you can point and click or surf your way all over the Web. You also can bookmark pages that you find, so you can find them again later.

Your Turn: Open a page on the Web. Surf the Web using the hyperlinks displayed on the page.

UNIT 21 LESSON

Designing Miscellaneous Office Forms

105

Goals

- Demonstrate improved speed and accuracy while typing.
- Demonstrate acceptable language arts skills in composing an e-mail message.
- Correctly format a directory form, a sign-in form, and a memo template.
- Successfully complete a Progress and Proofreading Check with zero errors on the first scored attempt.

A. WARMUP

```
alphabet       1 Xylophone wizards quickly begat a lively form of jive beat.
number/symbol  2 pnoe@att.net 270% Ivy & Day 3/8 Go! $17.59 *sic (#6423-145)
easy           3 The turkeys and hogs may spend the day in the mango fields.
```

Skillbuilding

B. 12-SECOND SPEED SPRINTS

Take three 12-second timed writings on each line.

```
4 The man with the rifle may signal us to take the sign down.
5 Hale saw a bible of the gospel in the chapel near the lake.
6 Half of the maps may be for the land and half for the lake.
7 The firm did not sign a form that may name me to the panel.
  ''''5''''10''''15''''20''''25''''30''''35''''40''''45''''50''''55''''60
```

C. PACED PRACTICE

Follow the GDP software directions for this exercise to improve keystroking speed and accuracy.

Language Arts

D. COMPOSING AN E-MAIL MESSAGE

Compose the body of an e-mail message to explain basic design guidelines. Refer to page 423—Section H, Designing a Form. Using your own wording, include the following ideas:

Paragraph 1. Explain that a simple, balanced design is essential and that typefaces (fonts), attributes, and sizes should be limited.

Paragraph 2. Explain that white space should be used to make text easier to read and graphics easier to see.

Paragraph 3. Explain that word processing software is a powerful tool that makes experimenting easy.

Document Processing

Form
105-12
Directory Form

1. Change the page orientation to landscape.
2. Change the top margin to 2 inches, the bottom margin to 0.75 inch, and the side margins to 0.5 inch.
3. Insert clip art associated with a home about the same size in the same position as the one in the illustration.
   Note: Change text wrap to In Front of Text before moving the clip art.
4. Click outside the clip art; then insert a text box, about the same size in the same position as the one in the illustration, to hold the headings.
5. Press ENTER 1 time, then change to Calibri 48 pt. Bold, Small Caps.
6. Center and type this:

   ARBOR STATION SUBDIVISION

7. Change the font color to complement the clip art inserted in step 3.
8. Press ENTER 1 time; then change to Calibri 24 pt. Bold, Small Caps.
9. Center and type DIRECTORY OF RESIDENTS as the subtitle.
10. Remove the border around the text box.
11. Click outside the text box; then insert a boxed table with 4 columns and 17 rows.
12. Move the table below the clip art and text box, as shown in the illustration.
13. Select the entire table, and change the font to Calibri 18 pt. Bold.
14. Type these column headings in Row 1: `Name` | `Address` | `Telephone` | `E-Mail`
15. Change the alignment in Row 1 to center.
16. Add shading to Row 1, using a color that complements the picture.
17. Change the font color to white.

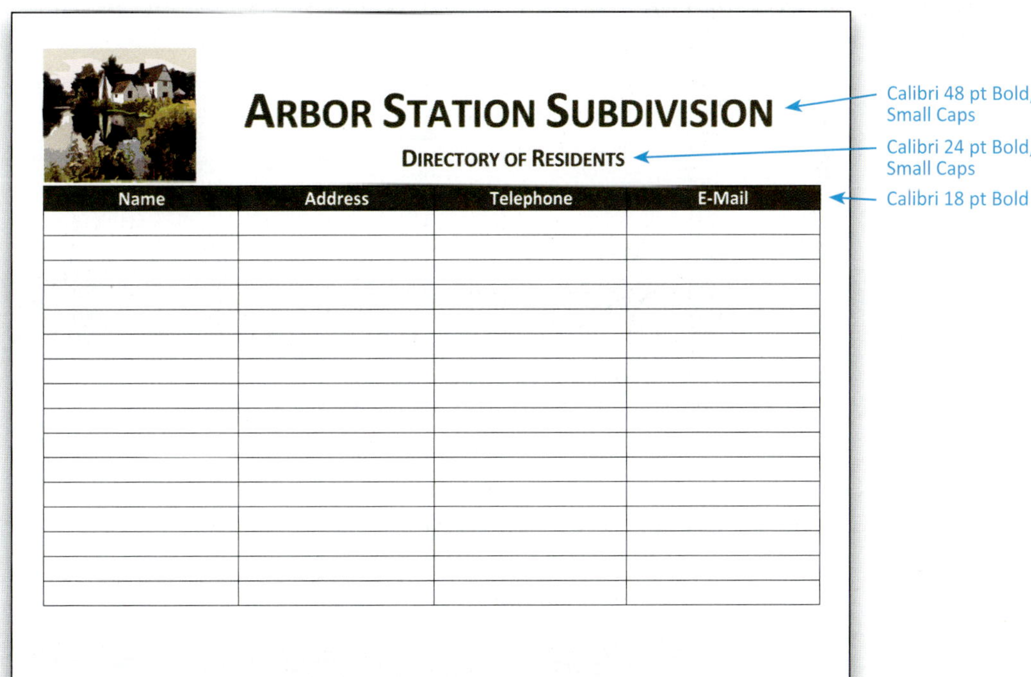

Form
105-13
Sign-In Form

1. Change the top margin to 2 inches, the bottom margin to 0.75 inch, and the side margins to 0.5 inch.
2. Insert a boxed table with 4 columns and 28 rows.
3. Select the entire table, and change the font to Calibri 16 pt. Bold.
4. Type these column headings in Row 1: `Name | Time In | Time Out | Date`, and then change the alignment in Row 1 to center.
5. Add shading of 25 percent to Row 1.
6. Move to the top of the document, and insert clip art, associated with a check mark, in the same position and about the same size as the one in the illustration that follows. **Note:** Before moving the clip art, set text wrapping so that the image appears on top of the text without rearranging the text.
7. Click outside the clip art, then insert a text box, about the same size and in the same position as the one in the illustration, to hold the heading and the doctors' names.
8. Remove the border around the text box.
9. Change to Calibri 36 pt. Bold, Small Caps; then center and type this:

   `PHYSICIAN SIGN-IN SHEET`

10. Press ENTER 1 time, and change the alignment to left.
11. Press TAB 2 times; turn off Small Caps; then insert a round bullet using Wingdings 20 pt. Bold.
12. Press TAB 1 time, then type `Dr. Eleanor Clemmons` and press ENTER 1 time.
13. Repeat steps 11 and 12 for the remaining names in the list: `Dr. Paul Davis` and `Dr. Jeanine Sordhoff`.

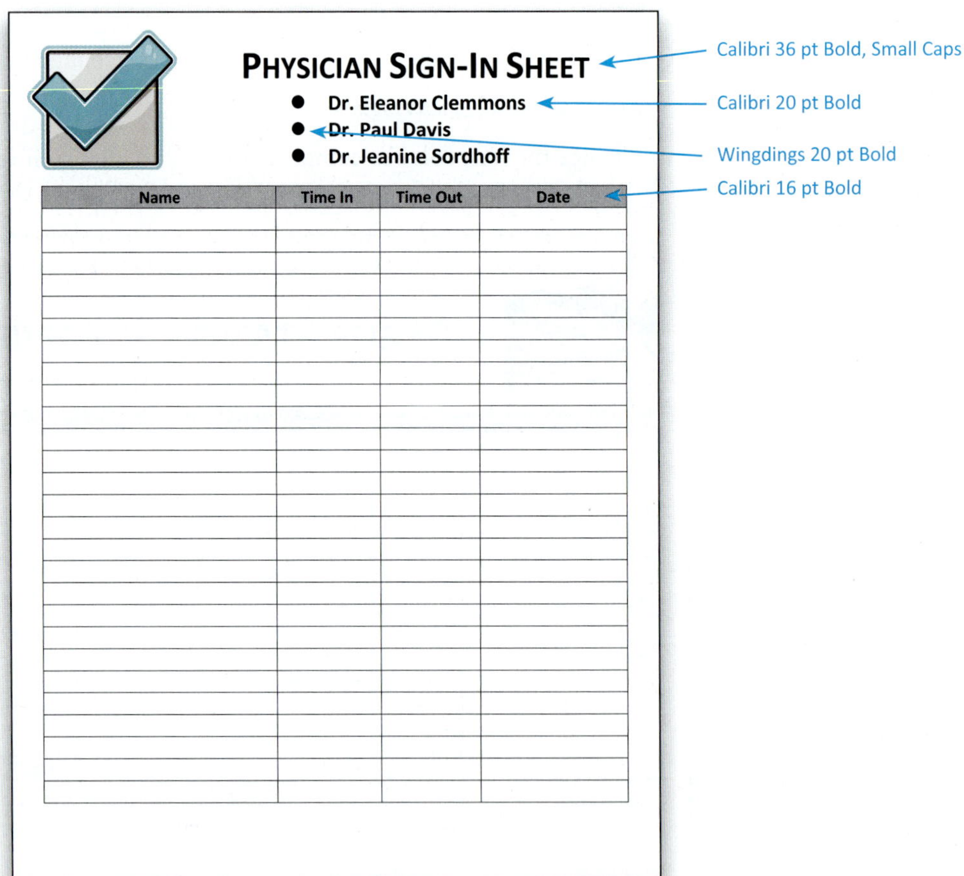

Form
105-14
Memo Template

Progress and Proofreading Check

Documents designated as Proofreading Checks serve as a check of your proofreading skill. Your goal is to have zero typographical errors when the GDP software first scores the document.

Type this memo using the preselected blank memo template that has opened automatically.

To: All Employees

CC: Shelley Castle, ~~Benefits~~ Department

From: Brett R. Cecoli, Human Resources Dept.

Date: November 10, 20--

Re: Company Well ness Program

¶ With the flue season just around the corner we are again planning to administer free flu shots to all company employees. Last year we administered a similar program, and employee absence due to illness was considerably reduced. ¶ A signup schedule will be distributed to all Departments on December 5th. The schedule will list all dates, times, and locations for flu shots to be ~~given~~ administered. Please put December 5 on your calender, and be sure to sign up for your flu shot. | urs

Keyboarding Connection

Choosing a Different Home Page

You don't have to start at the same home page every time you start your browser. You can change the browser's home page to start at one of your favorite Web pages or even a blank page. Refer to your browser's help feature for details.

Some companies require all browser windows to open with the company's home or internal use page. Check your company's Internet usage policy before making any changes to your computer or browser settings.

Your Turn: Using your browser, access a favorite Web page. Make it your browser's home page.

UNIT

22

Designing Office Publications

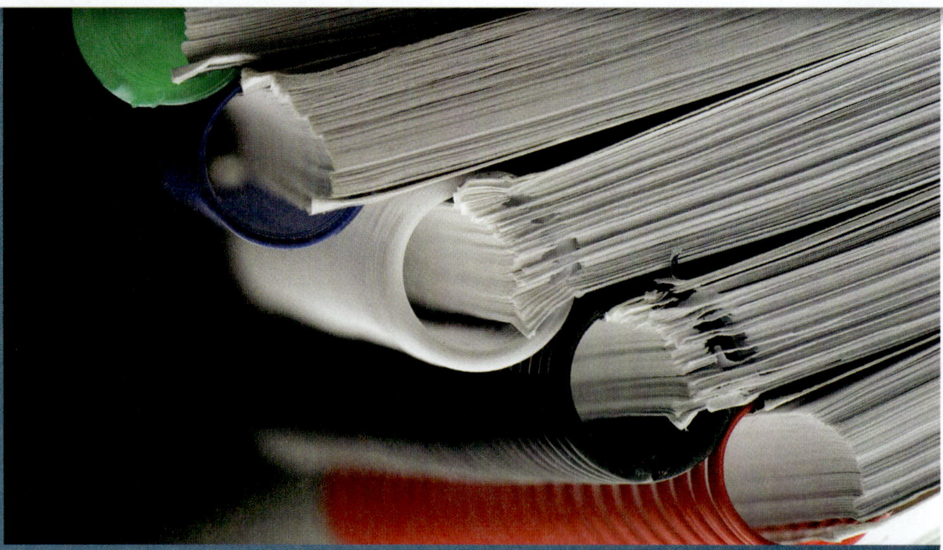

Designing Cover Pages

106

Goals

- Type at least 49wpm/5′/5e.
- Correctly use the WordArt feature.
- Correctly format a cover page.

A. WARMUP

alphabet 1 Few black taxis drove up major roads on a quiet hazy night.
concentration 2 nonrepresentational professionalization straightforwardness
easy 3 Glen may dismantle the authentic robot when he is downtown.

Skillbuilding

B. SUSTAINED PRACTICE: NUMBERS AND SYMBOLS

Take a 1-minute timed writing on the boxed paragraph to establish your base speed. Then take a 1-minute timed writing on the following paragraph. As soon as you equal or exceed your base speed on this paragraph, move to the next, more difficult paragraph.

4 Shopping in the comfort and convenience of your own 11
5 living room has never been more popular than it is right 22
6 now. Shopping clubs abound on cable channels. You could 33
7 buy anything from exotic pets to computers by mail order. 45

8 Sometimes you can find discounts as high as 20% off 11
9 the retail price; for example, a printer that sells for 22
10 $565 might be discounted 20% and be sold for $452. You 33
11 should always investigate quality before buying anything. 44

12 Sometimes hidden charges are involved; for example, 11
13 a printer costing $475.50 that promises a discount of 12% 22
14 ($57.06) has a net price of $418.44. However, if charges 34
15 for shipping range from 12% to 15%, you did not save money. 45

16 You must also check for errors. Several errors have 11
17 been noted so far: Invoice #223, #789, #273, and #904 had 22
18 errors totaling $21.35, $43.44, $79.23, and $91.23 for a 34
19 grand total of $235.25. As always, let the buyer beware. 45

1 | 2 | 3 | 4 | 5 | 6 | 7 | 8 | 9 | 10 | 11 | 12

Take two 5-minute timed writings.

Goal: At least 49wpm/5′/5e

C. 5-MINUTE TIMED WRITING

Why do people choose a particular career? Your first 11
instinct might likely be to say that people work to make 22
money. That may be true, but extensive research has shown 34
that many other factors are considered just as important 45
and that these factors should be carefully considered when 57
you are about to accept a new position. 65

There are many rewards that a job can provide, such 76
as a chance to be creative, the chance to spend time with 87
people whose company you enjoy, or the feeling that you are 99
doing something useful for yourself or for your employer. 111
The quality of the work environment is also an important 122
consideration in choosing a career, as is the chance to 134
work closely with people on a daily basis. 142

Obviously, your career should allow you to advance in 153
your field and to be competitive for promotions. You should 165
be able to see a clear line for advancement in your job and 177
be given a chance to demonstrate your abilities so that 188
your coworkers and supervisors recognize your strengths. 200

Parallel to these factors is the need for your job to 211
give you adequate challenges on a daily, continuing basis. 223
If your work is not challenging, boredom will set in, and 234
you might soon be looking for a change in your career. 245

1 | 2 | 3 | 4 | 5 | 6 | 7 | 8 | 9 | 10 | 11 | 12

Formatting

D. WORD PROCESSING: WORDART

GO TO Word Manual

Study Lesson 106 in your Word Manual. Complete all of the shaded steps while at your computer. Then format the documents that follow.

Document Processing

Report
106-78
Cover Page

1. Insert clip art related to health or the medical profession.
2. Drag and size the clip art so that it looks similar to the one shown in the illustration that follows.
3. Apply an attractive visual style of your choice for the clip art.
4. Insert WordArt, about the same size and in the same position as the one shown in the illustration. Type these words for the WordArt:

   `Health Care Basics`

5. Use Calibri 36 pt. Bold for the Word-Art text; choose a style and color for the WordArt to coordinate with the clip art.
6. Create a text box, about the same size and in the same position as the one below the clip art.
7. Type `"Making the Right Choice"` inside the text box using Cambria 36 pt. Bold Italic. Choose a font color for the text to coordinate with the clip art.
8. Remove the border around the text box.
9. Create a text box, about the same size and in the same position as the one at the bottom of the page shown in the illustration that follows.
10. Type `A SEMINAR SPONSORED BY BOYD MEDICAL CENTER` inside the text box using Calibri 24 pt. Bold, Small Caps.
11. Press ENTER 2 times, change to Calibri 20 pt. Bold, and then type this:

    `Tanner Auditorium`

12. Press ENTER 1 time; then type this:

    `1:00 to 2:30 p.m.`

13. Press ENTER 2 times; then type this:

    `July 10, 20--`

14. Remove the border around the text box.

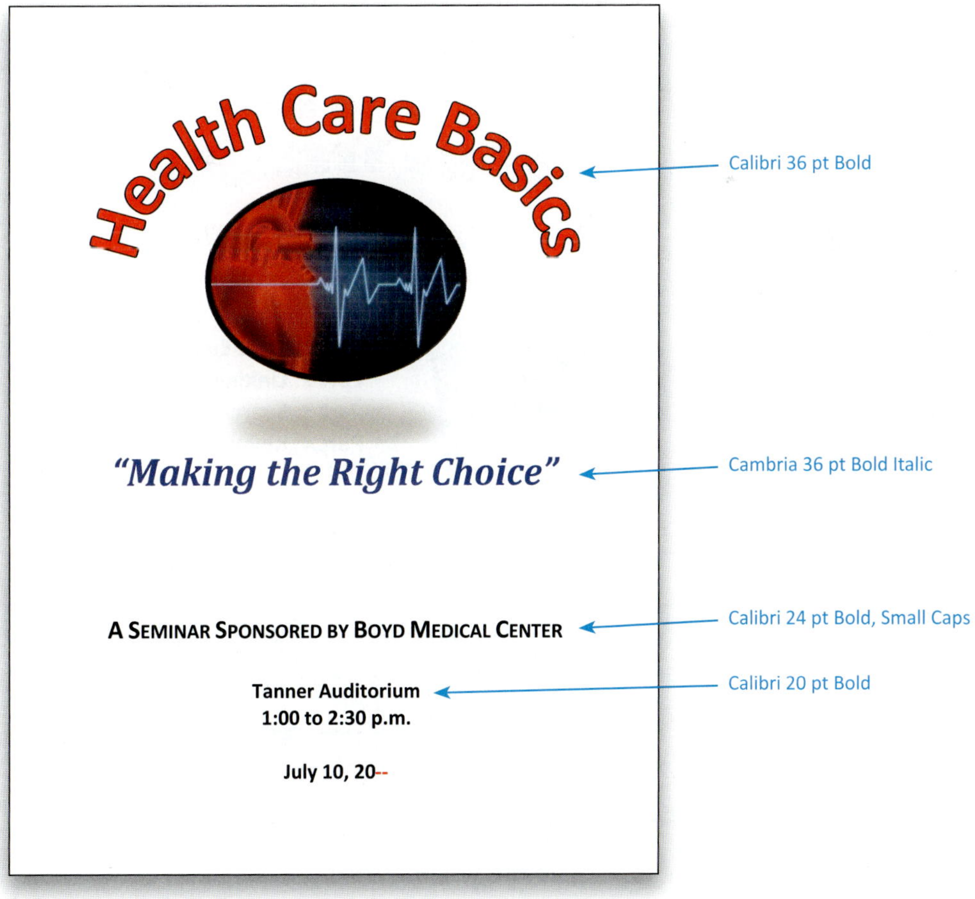

Report
106-79
Cover Page

1. Insert clip art related to the Internet or education.
2. Drag and size the clip art so that it looks similar to the one in the illustration that follows.
3. Apply an attractive visual style of your choice to the clip art.
4. Insert WordArt, about the same size and in the same position as the one at the top of the illustration, and then type `Web Page Design` on the first line and `Online Training` on the second line.
5. Use Impact 36 pt. Bold font for the WordArt text; choose a style and color for the WordArt to coordinate with the clip art.
6. Create a text box, about the same size and in the same position as the one shown in the illustration that follows.
7. Use Calibri 24 pt. Bold to type the following inside the text box:
   - `Part 1: Page Elements`
   - `Part 2: Linking Tools`
   - `Part 3: Search Engines`
   - `Part 4: Keyword Selection`
8. Remove the border around the text box.
9. Create a text box, about the same size and in the same position as the one shown at the bottom of the page in the illustration that follows.
10. Use Calibri 18 pt. Bold to center and type the following inside the text box:

    ```
    Cost of 16 hours of
    instruction is $300.
    Online training is scheduled
    for May 4 to May 7, 20--.
    Each daily program is
    scheduled from 1 to 5 p.m.
    ```

11. Press ENTER 2 times, and then center and type this:

    ```
    Enroll at
    www.webdesign.com/enroll.
    ```

12. Add a text box fill color that coordinates with the picture.

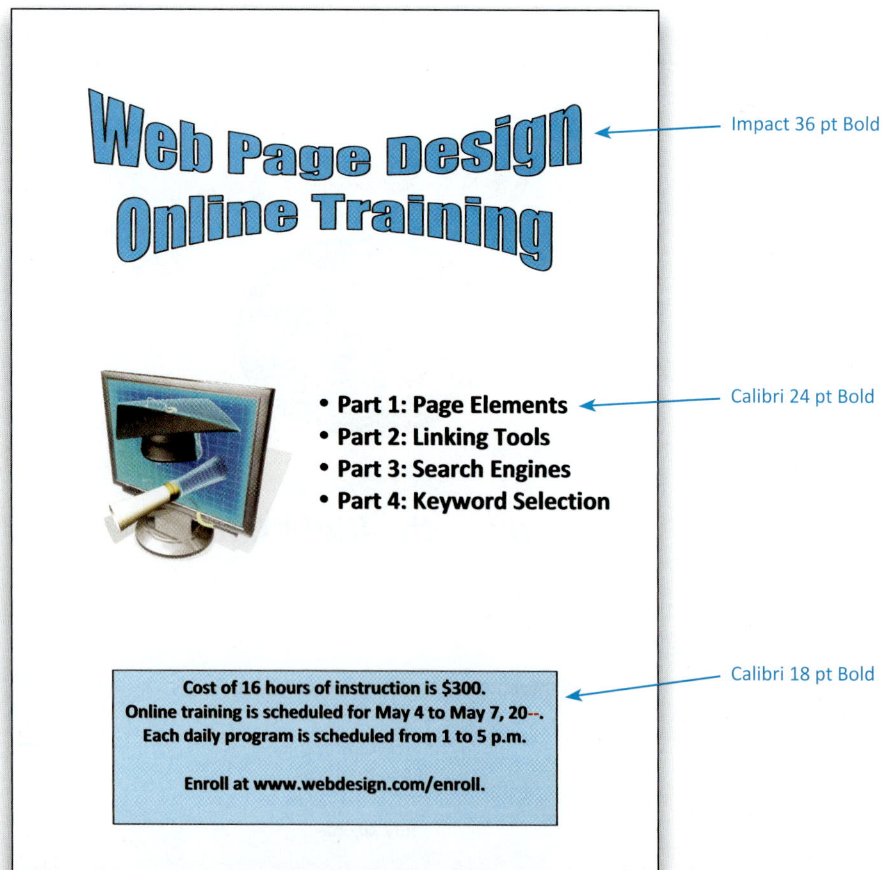

Report
106-80
Cover Page

1. Create a cover page design of your own to be used as the insert for a view binder that holds information for one of your courses.
2. Insert at least one picture related to the subject of the course.
3. Insert at least one text box with a fill.
4. Insert some WordArt.
5. Change any of the font colors to coordinate with the picture or WordArt as desired.

Designing Announcements and Flyers 107

Goals

- Demonstrate improved speed and accuracy while typing.
- Demonstrate acceptable language arts skills in pronoun usage.
- Correctly use Word's features to move a table and add a background page color.
- Correctly format an announcement and a flyer.

A. WARMUP

alphabet 1 Six big devils from Japan then quickly forgot how to waltz.
one hand 2 revert unhook act him access pumpkin gave lymph fever union
easy 3 Rob's work as the auditor in Lakeland may help us in a way.

Skillbuilding

B. MAP+: ALPHABET

Follow the GDP software directions for this exercise to improve keystroking accuracy.

C. PROGRESSIVE PRACTICE: ALPHABET

Follow the GDP software directions for this exercise to improve keystroking speed.

Language Arts

Study the rules at the right.

D. PRONOUNS

RULE
nominative pronoun

Use nominative pronouns (such as *I, he, she, we, they,* and *who*) as subjects of a sentence or clause.

The programmer and he are reviewing the code.
Barb is a person who can do the job.

RULE
objective pronoun

Use objective pronouns (such as *me, him, her, us, them,* and *whom*) as objects of a verb, preposition, or infinitive.

The code was reviewed by the programmer and him.
Barb is the type of person whom we can trust.

See applications of correct pronoun usage in Report 110-88 on pages 456–457.

Edit each sentence to correct any errors.

4 We hope they will take all of them to the concert tomorrow.

5 John gave the gift to she on Monday; her was very pleased.

6 If them do not hurry, Mary will not finish her work on time.

7 The book was proofread by her; the changes were made by he.

8 It is up to them to give us all the pages they read today.

9 Me cannot assure they that it will not rain for the picnic.

Formatting

E. WORD PROCESSING: TABLE—MOVE AND PAGE COLOR

GO TO Word Manual

Study Lesson 107 in your Word Manual. Complete all of the shaded steps while at your computer. Then format the documents that follow.

Document Processing

Report 107-81
Announcement

1. Insert WordArt, about the same size and in the same position as the one at the top of the illustration that follows.

2. Use a shape similar to the one shown in the illustration, with the words `Dade County`; choose the desired font and font size for the text.

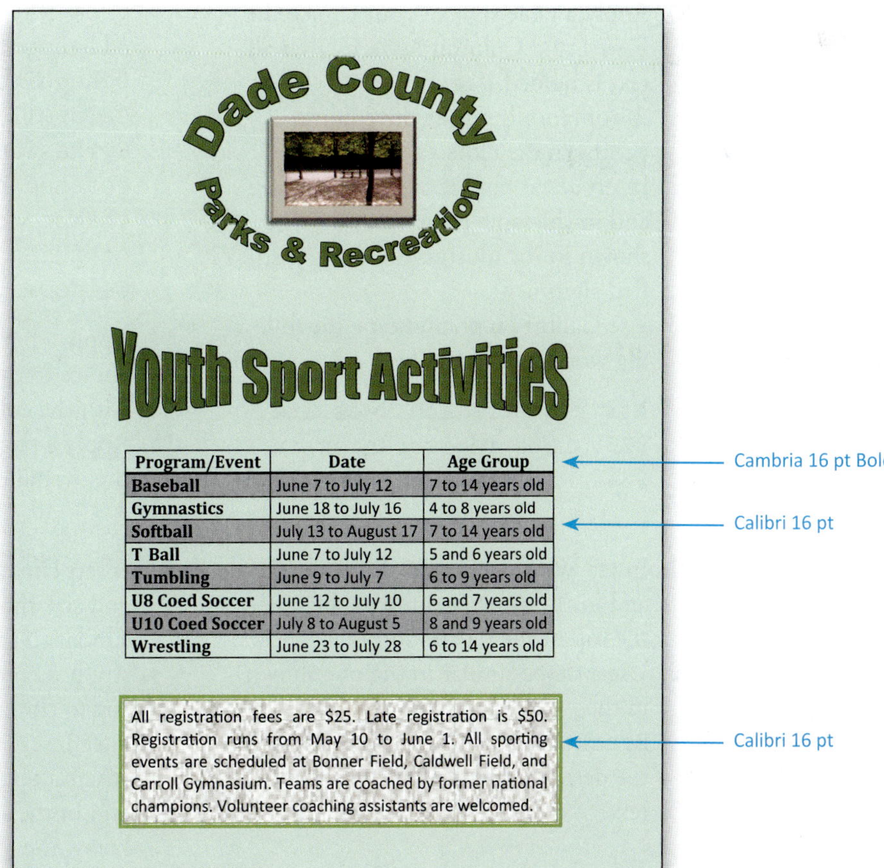

Program/Event	Date	Age Group
Baseball	June 7 to July 12	7 to 14 years old
Gymnastics	June 18 to July 16	4 to 8 years old
Softball	July 13 to August 17	7 to 14 years old
T Ball	June 7 to July 12	5 and 6 years old
Tumbling	June 9 to July 7	6 to 9 years old
U8 Coed Soccer	June 12 to July 10	6 and 7 years old
U10 Coed Soccer	July 8 to August 5	8 and 9 years old
Wrestling	June 23 to July 28	6 to 14 years old

All registration fees are $25. Late registration is $50. Registration runs from May 10 to June 1. All sporting events are scheduled at Bonner Field, Caldwell Field, and Carroll Gymnasium. Teams are coached by former national champions. Volunteer coaching assistants are welcomed.

3. Insert WordArt, similar in size and shape and in a position beneath the first WordArt you inserted in step 1. Use a shape similar to the one shown in the illustration, with the words `Parks & Recreation`; choose the desired font and font size for the text.
4. Insert clip art related to parks; drag and size the clip art so that it looks similar to the one in the illustration.
5. Select a picture style of your choice for the clip art.
6. Apply a color to the text in the WordArt to complement the clip art you have inserted.
7. Insert WordArt, about the same size and in the same position as the one below the WordArt you inserted in step 3. Type the words `Youth Sport Activities` and apply a font color that complements the overall design.
8. Insert a 3-column, 9-row boxed table. Drag the table to a position immediately below the WordArt inserted in step 7 as shown in the illustration that follows.
9. Use Calibri 16 pt. for all entries in the table. Type the following table entries:

Program/Event	**Date**	**Age Group**
Baseball	June 7 to July 12	7 to 14 years old
Gymnastics	June 18 to July 16	4 to 8 years old
Softball	July 13 to August 17	7 to 14 years old
T-Ball	June 7 to July 12	5 and 6 years old
Tumbling	June 9 to July 7	6 to 9 years old
U8 Coed Soccer	June 12 to July 10	6 and 7 years old
U10 Coed Soccer	July 8 to August 5	8 and 9 years old
Wrestling	June 23 to July 28	6 to 14 years old

10. Apply a table style of your choice. In Row 1 and Column A, verify that all text is bolded.
11. Automatically adjust the column widths in the table.
12. Insert a text box, about the same size and in the same position as the one shown in the illustration, using justified alignment.
13. Use Calibri 16 pt, and type the following words in the text box:

```
All registration fees are
$25. Late registration is
$50. Registration runs
from May 10 to June 1.
All sporting events are
scheduled at Bonner Field,
Caldwell Field, and Carroll
Gymnasium. Teams are
coached by former national
champions. Volunteer
coaching assistants are
welcomed.
```

14. Apply a border and a texture of your choice to the text box that coordinate with the color used in the WordArt.
15. Apply a page color that complements the overall design.

Report
107-82
Announcement

1. Insert WordArt, about the same size and in the same position as the one at the top of the illustration that follows.
2. Use a shape similar to the one shown in the illustration, with the words `Breckenridge Rentals`; choose the desired font and font size for the text.
3. Insert clip art related to skiing; drag and size the clip art so that it looks similar to the one in the illustration.
4. Apply a color to the text in the WordArt to complement the clip art you have inserted.
5. Insert a text box, about the same size and in the same position as the one below the clip art.

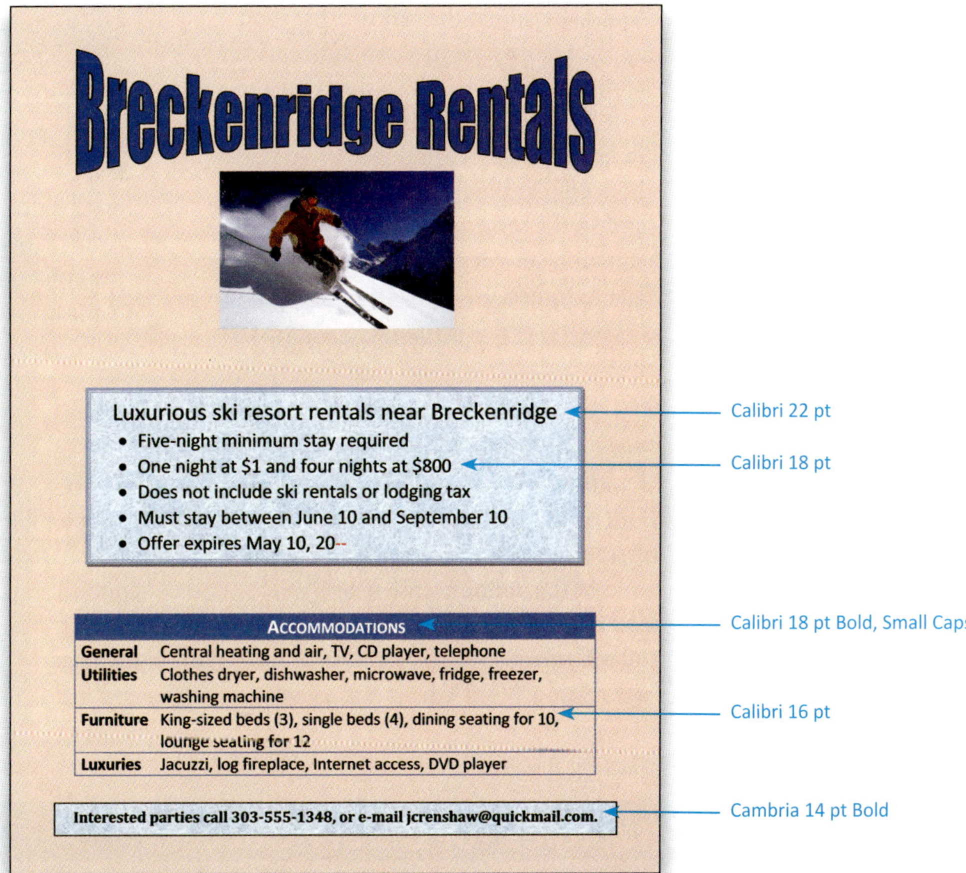

6. Type the following information in the text box. Use Calibri 22 pt. for the centered heading; then change to Calibri 18 pt. to format the remaining lines as a bulleted list:

   Luxurious ski resort rentals near Breckenridge
   - Five-night minimum stay required
   - One night at $1 and four nights at $800
   - Does not include ski rentals or lodging tax
   - Must stay between June 10 and September 10
   - Offer expires May 10, 20--

7. Apply a border and texture of your choice to the text box that coordinates with the colors used in the WordArt and clip art.
8. Insert a table with 2 columns and 5 rows. Drag the table to a position immediately below the text box created in step 5.
9. Merge the cells in Row 1.
10. Use Calibri 18 pt. Bold, Small Caps for Row 1; use Calibri 16 pt. for Rows 2 through 5. Type the following table entries:

Accommodations	
General	Central heating and air, TV, CD player, telephone
Utilities	Clothes dryer, dishwasher, microwave, fridge, freezer, washing machine
Furniture	King-sized beds (3), single beds (4), dining seating for 10, lounge seating for 12
Luxuries	Jacuzzi, log fireplace, Internet access, DVD player

11. Manually adjust the cell widths; then apply a table style of your choice. After applying the style, make sure that the text in Row 1 and Column A appears in bold.
12. Insert a text box, about the same size and in the same position as the one shown below the table.
13. Use Cambria 14 pt. Bold to type the following words centered in the text box:

```
Interested parties call
303-555-1348, or e-mail
jcrenshaw@quickmail.com.
```

14. Apply a border and a texture fill to the text box that match those used in the text box created in step 5.
15. Apply a page color that complements the colors used in the WordArt and clip art.

Report
107-83
Announcement or Flyer

1. Create an announcement or flyer design of your own for an upcoming event at work or on campus.
2. Insert at least one picture related to the topic of the announcement or flyer.
3. Insert at least one text box with a fill and a border.
4. Insert some WordArt.
5. Use a font color to coordinate with the clip art or WordArt.
6. Insert a table that contains information related to the topic of the flyer or announcement.
7. Apply a complementary page color to the page.

Strategies for Career Success

What to Exclude From Your Resume

What items should you omit from your resume? Don't list salary demands. If the job posting requires a salary history, create a separate page listing the salaries for each position you've held. If the job posting wants your salary requirements, in the application letter state, "Salary expectation is in the range . . . ," and provide a range (usually a $5,000 range).

Exclude personal information such as race, gender, health status, age, marital status, religious preference, political preference, national origin, and physical characteristics (for example, height and weight). Do not provide your Social Security number or your photograph.

Exceptions to listing personal information do exist. For example, if you are applying for a job at a political party's headquarters and you are a member of that party, listing your party affiliation might be important to your potential employer.

Your Turn: Review your resume. Have you included any personal information? If your answer is yes, does it serve a purpose for being in your resume?

Designing Newsletters—A

108

Goals

- Type at least 49wpm/5′/5e.
- Correctly format a newsletter masthead.

A. WARMUP

alphabet: In the North, quick waxy bugs jumped over the frozen veldt.

practice: *w* and *e*: wet were where we elbow wed dew wide ewe wee wade web endow

easy: Jane can buy fuel for the antique auto at the downtown lot.

Skillbuilding

B. PACED PRACTICE

Follow the GDP software directions for this exercise to improve keystroking speed and accuracy.

C. 5-MINUTE TIMED WRITING

Take two 5-minute timed writings.

Goal: At least 49wpm/5′/5e

Purchasing a home is probably one of the most major 11
financial decisions you will make in your lifetime. Dozens 22
of questions need to be answered when buying a home. For 34
example, how much of a down payment will you make and how 45
much of a monthly payment on your mortgage will you be able 57
to afford? 60
In addition to your mortgage payment, there are other 71
costs associated with buying a new home. The mortgage will 82
cover the principal and interest for your loan, but you 94
will also have homeowner's insurance and utilities to pay, 105
such as water, sewer, electricity, or gas. 114
You may want to purchase a home through a real estate 125
agent, and it is important that you find out how much of a 137
commission will be charged for that service. 146
When working with a real estate agent, you need to let 157
that person know about the kind of community in which you 169
would prefer to live. Do you want to be close to schools, 180
shopping centers, and restaurants, or would you rather 191
purchase a home in a secluded neighborhood away from the 203
noise and congestion of a metropolitan city? 212
When you find the home that you like, look at it very 223
carefully to see if it is structurally well built, if you 234
like the floor plan, and if it is big enough for you. 245

1 | 2 | 3 | 4 | 5 | 6 | 7 | 8 | 9 | 10 | 11 | 12

Formatting

D. NEWSLETTER DESIGN

Newsletters are an excellent forum for communicating information on a wide range of subjects. A well-planned newsletter will employ all the basic principles of good design. However, because newsletters usually include information on a wide variety of topics, they are generally complex in their layouts.

Most newsletters have the following elements in common: mastheads, main headings and subheadings, text arranged in flowing newspaper-column format using various column widths to add interest, text boxes to emphasize and summarize, pictures to draw readers' attention and interest to a topic, and a variety of borders and fills.

The design of a multipage newsletter must look consistent from one page to the next. This consistency provides unity to the newsletter design and is often achieved through the use of headers and footers.

Document Processing

Report
108-84
Newsletter

Follow these steps to create the masthead and footer for the first page of the newsletter shown on the next page.

1. Set all margins to 0.75 inch.
2. Create an open table with 2 columns and 2 rows. Drag the middle column border to the left so that Column A is about 2.0 inches wide.
3. Right-align Column B, Row 1.
4. In Column B, Row 1, change to Calibri 36 pt. Bold and type `Planning Today for a Fire Emergency` on two lines.
5. Press ENTER 1 time, change to Calibri 14 pt. Bold, and type `A Newsletter From HLS Security Systems`; then press ENTER 1 time.
6. Move to Column A, Row 2, change to Calibri 12 pt. Bold Italic, and type `Volume 5, Issue No. 2`
7. Move to Column B, Row 2, and change to right alignment; then change to Calibri 12 pt. Bold Italic and type this:

   `February 20--`
8. Apply a left, right, and bottom border to Row 2.
9. In Column A, Row 1, insert clip art associated with security. Drag and size the clip art so that it looks similar to the one shown in the illustration that follows.
10. Select the newsletter title, and change the font color to coordinate with the picture in Column A.
11. Apply a double-line border to Row 1 using a color that complements the color in the newsletter title.
12. Insert a blank footer, and center and type `Page` followed by 1 space.
13. Insert a page number and close the footer.
14. Apply a page color to coordinate with the picture and newsletter title.

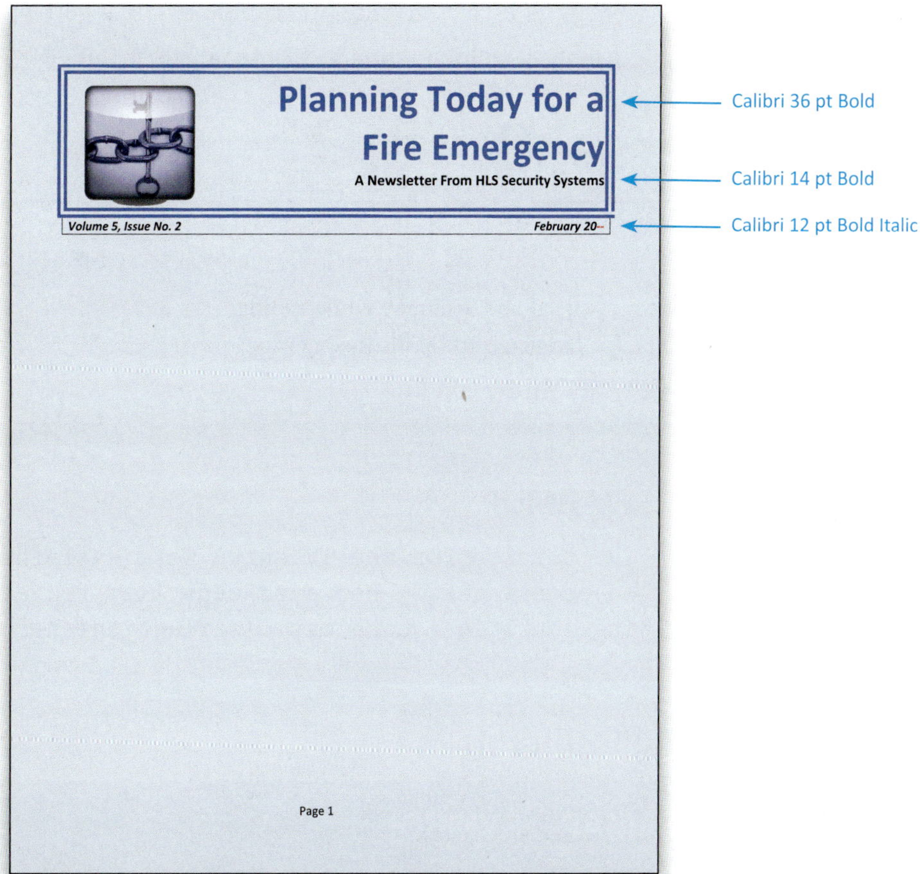

Report
108-85
Newsletter

1. Create a newsletter masthead of your own related to home safety.
2. Use any picture that enhances the purpose of your newsletter.

UNIT 22 | LESSON

Designing Newsletters—B

109

Goals

- Demonstrate improved speed and accuracy while typing.
- Demonstrate acceptable language arts skills in spelling.
- Correctly format a newsletter.

A. WARMUP

alphabet	1	The quizzes for the TV shows were explained by Mick Jagger.
frequent digraphs	2	ed edge wed Eddy bed eyed cede lied fed edited led axed red
easy	3	The neurotic iguana may disorient the neighbor and her dog.

Skillbuilding

B. MAP+: SYMBOL

Follow the GDP software directions for this exercise to improve keystroking accuracy.

PPP PRETEST » PRACTICE » POSTTEST

PRETEST

Take a 1-minute timed writing.

C. PRETEST: Alternate- and One-Hand Words

4 In their opinion, the ornamental bicycle from Honolulu 11
5 may be regarded as an authentic antique. It deserves to be 23
6 treated well because it may attract many new visitors from 35
7 Texas and Ohio to most downtown streets in July and August. 47
1 | 2 | 3 | 4 | 5 | 6 | 7 | 8 | 9 | 10 | 11 | 12

PRACTICE

Speed Emphasis:
If you made no more than 1 error on the Pretest, type each *individual* line 2 times.

Accuracy Emphasis:
If you made 2 or more errors, type each *group* of lines (as though it were a paragraph) 2 times.

D. PRACTICE: Alternate-Hand Words

8 maps visual suspend amendment turndown visible height signs
9 form profit penalty shamrocks blandish problem thrown chair
10 snap emblem dormant authentic clemency figment island usual
11 half signal auditor endowment ornament element handle amend

E. PRACTICE: One-Hand Words

12 serve uphill exceeds killjoy carefree homonym terrace onion
13 trade poplin greater pumpkin eastward plumply barrage holly
14 defer unhook reserve minimum attracts million scatter plump
15 exact kimono created phonily cassette opinion seaweed union

POSTTEST

Repeat the Pretest timed writing and compare performance.

F. POSTTEST: Alternate- and One-Hand Words

Language Arts

Type these frequently misspelled words, paying special attention to any spelling problems in each word.

G. SPELLING

```
16 operations health individual considered expenditures vendor
17 beginning internal pursuant president union written develop
18 hours enclosing situation function including standard shown
19 engineering payable suggested participants providing orders
20 toward nays total without paragraph meetings different vice
```

Edit the sentences to correct any misspellings.

```
21 The participents in the different meetings voted for hours.
22 The presdent of the union is working toward a resolution.
23 The health of each individal must be seriously considered.
24 Engineering has suggested providing orders for the vendor.
25 One expanditure has been written off as part of oparations.
26 He is inclosing the accounts payible record as shown today.
```

Document Processing

Report 109-86
Newsletter (Continued)

Open the file for Report 108-84. Follow these steps to continue the newsletter as shown below:

1. Move your insertion point to the end of the document; then press ENTER 1 time.
2. Insert File 109, and turn on automatic hyphenation.
3. Carefully place your insertion point in front of the first character of the text you inserted from File 109.
4. Select all the newly inserted text, including 1 blank line below the last line of text.
5. With the text still selected, create a 3-column page layout.
6. Select the following side headings in the newsletter, and change the font to Calibri 20 pt. Bold:

   ```
   Plan Ahead
   Make a Diagram
   Plan Your Escape
   Avoid Smoke
   ```

7. Insert clip art in the space below the first two side headings. The clip art should be related to the topic of each of the paragraphs (*plan* and *drawing*).
8. Set text wrapping to place text above and below the image, but not beside the image.
9. Set the clip art height to 1.8 inches; let the width adjust proportionally to the height.
10. Drag the clip art into a position similar to the clip art shown in the illustration.
11. Compare the placement of the columnar text to see if it's similar to that shown in the illustration. Check to see if the side heading "Plan Your Escape" appears at the top of Column C. If not, adjust the size and placement of the clip art.

Adjust the size and placement of the pictures on this page so that the heading **Plan Your Escape** displays at the top of Column C.

Highlighted words are spelling words from the language arts activities.

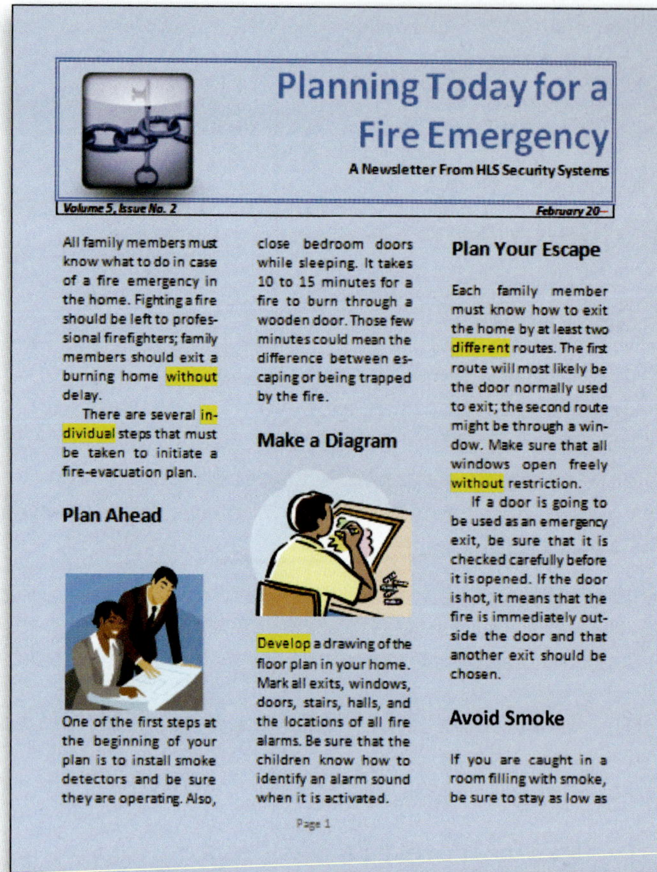

Planning Today for a Fire Emergency

A Newsletter From HLS Security Systems

Volume 5, Issue No. 2 | February 20—

All family members must know what to do in case of a fire emergency in the home. Fighting a fire should be left to professional firefighters; family members should exit a burning home without delay.

There are several individual steps that must be taken to initiate a fire-evacuation plan.

Plan Ahead

One of the first steps at the beginning of your plan is to install smoke detectors and be sure they are operating. Also, close bedroom doors while sleeping. It takes 10 to 15 minutes for a fire to burn through a wooden door. Those few minutes could mean the difference between escaping or being trapped by the fire.

Make a Diagram

Develop a drawing of the floor plan in your home. Mark all exits, windows, doors, stairs, halls, and the locations of all fire alarms. Be sure that the children know how to identify an alarm sound when it is activated.

Plan Your Escape

Each family member must know how to exit the home by at least two different routes. The first route will most likely be the door normally used to exit; the second route might be through a window. Make sure that all windows open freely without restriction.

If a door is going to be used as an emergency exit, be sure that it is checked carefully before it is opened. If the door is hot, it means that the fire is immediately outside the door and that another exit should be chosen.

Avoid Smoke

If you are caught in a room filling with smoke, be sure to stay as low as

Page 1

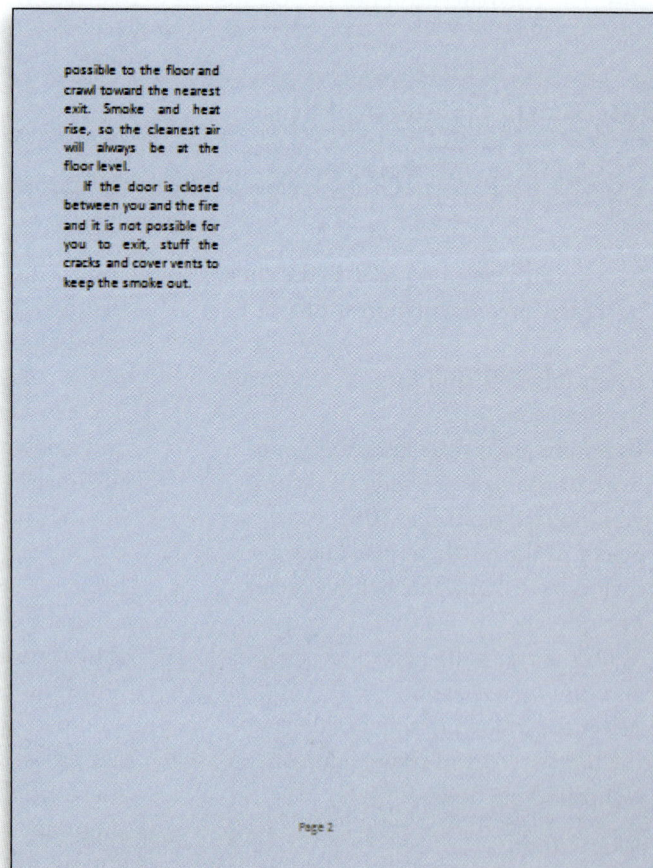

possible to the floor and crawl toward the nearest exit. Smoke and heat rise, so the cleanest air will always be at the floor level.

If the door is closed between you and the fire and it is not possible for you to exit, stuff the cracks and cover vents to keep the smoke out.

Page 2

Report
109-87
Newsletter (Continued)

1. Open the file for Report 108-85 with the newsletter masthead you created.
2. Follow the steps for Report 109-86, and then delete the "Avoid Smoke" section at the bottom of Column C.
3. Insert a picture after the side heading "Plan Your Escape."
4. Drag and size the picture so that it is similar to the ones previously inserted on the page. Make certain that all of the text remains on that page and does not wrap to a second page.

Keyboarding Connection

E-Mail Privacy

How private are your e-mail messages? Although there has been a lot of discussion about hacking and Internet security, e-mail may be more secure than your phone or postal mail. In fact, most new-generation e-mail programs have some kind of encryption built in.

It is not hackers who are most likely to read your e-mail. It is anyone with access to your incoming mail server or your computer. If your computer and incoming server are at work, then you can assume your supervisor can read your e-mail. In some companies, it is normal practice to monitor employees' e-mail. Therefore, you should not send e-mail from work that you don't want anyone there to read.

If you are serious about e-mail privacy, you may want to examine other encryption methods. Different products are available to ensure that your e-mail is read only by the intended recipient(s). However, some companies don't allow employees to add software to their computers for legal reasons, so check your company's computer policies. It may be wiser to send personal e-mail from your own computer outside of work.

Your Turn: Perform a keyword search using a search engine for information on different products that are available to protect your e-mail privacy.

Designing Newsletters—C

110

Goals

- Type at least 49wpm/5′/5e.
- Correctly format a newsletter.
- Successfully complete a Progress and Proofreading Check with zero errors on the first scored attempt.

A. WARMUP

alphabet	1	The glum, wavy-haired ex-cons bequeathed fake topaz jewels.
number/symbol	2	gilp@comcast.net (11%) Ng & Ma 4/5 No! $13.86 *Est. #20-972
easy	3	Nancy and Blanche cut six bushels of corn in the cornfield.

Skillbuilding

B. 12-SECOND SPEED SPRINTS

Take three 12-second timed writings on each line.

4 He may go with us to the giant dock down by the handy lake.
5 The old chapel at the end of the big lake has an odd shape.
6 His body of work may charm the guests who visit the chapel.
7 His civic goal for the city is for them to endow the chair.

' ' ' ' 5 ' ' ' '10' ' ' '15' ' ' '20' ' ' '25' ' ' '30' ' ' '35' ' ' '40' ' ' '45' ' ' '50' ' ' '55' ' ' '60

C. TECHNIQUE PRACTICE: ENTER KEY

Type each line 2 times. Type each sentence on a separate line by pressing ENTER after each sentence.

8 Don't! We are. Give. Speak. Type it. Beg. Be there. We did?
9 Step on it. See to it. Wait. Find it? Says who? We do. Sit.
10 Who knows? See me. Get up. Eat! Where? Who is he? Finished?
11 When? Today. Do it now. We are up. Al saw her. Do not. All?

Take two 5-minute timed writings.

Goal: At least 49wpm/5'/5e

D. 5-MINUTE TIMED WRITING

When the rate of unemployment is very low, jobs are 11
easier to find. Although you may find a job easily, what 22
can you do to make sure your job is one you will enjoy? 33
Here are some suggestions to assist you. 41
First, be certain you receive a job description when 52
you are hired. The job description should list all of the 64
requirements of the job and the details of what you will be 78
expected to do. 79
Second, you should receive some type of orientation to 90
your job and the company. During orientation, you will fill 102
out various tax forms, benefit forms, and insurance papers. 114
You may view a video that will help you learn more about 126
the company and available benefits. 133
Third, when you start your training, you should take 144
notes, pay attention, and ask questions. You should also 155
have your trainer check your work for a period of time to 167
be sure you are performing your duties correctly. If your 178
tasks are complex, you can break them down into smaller 189
parts so you can remember all aspects of your job. 200
Finally, when you know your job requirements, chart 210
your work each day. Concentrate on being part of the team. 222
Be zealous in striving to work beyond the expectations of 234
your supervisor. Then, you will achieve job satisfaction. 245

1 | 2 | 3 | 4 | 5 | 6 | 7 | 8 | 9 | 10 | 11 | 12

Document Processing

Report 110-88
Newsletter (Continued)

Open the file for Report 109-86. Follow these steps to finish creating the newsletter shown below.

1. Verify that automatic hyphenation is on.
2. Place your insertion point directly after the final period at the end of the sentence in Column A. Then press ENTER 2 times.
3. Change to Calibri 20 pt. Bold, and type `Practice the Plan` as a side heading. Then press ENTER 1 time.
4. Change to Calibri 14 pt., press ENTER 1 time, and then type the following paragraph:

Effective fire evacuation is only as good as family members are aware of how it is supposed to function. Have them practice the plan, and be certain all family members are aware of all escape routes. Practice the escape plan at different hours.

5. With your insertion point after the final period you typed in step 3, press ENTER 2 times; then insert File 110.
6. Select the following side headings in the text that was inserted, and change the font to Calibri 20 pt. Bold:

```
Exit Safely
Plan to Meet
Assist Others
```

7. Insert clip art in the space below the side heading "Exit Safely." The clip art should be associated with the topic of the paragraph (*exit*).
8. Set the clip art with a height of 1.55 inches; let the width adjust proportionally to the height.
9. Apply the same picture style to the clip art that was used for the clip art on page 1 of the newsletter.
10. Drag the clip art into a position similar to the clip art shown in the illustration below. Set text wrapping to place text above and below the image, but not beside the image.
11. Move your insertion point to the end of the newsletter.
12. Insert a text box at the bottom of Column C, about the same size and shape and in the same position as the one shown in the illustration.
13. Change to Calibri 16 pt. Bold; then center and type this in the text box:

```
Future Issues
```

14. Press ENTER 1 time, change to Calibri 11 pt. Bold, and then center and type this:

```
March: Homeland Security
April: Updating Your System
May: Emergency Supplies
June: Safety Seminars
```

15. Apply a textured fill to the text box that complements the page color of the newsletter.
16. Change the shape of the text box to complement the shape used for the clip art in the newsletter.
17. Make whatever adjustments are needed to make your newsletter look attractive.
18. The newsletter should look similar to the illustrations that follow.

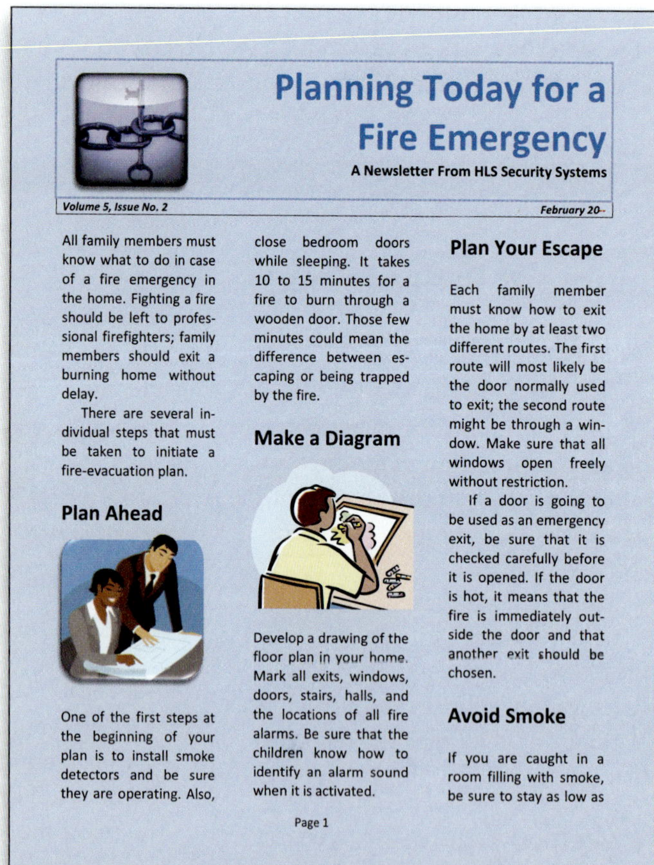

Planning Today for a Fire Emergency

A Newsletter From HLS Security Systems

Volume 5, Issue No. 2 *February 20--*

All family members must know what to do in case of a fire emergency in the home. Fighting a fire should be left to professional firefighters; family members should exit a burning home without delay.

There are several individual steps that must be taken to initiate a fire-evacuation plan.

Plan Ahead

One of the first steps at the beginning of your plan is to install smoke detectors and be sure they are operating. Also, close bedroom doors while sleeping. It takes 10 to 15 minutes for a fire to burn through a wooden door. Those few minutes could mean the difference between escaping or being trapped by the fire.

Make a Diagram

Develop a drawing of the floor plan in your home. Mark all exits, windows, doors, stairs, halls, and the locations of all fire alarms. Be sure that the children know how to identify an alarm sound when it is activated.

Plan Your Escape

Each family member must know how to exit the home by at least two different routes. The first route will most likely be the door normally used to exit; the second route might be through a window. Make sure that all windows open freely without restriction.

If a door is going to be used as an emergency exit, be sure that it is checked carefully before it is opened. If the door is hot, it means that the fire is immediately outside the door and that another exit should be chosen.

Avoid Smoke

If you are caught in a room filling with smoke, be sure to stay as low as

Page 1

nominative pronoun
Column A (*"they"*)

nominative pronoun Column B (*"they"*)
objective pronoun Column C (*"them"*)
objective pronoun Column A (*"them"*)

objective pronoun Column C (*"themselves"*)
nominative pronoun Column C (*"who"*)

possible to the floor and crawl toward the nearest exit. Smoke and heat rise, so the cleanest air will always be at the floor level.

If the door is closed between you and the fire and it is not possible for you to exit, stuff the cracks and cover vents to keep the smoke out.

Practice the Plan

Effective fire evacuation is only as good as family members are aware of how it is supposed to function. Have them practice the plan, and be certain all family members are aware of all escape routes. Practice the escape plan at different hours.

Exit Safely

Exiting safely through a ground-floor window or door is usually uneventful. However, if you are on the second floor or higher, exiting will require you to take some precautions. If you attempt to jump from an upper floor, you might injure an ankle or leg. One suggested solution would be to purchase a ladder for the upstairs bedrooms to use for emergency exits. Make sure to inspect the ladders annually to be sure they operate properly.

If living in an apartment, never use an elevator in case of fire. An elevator may cease operating during a fire and stop between floors or at a floor where the fire is located. As an alternative, use a fire escape or stairwell to escape.

Teach your family that, once they are outside a burning building, they should never go back into the building.

Plan to Meet

A special meeting place should be considered that is always located a safe distance from the house. Knowing where this meeting place is will assist all family members in determining where to meet to see if everyone is safe and has exited the home.

Assist Others

You may have to provide some special assistance to young children.

If children are afraid, they may choose to hide under a bed or in the closet. Encourage them to exit outside the home, a safe distance away from the fire. Make certain that your children can operate all windows, open all doors, descend a ladder, or lower themselves to the ground.

You may also need to consider assistance for the elderly, who may have difficulty in exiting the premises.

Future Issues

March: Homeland Security
April: Updating Your System
May: Emergency Supplies
June: Safety Seminars

Page 2

Report
110-89
Flyer

Progress and Proofreading Check

Documents designated as Proofreading Checks serve as a check of your proofreading skill. Your goal is to have zero typographical errors when the GDP software first scores the document.

1. Insert WordArt about the same size as the one in the illustration that follows. Center the WordArt horizontally, and apply a color of your choice for the text. Use the following text for the WordArt:

   `Premier Real Estate`

2. Insert clip art related to homes; drag and size the clip art so that it looks similar to the one in the illustration.
3. Select an attractive visual style of your choice for the clip art.
4. Apply a font color to the text in the WordArt to complement the clip art you have inserted.
5. Create a text box, about the same size and in the same position as the one in the illustration. Use Calibri 20 pt. Bold Italic to type and center the words `"Serving the Canton area for 55 years"` in the text box. Use a shape fill that complements the color of the WordArt.
6. Create a boxed table with 3 columns and 9 rows. Drag the table to a position immediately below the text box created in step 5.
7. Use Calibri 16 pt. for Row 1; use Calibri 14 pt. for Rows 2 through 9. Type the table entries as follows:

Weekly Specials: April 10 Through April 16		
Address	**Price**	**Agent**
224 Birchfield Run, Green Bay	$242,000	Angie Summers
4134 Diamond Court, DePere	$257,000	Doug McClure
812 Eagles Nest Circle, Allouez	$263,000	Angie Summers
427 Matthews Avenue, Green Bay	$269,000	Connie McCormack
1280 Timbermill Circle, Allouez	$283,000	Doug McClure
628 Clifton Terrace, DePere	$297,000	Chad Burnett
829 Cypress Court, Green Bay	$323,000	Angie Summers

8. Apply a style of your choice to the table. After applying the style, make sure that the text in Row 1, Row 2, and Column A appear in bold.

9. Apply a page color that complements the colors used in the WordArt and clip art.

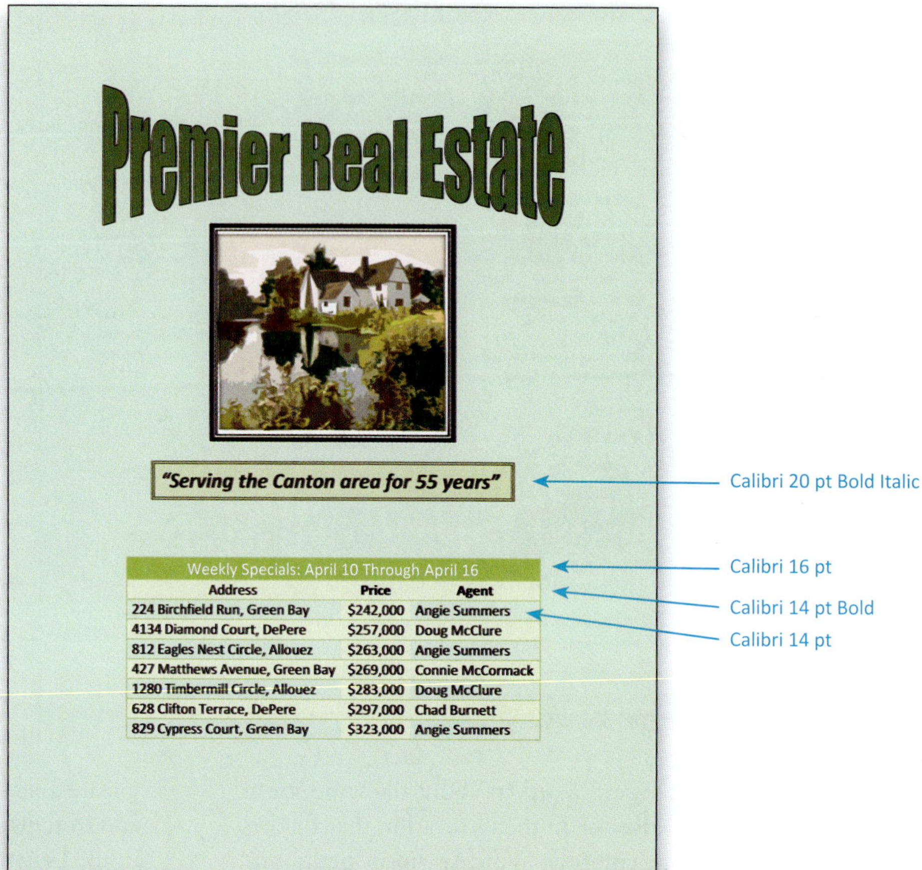

Address	Price	Agent
224 Birchfield Run, Green Bay	$242,000	Angie Summers
4134 Diamond Court, DePere	$257,000	Doug McClure
812 Eagles Nest Circle, Allouez	$263,000	Angie Summers
427 Matthews Avenue, Green Bay	$269,000	Connie McCormack
1280 Timbermill Circle, Allouez	$283,000	Doug McClure
628 Clifton Terrace, DePere	$297,000	Chad Burnett
829 Cypress Court, Green Bay	$323,000	Angie Summers

UNIT 23

Online Resumes and Merged Documents

UNIT 23 LESSON

111

Designing an Online Resume

Goals

- Demonstrate improved speed and accuracy while typing.
- Demonstrate acceptable language arts skills in capitalization.
- Correctly use Word's custom borders and shading feature.
- Correctly format an online resume.

A. WARMUP

alphabet	1	`Big July earthquakes confounded the zany experimental vows.`
concentration	2	`uncommunicativeness departmentalization electrocardiography`
easy	3	`It is the duty of the busy ensigns to dismantle the panels.`

Skillbuilding

B. MAP+: ALPHABET

Follow the GDP software directions for this exercise to improve keystroking accuracy.

C. PROGRESSIVE PRACTICE: ALPHABET

Follow the GDP software directions for this exercise to improve keystroking speed.

Language Arts

D. CAPITALIZATION

Study the rules at the right.

RULE
= organization

Capitalize common organizational terms (such as *advertising department* and *finance committee*) only when they are the actual names of the units in the writer's own organization and when they are preceded by the word *the*.

The report from the Advertising Department is due today.

But: Our advertising department will submit its report today.

RULE
= course

Capitalize the names of specific course titles but not the names of subjects or areas of study.

I have enrolled in Accounting 201 and will also take the marketing course.

Edit each sentence to correct any errors.

```
The advertising department at their firm is excellent.

The Finance Committee here at Irwin will meet today.

I think I am going to pass keyboarding 1 with flying colors.

Their marketing department must approve the proposal first.

A class in Business Communications would be very helpful.

To take Math 102, you must have taken a beginning math course.
```

Formatting

E. ONLINE RESUME

REFER TO Word Manual

Appendix C: Saving a Word File in PDF Format.

An online resume is an opportunity to showcase your technical expertise and creativity in Word as you use customized borders and shading. Also, because an online resume is electronically available and could be posted online in PDF format, your resume is accessible to a wider range of prospective employers.

If desired, you can include hyperlinks to actual documents if those documents are available with your resume or posted on the Internet. Text shown in square brackets on an electronic resume, such as [Transcript], would be converted to a hyperlink to jump to the related item.

F. WORD PROCESSING: TABLE—BORDERS AND SHADING, CUSTOM

GO TO Word Manual

Study Lesson 111 in your Word Manual. Complete all of the shaded steps while at your computer. Then format the documents that follow.

Document Processing

Report 111-90
Online Resume

1. Create a table structure, and type in the information as shown in the completed resume. Use the default Calibri 12-pt. font unless directed otherwise.
2. Select Row 1, set a right tab at the right margin, and apply italic.
3. Type the information in Row 1, aligning the phone number and e-mail address at the right margin.
4. Select "Ted C. Campos," and change the font to Calibri 24 pt. Bold.
5. Type the headings in the appropriate rows using Calibri 14 pt. Bold.
6. Type the information under each heading in the corresponding rows.
7. Type the bulleted lists in Calibri 11 pt.
8. Italicize the job titles in the "Experience" section.
9. Increase the indent on the line under the "References" section to align with the text following the bullets in the bulleted lists.
10. Type the last line of text in the resume, center it, and change the font to Calibri 9 pt. Italic.
11. Apply custom borders and shading as desired.
12. Apply a theme color palette and theme font of your choice.

24 pt Bold Italic (name only)

Italic

14 pt Bold

11 pt

Italic

→ indent 0.5″

9 pt Italic

Ted C. Campos → tab 6.5″ *401-555-7880*

29 Americas Cup Avenue, Newport, RI 02840 → tab 6.5″ *tcampos@speedmail.com*

OBJECTIVE

To obtain a full-time position as a fitness trainer with an opportunity to work as an exercise therapist in a rehabilitation clinic.

EDUCATION

University of Rhode Island, [Accreditation], Kingston, Rhode Island
Bachelor of Science Degree

- Graduated: June 2010
- Major: Exercise Science
- GPA: 3.9 in major on 4.0 scale [Transcript] [Skills Checklist]

EXPERIENCE

Personal Trainer (part-time), Oakwood Fitness Center
Kingston, Rhode Island
June 2008 to present

- Help clients assess their level of physical fitness and set and reach fitness goals, and demonstrate various exercises to help clients improve their exercise techniques.
- Keep records of exercise sessions to monitor clients' progress toward physical fitness and evaluate clients' responses.

Volunteer, YMCA
Newport, Rhode Island
December 2007 to May 2008

- Taught first aid and CPR [Instructor Certification].
- Interacted with youth through adult population.

SKILLS

- Youth Sports Clinic Referee [Certification]
- Tae Kwon Do instructor [Certification]

REFERENCES

Available on request.

(Created on July 13, 2010; last updated on August 15, 2010.)

Your completed resume may look different from the one shown. This table is shown with "View Gridlines" active.

Report
111-91
Online Resume

1. Open Report 111-90.
2. Apply borders and shading with customized widths and colors of your choice different from the ones used in Report 111-90.
3. Apply a theme color palette and theme font of your choice different from the ones used in Report 111-90.
4. Change the content of the first bulleted item in the first portion of the EXPERIENCE section to this:

   Help clients set and reach fitness goals and improve their exercise techniques.

5. Change the content of the second portion of the EXPERIENCE section to this:

   Strength Coach (part-time), Fitness Emporium
   Jamestown, Rhode Island
   January 2007 to April 2008
   - Selected fitness equipment; coordinated personal training programs.
   - Demonstrated several methods of strength training.

Mail Merge—A

Goals

- Type at least 50wpm/5′/5e.
- Correctly use Word's mail merge feature to create merged letters.
- Correctly format a form letter in block style.

A. WARMUP

alphabet 1 Dr. Jekyll vowed to finish zapping the quixotic bumblebees.
one hand 2 secret hominy dew hip beasts nonunion edge monk staff nylon
easy 3 Susie's sorority is proficient in their work with the city.

Skillbuilding

B. SUSTAINED PRACTICE: CAPITALS

Take a 1-minute timed writing on the boxed paragraph to establish your base speed. Then take a 1-minute timed writing on the following paragraph. As soon as you equal or exceed your base speed on this paragraph, move to the next, more difficult paragraph.

4 Even though he was only about thirty years old, Jason 11
5 knew that it was not too soon to begin thinking about his 23
6 retirement. He soon found out that there were many things 34
7 involved in his plans for an early and long retirement. 45

8 Even without considering the uncertainty of social 10
9 security, Jason knew that he should plan his career moves 22
10 so that he would have a strong company retirement plan. He 33
11 realized that he should have an Individual Retirement Plan. 45

12 When he became aware that The Longman Company, the 10
13 firm that employed him, would match his contributions to a 22
14 supplemental retirement account, he began saving even more. 34
15 He used the Payroll Department funds from the Goplin Group. 46

16 He also learned that The Longman Company retirement 11
17 plan, his Individual Retirement Plan, and his supplemental 22
18 retirement account are all deferred savings. With those 34
19 tax-dollar savings, Jason bought New Venture Group funds. 45

1 | 2 | 3 | 4 | 5 | 6 | 7 | 8 | 9 | 10 | 11 | 12

Take two 5-minute timed writings.

Goal: At least 50wpm/5′/5e

C. 5-MINUTE TIMED WRITING

Employers want the people who work for them to have 11
many qualities of good character. Character is defined as a 23
distinctive feature of a person or thing. Character may be 34
what you are known for and may be why you remember someone 46
else. What are some of the traits you think of that are 57
linked with good character? A few traits might be respect, 69
honesty, trust, caring, leadership, attitude, tolerance, 81
fairness, and patience. 85

All people should have respect for themselves and for 96
others. If you respect people, you have a high regard for 108
the way they conduct themselves in all aspects of life. 119
However, before you can respect others, you need to have 131
respect for yourself. 135

Honesty and trustworthiness are similar traits. In 145
business dealings, people expect honesty and will admire 157
people who have this quality. They like to build business 168
relationships with companies whose employees are honest, 180
just, and trustworthy. 184

Your attitude is reflected in the way you act toward 195
other people or in the way you speak to them. You can make 207
great strides in advancing your career by taking a look at 219
the way you interact with people. You may want to take a 230
closer look at some character traits you want to improve. 242
Such improvements in life will amaze you. 250

1 | 2 | 3 | 4 | 5 | 6 | 7 | 8 | 9 | 10 | 11 | 12

Formatting

D. FORM LETTERS

A form letter is a letter that combines standard and variable information for a number of different recipients to create a set of merged documents. Mail merge is also very useful when creating corresponding envelopes and labels for a form letter. The same variable information used to create the address block in the form letter may be used to create the address block in envelopes or labels.

Two files must be created before a merge can occur. The main document (in this example, a form letter) contains generic content that doesn't change. The data source file contains variable information specific to the recipient (the person receiving the finalized merged document), such as the inside address block and the first and last name in the salutation.

After these two files are created, placeholder fields (codes that will be replaced with actual text after the files are merged) are inserted into the main document. These fields link the variable content from the data source file to the generic text in the main document. Finally, the main document file is merged with the data source file to create a number of finished documents that combine generic text from the main document with variable text from the data source file into a single file.

When the main document or data source is updated, all changes will be reflected in each new merged document. The following illustration shows a letter created as a main document with corresponding placeholder fields inserted.

Placeholder field codes for the inside address and salutation in the main document

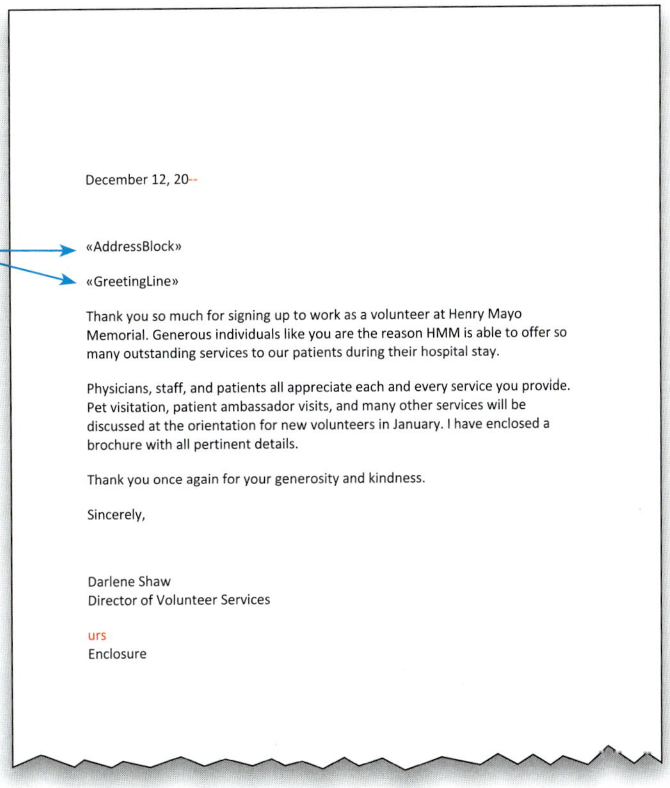

December 12, 20--

«AddressBlock»

«GreetingLine»

Thank you so much for signing up to work as a volunteer at Henry Mayo Memorial. Generous individuals like you are the reason HMM is able to offer so many outstanding services to our patients during their hospital stay.

Physicians, staff, and patients all appreciate each and every service you provide. Pet visitation, patient ambassador visits, and many other services will be discussed at the orientation for new volunteers in January. I have enclosed a brochure with all pertinent details.

Thank you once again for your generosity and kindness.

Sincerely,

Darlene Shaw
Director of Volunteer Services

urs
Enclosure

E. WORD PROCESSING: MAIL MERGE—LETTERS

GO TO Word Manual

Study Lesson 112 in your Word Manual. Complete all of the shaded steps while at your computer. Then format the documents that follow.

Document Processing

Correspondence 112-95
Business Letter in Block Style

1. Create the main document without any placeholder fields, and save the main document file as *Correspondence 112-95-main.*
2. Create a data source file for each recipient listed, and save the data source file as *Correspondence 112-95-data.*
3. Insert the appropriate placeholder fields in the form letter; select a colon as the punctuation mark for the salutation.
4. Adjust the blank lines above or below the placeholder fields as needed to format the inside address and salutation correctly.
5. Preview your results and make any adjustments as needed.
6. Merge the main document and the data source file to create one file with the four merged letters, and save the file as *Correspondence 112-95.*

Main Document

February 14, 20--
«AddressBlock»
«GreetingLine»
¶ Welcome to Lakeshore Terrace! I hope you are enjoying the stunning vistas of nearby Lake Tahoe, the golf course, and the recreation center that are all part of the amenities available to every homeowner in our planned community.
¶ Be assured that the Lakeshore Terrace Residential Community Association is committed to maintaining the guidelines set forth by our association so that our

(continued on next page)

residents will continue to enjoy all the amenities of this community for many years to come.

¶ If you have any questions at all, please feel free to e-mail me at cbrown@ltrca.com or call me at 530-555-2992. Also, check our Web site at http://ltrca.org for upcoming community events and other items of interest.

¶ Once again, welcome to the neighborhood!

Sincerely, | Carly Brown | Assistant Association Manager | urs

Data Source

Type the data shown in the table in the appropriate fields in the dialog box.

Title	First Name	Last Name	Address Line 1	City	State	ZIP Code
Dr.	Karen	Simpson	4309 Pine Bouquet Road	Lake Tahoe	CA	96150
Ms.	Gloria	Freeman	4135 Zephyr Road	Lake Tahoe	CA	96150
Mr.	Justin	Frazier	1900 Jansen Beach Road	Lake Tahoe	CA	96150
Mrs.	Lillian	Hunt	1135 Pioneer Trail Road	Lake Tahoe	CA	96150

Mail Merge—B 113

Goals

- Demonstrate improved speed and accuracy while typing.
- Demonstrate acceptable proofreading skills by editing lines.
- Correctly format a form letter in modified-block style.

A. WARMUP

alphabet
1 Prized waxy jonquils choked the weeds in the big farm vats.

practice: *f* and *g*
2 fig finger flag frogs gift golf gulf goofs gruff fogs flags

easy
3 The new formal audit may be paid for by the downtown firms.

Skillbuilding

B. MAP+: NUMBERS

Follow the GDP software directions for this exercise to improve keystroking accuracy.

PPP PRETEST » PRACTICE » POSTTEST

C. PRETEST: Common Letter Combinations

PRETEST
Take a 1-minute timed writing.

4 The condo committee was hoping the motion would not be 11
5 forced upon it, realizing that viable solutions ought to be 23
6 developed. It was forceful in seeking a period of time for 35
7 tensions to cool. All concerned wanted the problem solved. 47

1 | 2 | 3 | 4 | 5 | 6 | 7 | 8 | 9 | 10 | 11 | 12

D. PRACTICE: Word Beginnings

PRACTICE
Speed Emphasis:
If you made no more than 1 error on the Pretest, type each *individual* line 2 times.
Accuracy Emphasis:
If you made 2 or more errors, type each *group* of lines (as though it were a paragraph) 2 times.

8 for forum forge forced forgot formal forest foreign forerun
9 con conks conic consul confer convey convex contact concern
10 per perks peril person period perish permit percale percent
11 com combs comet combat comedy comics common compete complex

E. PRACTICE: Word Endings

12 ing tying hiking liking edging bowing hoping having nursing
13 ble fable pebble treble tumble viable dabble fumble fusible
14 ion union legion nation region motion potion option bastion
15 ful awful cupful fitful joyful lawful earful artful tearful

POSTTEST

Repeat the Pretest timed writing and compare performance.

F. POSTTEST: Common Letter Combinations

Language Arts

Edit this paragraph to correct any errors.

G. PROOFREADING

The idea and practise of sharing risk originated in antiquetry. Many years ago, Chinesemerchants deviced an injenious way of protecting themselves against the chance of a financialy ruinous accadent in the dangerous river along the trade routes when they were delivring goods.

Document Processing

Correspondence 113-96

Business Letter in Modified-Block Style

1. Create the main document without any placeholder fields, and save the main document file as *Correspondence 113-96-main.*
2. Create a data source file for each recipient listed, and save the data source file as *Correspondence 113-96-data.*
3. Insert the appropriate placeholder fields in the form letter; select a colon as the punctuation mark for the salutation.
4. Adjust the blank lines above or below the placeholder fields as needed to format the inside address and salutation correctly.
5. Preview your results and make any adjustments as needed.
6. Merge the main document and the data source file to create one file with the four merged letters, and save the file as *Correspondence 113-96.*

Main Document

July 21, 20--

«AddressBlock»

«GreetingLine»

¶ Thank you for registering for the American Association of Retired Teachers annual convention to be held in Las Vegas, Nevada, on October 10-12.

¶ You can look forward to three days of noted speakers, engaging educational presentations, interactive exhibitors, prizes, and events. Your evenings will be filled with concerts, dinners, and Las Vegas entertainment! If you wish to take some excursions to nearby attractions, such as Hoover Dam and Red Rock Canyon, visit the concierge booth upon arrival to make all the necessary arrangements.

(continued on next page)

¶ AART has contracted with several Las Vegas hotels to provide you with luxury accommodations at a price you can afford. Reserve your hotel room soon to secure your accommodations. Visit our Web site at http://www.aart.org for details and online reservations.
¶ Please feel free to e-mail me at rholt@aart.org if you have any further questions.
Sincerely, / Ms. Robbie Holt / Event Coordinator / urs

Data Source

First Entry
Mr. / Richard / Lampman / 1237 Winterson Road / Baltimore / MD / 21201

Second Entry
Ms. / Penny / Cutler / 915 Fairmont Boulevard / Rapid City / SD / 57701

Third Entry
Dr. / Todd / Dabney / 1531 Paseo de Peralta / Santa Fe / NM / 87501

Fourth Entry
Mrs. / Tanya / Benjamin / 931 Talbot Street / Taylor / TX / 76574

Mail Merge—C 114

Goals

- Type at least 50wpm/5′/5e.
- Correctly format a form letter in block style.

A. WARMUP

alphabet 1 Why did Max become eloquent over a zany gift like jodhpurs?
frequent digraphs 2 te tee ate byte tell tea termite ten Ute tent teed teen Ted
easy 3 The auditor's panel had the right to risk a firm's profits.

Skillbuilding

B. PROGRESSIVE PRACTICE: NUMBERS

Follow the GDP software directions for this exercise to improve keystroking speed.

C. TECHNIQUE PRACTICE: SHIFT KEY

Type each line 2 times. After striking the capitalized letter, return the SHIFT KEY finger immediately to home-row position.

4 Alex Bly and Clara Dye wed. Ella Fochs and Gil Hall talked.
5 Ida Jackson met Kay Lang for a fast lunch at Mamma Nancy's.
6 Otis Pike should call Quint Richards about Sophia Townsend.
7 Urich Volte will take Winona Xie to visit Yadkin in Zurich.

Take two 5-minute timed writings.

Goal: At least 50wpm/5'/5e

D. 5-MINUTE TIMED WRITING

```
     Before you apply for a job, you will want to do some       11
detective work. First, choose a company where you want to       23
work, and then use the Internet to find out about the firm.     34
If you find a site for the business, then you can learn all     46
about the company, its hiring policies, the job listings,       58
or ways to apply for a job there.                               65
     When you are researching a business, you want to           75
learn about the history of the company. You may be able         86
to find out how stock analysts expect the company stock         97
to perform in the coming months if the firm is publicly        108
traded. When you find a job opening for which you know that    120
you want to apply, read carefully to see what type of work     132
experience and education the business requires for the job.    144
     When you prepare your resume, emphasize your major        155
qualifications based on the requirements listed for the        166
job. If the person who will receive the job inquiries is       177
not listed, contact the company by phone or e-mail to learn    189
his or her name. You should personalize the cover letter       201
and resume to stress what the firm needs.                      209
     The information you find in your research will be         219
very helpful during the interview with a manager at the        230
company. Ask good questions and speak confidently about        242
the job. Emphasize how your skills fit in.                     250
   1 | 2 | 3 | 4 | 5 | 6 | 7 | 8 | 9 | 10 | 11 | 12
```

Document Processing

Correspondence 114-97
Business Letter in Block Style

1. Create the main document without any placeholder fields, and save the main document file as *Correspondence 114-97-main.*
2. Create a data source file for each recipient listed, and save the data source file as *Correspondence 114-97-data.*
3. Insert the appropriate placeholder fields in the form letter; select a colon as the punctuation mark for the salutation.
4. Adjust the blank lines above or below the placeholder fields as needed to format the inside address and salutation correctly.
5. Preview your results and make any adjustments as needed.
6. Merge the main document and the data source file to create one file with the four merged letters, and save the file as *Correspondence 114-97.*

Main Document

Nov. 1, 20--

<<GreetingLine>>

<<AddressBlock>>

¶ Welcome to Movie Flix! As a new member youre entitled to 6 months of free dvds by mail. Because we have over 150 shipping points across the Nation you can count on receiving ~~your~~ a DVD in about one business day. Due dates and late fees are a thing of the past. For every new member yuo refer, you will receive anadditional 2 months of free premium membership. You have a wide array of DVDs from which to choose ~~from~~. Many new-release movies and and current-season TV episodes are available. If you prefer, we can stream all your entertainment to you via a Movieflix device or directly online to your personal computer at no extra charge. Please visit our Web site at www.mflix.com for complete listings and details.

¶ If you have any questions or concerns whatsoever, don't hesitate to contact me at 800-555-7662 or e-mail me at rphillips@mflix.com. I'm at your service.

Sincerely, | Roy Phillips | Subscriber RelationsSpecialist | urs

Data Source

Mr. | Estrada | Andres | 123 N. Thomas Road | Phoenix | AZ | 85400

Ms. Joyce | Evans | 1172 Yellowstone High way | Cody | WY | 82414

Mr. | Ken | Newwton | 459 South Meridian | Oklahoma City | OK | 73108

~~Mr.~~ Mrs. | Brandy | Burgess | 29 Riverside Dr. | Corning | NY | 14830

Mail Merge—D

Goals

- Demonstrate improved speed and accuracy while typing.
- Demonstrate acceptable language arts skills in composing a personal business letter.
- Correctly use Word's mail merge feature to create merged envelopes and labels.
- Correctly format merged envelopes and labels.
- Correctly format a form letter in block style.
- Successfully complete a Progress and Proofreading check with zero errors on the first scored attempt.

A. WARMUP

alphabet
1 I have just quoted for nine dozen boxes of gray lamp wicks.

number/symbol
2 wroe@gmail.com 82% Dye & Cox (5/7) Oh! ($6.90) *8:45 #12-63

easy
3 My mangy dog then ran to his bowl in the den to take a sip.

Skillbuilding

B. 12-SECOND SPEED SPRINTS

Take three 12-second timed writings on each line.

4 I am at my best when I am on a boat on an icy lake at home.
5 Ray may work in the field of coal when he is not busy here.
6 If they work in town, they may make a visit to the old gym.
7 Jake may try to fix the leaks in the pipes in the city gym.

' ' ' ' 5 ' ' ' ' 10 ' ' ' ' 15 ' ' ' ' 20 ' ' ' ' 25 ' ' ' ' 30 ' ' ' ' 35 ' ' ' ' 40 ' ' ' ' 45 ' ' ' ' 50 ' ' ' ' 55 ' ' ' ' 60

C. PACED PRACTICE

Follow the GDP software directions for this exercise to improve keystroking speed and accuracy.

Language Arts

D. COMPOSING A PERSONAL BUSINESS LETTER

Compose the body of a letter to a former instructor of yours. You want him or her to agree to serve as a reference for you when you apply for jobs after college. In the letter, discuss the following:

Paragraph 1: Start with a pleasant introduction, and remind the instructor of which class(es) you had with him or her and perhaps something specific about yourself to help the instructor remember you.

Paragraph 2: Describe the kind of position for which you're applying so that the instructor will know what to include in the letter of reference.

Paragraph 3: Close on a positive, appreciative note.

Formatting

E. MERGED ENVELOPES AND LABELS

Creating a set of merged envelopes and labels is very similar to creating a set of merged letters. The basic difference is that the main document is a blank envelope, an envelope with a return address, or a blank label rather than a letter with generic content. A new data source can also be created and used, or an existing data source can be reused.

F. WORD PROCESSING: MAIL MERGE—ENVELOPES AND LABELS

GO TO Word Manual

Study Lesson 115 in your Word Manual. Complete all of the shaded steps while at your computer. Then format the documents that follow.

Document Processing

Correspondence 115-98
Envelopes

Main Document

1. Create the main document without any placeholder fields, and save the main document file as *Correspondence 115-98-main.*
2. Delete any return address that might appear.
3. Create a data source file for each recipient listed, and save the data source file as *Correspondence 115-98-data.*
4. Insert the appropriate placeholder fields in the inside address area of the envelope.
5. Preview your results and make any adjustments as needed.
6. Merge the main document and the data source file to create one file with the four merged envelopes, and save the file as *Correspondence 115-98.*

Data Source

First Entry

Mrs. | Esther | Page | Alpha Sound Systems | 720 East Adams Street | Springfield | IL | 62701

Second Entry

Ms. | Jennie | Guthrie | Advanced Solar Heating Systems | 3421 West Markham Street | Little Rock | AR | 72201

Third Entry

Dr. | Ruth | Mendoza | Henry Mayo Hospital | 6439 Vista Way | Carlsbad | CA | 92008

Fourth Entry

Mr. | Benjamin | Ong | World Appliance Service | 2394 Graves Road | Tallahassee | FL | 32303

Correspondence
115-99
Mailing Labels

Main Document

1. Create the main document without any placeholder fields, and save the main document file as *Correspondence 115-99-main.*
2. Choose Avery US Letter as the label vendor and 5160 as the product number.
3. Create a data source file for each recipient listed, and save the data source file as *Correspondence 115-99-data.*
4. Insert the appropriate placeholder fields in the label.
5. Preview your results and make any adjustments as needed.
6. Merge the main document and the data source file to create one file with the four merged labels, and save the file as *Correspondence 115-99.*

Data Source

First Entry

Mr. | Carlos | Bedolla | 500 Stoneridge Drive | Columbia | SC | 29210

Second Entry

Dr. | Julie | Bergman | 5331 Grand Canyon Drive | Madison | WI | 53713

Third Entry

Ms. | Shannon | Beckam | 111 North Grand Avenue | Lansing | MI | 48917

Fourth Entry

Mrs. | Debra | Mack | 1444 Fairview Avenue | Boise | ID | 83702

Correspondence
115-100
Business Letter in Block Style

1. Create the main document without any placeholder fields, and save the main document file as *Correspondence 115-100-main.*
2. Create a data source file for each recipient listed, and save the data source file as *Correspondence 115-100-data.*
3. Insert the appropriate placeholder fields in the form letter; select a colon as the punctuation mark for the salutation.
4. Adjust the blank lines above or below the placeholder fields as needed to format the inside address and salutation correctly.
5. Preview your results and make any adjustments as needed.
6. Merge the main document and the data source file to create one file with the four merged letters, and save the file as *Correspondence 115-100.*

Main Document

March 28, 20--
«AddressBlock»
«GreetingLine»
¶ Summer is rapidly approaching, and Southern California Electrical has a great idea to help save you money on your electric bill. SCE is offering a special Summer Discount Plan to help conserve energy and prevent power emergencies.
¶ If you agree to enroll in our plan, we will install a remote-controlled device on your air-conditioning unit. During hours of peak demand, this remote device will cycle your air conditioning on and off based on an interval of your choosing. You will be interested to know that a temperature shift of only a few degrees is typical—you probably won't even notice it. But you will notice the savings in your energy bill.
¶ There are two convenient options to choose from—one plan will maximize your savings and the other plan will maximize your comfort. Log on to www.scelectrical.com/sdp to enroll online and to review all details of each plan. The earlier you sign up, the faster you'll begin saving money.
Sincerely, | George Morimoto | Customer Programs Representative | urs

Data Source

Progress and Proofreading Check

Documents designated as Proofreading Checks serve as a check of your proofreading skill. Your goal is to have zero typographical errors when the GDP software first scores the document.

First Entry
Mr. | Martin | Galindo | 1599 South Raymond Avenue | Fullerton | CA | 92831

Second Entry
Ms. | Colleen | Westridge | 1029 West Ball Road | Anaheim | CA | 92802

Third Entry
Dr. | Michelle | Hardey | 431 North Doheny Drive | Beverly Hills | CA | 90210

Fourth Entry
Mrs. | Carolyn | Wong | 325 North Pass Avenue | Burbank | CA | 91505

UNIT 24

Skillbuilding and In-Basket Review

UNIT 24 LESSON

Skillbuilding and In-Basket Review—Banking

116

Goals

- Type at least 50wpm/5′/5e.
- Correctly format a memo template, boxed table, and letterhead form.

A. WARMUP

alphabet — We promptly judge antique ivory buckles for the next prize.

concentration — gastroenterologists interdenominational individualistically

easy — Dirk may visit the island by the oaks with his tan bicycle.

Skillbuilding

B. SUSTAINED PRACTICE: PUNCTUATION

Take a 1-minute timed writing on the boxed paragraph to establish your base speed. Then take a 1-minute timed writing on the following paragraph. As soon as you equal or exceed your base speed on this paragraph, move to the next, more difficult paragraph.

Have you ever noticed that a good laugh every now and 11
then really makes you feel better? Research has shown that 22
laughter can have a very healing effect on our bodies. It 33
is an excellent way to relieve tension and stress all over. 46

When you laugh, your heart beats faster, you breathe 11
deeper, and you exercise your lungs. When you laugh, your 22
body produces endorphins--a natural painkiller that gives 34
you a sense of euphoria that is very powerful and pleasant. 46

Someone said, "Laugh in the face of adversity." As it 11
happens, this is first-rate advice. It's a great way to 22
cope with life's trials and tribulations; it's also a good 34
way to raise other people's spirits and relieve tension. 45

Finding "humor" in any situation takes practice--try 11
to make it a full-time habit. We're all looking for ways 22
to relieve stress. Any exercise--jogging, tennis, biking, 34
swimming, or golfing--is a proven remedy for "the blues." 45

1 | 2 | 3 | 4 | 5 | 6 | 7 | 8 | 9 | 10 | 11 | 12

Take two 5-minute timed writings.

Goal: At least 50wpm/5′/5e

C. 5-MINUTE TIMED WRITING

```
     A few factors should be considered before you buy a         11
new printer for your computer. First, decide how you will       22
use your new printer. If you plan to use the printer for        34
typing letters and reports, you may decide you want a laser     45
printer at a reasonable price and that is capable of doing      57
general tasks you will need.                                    63
     If you are buying the printer for office use, you may      74
decide to shop for a printer that prints documents more         85
quickly and is of exceptional value. Then, if you plan to       97
use a digital camera with the printer, you will want to get    109
a printer that is made to print documents of photo quality.    121
     Resolution, speed, and paper handling are some other      132
factors you should consider when you buy a new printer.        143
Resolution refers to how sharp the image appears on the        154
paper. With printers that have a higher resolution, the        165
image gives you output of higher quality. You will see an      177
amazing difference when you compare some samples of print      188
from the other kinds of printers.                              195
     If you expect to print long documents, then you will      206
want to search for a reliable printer with a feed tray that    218
holds a large amount of paper. The more expensive printers     230
are usually faster printers. After assessing your printer      241
needs, you are ready to make your purchase.                    250
     1 | 2 | 3 | 4 | 5 | 6 | 7 | 8 | 9 | 10 | 11 | 12
```

Document Processing

Situation: Today is October 10. You are employed in the office of First National Savings in Del Mar, California. Ms. Sabrina Talavaro, vice president, has written the memo shown next. Type it using a memo template; send it to all bank employees with a copy to T. J. Hurley, president. Ms. Talavaro prefers to use her name and title in the From field. The subject of the memo is "Revision to Online Access Agreement."

Form 116-15
Memo Template

¶ The revised OAA (Online-Access Agreement) becomes effective on October 20. Our customers have been notified of the new agreement via e-mail and letters. However, we do anticipate customer inquiries for specific details and individual account questions. Below is a recap of significant changes made to the OAA.

(continued on next page)

¶ The agreement was simplified and includes two important changes. First, the rights and responsibilities of account owners and delegates have been amended to add an option for an account owner to delegate account-management authority to another person. Second , online banking terms and conditions have been incorporated into the OAA for the convenience of our customers.

¶ The revised OAA also specifically clarifies details regarding the "Payment-Send-on Date" for Automatic Bill Pay that has historically been a source of confusion. Also, the sections related to online banking were revised to better describe the enrollment process.

¶ Please visit www.fns.com/oaa/about to review all changes in depth. I have also attached a table that can be used as a quick reference to relevant sections in the OAA. Contact me at stalavaro@fns.com if you have any questions.

When the memo is distributed, the table below should be attached. Ms. Talavaro asks you to use attractive borders and shading to give this table a desktop-published appearance.

Table
116-55
Boxed Table

Your completed table may look different from the one shown.

ONLINE ACCESS AGREEMENT* First National Savings	
Topic	**Section**
Online banking terms and conditions	1, 3, 4, and 29
Guest users and authorized users defined	2A, 2B, and 5D
Bill Pay Account name change	7A
Bill Pay Account number changes	10A
Online billing provider definition	6A
Enrollment process for eligible accounts	10
Legal disclosures	20A and 20B
*Update effective October 20, 20--.	

Ms. Talavaro has sketched out a letterhead form and wants you to design the finished letterhead for First National Savings. The top of the letterhead should include the company name, address, phone number, and Web site address with each element separated by a diamond-shaped symbol. The main office address is 1701 Coast Boulevard, Del Mar, CA 92014; the phone number is 800-555-2447, and the Web site address is www.fns.com. Type the company slogan `First National Savings: the key to your financial future` at the bottom of the letterhead form.

Form
116-16
Letterhead Form

To begin the form, change all margins to 0.6 inch.

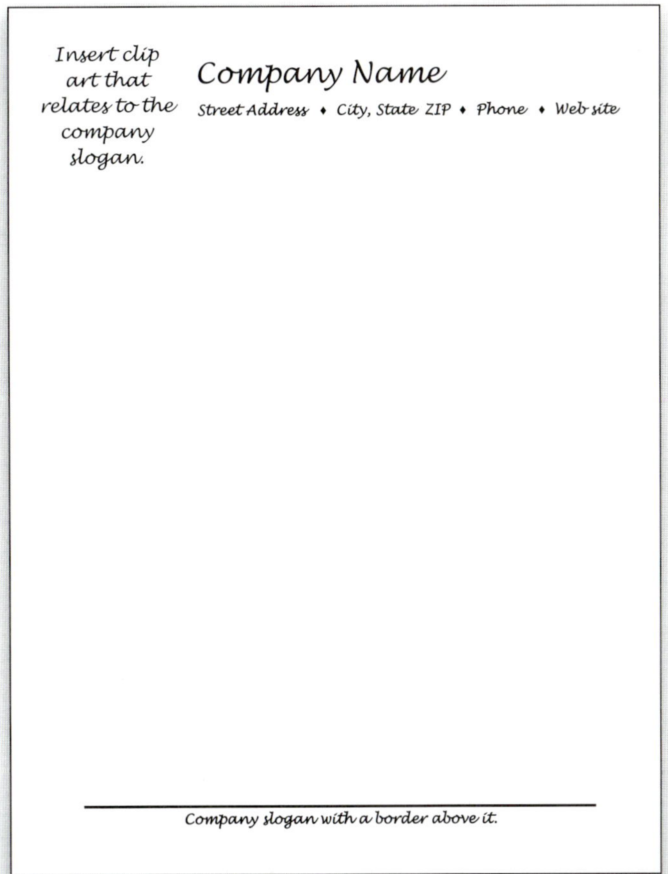
Insert clip art that relates to the company slogan.

Company Name

Street Address ♦ City, State ZIP ♦ Phone ♦ Web site

Company slogan with a border above it.

Skillbuilding and In-Basket Review—Education

Goals

- Demonstrate improved speed and accuracy while typing.
- Demonstrate acceptable language arts skills in word usage.
- Correctly format an academic report, a flyer, and a left-bound business report.

A. WARMUP

alphabet	1	`Jackie quietly gave the dog owner most of his prize boxers.`
one hand	2	`stages phylum wet pop affect jumpily tact junky beard pinky`
easy	3	`Duane's handy bicycle is to be thrown in the dormant field.`

Skillbuilding

B. MAP+: ALPHABET

Follow the GDP software directions for this exercise to improve keystroking accuracy.

C. PROGRESSIVE PRACTICE: ALPHABET

Follow the GDP software directions for this exercise to improve keystroking speed.

Language Arts

D. WORD USAGE

Study the rules at the right.

RULE accept/except

***Accept* means "to agree to"; *except* means "to leave out."**

All employees except the maintenance staff should accept the agreement.

RULE affect/effect

***Affect* is most often used as a verb meaning "to influence"; *effect* is most often used as a noun meaning "result."**

The ruling will affect our domestic operations but will have no effect on Asian operations.

RULE farther/further

***Farther* refers to distance; *further* refers to extent or degree.**

The farther we drove, the further agitated he became.

RULE personal/personnel

***Personal* means "private"; *personnel* means "employees."**

All personnel agreed not to use personal e-mail for business.

RULE principal/principle

***Principal* means "primary"; *principle* means "rule."**

The principle of fairness is our principal means of dealing with customers.

Edit each sentence to correct any errors.

4 The company cannot accept any collect calls, except for his.

5 The affect of the speech was dramatic; everyone was affected.

6 Further discussion by office personal was not appropriate.

7 Comments made during any meeting should never be personal.

8 If the meeting is held any further away, no one will attend.

9 The principle reason for the decision was to save money.

10 Office ethics are basic principles that should be practiced.

11 He cannot except the fact that the job was delegated to Jack.

12 Any further effects on office personnel will be evaluated.

Document Processing

Situation: Today is September 25. You are employed in the office of Dr. Daniel Lopez, dean of online education, at Arizona Technical College in Phoenix. Dr. Lopez has written the report shown next and left it in your in-basket for you to type and format. The title of the report is "PREPARING TO TEACH ONLINE." In his reports, he uses "Dr. Daniel V. Lopez, Dean" as the byline followed by the complete date.

Report 117-92
Academic Report

affect/effect
principal/principle

There are many strategies for becoming a successful online instructor. Adapting class management strategies and developing related course management systems will affect the outcome and success of any online course. A few basic principles are discussed here.

CLASS MANAGEMENT STRATEGIES

affect/effect

To make a successful transition from a traditional class setting to an online class setting, you must be very cognizant that class management strategies must be adapted. In particular, course policies related to due dates and timelines as well as the effects of late work on student success must be spelled out and strictly enforced.

principal/principle
affect/effect

Dr. Bill Maedke, a principal expert in online teaching, says that if students are not held accountable for delivering assignments on time, student success is greatly affected.

(continued on next page)

	Attrition increases as they procrastinate beyond the point of
farther/further	no return. When they finally realize they are getting further
accept/except	and further behind, many will drop out rather than accept
	a failing grade.[1]

COURSE MANAGEMENT SYSTEMS

	A course management system that supports the course requirements and facilitates the exchange of work between instructor and student is critical. Take time to research the various courseware management systems and compare their features. For a comprehensive list of
accept/except	accepted course management systems at ATC, visit www.atc.edu/online/courseware. The article "The Fine Art of Teaching at a Distance" by Dana Evans is another excellent resource.[2]

STAFF-DEVELOPMENT TRAINING SESSIONS

	The best way to prepare to teach online at Arizona Tech is to attend a series of upcoming staff-development training sessions entitled "Teaching Online @ ATC" that will be
personal/personnel	available to all interested instructional personnel. Look for a flyer in your mailbox and in your school e-mail soon that
farther/further	will provide further details on these training sessions.

	[1]Bill Maedke, "Class Management Strategies for Teaching at
Italicize publication titles.	a Distance," The Collegian Journal, February 1, 2010, p. 29.
	[2]Dana Evans, "The Fine Art of Teaching Online," Education Today, April 17, 2010, pp. 85-91.

Dr. Lopez has left a sketch of a flyer for the staff-development workshop entitled "Teaching Online @ ATC" that he would like you to design. He has asked you to use WordArt for the title, a rounded text box for the announcement, a predesigned table format for the workshop schedule, and landscape orientation for the page layout.

Report 117-93
Flyer

personal/personnel

Teaching Online @ ATC

Insert a picture that relates to the @ symbol.

Dr. Daniel V. Lopez, dean of online education, would like to extend a personal invitation to all instructional personnel to attend a series of staff-development workshops that will focus on strategies for teaching at a distance.

- *The workshops will be held at the Faculty Conference Center at Arizona Technical College beginning November 2.*
- *The schedule and topics are listed below.*

Date, Time, and Location	*Topic*
Monday, November 2, Room 1A	*Online Pedagogy*
Tuesday, November 10, Room 1B	*Course Design*
Wednesday, November 18, Room 2A	*Learning Objects*
Monday, November 30, Room 2C	*Online Resources*
For further details, visit www.atc.edu/online/workshops.	

farther/further

Report 117-94
Left-Bound Business Report

Open the file for Report 117-92, and make the following changes:

1. Change the format from an academic report to a left-bound business report.
2. Change the report title to this: `ONLINE TEACHING AND LEARNING RESOURCES`.
3. Change the date to `September 30, 20--`.
4. Delete the second sentence in the first paragraph.
5. Insert this side heading and the paragraph that follows it into the report just above the "COURSE MANAGEMENT SYSTEMS" heading:

   `INSTRUCTIONAL TECHNOLOGY`
   `A learning object is an online instructional resource that supports learning via the use and reuse of digital instructional components designed to deliver small amounts of information in different contexts. For example, a set of digital flash cards might include a course concept on one side of the card and the corresponding definition on the other side. The flash card content could be written by an instructor or purchased as part of a digital instructional package.`

UNIT 24 LESSON

Skillbuilding and In-Basket Review—Nursing Facility

118

Goals

- Type at least 50wpm/5′/5e.
- Correctly format a business letter in block style, an itinerary, and a newsletter.

A. WARMUP

alphabet
Jacqueline was vexed by the folks who got the money prizes.

practice: *o* and *i*
oil boil folio polio Rio coin icon into Ohio olio silo void

easy
Her ruby handiwork is fine, and she is so proficient at it.

Skillbuilding

B. PACED PRACTICE

Follow the GDP software directions for this exercise to improve keystroking speed and accuracy.

C. 5-MINUTE TIMED WRITING

Take two 5-minute timed writings.

Goal: At least 50wpm/5′/5e

Job sharing is a current concept that many places are 11
using to keep valued workers. People are finding a wide 22
range of reasons for not wanting to work full time. Here 34
are some tips on how to approach your boss if you would 45
like to attempt job sharing. 51

First, check your company handbook for an authorized 61
policy regarding this concept. If there is no rule that 73
prohibits the concept, then try to enlist a coworker who 84
would like to job-share and help you in writing a proposal 96
for job sharing where you work. 102

Next, define your needs and your goals. Develop a work 113
schedule that will meet all of your personal and monetary 125
needs. Be sure that you include enough time to get the work 137
done. If you want to work at your home on occasion, be sure 149
to state your desires. 154

You might find it is often quite helpful to maintain a 165
journal of your job duties, noting how much time is devoted 177
to each task. Your plan must also include details about the 189
logistics of the proposal. Decide how to handle unexpected 201
crisis situations. 205

Finally, time your presentation so there will be no 215
unnecessary interruptions. Be organized, persistent, and 227
professional in your presentation. Prepare to be successful 239
by compiling clearly defined ideas to support your plans. 250

1 | 2 | 3 | 4 | 5 | 6 | 7 | 8 | 9 | 10 | 11 | 12

Document Processing

Situation: Today is February 10. You work at The Meadows at Ivy Glen, an assisted-living residence in Connecticut, for Ms. Angelica Casillas, director. Ms. Casillas has written the letter shown next. It should be sent to Mrs. Sandra Elliott, 1122 King Street, Greenwich, CT 06831. Ms. Casillas uses "Sincerely yours" as her standard complimentary closing, uses "Ms. Angelica Casillas" as her writer's identification, and prefers her business title typed under her name in the closing lines.

Correspondence
118-101
Business Letter in Block Style

¶ Thank you for your inquiry regarding the assisted-living facilities here at The Meadows at Ivy Glen. We know that you, like so many of our residents, wish to live as independently as possible for as long as possible. We're here to help bridge the gap between independent living and living with assistance.

¶ I've spoken with Molly Fitzgerald, your dear friend who has been a resident for the past six months. She speaks fondly of you and believes that you would be very happy living here. I would like to meet with you in person to evaluate which level of assistance would best meet your needs. Based on the information in your application, I believe that you would benefit from basic assistance with laundry, housekeeping, and medications.

¶ Please call me at your earliest convenience at 203-555-2435 to set up an appointment. I will be happy to give you a personal tour of our lovely grounds and review our range of services and facilities at that time. I will also arrange for Molly to join us for a leisurely lunch.

¶ Thank you again for your interest in The Meadows at Ivy Glen, and I look forward to meeting you very soon.

Report
118-95
Itinerary

Ms. Casillas will be attending the Assisted-Living Federation of America Conference in Philadelphia in June and has asked you to prepare an itinerary with the title `ASSISTED-LIVING FEDERATION OF AMERICA CONFERENCE`. Type `Itinerary for Angelica Casillas` as the subtitle. The inclusive trip dates are June 12–14.

THURSDAY, JUNE 12

7:09 a.m. - 8:28 a.m.	Flight from New York city, La Guardia Airport, to Philadelphia; Continental 1282 (800-555-3668); eticket; Seat 24C; nonstop.
	¶ Roz Jorgensen (Cell: 215-555-7635; Office: 215-555-2121) will meet your flight on Thrusday, provide transportation during your visit, and arrange for transportation back *to the airport* on Saturday morning
	¶ Philadelphia Courtyard Suites (215-555-1200)
	King-sized bed, *non* smoking room; late arrival guaranteed; Reservation No. 35762-M1.
Friday, MARCH 13	ALFA Conference and Expo Philadelphia Royale Hotel 1239 Market St. Philadelphia, PA 19107 (215-555-1876)
8 p. m.	Dinner at the Amalfi Eatery next door to the Philadelphia *Hotel* Royale
SAT., MARCH 14	
6:30 a.m.	Meet ~~Tom Clinton~~ *Roz Jorgensen* in the ~~hotel restaurant~~ *lobby* of the Philadelphia Courtyard Suites for transportation to the airport.
9:30 a.m.-10:40 ~~p~~.m. *a*	Flight from New York City to Philadelphia, LaGuardia Airport; Continental 1541; e-ticket; Seat 11A; nonstop.

Report
118-96
Newsletter

Ms. Casillas has written the spring newsletter and has sketched out a masthead. She would like you to design the newsletter using these guidelines:

1. Set all margins at 0.75 inch.
2. For the masthead table, use clip art that is inspired by the spring season, and set the height to 2 inches.
3. Press Enter 2 times outside the masthead table to begin typing the body.
4. Select a page color and font colors for titles and headings that complement the clip art.
5. Add or remove borders to enhance the design.
6. For the 2-column body, use automatic hyphenation, full justification, and Calibri 16 pt. so the residents will be able to read the newsletter more easily.
7. After you type the body, format the headings in bold and change the font to Cambria 24 pt.

Insert clip art that relates to spring. Set the height to 2 inches.

The Meadows at Ivy Glen

Spring 20--

With summer just around the corner, it's time to pull out your social calendars and reserve time for the great activities we have planned. Read on, and let Joyce Fontana know if you plan to participate.

Healthy Sleep

Are you getting enough sleep? Sleep debt might be keeping you from having the energy you need to participate in our fitness fun. Try this to improve your sleep time:

- Exercise early in the day to help you relax at night.
- Avoid coffee and nicotine as they can both disturb the quality of your sleep.
- Take a warm bath or shower just before bed.
- Establish a sleep pattern by going to bed and getting up at the same time each day.

Spring Fitness Fun

With the warmer months approaching, many folks are thinking about stepping up their exercise regimen. Join Ray Kirk in the rose garden for an energizing fitness walk beginning March 20 at 9 a.m.

Tee Time

Beginning April 1, join Alex Taylor on the putting green each day at 10-11 a.m. for two weeks for some golf instruction. At that time, you can sign up for excursions to our fabulous local golf courses.

Fat Burners

We've added new items to our menu that are low in calories but high in taste and are nutritious! Give them a try.

Skillbuilding and In-Basket Review—Government

Goals

- Demonstrate improved speed and accuracy while typing.
- Demonstrate acceptable language arts skills in spelling.
- Correctly format a business letter in block style, a ruled table, and an e-mail message.

A. WARMUP

alphabet	1	My grandfathers picked up quartz and a valuable onyx jewel.
frequent digraphs	2	at ate bat cat eat tat fat hat mat oat pat rat sat vat beat
easy	3	The girls may fish for cod in the lake or buy them in town.

Skillbuilding

B. MAP+: SYMBOL

Follow the GDP software directions for this exercise to improve keystroking accuracy.

PPP PRETEST » PRACTICE » POSTTEST

C. PRETEST: Close Reaches

PRETEST

Take a 1-minute timed writing.

```
4      Casey hoped that we were not wasting good grub. After 11
5 the sun went down, he swiftly put the oleo and plums in the 23
6 cart. Bart opened a copy of an old book, Grant had a swim,  35
7 and Curt unearthed a sword in a hole in that grassy dune.   46
    1 | 2 | 3 | 4 | 5 | 6 | 7 | 8 | 9 | 10 | 11 | 12
```

D. PRACTICE: Adjacent Keys

PRACTICE

Speed Emphasis:
If you made no more than 1 error on the Pretest, type each *individual* line 2 times.

Accuracy Emphasis:
If you made 2 or more errors, type each *group* of lines (as though it were a paragraph) 2 times.

```
8 as mask last past easy vase beast waste toast reason castle
9 op hope flop open mops rope opera droop scope copier trophy
10 we west owed went weld weep weigh weary wedge wealth plowed
11 rt hurt port cart dirt fort court party start hearty parted
```

E. PRACTICE: Consecutive Fingers

```
12 sw swat swim swan swig swap swift sweet sword switch swirly
13 un tune spun unit dune punt under prune sunny hunter uneasy
14 gr grow grim grab grub grew great graze gripe greasy grassy
15 ol role oleo pool sold hole troll folly polka stolen oldest
```

POSTTEST

Repeat the Pretest timed writing and compare performance.

F. POSTTEST: Close Reaches

Language Arts

Type these frequently misspelled words, paying special attention to any spelling problems in each word.

G. SPELLING

16 practice continue regular entitled course resolution assist
17 weeks preparation purposes referred communication potential
18 environmental specifications original contractor associated
19 principal systems client excellent estimated administration
20 responsibility mentioned utilized materials criteria campus

Edit the sentences to correct any misspellings.

21 It is the responsability of the administration to assist.

22 The principle client prepared the excellent specifications.

23 He mentioned that the critiria for the decision were clear.

24 The contractor associated with the project referred them.

25 He estamated that the potential for resolution was great.

26 I was told that weeks of reguler practice were required.

Document Processing

Situation: Today is April 25. You work as an administrative assistant at the Centers for Disease Control and Prevention for Ms. Tina Min, traveler health specialist. Ms. Min has written the letter shown next. The letter should be sent to Mr. Carlos De Leon, 539 Locust Street, Des Moines, IA 50309. Ms. Min uses "Sincerely" as her standard complimentary closing, uses "Ms. Tina Min" as her writer's identification, and prefers her title typed under her name in the closing lines.

Correspondence 119-102
Business Letter in Block Style

¶ Your inquiry regarding vaccinations required for international travel was referred to me, and I am happy to answer your excellent questions. Preparation for a trip abroad does require a few weeks of planning to avoid potential problems associated with the timing of vaccinations.

¶ You mentioned that you are leaving in three months. Have you scheduled a visit to your doctor? Ideally, you should

(continued on next page)

set up a visit at least four to six weeks before your trip. Because so many environmental factors are at play when international travel is involved, you would be wise to go to a travel medicine provider specialist who can assist you with all details related to vaccinations. A principal responsibility of a provider of this type is to inform patients about the latest specifications for all health-related aspects of international travel.

¶ Please visit http://www.cdc.gov/travel.aspx for more helpful details and informative travel podcasts, or call CDC at 1-800-CDC-INFO. Enjoy your vacation, and I wish you continued good health.

Table
119-56
Ruled Table

HEALTH INFORMATION FOR TRAVELERS TO AUSTRALIA

Vaccination or Disease	Recommendations or Requirements for Vaccine-Preventable Disease
Routine	Recommended if you are not up to date with routine shots, such as measles/mumps/rubella (MMR) vaccine and the diphtheria/pertussis/tetanus (DPT) vaccine.
Hepatitis B	Recommended for all unvaccinated persons who might be exposed to blood or body fluids, have sexual contact with the local population, or be exposed through medical treatment, such as for an accident, even in developed countries, and for all adults for the purpose of protection from HBV infection.
Japanese encephalitis	Recommended if you visit Torres Strait and any zones associated with far Northern Australia.

This e-mail message should be sent to Regina Crawford, a close associate of Ms. Min. They address each other on a first-name basis. Ms. Min's e-mail address is tmin@cdc.gov. Her office phone number is 323-555-1876.

Correspondence
119-103
E-Mail Message

Hi, Regina:

¶ I mentioned to you yesterday that I am researching an inquiry related to health information for travelers to Australia. Please review the attached table, and let me know if it is complete or requires further information. I utilized the CDC Web site as my principal resource.

¶ Thank you, Regina, for your excellent assistance.

Skillbuilding and In-Basket Review—Software Development 120

Goals

- Type at least 50wpm/5′/5e.
- Correctly format a business report and a business letter in modified-block style.
- Successfully complete a Progress and Proofreading check with zero errors on the first scored attempt.

A. WARMUP

alphabet
1 Brown jars prevented the mixture from freezing too quickly.

number/symbol
2 coy20@cox.net 70% Hsu & Van 5/7 Win! ($4.93) *op. cit #16-8

easy
3 Jay may ask if my own neighbor is proficient in such a job.

Skillbuilding

B. 12-SECOND SPEED SPRINTS

Take three 12-second timed writings on each line.

4 Leo may visit the island by the giant oaks on his tan bike.
5 Nan may sign over the title to her car when she is in town.
6 She is so good at her work and likes what she does as well.
7 The old men may have a duel down by the lake at noon today.
| | | | 5 | | | | 10 | | | | 15 | | | | 20 | | | | 25 | | | | 30 | | | | 35 | | | | 40 | | | | 45 | | | | 50 | | | | 55 | | | | 60

C. TECHNIQUE PRACTICE: BACKSPACE KEY

Type each line 2 times, using your Sem finger to strike the BACKSPACE key when you see the ← symbol. For example, type *kid*, backspace, and type *n*, thus changing *kid* to *kin*.

8 kid←n jag←m law←y oaf←k pat←y tag←m hid←m ice←y inn←k
9 fro←y mud←m rat←p sue←m flu←y bog←o gym←p big←n hug←m
10 dug←n and←y zag←p hex←y mow←p art←m tow←y age←o her←n
11 dad←m fur←n sin←p elf←k bar←n bud←m spa←y log←o fad←n

Take two 5-minute timed writings.

Goal: At least 50wpm/5′/5e

D. 5-MINUTE TIMED WRITING

```
     With modern technology, it is possible to work at a        11
job full time and never leave your house. You can set up a      22
home office with a phone line, a facsimile, and a computer      34
system. Before choosing to work at home, however, you will      46
want to examine carefully your reasons for working at home.     58
     Some people think about working at home so they can        69
have more time to spend with their families. Other people       80
like to have more flexibility in their work schedule. They      92
are looking for the opportunity to enjoy a better quality      104
of life or to participate in other activities.                 113
     There are some factors to consider before you make        123
the decision to work at home. You will want to consider the    135
ultimate cost of benefits that you could give up if you        147
change your place of work. You will want to check with your    159
employer to see if you are entitled to paid vacation days      170
and health insurance or if you can make contributions to       182
your retirement plan. Another factor to consider is the        193
limited contact with peers.                                    198
     Before making the ultimate decision to work at home,      209
develop some realistic expectations of how you will spend      221
each day. Although you can organize your work to fit your      232
schedule, you will find the real challenge is to determine     244
a routine that works for you.                                  250
   1 | 2 | 3 | 4 | 5 | 6 | 7 | 8 | 9 | 10 | 11 | 12
```

Document Processing

Situation: Today is September 1. You work for Software Solutions, a software development company in Washington. Your boss is Mr. Jeffrey Hill, software development manager. Mr. Hill has written the business report shown next and left it in your in-basket for you to type and format. The title of the report is "NEW PROJECT-DEVELOPMENT STRATEGIES." He prefers to use "Jeffrey Hill, Software Development Manager" as the report byline followed by the above date and the current year.

Report 120-97
Business Report

¶ In january our company was given the Bantam and Jones Project. As you know, this project was critical from a monetary stand point. We also knew that ~~Bantam and Jones~~ *our customer* was carefully scrutinizing the quality of this project. Because this was a fixed-price project, ~~and~~ we had to deliverthe work by the end of July *in* order to avoid huge customer fees. The problem was that the project was out sourced to a different project team in a different location and the quality of the end product that was turned over *to us* for final review was questionable. ¶ As we later found out, the

(continued on next page)

project remote team had slowly disintegrated, and our home-based Seattle team had to come in at the last moment to rescue this project. In order to avoid this type of in the future, we will be implementing some new development project strategies.

TEAM COMMUNICATION

The design phase of any project is always exciting and energizing. Our analysts are talking to our clients, softwarearchitects are meeting with developers and managers are coordinating the flow of communication. As the porject progresses, communication breaks down. The analysts has moved on to the next project, the architects have finished their design, and the manager is reviewing status reports only occasionally. The developers are working at a feverish pace to get the project out on time, and the team is no longer working in unison. The following changes are going to be implemented to avoid this type of communication breakdown:

Pair Programming. Studies show that 2 programmers work harder on a given task than they would if they were working independently and produce 15 % fewer bugs. On all future projects programmers will work to keep each other in check. One person will type in code while the other reviews each line of code as it is being typed at the same keyboard. We will provide programmers with "people-skills training, since issues related to personal interaction are the biggest drawback to successful pair programming.

Customer Status Reports. Our customer is going to be an integral part of this team approach. A weekly status report will keep our customer in the loop and hold our teams account able for both content and deadlines. The project manager will oversee and coordinate communication between all parties.

CONCLUSION

Our company has earned a reputation for exceptional control quality in this industry. We are makinga renewed commitment to maintain that reputation and hopefully surpass our own impressive standards. Another Status Report will be issued in 2 weeks regarding how these meas ures will be implemented on what the effects will be for specific projects currently underway.

Correspondence
120-104
Business Letter in Modified-Block Style

Mr. Hill has written the letter shown next. The letter should be sent to Ms. Patty Chang, Project Director, Silicon Valley Consulting Services, 15125 South Market Street, San Jose, CA 95113. Mr. Hill uses "Sincerely" as his standard complimentary closing and prefers his title typed under his name in the writer's identification. Add this postscript to the letter: `Our president is very impressed with all your recommendations to date.` Send a blind copy to Hong Chan Cho.

Progress and Proofreading Check

Documents designated as Proofreading Checks serve as a check of your proofreading skill. Your goal is to have zero typographical errors when the GDP software first scores the document.

¶ Thank you for your prompt input as we have worked through ideas on the Bantam and Jones project. Your recommendations are sure to have a very powerful and positive impact on future projects.

¶ I have enclosed a copy of the report that was distributed to all Software Solutions employees involved in project development. Please review it and let me have your reactions. I feel confident that once our teams are comfortable with the new strategies and see the positive outcomes, they will embrace the recommendations.

¶ Please let me have your recommendations regarding training for our programmers as we implement our new pair-programming strategy. Here is a table with the proposed training schedule:

PROPOSED TRAINING SCHEDULE Pair Programming, Phase I	
Date	**Workshop Topic**
September 30	Communication Techniques
October 10	Tools for Pair Programming
October 20	Refactoring to Patterns
October 30	Design Patterns

¶ I need your final recommendations no later than September 15. I would assume that it makes more sense to begin with a workshop on communications techniques since the typical reaction to change by most employees is resistance. Perhaps if our programmers realize that the transition to pair programming will take place in phases, they will be more likely to accept the new approach and react positively.

(continued on next page)

¶ We need to arrange a face-to-face meeting for in-depth discussions on this very important transition. The following individuals will be invited to attend as they will play key roles during this transitional period:

- Hong Chan Cho
- Alicia King
- Barry Kidd
- Steven Cozell
- Colleen Cunningham

¶ Please call me when you receive this letter so that we can make the proper arrangements and coordinate schedules.

Outcomes Assessment on Part 6

Test 6

5-Minute Timed Writing

```
     The potential to reach your career goals has never        10
been better. The person who will move forward in a career      22
is the one who will make the bold moves to follow his or       33
her dreams. He or she will have the required attributes of     45
initiative and motivation to put forth maximum efforts in      57
order to realize a fulfilling position.                        65
     If you want to get ahead in the highly competitive        75
business world today, you need a personal coach or mentor      87
who is experienced in motivating people who want to reach      98
their potential. You may be afraid to go after your dream     110
career because you are afraid of failure. Your personal       121
mentor will help you to minimize any problems you incur. He   132
or she will encourage you to strive for more.                 142
     When you decide to work with a qualified coach, you      153
are investing in yourself. You can trust your coach to help   165
you through this joyful process of expanding your horizons    177
until you reach your goals.                                   182
     When you think you have reached your limit, your coach   194
will make suggestions for additional improvement. He or she   206
will present the strategies you can use to be successful.     217
Your coach will guide you in making the critical decisions    229
for advancing your career. The final decision to improve      240
your skills and be successful is yours, however.              250
     1 | 2 | 3 | 4 | 5 | 6 | 7 | 8 | 9 | 10 | 11 | 12
```

Form Test
6-17
Memo Template

Type this memo using the preselected blank memo template that opens automatically.

To: Brian Collins, Director of human resources

CC: Vincent Alvarez, President

From: April Mendoza, Chair Committee

Date: May 15, 20--

Re: Sierra Madre Health Run

The Sierra Madre Health Run is being scheduled again this year on June 17, 20--. As you may recall, last year we were able to raise 12,000 for the Sierra Madre home for youth. Since its inception 5 years ago, we have raised over $75,00 that has gone [directly] to the building fund at the home.

(continued on next page)

We Thank you for participating in this annual event and a special thanks goes to all those who donated ~~there~~ their time and effort to make this event such a ~~tremendous~~ success over the years.

As Human Resources Director, ~~we~~ I hope you'll again encourage all your employes to participate in the Health Run. We hope we will be able to exceed last year's donations by 10%. With Crosby international's participation, we know that will be a very reasonable goal to reach.

urs

Report Test
6-98
Online Resume

Your completed resume may look different from the one shown. This table is shown with "View Gridlines" active.

Marilyn Alexander *607-555-6475*
8142 Lawton Avenue, Binghamton, NY 13901 *malexander@quickmail.com*

OBJECTIVE
To obtain a full-time position as an event or meeting planner.

EDUCATION
Ithaca College, Ithaca, New York
Bachelor of Science Degree
- Graduated: August 2010
- Major: Event Planning
- GPA: 3.85 in major; 3.75 overall [Transcript] [Skills Checklist]

EXPERIENCE
Event Planner, Empire Facilities Inc.
Binghamton, New York
June 2006 to present
- Inspect and evaluate meeting space, lodging, and related venues and services to ensure a high standard of quality for scheduled events.
- Select key suppliers, prepare budgets, and negotiate contracts.
- Develop and maintain strong business relationships with hotels, conference centers, restaurants, gift suppliers, and audiovisual companies.

Administrative Assistant to Event Planner, Kramer Conferences Inc.
Flushing, New York
June 2005 to May 2006
- Scheduled conference calls and conference rooms for events.
- Ordered computer equipment and software used to plan events.
- Arranged for Web site and brochure updates; scheduled monthly meetings.

SKILLS
- Computing skills in Microsoft Word, Excel, and PowerPoint.
- Strong Interpersonal and organizational skills.

REFERENCES
Available on request.

(Created on July 13, 2010; last updated on August 15, 2010.)

Report Test
6-99
Flyer

Use a predesigned table style of your choice.

WordArt

Page color

Calibri 24 pt Bold

Calibri 20 pt

Calibri 16 pt Bold

Calibri 14 pt

Picture related to a mountain

Sierra Madre Health Run

Schedule of Events Wednesday, June 17, 20--			
Event	**Start Time**	**Participants**	**Cost**
10K Run	8:15 a.m.	All ages	$10
5K Run	10:30 a.m.	14 to adult	5
2-Mile Walk	9:00 a.m.	All ages	8
Kids' Dash	9:45 a.m.	5 to 9 years old	5
Seniors' Run	10:15 a.m.	65 and older	8

All participants should arrive early to register for individual events.

All proceeds will be donated to the Sierra Madre Home for Youth.

Use a shape fill that complements the page color

Calibri 16 pt Bold

Text box with double line border

Skillbuilding

Progressive Practice: Alphabet

This skillbuilding routine contains a series of 30-second timed writings that range from 16 wpm to 104 wpm. The first time you use these timed writings, take a 1-minute timed writing with 3 or fewer errors on the Entry Timed Writing paragraph. Push moderately for speed.

Select a passage that is 1 to 2 wpm *higher* than your Entry Timed Writing speed. Then take up to six 30-second timed writings on the passage.

Your goal each time is to complete the passage within 30 seconds with no errors. When you have achieved your goal, move on to the next passage and repeat the procedure.

Entry Timed Writing

Bev was very lucky when she found extra quality in the 11
home she was buying. She quietly told the builder that she 23
was extremely satisfied with the work done on her new home. 35
The builder said she can move into her new house next month. 47

1 | 2 | 3 | 4 | 5 | 6 | 7 | 8 | 9 | 10 | 11 | 12

16 wpm
The author is the creator of a document.

18 wpm
Open means to access a previously saved file.

20 wpm
A byte represents one character to every computer.

22 wpm
Hard copy is usually text that is printed out on paper.

24 wpm
Soft copy is text that is displayed on your computer screen.

26 wpm
Memory is that part of your word processor that stores your data.

28 wpm
The menu is a list of choices used to guide a user through a function.

30 wpm
A sheet feeder is a device that will insert sheets of paper into a printer.

32 wpm
An icon is a small picture that illustrates a function or an object in software.

34 wpm
Active icons on your desktop represent the programs that can be run on your computer.

Skillbuilding

36 wpm	To execute means to perform an action specified by the user or also by a computer program.
38 wpm	Output is the result of a word processing operation. It can be either printed or magnetic form.
40 wpm	Format refers to the physical features which affect the appearance and arrangement of your document.
42 wpm	A font is a type style of a particular size or kind that includes letters, numbers, or punctuation marks.
44 wpm	Ergonomics is the science of adapting working conditions or equipment to meet the physical needs of employees.
46 wpm	Home position is the starting position of a document; it is typically the upper left corner of the display monitor.
48 wpm	The purpose of a virus checker is to find those programs that may cause your computer to stop working as you want it to.
50 wpm	An optical scanner is a device that can read text and enter it into a word processor without the need to type the data again.
52 wpm	Hardware refers to all the physical equipment you use while computing, such as the display screen, keyboard, printer, and scanner.
54 wpm	A peripheral device is any piece of equipment that will extend the capabilities of a computer system but is not required for operation.
56 wpm	A split screen displays two or more different images at the same time; it can, for example, display two different pages of a legal document.
58 wpm	To defrag the computer means that you are reorganizing the files so that related files will be located in the same general place on a hard drive.
60 wpm	With the click of a mouse, one can use a button bar or a toolbar for fast access to features that are frequently applied when using a Windows program.

62 wpm

Gadgets are typically controls which are placed on your desktop to allow you to have immediate access to frequently used information such as time and date.

64 wpm

Turnaround time is the length of time needed for a document to be keyboarded, edited, proofread, corrected if required, printed, and returned to the originator.

66 wpm

A local area network is a system that uses cable or another means to allow high-speed communication among many kinds of electronic equipment within particular areas.

68 wpm

To search and replace means to direct the word processor to locate a character, word, or group of words wherever it occurs in the document and replace it with newer text.

70 wpm

Indexing is the ability of a word processor to accumulate a list of words that appear in a document, including page numbers, and then print a revised list in alphabetic order.

72 wpm

When a program needs information from you, a dialog box will appear on the desktop. Once the dialog box appears, you must identify the option you desire and then choose the option.

74 wpm

A facsimile is an exact copy of a document, and it is also a process by which images, such as typed letters, graphs, and signatures, are scanned, transmitted, and then printed on paper.

76 wpm

Compatibility refers to when a computer is able to share information with other computers or also to communicate with different hardware. It could be accomplished by other methods.

78 wpm

Some operators like to personalize their desktops when they use Windows by making various changes. For example, they can change their screen colors or the pointer so that they will have more fun.

80 wpm

Wraparound is the ability of a word processor to move words from one line to another line and from one page to the next page as a result of inserting and deleting text or changing the size of margins.

82 wpm

It is possible when using Windows to evaluate the contents of different directories on the screen at the very same time. You can then choose to copy or move a particular file from one directory to another.

84 wpm

List processing is a capability of a word processor to keep lists of data that can be updated and sorted in alphabetic or numeric order. A list can also be added to any document that is stored in your computer.

86 wpm

A computer is a device that accepts data that are input and then processes those data to produce the output. A computer performs its work by using various stored programs that provide all the necessary instructions.

88 wpm

A word processor is more than a program that can process words. Word processors have many other capabilities such as merging documents; executing some mathematical equations; and inserting clip art, shapes, and pictures.

90 wpm

Help and support in Windows are available to assist you in finding answers to questions you may have about just how the computer functions. You can find help on topics like security, files, folders, printing, and maintenance.

92 wpm

When you want to look at the contents of two windows when using Windows, you might want to reduce the window size. Do this by pointing to a border or a corner of a window and dragging it until the window is the size that you want.

94 wpm

Scrolling means to display a very large quantity of text by rolling it horizontally or vertically past your display screen. As text disappears from the top section of your screen, new text will appear in the bottom area of your screen.

96 wpm

You have several options available to you when you print a document. For example, you can determine which printer to use, the pages you desire to print, the number of copies to be printed, the print quality desired, and the paper size used.

98 wpm

An ink-jet printer and a laser printer are popular printers used in a home office. Many users prefer an ink-jet printer because it is not as expensive to buy. But a laser printer provides a higher-quality print and is often the preferred choice.

100 wpm

E-mail, text messaging, cell phones, and chat rooms have enabled us to communicate quickly with people all around the globe. We can transmit a call or a message on the spur of the moment and receive a response to our call or message almost instantly.

102 wpm

Many different graphics software programs have been brought on the market in past years. These programs can be very powerful in helping with a business presentation. If there is a requirement to share data, using programs like these could be very helpful.

104 wpm

Voice mail is an essential service used by many people in the business world. This technology enables anyone placing a call to your phone to leave you a message if you cannot answer it at that time. This unique feature can help many workers be more productive.

Progressive Practice: Numbers

This skillbuilding routine contains a series of 30-second timed writings that range from 16 wpm to 80 wpm. The first time you use these timed writings, take a 1-minute timed writing with 3 or fewer errors on the Entry Timed Writing paragraph. Push moderately for speed.

Select a passage that is 1 to 2 wpm *higher* than your Entry Timed Writing speed. Then take up to six 30-second timed writings on the passage.

Your goal each time is to complete the passage within 30 seconds with no errors. When you have achieved your goal, move on to the next passage and repeat the procedure.

Entry Timed Writing

Their bags were filled with 10 sets of jars, 23 cookie 11
cutters, 4 baking pans, 6 coffee mugs, 25 plates, 9 dessert 23
plates, 7 soup bowls, 125 recipe cards, and 8 recipe boxes. 35
David delivered these 217 items to 20487 Mountain Boulevard. 47

1 | 2 | 3 | 4 | 5 | 6 | 7 | 8 | 9 | 10 | 11 | 12

16 wpm There are 37 chairs in Rooms 24 and 156.

18 wpm About 10 of the 39 boxes were torn on June 8.

20 wpm Only 3 papers had errors on pages 28, 40, and 197.

22 wpm My 46 letters were sent on May 10, June 3, and June 27.

24 wpm The 79 freshmen, 86 juniors, and 54 seniors arrived at home.

26 wpm The school needs 150 pens, 38 reams of paper, and 42 new folders.

28 wpm Only 1 or 2 of the 305 new books had errors on pages 46, 178, and 192.

30 wpm They met 10 of the 23 tennis players who received 4 awards from 5 trainers.

32 wpm Those 8 vans carried 75 passengers on the first trip and 64 on the next 3 trips.

34 wpm I saw 2 eagles on Route 86 and then 4 eagles on Route 53 at 9 a.m. on Monday, May 10.

36 wpm	The 17 firms produced 50 of the 62 records that received awards for 3 of the 4 categories.
38 wpm	The 12 trucks hauled 87 cows, 65 horses, and 49 pigs to the farm, which was 30 miles northeast.
40 wpm	She moved from 87 Bayview Drive to 659 Bay Street and then 3 blocks south to 4012 Gulbranson Avenue.
42 wpm	My 2 or 3 buyers ordered 5 dozen in sizes 6, 7, 8, and 9 after the 10 to 14 percent discounts were added.
44 wpm	There were 134 men and 121 women waiting in line at Gate 206 for the 58 to 79 tickets to the Cape Cod concert.
46 wpm	Steve had listed 5, 6, or 7 items on Purchase Order 243 when he saw that Purchase Requisition 89 contained 10 more.
48 wpm	Your items numbered 278 will sell for about 90 percent of the value of the 16 items that have code numbers shown as 435.
50 wpm	The managers stated that 98 of those 750 randomly selected new valves had about 264 defects, far exceeding the usual 31 norm.
52 wpm	Half of the 625 volunteers received over 90 percent of the charity pledges. Approximately 38 of the 147 agencies might enjoy this.
54 wpm	Merico hired 94 part-time workers to help the 378 full-time employees during the 62-day period when sales go up by 150 percent or more.
56 wpm	Kaye only hit 1 for 4 in the first 29 games after an 8-game streak in which she batted 3 for 4. She then hit at a .570 average for 16 games.
58 wpm	The mail carrier delivered 98 letters during the week to 734 Oak Street and also took 52 letters to 610 Faulkner Road as he returned on Route 58.
60 wpm	Pat said that about 1 in 5 of the 379 swimmers had a chance of being among the top 20. The best 6 of these 48 divers will receive special recognition.

62 wpm	It rained from 3 to 6 inches, and 18 of those 20 farmers were fearful that 4 to 7 inches more would flood about 95 acres along 3 miles of the new Route 79.
64 wpm	Those 17 sacks weighed 48 pounds, more than the 30 pounds that I had thought. All 24 believe the 92-pound bag is at least 15 or 16 pounds above its true weight.
66 wpm	They bought 7 of the 8 options for 54 of the 63 vehicles last month. They now have over 120 dump trucks for use in 9 of the 15 new regions in the big 20-county area.
68 wpm	Andy was 8 or 9 years old when they moved to 612 Glendale Street and away from the 700 block of Henry Lane, which is about 45 miles directly west of Boca Raton, FL 33434.
70 wpm	Doug had read 575 pages in the 760-page book by August 30; Darlene had read only 468 pages. Darlene has read 29 of those optional books since October 19, and Doug has read 18.
72 wpm	The school district has 985 elementary students, 507 middle school students, and 463 high school students. This total represents the greatest increase in total enrollment for us.
74 wpm	Attendance at last year's meeting was 10,835. Your goal for this year is to have 11,764 people. This might enable us to plan for an increase of 929 participants, a rise of 8.57 percent.
76 wpm	David's firm has 158 stores, located in 109 cities in the South. The company employs 3,540 males and 2,624 females, a total of 6,164 employees. About 4,750 of those employees work part-time.
78 wpm	Memberships were as follows: 98 members in the Drama Guild, 90 members in Zeta Tau, 82 members in Theta Phi, 75 in the Bowling Club, and 136 in the Ski Club. This meant that 481 joined the group.
80 wpm	The association had 684 members from the South, 830 members from the North, 1,023 members from the East, and 751 from the West. This total membership was 3,288; these numbers increased by 9.8 percent.

Paced Practice

The Paced Practice skillbuilding routine builds speed and accuracy in short, easy steps by using individualized goals and immediate feedback. You may use this program at any time after completing Lesson 9.

This section contains a series of 2-minute timed writings for speeds ranging from 16 wpm to 96 wpm. The first time you use these timed writings, take the 1-minute Entry Timed Writing with 2 or fewer uncorrected errors to establish your base speed.

Select a passage that is 2 wpm higher than your Entry Timed Writing speed. Then use this two-stage practice pattern to achieve each speed goal: (1) concentrate on speed and (2) work on accuracy.

Speed Goal. To determine your speed goal, take three 2-minute timed writings in total. Your goal each time is to complete the passage in 2 minutes without regard to errors. When you have achieved your speed goal, work on accuracy.

Accuracy Goal. To type accurately, you need to slow down—just a bit. Therefore, to reach your accuracy goal, drop back 2 wpm from the previous passage. Take consecutive timed writings on this passage until you can complete the passage in 2 minutes with no more than 2 errors.

For example, if you achieved a speed goal of 54 wpm, you should then work on an accuracy goal of 52 wpm. When you have achieved 52 wpm for accuracy, move up 4 wpm (for example, to the 56-wpm passage) and work for speed again.

Entry Timed Writing

If you can dream it, you can live it. Just follow your heart. There are many careers, which range from the mundane to the exotic to the sublime.

Start your career planning now by quizzing yourself about your talents, skills, and personal interests.

1 | 2 | 3 | 4 | 5 | 6 | 7 | 8 | 9 | 10 | 11 | 12

16 wpm

Your future is now, so you must seize every day.

After exploring your interests, quickly check the sixteen career clusters for a wide range of potential jobs.

18 wpm

When exploring various career options, think about what a job means for you.

Recognize that it can mean what you do just to earn money or what you find quite challenging overall.

20 wpm

If you acquire a job that you enjoy, then it means even more than simply earning an excellent wage.

It also means making a contribution, taking pride in your work, and utilizing all of your talents.

22 wpm

What is the difference between[1] a job and a career? Think[2] carefully. A job is work[3] that you have to do for money[4].

A career is a sequence[5] of related jobs that optimize[6] your interests, experience[7], knowledge, and training[8].

24 wpm

Learn all about the world of work[1] by looking at the sixteen[2] career clusters. Most jobs are[3] included in one of the clusters[4] that have been organized by[5] the government.

When exploring[6] careers, list all the unique[7] clusters that interest you[8].

26 wpm

Once you identify the career clusters[1] that interest you, look at[2] the jobs that are within each cluster[3].

Analyze exactly what skills[4] and aptitudes are needed, what[5] training is required, what the[6] work setting is like, and what your[7] chances for advancement are[8].

28 wpm

Use your career center and your school[1] or a public library to research[2] your career choice. Go on the Internet[3], and ask experts for their unique[4] views of certain careers.

As you[5] gather data about your job options[6], you might learn about new career[7] options that are on the horizon[8].

30 wpm

You must gain insight into a career[1]. You can become a volunteer, sign up for[2] an internship, or even work in a part-time[3] job in the field.

You will become[4] more familiar with a specific job[5] while you develop your skills. You[6] will quickly gain prized experience, whether[7] you choose that career or not[8].

Skillbuilding

32 wpm

No matter which path you choose, strive[1] for a high level of pride in yourself and[2] in your job. Your image is affected by[3] what other people think of you as well[4] as by what you think of yourself.

Next,[5] analyze your level of confidence. If you[6] have any self-doubts, strive to acquire[7] more self-confidence and self-esteem.[8]

34 wpm

Confidence is required for a positive attitude,[1] and a positive attitude is required[2] for success at work. While you may not control[3] all that happens at work, recognize that[4] you must control how you react to what[5] happens.

Become more confident and cultivate[6] positive thoughts, which will provide you[7] with extra power in life and on the job.[8]

36 wpm

Quite a few factors lead to success on the job.[1] People who have analyzed these factors say[2] that it is the personal traits one exhibits[3] that determine who is promoted and who is not.[4]

One of the best traits a person can have[5] is the trait of being likable. That means that[6] you are honest, loyal, courteous, thoughtful,[7] pleasant, kind, considerate, and positive.[8]

38 wpm

If you are likable, you will relate well with[1] most people. If you have excellent social contact[2] with others, it will humanize the workplace and[3] make your work there more enjoyable. Think of[4] all the hours you are required to spend with one[5] another each day.

If you show that you are willing[6] to collaborate with your coworkers, most[7] likely you will also receive their cooperation.[8]

40 wpm

Cooperation begins on the first day of your new job. When you work for a firm, you quickly become a part of that team. Meeting people and learning new skills can be quite exciting.

For some people, though, a new situation can trigger some anxiety. The best advice is to remain calm, do your job with zeal, learn the workplace policies, be flexible, avoid being too critical, and always be positive.

42 wpm

When you begin a new job, even if you have recently received your college degree, chances are you will start at the bottom of the organizational chart. Each of us has to start somewhere. Do not despair or become lazy.

With hard work, you should start your climb up the corporate ladder. If you are smart, you will quietly take on even the most tedious task, take everything in stride, and exercise any chance to learn.

44 wpm

If you think learning is restricted to an academic setting, think again. You have much to learn on the job, even if it is a position for which you have been trained.

As a new employee, you will not be expected to know everything. When necessary, do not hesitate to ask your employer questions. Learn all you can about your job and the company. Capitalize on the new information to enhance your job performance and to build toward success.

46 wpm

Begin every valuable workday by prioritizing all of your tasks. Decide which tasks must be done immediately and which can wait. List the most important items first; then determine the order in which each item must be done.

After you complete a task, then quickly cross it off your priority list. Maximize your time; that is, do not put off work you should do. If a job must be done, just do it. You will stay on top of your list when you utilize time wisely.

Skillbuilding

48 wpm

Do not let the phone control your time. Learn how to manage[1] all your phone calls. Phone calls can be extremely distracting[2] from other duties, so be jealous of your quiet time. When[3] making a phone call, organize the topics you want to discuss[4]. Gather needed supplies such as pencils, papers, and files[5].

Set a time limit and stick to the topic. Give concise answers[6], summarize the points discussed, and end your talk politely[7]. Efficient phone usage will help you manage your time[8].

50 wpm

As with everything, practice makes perfect, but along the way[1], we have all made some mistakes. Realize that the difference between[2] successful people and those who are less successful is[3] not that the successful people make fewer mistakes. It is just[4] that they will never quit.

Instead of letting mistakes bring[5] you down, use your mistakes as opportunities to grow. If you make[6] a mistake, be patient with yourself. You might be able to fix[7] your mistake. Look for success to be just around the corner.[8]

52 wpm

Be patient as you learn how to take care of problems and accept[1] criticism. Accepting criticism may be quite a test for you. Still[2], it is vital to many of us at work. Criticism that is given in a[3] way to help you learn, expand, or grow is called constructive criticism[4].

If you look at criticism as being helpful, it will be easier[5] to deal with. You might be amazed to learn that some people[6] welcome it since it teaches them the best way to succeed on the[7] job. Try to improve how you accept helpful criticism from others.[8]

54 wpm

People experience continuous growth during a career. Goal setting is a key tool to acquire for any job. Some people believe that goals provide the motivation we need to get to the place we want to be. Setting goals encourages greater achievements. The higher that we set our goals, the greater the effort we need to reach them.

Each time we reach a target or come closer to a goal, we should realize an increase in our confidence and in our performance, which leads to greater accomplishments. And the cycle continues to spiral for years.

56 wpm

One goal we must all strive for is punctuality. When employees are absent or just tardy, it costs the company money. If you are frequently tardy or absent, others have to do extra work to cover for you. If you are absent often, your peers may begin to resent you, which causes everyone stress in the department.

Being late and missing work might penalize your own relationship with your manager and have a negative effect on your career. To avoid such potential problems, develop a personal plan to ensure that you arrive every day on time and ready to work.

58 wpm

To hold a job is a chief part of being an adult. Some people start their work careers as teens. From the start, a range of work habits are developed that are as crucial to success as the actual job skills and knowledge that someone brings to his or her job.

What traits are expected of workers? What do employers look for when they rate their own workers? Vital personal traits would include being confident, helpful, positive, and loyal. If you are also kind, passionate, and organized, you may now have many of these qualities that employers value most of all in their staffs.

60 wpm

Being dependable is a required work trait. If a job must be done by a special time, the manager will be pleased to learn that his or her workers are going to meet that deadline. Those who are dependable learn to utilize their time to attain maximum results. Loyal workers can also be counted on, they have good attendance records, they are well prepared, and they get to work on time and ready to start.

If the firm wants to meet its goals, it must have a team of loyal and dependable workers. You, your peers, your supervisors, and your managers are all team members who work to reach their goals.

62 wpm

The ability to organize is an important quality for the worker who would like to display good work habits. The worker should have the ability to plan the work that needs to be done and then to be able to execute that plan in a timely manner.

An employer requires a competent worker to be well organized. If the office worker is efficient, he or she handles requests swiftly and deals with messages without delay. The organized worker does not allow his or her work to accumulate on the desk. Also, the organized worker will return all phone calls quickly and make lists of the jobs that still need to be done each day.

Skillbuilding

64 wpm

Efficiency is one work habit that is important. The efficient worker does each [1] task quickly and starts work on the next task eagerly. He or she thinks about ways [2] to save steps or time. For example, an efficient worker may plan just one trip [3] to the copier with a number of copying jobs rather than take many trips to do [4] each separate job.

Being efficient also means that you have all of the required [5] supplies to finish each job. An efficient worker zips along on each project, uses [6] his or her time wisely, and then stays focused on that one task. With careful [7] and detailed planning, a worker who is efficient can finish tasks in less time. [8]

66 wpm

Cooperation is another ideal work habit. It begins on the first day of the job and [1] means that you quietly think of all team members when you make a decision. A person [2] who cooperates is willing to do what is needed for the good of the whole group. [3] For you to be a team player, you must take the extra steps to cooperate.

Cooperation [4] may mean that you need to be a good sport if you are asked to do something you [5] would rather not do. It may mean that you have to correct some mistakes made by another [6] person in the office. When each employee has the interests of the company at [7] heart and works well with other workers, then everyone is a good corporate citizen. [8]

68 wpm

Enthusiasm is still another work trait that is eagerly sought after by employers. If[1] you are enthusiastic, then you have lots of positive energy. This is reflected in your[2] actions toward your work, coworkers, and employer. It has been noted that eagerness[3] can be catching. If you show you are excited to try any project, then you may quickly[4] not only achieve the highest praise but also will be considered for career advancement[5].

How much enthusiasm do you show at the workplace? Do you encourage people or complain[6] to people? There should always be lots of good jobs for workers who are known[7] to have a wealth of zeal and a positive approach to the jobs that they are assigned.[8]

70 wpm

Acceptance is a work trait required of all of us. In the work world of today, each business[1] includes both men and women of different religions, races, cultures, skills, and beliefs[2]. You will interact with many types of people as customers, coworkers, and owners[3]. Treat each one fairly, openly, and honestly.

All types of prejudice are hurtful, hateful[4], and, in short, unacceptable. Prejudice is not allowed at work. Each of us must learn[5] to accept and even prize the many kinds of differences that are exhibited by all of us[6]. Since so many diverse groups work side by side in the work world, it is vital that all[7] workers maintain a high degree of shared insights. Embrace each of us for who we are.[8]

72 wpm

It can be concluded that certain work habits or traits should play the major role in deciding [1] the success of all workers. Most managers would be quick to agree on the high importance [2] of these traits. It is most likely that these habits would be analyzed on performance [3] appraisal forms. Promotions, pay increases, new duties, and your future with the company may [4] be based on these yearly job assessments.

You should request regular job performance assessments [5] even if your company does not conduct them. This feedback might then expand your [6] job skills and career development by helping you grow. If you always look for ways to improve [7] your work habits and skills, you will enjoy success in the world of work and beyond. [8]

74 wpm

You can be sure that no matter where you work, you will use some form of technology. Almost [1] every business depends on computers. Firms use such devices as voice mail, fax machines, cell [2] phones, and personal digital assistants. These tools help us to do our work quickly and efficiently. [3] They also take some of the drudgery out of our lives.

One result of the use of these [4] tools is globalization, which means worldwide communication links between people. Our world [5] has turned into one global village. We should expand our thinking beyond the office walls. [6] We must become aware of what happens in other parts of the world. These events may directly [7] affect you and your job. The more you know, the more valuable you will become to a company. [8]

Skillbuilding

76 wpm

Each advance in technology has had an effect on all aspects of our lives. For example, the [1] dawn of the age of the Internet has changed how people get and send data. It is the largest data [2] network in the world. It is called the information superhighway since it is a vast network of [3] big computers that can link people and resources around the world. It is an exciting medium to [4] help you access current data and be more useful on the job and at home.

Without a doubt, we are [5] all globally linked, and data technology services can support those links. The industry offers [6] different job opportunities in dozens of fields. Keep in mind that keyboarding skills are [7] required in this field as well as in most others. Touch-typing skills are just assumed in most jobs. [8]

78 wpm

It is amazing to learn about the many jobs in which keyboarding skill is needed today. The use [1] of a computer keyboard by executive chefs is a prime example. The chefs in large restaurants must [2] prepare parts or all of the meals served while they direct the work of their staff of chefs, [3] cooks, and others in and near the kitchens.

The computer has become a prime tool for a wide range of [4] tasks, including tracking stocks of their food supplies. By seeing which items are favorites and [5] which items are not requested, the chef can work out the food requirements, order food, and [6] supervise the purchase of foods. Also, the computer has proved to be a very practical tool for such [7] tasks as helping to plan budgets, prepare purchase orders for vendors, write menus, and print reports. [8]

80 wpm

Advanced technology has opened the doors to a wide variety of amazing new products and services to[1] sell. It seems that the more complex the products get, the higher the price of the products is and [2]that the larger the sales commission is, the stiffer the competition is. To sell a technical product[3] requires detailed product knowledge, good verbal skills, smooth sales rapport, and also expert typing[4] skills.

Business favors those who have special training. For example, a pharmacy company may choose[5] a person who has a strong knowledge of chemistry to sell its products. Sales is for those who enjoy[6] using their command of persuasion to make the sales. The potential for good pay and commissions [7]is quite high for the salesperson who is trained well. You should perhaps think about a job in sales.[8]

82 wpm

As you travel about in your sales job or type a report at the office or create the Friday night pizza[1] special for your new diner, you should always plan to put safety first. Accidents happen, but they do[2] not have to happen regularly or to have such severe results. Accidents cost businesses billions of dollars[3] each year in medical expenses, lost wages, and insurance claims.

Part of your job is to make certain[4] that you are not one of the millions of people injured on the job each year. You may believe you [5]work in a safe place, but accidents occur in all types of businesses. A few careless people cause most [6]accidents, so ensure your safety on the job. Safety does not just happen. It is the result of the very[7] careful awareness of those people who plan and put into action a safety program that benefits everyone.[8]

84 wpm

In the world of today, you need more than the needed skills or the personal qualities to succeed on the job. Managers also expect all workers to have ethics. Ethics are the codes of conduct that tell a person or a group how to act. Workers who act ethically do not lie, cheat, or steal. They are honest and fair in all their dealings with others. In short, they are good citizens.

Workers who act ethically gain a good reputation for themselves and for their companies. They are known to be dependable. Unethical behavior can have a spiraling effect. A single act can do a lot of damage. Even if you have not held a job yet, you have had some experience with ethical problems. Life is full of a range of occasions to behave ethically. Do the right thing when faced with decisions. The ethics you follow will carry over into the workplace.

86 wpm

Now that you know what will be expected of you on the job, how do you make sure you will get the job in the first place? Almost everyone has at least once gone through the interview process for a job. For some, the interview is a traumatic event, but it does not have to be so stressful. Research is the key. Learn about the firm with whom you are seeking a job. Form a list of questions to ask. Interviews also provide you the chance to interview the organization.

Take a folder of items with you. Include copies of your data sheet with a list of three or more professional references, your academic transcript, and your certificates and licenses. Be sure to wear appropriate business attire. The outcome of the interview will be positive if you have enthusiasm for the job, match your skills to the needs of the company, ask relevant questions, and listen.

88 wpm

How can you be the strongest candidate for the job? Be sure that your skills in reading, writing, math, speaking,[1] and listening are strong. These skills should enable you to listen well and communicate clearly, not only[2] during the job interview but also at your place of work. This exchange of information between a sender and a[3] receiver is known as communication.

It does not matter which career you choose; you will still spend most of[4] your time using these basic skills to communicate with others. You should use the skills as tools to gain information,[5] solve problems, and share ideas. You can also use these skills to help you meet the needs of your customers.[6] Most of the new jobs in the next few years will be in industries that will require direct customer contact.[7] Do not jeopardize your chances for success; make sure that you are able to communicate well with others.[8]

90 wpm

Writing well can help you gain a competitive edge in your job search and throughout your career. Most of us have[1] had occasion to write business letters whether to apply for a job, to comment on a product or service, or to place[2] an order. Often it seems easy to sit back and let our thoughts flow freely. At other times, we seem to struggle[3] to find the best words to use to express our thoughts in precisely the correct way. We all sometimes have these[4] issues.

Writing skills can improve with practice. Use these principles to develop your writing skills. Try to[5] use words that you would be comfortable using in person. Use words that are simple, direct, kind, and confident.[6] When it is possible, use words that emphasize only the positive side. Remember to proofread your work. Well-organized[7] thoughts and proper grammar, spelling, and punctuation will show your reader that you care about quality.[8]

92 wpm

Listening is such a vital part of the communication process. It is the key for learning, getting along, and forming[1] rapport. Do you think that you are an active or a passive listener? Listening should not be just a passive process.[2] To listen actively means to analyze what is being said and to interpret what it means. Active listening makes you[3] a more effective worker because you react to what you have heard as well as to what you have not heard.

Study these[4] steps to expand your listening skills: Do not cut people off; let them finish their remarks before you speak.[5] If what they said is unclear, write down your questions, and wait for the discussion to be finished until you ask them.[6] Reduce personal and environmental noise so you can focus on the message. Keep an open mind. Remain attentive and[7] maintain eye contact when possible. By using these skills, you can become even more confident and more effective.[8]

94 wpm

Speaking is also a form of communication. In the world of work, speaking is an important way in which to share information.[1] Regardless of whether you are speaking to an audience of one or one hundred, you will want to be sure that your[2] listeners hear your message. Be clear about your purpose, your audience, and your subject. A purpose is the overall[3] goal or reason for speaking. An audience is anyone who receives information. The subject is the main topic or key idea[4] that you wish to analyze.

Research your subject. Use specific facts and examples to give you credibility. As you speak,[5] be brief and direct. Progress logically from point to point.[6] Speak slowly and pronounce clearly all your words. Is the quality of your voice friendly and pleasant or is it shrill and offensive? These factors influence how your message[7] is received. A good idea is worthless if you cannot present it well, so take all the time you need to get ready.[8]

96 wpm

Building a career is a process. You have looked at all your interests, values, skills, talents, and feelings. Your look into the world of work has begun, but the journey does not stop here, for the present is the perfect place to start thinking about the future. It is where you start to take steps toward your goals. It is where you can really make a difference.

As you set personal and career goals, remember the importance of small steps. Each step toward a personal goal or a career goal is a small victory. The feeling of success encourages you to take other small steps. Each step builds onto the next. Continue analyzing your personal world as well as the world you share with others. Expect the best as you go forward. Expect a happy life, loving relationships, success in life, and fulfilling and satisfying work in a job that you really love. Last but not least, expect that you have something unique and special to offer the world, because you do.

Supplementary Timed Writings

Supplementary Timed Writing 1

All problem solving, whether or not it is personal or 11
academic, involves decision making. You make decisions in 23
order to solve problems. On occasion, a problem occurs as a 35
result of a decision you have made. For example, you may 46
decide to smoke, but later in life, you might then face the 58
problem of nicotine addiction. You may decide not to study 70
math and science because you think that they are difficult. 82

Because of this choice, some career options may be 93
closed to you. There is a consequence for each action. Do 108
you see that events in your life do not just happen, but 116
that they are the result of your choices and decisions? 127

How can you best prepare your mind to help you solve 138
problems? A positive attitude is a great start. Indeed, 149
your attitude will determine the way in which you may solve 161
a problem or make a decision. Approach your studies, such 173
as science and math courses, with a positive attitude. Try 185
to think of academic problems as puzzles to be solved and 195
not just as work to be avoided. 203

Critical thinking is a type of problem solving that 213
allows you to decode, analyze, reason, assess, and process 224
data. Since it is basic for all successful problem solving, 235
you should try to explore, probe, question, and search for 248
all the right answers. 253

A problem may not always be solved on the first try, 263
so do not give up. Try, try again. To find a solution may 275
take a real effort. Use your critical thinking skills to 286
achieve success in a world that is highly competitive and 298
demanding. 300

1 | 2 | 3 | 4 | 5 | 6 | 7 | 8 | 9 | 10 | 11 | 12

Supplementary Timed Writing 2

For many of us, the Internet is an important resource 11
in our private and public lives. The Internet provides us 23
with quick access to countless Web sites that may contain 34
news, products, games, and other types of data. The Web 45
pages on these sites can be designed, authored, and posted 57
by anyone from anywhere around the world, so you must use 69
critical thinking skills when reviewing these Web sites. 80

Just because something is said on the radio, printed 91
in the newspaper, or shown on television does not mean that 103
it is true. This applies to data found on the Internet as 115
well. Do not fall into the trap of believing that if it is 126
on the Net, it must be true. A wise user of the Internet 138
thinks critically about data found on the Net and evaluates 150
this material before he or she decides to use it. 160

When you assess a new Web site, think about who, what, 171
how, when, and where. Who refers to the author of the Web 183
site. The author may be a business firm, an organization, 194
or a person. What refers to the validity of the data. Can 206
this data be verified by a reputable source? 215

How refers to the viewpoint of the author. Are your 225
data presented without prejudice? When refers to the time 237
frame of your data. Do you have recent data? Where refers 249
to your data source. Are the data from a trusted source? 260

By answering these critical questions, you will learn 271
more about the accuracy and dependability of a Web site. 283
When you surf the Net next time, be quite cautious. Anyone 294
can publish on the Internet. 300

1 | 2 | 3 | 4 | 5 | 6 | 7 | 8 | 9 | 10 | 11 | 12

Supplementary Timed Writing 3

Most office workers perform a wide range of tasks in 11
their workday. These tasks may require them to handle phone 23
calls or forward personal messages, to send short e-mail 34
notes or compile complex office reports, or to write simple 46
letters or assemble detailed letters with tables, graphics, 58
and imported data. Office workers are thus a basic part of 70
the structure of the firm. 75

The office worker must use critical thinking in order 86
to carry out a wide array of daily tasks. Some of the tasks 98
are more urgent than other tasks and should be done first. 110
Some tasks take only a short time, while others take a lot 122
more time. Some tasks demand a quick response, while others 134
may be taken up as time permits or even postponed until the 146
future. Some of these tasks might require input from other 158
people. 159

Whether a job is simple or complex or big or small, 170
the office worker must decide what is to be done first by 182
setting the priority for each task. 189

When setting priorities, critical thinking skills are 200
essential. The office worker must assess each aspect of the 212
task. It is a good idea to identify the size of the task, 223
learn about its complexity, estimate the effort needed, 235
judge its importance, and set its deadline. 243

Once the office worker assesses a task that is to be 254
done within a certain span of time, then the priority for 266
completing all those tasks can be set. Critical thinking 277
skills, if applied well, can save the employer money, but 289
if they are applied poorly, they might cost an employer. 300

1 | 2 | 3 | 4 | 5 | 6 | 7 | 8 | 9 | 10 | 11 | 12

Supplementary Timed Writing 4

Each day business managers must make choices that keep 11
their firms running in a smooth, skillful, and gainful way. 23
Every decision needs to be quick and sure. 32

To make good decisions, all managers must use critical 43
thinking. They must gather all the needed facts so that 54
they can make sound, well-informed choices. Over time, they 66
can refine their skills. Then, when they face a similar 77
problem, they can use their knowledge to help them solve 89
new problems with ease and in less time. 97

What types of decisions do you think managers make 107
that involve critical thinking? Human resource managers 119
need to decide whom to hire, what to pay the new worker, 130
and where to place him or her. In addition, human resource 142
managers should be able to help resolve conflicts between 153
workers. 155

Office managers must purchase copy machines, software, 166
computers, and supplies. Top executives must make business 178
policies, appoint other managers, and assess the success of 190
the firm. Plant supervisors must set schedules, gauge work 202
quality, and assess workers. Sales managers must study all 214
of the new sales trends, as well as provide sales training. 226

Most managers use critical thinking to make wise and 237
well-thought-out decisions. They carefully check all the 248
facts, analyze these facts, and then make a final judgment 259
based upon these facts. They should also be able to clearly 271
discern fact from fiction. Through trial and error, most 283
managers learn their own ways to solve problems and find a 294
solution for their firms. 300

1 | 2 | 3 | 4 | 5 | 6 | 7 | 8 | 9 | 10 | 11 | 12

Supplementary Timed Writing 5

In most classes, teachers just want the students to 11
analyze situations, draw conclusions, and solve problems. 22
Each of these tasks requires students to use good thinking 34
skills. How do students acquire these skills? What process 46
do students follow to develop these skills? 55

During early years of life, children learn words and 65
then combine these words into sentences. From there, they 77
learn to declare ideas, share thoughts, and express their 89
feelings. Students learn numbers and math concepts. They 100
may learn to read musical notes, to keep rhythm, to sing 111
songs, and to recognize popular and classical pieces of 123
music. Students learn colors and shapes and start to draw. 134

During their early years, students learn the basic 145
models of problem solving. One way for students to solve 156
problems and apply thinking skills is to use the scientific 168
approach. This approach requires a student to state the 179
problem to be solved, collect the known facts about that 191
problem, analyze the problem, and pose viable solutions. 202
Throughout this process, teachers ask questions that force 214
students to expand their thinking skills. 222

Teachers may want to ask questions such as these: Did 233
you clearly state the problem? Did you get all the facts? 245
Did you get the facts from the right place? Did you assume 257
anything? Did you pose other possible answers? Did you keep 269
an open mind to all solutions? Did you let your bias come 280
into play? Did you take the time to listen to other people? 292
Finally, does the solution make sense? 300

1 | 2 | 3 | 4 | 5 | 6 | 7 | 8 | 9 | 10 | 11 | 12

Supplementary Timed Writing 6

A major goal for all instructors in school is to teach 11
critical thinking skills to their class. This skill is the 23
process of deciding in a logical way what we should do or 35
believe, and it also involves an ability to compare and 46
contrast, solve problems, make decisions, analyze results, 58
and combine and use knowledge. Can you see that these are 69
important skills you can use all your life? 78

These skills help the student who later becomes a part 89
of the workforce. Whether someone is in a small business, 101
is in a corporate setting, or is self-employed, the world 112
of today is a competitive one, and skilled employees are 124
always in demand. 127

One part of gaining success in the workforce is having 139
the skill to deal with the mixed demands of the fast-paced 150
business world. A few of the required skills are insightful 162
decision making, creative problem solving, and productive 174
contact among diverse groups. 180

In school, we learn the basics of critical thinking. 191
This skill extends far beyond the borders of the classroom 203
and lasts a lifetime. We use critical thinking in all of 214
our daily lives. We constantly analyze and assess pursuits 226
such as music, movies, speech, fashion, magazine articles, 238
and television shows. 242

We all had experience using critical thinking skills 253
well before we even knew what they were. So you should keep 265
on learning and growing. The classroom can be the perfect 276
place for your exploration, so use that time to learn how 288
others solve problems. There are always new goals to reach. 300

1 | 2 | 3 | 4 | 5 | 6 | 7 | 8 | 9 | 10 | 11 | 12

Supplementary Timed Writing 7

One of the first steps you should take to unlock your 11
creativity is to realize that you have control over your 22
mind; your mind does not control you. Creativity is just 34
using a new or different way to solve a problem. 44

Many of our inventions have involved breakthroughs in 55
traditional ways of thinking, and the result has often been 67
amazing. For example, Einstein broke with the old ways and 78
tried obscure formulas that have changed all scientific 90
thought. Your attitude can form a mental block that may 101
keep you from exercising creativity. When you free up your 113
mind, the rest will follow. 118

Do your best to unleash your mind's innate creativity 129
by turning problems into puzzles. When you think of the 140
task as a puzzle, a challenge, or a game instead of as a 152
difficult problem, you will open up your mind and free your 164
creative side to operate. Creative ideas come when you are 176
enjoying yourself and are involved in unrelated tasks. 187

Old habits often restrict you from trying new ways of 198
solving problems. There is often more than one solution, so 210
strive to see each situation in a fresh, new light. How 221
many times have you told yourself that you must follow the 233
rules and perform tasks only in a certain way? 242

If you want to be creative, then look at situations in 253
a new light, break the pattern, explore new opportunities, 265
and challenge old rules. If you are facing a hard problem 277
and cannot find an answer, take a quick walk or relax for a 289
few minutes; you can then go back to the problem renewed. 300

1 | 2 | 3 | 4 | 5 | 6 | 7 | 8 | 9 | 10 | 11 | 12

Supplementary Timed Writing 8

Keyboarding is a very popular business course that 10
most students take. The major goals of a keyboarding course 22
are to develop touch control of the keyboard, to use proper 34
typing techniques, to build basic speed and accuracy, and 46
to receive considerable practice in applying those basic 57
skills to format letters, reports, tables, memos, and other 69
kinds of personal and business documents. 78

In the first part of a keyboarding course, you must 88
learn to stroke the keys by touch, using proven techniques. 100
You learn to strike the keys in a quick and accurate way. 112
After the keys are learned, you then focus your attention 123
on producing documents of many sizes and types. 133

When you first learn to keyboard, there may be certain 144
steps, guidelines, and exercises that should be followed. 156
There are rules to help you learn and in due time to master 168
the keyboard. To create each document requires that you 179
apply critical thinking. What format or layout should be 190
used? What font and font size would be best? Are all the 202
words spelled correctly? Does the document look neat on the 214
page? Are the figures accurate? Are the punctuation and 225
grammar correct? 228

Being creative also has a lot to do with risk taking 239
and courage. It takes courage to explore new ways to think 251
and to risk looking different and even to risk being wrong. 263
Your path to creativity is such a vital component of your 274
critical thinking skills. Allow your creative thoughts to 286
flow freely when you produce each keyboarding task. Enjoy 298
the journey. 300

1 | 2 | 3 | 4 | 5 | 6 | 7 | 8 | 9 | 10 | 11 | 12

Supplementary Timed Writing 9

More employees are injured using the computer keyboard 11
in the United States than using any other equipment in the 23
workplace. Therefore, you should find the most comfortable 35
and ergonomic position when you are keyboarding. 45

Your chair should be on rollers, be adjustable to fit 56
your individual height, and have substantial support for 67
your lower back. You should sit with your hips pushed as 78
far back in the chair as possible, and your thighs should 90
not touch the underside of the workstation. 99

Your monitor should be aligned with your keyboard and 110
centered opposite you. The display should be just slightly 122
below eye level and tilted away from you slightly. When you 134
sit back in the chair and hold your arm out horizontally, 145
your middle finger should touch the middle of the monitor. 157
That way you won't need to make excessive head movements to 169
see the viewing area of your screen. 176

A document holder should be positioned at the same 187
height and distance as the screen in order to minimize any 199
head movements and at the same angle as the screen. Place 210
the document holder to the side of the screen opposite the 222
mouse. Position the mouse at the identical height as the 233
keyboard, and you should move the mouse with your whole arm 245
and not just with your wrist. 251

There's no research to show that an ergonomic keyboard 263
is any more beneficial than the standard keyboard layout. 274
If your keyboard has pop-up legs, these should not be used 286
because a negative slope to the keyboard is by far the most 298
healthful. 300

1 | 2 | 3 | 4 | 5 | 6 | 7 | 8 | 9 | 10 | 11 | 12

Supplementary Timed Writing 10

One of the most important decisions we all have to 10
face is choosing a career. Your options can appear to be a 22
bit overwhelming at first. But you should not worry because 34
your critical thinking skills will help. 42

Start with a self-assessment. What are your interests? 54
Would you prefer to work inside or outdoors? Would you like 66
to work with numbers or with words? Are you an independent 77
type or would you rather work within a group? What are your 89
preferred courses? Think about each of these questions, and 101
then make a list of your interests, skills, aptitudes, and 113
values. What you learn about yourself might help you find 125
the career that is just right for you. 133

After you have explored your own interests, look at 143
the sixteen career clusters for a wide range of possible 155
jobs. Most jobs are included in one of these clusters that 166
have been organized by the government. During your search, 178
make a note of the clusters that interest you and look into 190
all the clusters. 194

Get as much information as you can by making use of 204
all available resources. Scan the employment section in the 216
major Sunday newspapers for job descriptions and salaries. 228
Search the Internet, which provides access to job listings 240
around the world. If you want to evaluate closely a certain 252
company, access its home page and look around. 261

Sign up for interviews with companies that visit your 272
campus. Talk with people in your field of interest to ask 284
questions and get advice. Taking the initiative in your job 296
search will pay off. 300

1 | 2 | 3 | 4 | 5 | 6 | 7 | 8 | 9 | 10 | 11 | 12

Index

NOTE: Page numbers preceded by R- indicate material in References Manual; page numbers preceded by SB- indicate material in Skillbuilding supplement.

C

M

Q

R

S

U

V

W

Y

PHOTO CREDITS

it Stock/Punchstock xiii, 234; Brooklyn Production/Corbis xv, 368; Flying Colurs/Getty xvii, 414; Eric Audras/PhotoAlto/PictureQuest xxi; Mark Dierker, McGraw-Hill Companies R-2; Ryan McVay/Getty 244, 279, 287, 299, 309, 319, 339, 367, 377, 385, 398, 426, 446; Corbis 245, 477; Jason Reed/Getty 247, 266, 290, 304, 329, 346, 359, 372, 383, 393, 401, 427, 435, 453; Thinkstock 251; Artifacts Images 264, 366; Anderson Ross/Getty 275; DigitalVision/Getty 282; Comstock/PictureQuest 300; Steve Ide 307; Stockbyte/Getty 324, 347; Joseph Sohm/Visions of America/Corbis 334; Ross Anania 343; DigitalVision 350; Stockbyte 361, 481; Comstock/Jupiter Images 381; Veer 382; Steve Cole/Getty 389, 469; Jack Star/Photolink/Getty 394; Comstock Images 403, 406; Getty Images/PhotoDisc 423; Tetra Images 428; PhotoDisc/Getty 431; Ingram Publishing/Superstock 436; AbleStock/Alamy 441; Moodboard/Corbis 449; AFP/GETTY 453; Banana Stock/Jupiter Images 458; Image Source/Jupiter Images 459; Stockbyte/Punchstock 466; InDeed 476; Ingram Publishing/AGE Photostock 489; Red Chopsticks 497; Barbara Penoyar/Getty SB-1.